Jacek Błazewicz · Klaus Ecker
Günter Schmidt · Jan Węglarz

Scheduling in Computer
and Manufacturing Systems

With 97 Figures

Springer-Verlag

Berlin Heidelberg New York
London Paris Tokyo
Hong Kong Barcelona
Budapest

Prof.Dr. Jacek Błazewicz
Instytut Informatyki
Politechnika Poznanska
ul. Piotrowo 3a
60-965 Poznań
Poland

Prof.Dr. Klaus Ecker
Institut für Informatik
Technische Universität Clausthal
Leibnizstr. 19
3392 Clausthal-Zellerfeld
FRG

Prof.Dr. Günter Schmidt
Rechts- und Wirtschaftswissenschaftliche Fakultät
Lehrstuhl für Betriebswirtschaftslehre
insbesondere Wirtschaftsinformatik II
Universität des Saarlandes, Bau 30
Im Stadtwald
6600 Saarbrücken
FRG

Prof.Dr. Jan Węglarz
Instytut Informatyki
Politechnika Poznanska
ul. Piotrowo 3a
60-965 Poznań
Poland

ISBN 3-540-55958-2 Springer-Verlag Berlin Heidelberg New York Tokyo
ISBN 0-387-55958-2 Springer-Verlag New York Heidelberg Berlin Tokyo

© Springer-Verlag Berlin · Heidelberg 1993
Printed in Germany

The use of registered names, trademarks, etc. in this publication does not imply, even in the absence of a specific statement, that such names are exempt from the relevant protective laws and regulations and therefore free for general use.

42/7130-543210 - Printed on acid-free paper

FOREWORD

This book is the result of a joint German-Polish project which has been partially supported by the Committee for Scientific Research [1] and the Deutsche Forschungsgemeinschaft [2]. We appreciate the help of both institutions.

The planning and preparation of the manuscript was an iterative and rather lengthy process which we had to stop at a certain stage, but it does not mean that we were fully satisfied with the output. Thus, comments and improvements will be appreciated. In the meantime we would like to thank many colleagues who already discussed with us different topics presented in the book. We are not able to list all of them but we would like to express our special gratitude toward Peter Brucker, Gerd Finke, Adam Janiak, Wiesław Kubiak, Kathryn Stecke, and Dominique de Werra.

As to the technical help in preparing the manuscript our thanks are due to Barbara Błażewicz, Brigitte Ecker, Maria Kamińska, and Brigitte Sand, especially for their typing efforts.

[1] Supported by grant KBN-302279101 and Project CRIT

[2] Grant 436 pol-11345/3.

Contents

1 Introduction

Let us start with the description of the purpose of this book. Firstly we should explain how we understand its title. In general, scheduling problems can be understood very broadly as the problems of the allocation of resources over time to perform a set of tasks. By resources we understand arbitrary means tasks compete for. They can be of a very different nature, e.g. manpower, money, processors (machines), energy, tools. Also tasks can have a variety of interpretations starting from machining parts in manufacturing systems up to processing information in computer systems. The same is true for task characteristics, e. g. ready times, due dates, relative urgency weights, functions describing task processing in relation to allotted resources. Moreover, a structure of a set of tasks, reflecting precedence contraints among them, can be defined in different ways. In addition, different criteria which measure the quality of the performance of a set of tasks can be taken into account.

It is easy to imagine that scheduling problems understood so generally appear almost everywhere in real-world situations. Of course, there are many aspects concerning approaches for modelling and solving these problems which are of general methodological importance. On the other hand, however, some classes of scheduling problems have their own specificity which should be taken into account. Since it is rather impossible to treat all these classes with the same attention in a framework of one book, some constraints must be put on the subject area considered. In the case of this book these constraints are as follows.

First of all we deal with deterministic scheduling problems (cf. [Bak74, BCSW86, CMM67, Cof76, Eck77, Fre82, GK87, Len77, LLRKS89, Rin76]), i.e. those in which no variable with a non-deterministic (e. g. probabilistic) description appears. Let us stress that this assumption does not necessarily mean that we deal only with static problems in which all characteristics of a set of tasks and a set of resources are known in advance. We consider also dynamic problems in which some parameters such as task ready times are unknown in advance, and we do not assume any knowledge about them, which is even more realistic in many practical situations. Secondly, we consider problems in which a set of resources always contains processors (machines). This means that we take into account the specificity of these particular resources in modeling and solving corresponding scheduling problems, but it does not mean that all presented methods and approaches are restricted to this specificity only. The main reason for which we differentiate processors (we even do not call them "resources" for the convenience of a reader) is that we like to expose especially two broad (and not exclusive) areas of practical applications of the considered problems, namely computer and manufacturing systems.

After the explanation of the book's title, we can pass to the description of some of its deeper specificities. They can be meant as compromises we accepted in multi-objective decision situations we had to deal with before and during the preparation of the text. At the beginning, we found a compromise between algorithmic (rather quantitative) and knowledge-based (rather qualitative) approaches to scheduling. We decided to present in the first chapters the algorithmic approach, and at the end to show how it can be integrated with the approach coming from the area of Artificial Intelligence, in order to create a pretty general and efficient tool for solving a broad class of practical problems. In this way we also hopefully found a compromise between rather computer and more manufacturing oriented audience.

The second compromise was concerned with the way of presenting algorithms: formal or descriptive. Basically we decided to adopt a Pascal-like notation, although we allowed for few exceptions in cases where such a presentation would be not efficient.

Next we agreed that the presented material should realize a reasonable compromise betweeen the needs of readers coming from different areas, starting from those who are beginners in the field of scheduling and related topics, and ending with specialists in the area. Thus we included some preliminaries concerning basic notions from discrete mathematics (problems, algorithms and methods), as well as, besides the most recent, also the most important classical results.

Summing up the above compromises, we think that the book can be addressed to a quite broad audience, including practitioners and researchers interested in scheduling, and also to graduate or advanced undergraduate students in computer science/engineering, operations research, industrial engineering, management science, business administration, information systems, and applied mathematics curricula.

Finally, we present briefly the outline of the book.

In **Chapter 2** basic definitions and concepts used throughout the book are introduced. One of the basic issues studied here is the complexity analysis of combinatorial problems. As a unified framework for this presentation the concept of a combinatorial search problem is used. Such notions as: decision and optimization problems, their encoding schemes, input length, complexity of optimization algorithms solving search problems, complexity classes of problems, are discussed and illustrated by several examples. Since majority of scheduling problems are computationally hard, two general approaches dealing with such problems are briefly discussed: enumerative and heuristic. Firstly, general enumerative approaches, i. e. dynamic programming and branch and bound method are shortly presented. Secondly, heuristic algorithms are introduced and the ways of analysis of their accuracy in the worst case and on the average are described. Then, the two general heuristic approaches simulated annealing and tabu search are presented and some hints for their applications are given. The above considerations are complemented by a presentation of basic notions from sets and relations, as well as graphs and networks, which will be used in the later chapters.

In **Chapter 3** basic definitions, assumptions and motivations for deterministic scheduling problems are introduced. We start with the set of tasks, the set of processors (machines) and the set of resources, and with two basic models in deterministic scheduling, i.e. parallel processors and dedicated processors. Then, schedules and their performance measures (optimality criteria) are described. After this introduction, possible ways of analysis of scheduling problems are described with a special emphasis put to solution strategies of computationally hard problems. Finally, motivations for the use of the deterministic scheduling model as well as an interpretation of results, are discussed. Two major areas of applications, i.e. computer and manufacturing systems are especially taken into account. These considerations are complemented by a presentation of a classification scheme which enables one to present deterministic scheduling problems in a short and elegant way.

Chapter 4 deals with single-processor scheduling. The results presented here are mainly concerned with polynomial-time optimization algorithms. Their presentation is divided into several sections taking into account especially the following optimality criteria: schedule length, mean (and mean weighted) flow time, and due date involving criteria, such as maximum lateness, number of tardy tasks, mean (and mean weighted) tardiness and a combination of earliness and lateness. In each case polynomial-time optimization algorithms are presented, taking into account problem parameters such as type of precedence constraints, possibility of task preemption, processing and arrival times of tasks, etc. These basic results are complemented by some more advanced ones which take into account change-over cost and more general cost functions. Let us stress that in this chapter we present a more detailed classification of subcases as compared to the following chapters. This follows from the fact that the algorithms for the single-processor model are useful also in more complicated cases, whenever a proper decomposition of the latter is carried out. On the other hand, its relative easiness makes it possible to solve optimally in polynomial time many more subcases than in the case of multiple processors.

Chapter 5 carries on an analysis of scheduling problems where multiple parallel processors are involved. As in Chapter 4, a presentation of the results is divided into several subsections depending mainly on the criterion considered and then on problem parameters. Three main criteria are analyzed: schedule length, mean flow time and maximum lateness. A further division of the presented results takes in particular into account the type of processors considered, i.e. identical, uniform or unrelated processors, and then parameters of a set of tasks. Here, scheduling problems are more complicated than in Chapter 4, so not as many optimization polynomial-time algorithms are available as before. Hence, more attention is paid to the presentation of polynomial-time heuristic algorithms with guaranteed accuracy, as well as to the description of some enumerative algorithms. At the end of the chapter some more advanced models of processor systems are considered. They include semi-indentical processor systems that are available for processing tasks in different time intervals, and scheduling so-called multiprocessor tasks each of which may require for its processing more than one processor at a time. This last new model of tasks processing is useful in some manufacturing as well as multi-microprocessor applications.

In **Chapter 6** static shop scheduling problems are investigated. The application of these models focuses mainly on manufacturing systems. The classical flow shop and job shop scheduling problems are described in greater detail, but also easy solvable cases of open shop scheduling are reviewed. For flow shop scheduling the emphasis is put on approximation algorithms. A branch and bound algorithm and a quite general heuristic based on simulated annealing are presented for job shop scheduling. An evaluation of these algorithms is given concerning solution quality and computational time. Based on these results corresponding comparisons are performed.

Chapter 7 deals with resource constrained scheduling. In the first two sections it is assumed that tasks require for their processing processors and certain fixed amounts of discrete resources. The first section presents the classical model where schedule length is to be minimized. In this context several polynomial-time optimization algorithms are described. In the next section this model is generalized to cover also the case of multiprocessor tasks. Two algorithms are presented that minimize schedule length for preemptable tasks under different assumptions concerning resource requirements. The last section deals with problems in which additional resources are continuous, i.e. continuosly-divisible. We study three classes of scheduling problems of that type. The first one contains problems with parallel processors, and tasks described by continuous functions relating their processing speeds to the resource amount allotted at a time. The next two classes are concerned with single processor problems where task processing times or ready times, respectively, are continuous functions of the allotted resource amount.

Chapter 8 is devoted to problems which perhaps closer reflect some specific features of scheduling in flexible manufacturing systems than other chapters do. We start from so-called flexible flow shops which consist of machine stages or centers with given numbers of parallel, identical machines at each stage. For some simple cases we present heuristics with known worst case performance and then describe a branch and bound algorithm for the general case. In the next section dynamic job shops are considered, i. e. such in which some events, particularly job arrivals, occur at unknown times. A heuristic for a static problem with mean tardiness as a criterion is described. It solves the problem at each time when necessary, and the solution is implemented on a rolling horizon basis. The last section deals with simultaneous assignment of machines and vehicles to jobs. Firstly we solve in polynomial time the problem of finding a feasible vehicle schedule for a given assignment of jobs to machines, and then present a dynamic programming algorithm for the general case.

The goal of **Chapter 9** is two-fold. On one hand we want to review some results concerning the solution approaches for quite general scheduling problems. The corresponding ideas come mainly from the area of Artificial Intelligence. On the other hand we focus on a general approach for the solution of scheduling problems as they appear in manufacturing environments. For this some broader aspects are considered, which come from computer integrated manufacturing. The common goal of this chapter is to combine solution approaches for scheduling problems from different areas in order to solve quite practical questions. To achieve the above goals we firstly concentrate on the relationship between the ideas of computer integrated manufacturing and the requirements concerning solutions of scheduling problems. We discuss open loop interactive scheduling and closed loop knowledge-based systems. Finally, we make some proposals concerning the integration of solution approaches discussed in the preceding chapters with the ideas developed in this chapter. We concentrate on intelligent production scheduling and use an example to clarify the approach. Finally we discuss the impact of intelligent production scheduling for computer integrated manufacturing (CIM).

References

Bak74   K. Baker, *Introduction to Sequencing and Scheduling*, J. Wiley, New York, 1974.

BCSW86   J. Błażewicz, W. Cellary, R. Słowiński, J. Węglarz, *Scheduling under Resource Constraints: Deterministic Models*, J. C. Baltzer, Basel, 1986.

CMM67   R. W. Conway, W. L. Maxwell, L. W. Miller, *Theory of Scheduling*. Addison-Wesley, Reading, Mass., 1967.

Cof76   E. G. Coffman, Jr. (ed.), *Scheduling in Computer and Job Shop Systems*, J. Wiley, New York, 1976.

Eck77   K. Ecker, *Theorie Deterministischer Schedules*, Bibliographisches Institut Mannheim, Reihe Informatik, 1977.

Fre82   S. French, *Sequencing and Scheduling: An Introduction to the Mathematics of the Job-Shop*, Horwood, Chichester, 1982.

GK87   S. K. Gupta, and J. Kyparisis, Single machine scheduling research, *OMEGA Internat. J. Management Sci.* 15, 1987, 207-227.

Len77   J. K. Lenstra, *Sequencing by Enumerative Methods*, Mathematical Centre Tracts 69, Amsterdam, 1977.

LLRKS89   E. L. Lawler, J. K. Lenstra, A. H. G. Rinnooy Kan, D. B. Shmoys, Sequencing and scheduling: algorithms and complexity, Report Centre Mathematics and Computer Science, Amsterdam, 1989.

Rin76   A. H. G. Rinnooy Kan, *Machine Scheduling Problems: Classification, Complexity and Computations*. Martinus Nijhoff, The Hague, 1976.

2 Preliminaries

In this chapter we provide the reader with basic notions used throughout the book. After a short introduction into sets and relations, decision problems, optimization problems and the encoding of problem instances are discussed. The way algorithms will be represented, and problem membership of complexity classes are other issues that are essential because algorithms for scheduling problems and their properties will be discussed from the complexity point of view. Afterwards graphs, especially certain types such as precedence graphs and networks that are important for scheduling problems, are presented. The last two sections deal with algorithmic methods used in scheduling such as enumerative algorithms (e. g. dynamic programming and branch and bound) and heuristic approaches.

2.1 Sets and Relations

Sets are understood to be any collection of distinguishable objects, such as the set $\{1, 2, \cdots\}$ of natural numbers, denoted by $I\!N$, the set $I\!N^0$ of nonnegative integers, the set of real numbers, $I\!R$, or the set of nonnegative reals $I\!R^{\geq 0}$. Given real numbers a and b, $a \leq b$, then $[a, b]$ denotes the *closed interval* from a to b, i.e. the set of reals $\{x \mid a \leq x \leq b\}$. *Open intervals* $((a, b) := \{x \mid a < x < b\})$ and *half open intervals* are defined similarly.

In scheduling theory we are normally concerned with finite sets; so, unless infinity is stated explicitly, the sets are assumed to be finite.

For set S, $|S|$ denotes its *cardinality*. The *power set* of S (i.e. the set of all subsets of S) is denoted by $\mathcal{P}(S)$. For an integer k, $0 \leq k \leq |S|$, the set of all subsets of cardinality k is denoted by $\mathcal{P}_k(S)$.

The *cartesian product* $S_1 \times \cdots \times S_k$ of sets $S_1, \cdots, S_k$ is the set of all tuples of the form $(s_1, s_2, \cdots, s_k)$ where $s_i \in S_i$, $i = 1, \cdots, k$, i.e. $S_1 \times \cdots \times S_k = \{(s_1, \cdots, s_k) \mid s_i \in S_i, i = 1, \cdots, k\}$.

Given sets $S_1, \cdots, S_k$, a subset $\mathcal{R}$ of $S_1 \times \cdots \times S_k$ is called a *relation over* $S_1, \cdots, S_k$. In the case $k = 2$, $\mathcal{R}$ is called a *binary relation*. For a binary relation $\mathcal{R}$ over S_1 and S_2, the sets S_1 and S_2 are called *domain* and *range*, respectively. If $\mathcal{R}$ is a relation over $S_1, \cdots, S_k$, with $S_1 = \cdots = S_k = S$, then we simply say: $\mathcal{R}$ is a *(k-ary) relation over* S. For example, the set of edges of a directed graph (see Section 2.3) is a binary relation over the vertices of the graph.

Let S be a set, and $\mathcal{R}$ be a binary relation over S. Then, $\mathcal{R}^{-1} = \{(a, b) \mid (b, a) \in \mathcal{R}\}$ is the *inverse* to $\mathcal{R}$. Relation $\mathcal{R}$ is *symmetric* if $(a, b) \in \mathcal{R}$ implies $(b, a) \in \mathcal{R}$. $\mathcal{R}$ is *asymmetric* if for $a \neq b$, $(a, b) \in \mathcal{R}$ implies $(b, a) \notin \mathcal{R}$. $\mathcal{R}$ is *reflexive* if $(a, a) \in \mathcal{R}$ for all $a \in S$. $\mathcal{R}$ is *irreflexive* if $(a, a) \notin \mathcal{R}$ for all $a \in S$. $\mathcal{R}$ is *transitive* if for all $a, b, c \in S$, $(a, b) \in \mathcal{R}$ and $(b, c) \in \mathcal{R}$ implies $(a, c) \in \mathcal{R}$.

A binary relation over S is called a *partial order* (partially ordered set, *poset*) if it is reflexive, asymmetric and transitive. A binary relation over S is called an *equivalence* relation (over S) if it is reflexive, symmetric, and transitive.

Given set J of n closed intervals of reals, $J = \{I_i \mid I_i = [a_i, b_i], a_i \leq b_i, i = 1, \cdots, n\}$, a partial order $<_I$ on J can be defined by:

$$I_i <_I I_j \Leftrightarrow b_i < a_j, i, j \in \{1, \cdots, n\} .$$

A poset is called *interval order* if there is a set of intervals whose partial order $<_I$ represents the poset.

Let $l = (n_1, \cdots, n_k)$ and $l' = (n'_1, \cdots, n'_{k'})$ be sequences of integers, and $k, k' \geq 0$. If $k = 0$ then l is the empty sequence. We say that l is *lexicographically smaller* than l', written $l \lessdot l'$, if

(i) the two sequences agree up to some index j, but $n_{j+1} < n'_{j+1}$ (i.e. there exists j, $1 \leq j \leq k$, such that for all i, $1 \leq i \leq j$, $n_i = n'_i$ and $n_{j+1} < n'_{j+1}$), or

(ii) sequence l is shorter, and the two sequences agree up to the length of l (i.e. $k \leq k'$ and $n_i = n'_i$ for all i, $1 \leq i \leq k$).

If $\mathcal{R}$ is a binary relation over set S, then $\mathcal{R}^2 = \mathcal{R} \circ \mathcal{R}$ is the relational product of $\mathcal{R}$ and $\mathcal{R}$. Generally, we write $\mathcal{R}^0$ for $\{(a, a) \mid a \in S\}$, $\mathcal{R}^1 = \mathcal{R}$, and $\mathcal{R}^{i+1} = \mathcal{R}^i \circ \mathcal{R}$ for $i > 1$. The union $\mathcal{R}^* = \cup \{\mathcal{R}^i \mid i \geq 0\}$ is called the *transitive closure* of $\mathcal{R}$.

A *function* from $\mathcal{A}$ to $\mathcal{B}$ ($\mathcal{A} \to \mathcal{B}$; $\mathcal{A}$ and $\mathcal{B}$ are not necessarily finite) is a relation F over $\mathcal{A}$ and $\mathcal{B}$ such that for each $a \in \mathcal{A}$ there exists just one $b \in \mathcal{B}$ for which $(a, b) \in F$; instead of $(a, b) \in F$ we usually write $F(a) = b$. Set $\mathcal{A}$ is called the *domain* of F and set $\{b \mid b \in \mathcal{B}, \exists a \in \mathcal{A}, (a, b) \in F\}$ is called the *range* of F. F is called *surjective*, or *onto* $\mathcal{B}$ if for each element $b \in \mathcal{B}$ there is at least one element $a \in \mathcal{A}$ such that $F(a) = b$. Function F is said to be *injective*, or *one-one* if for each pair of elements, $a_1, a_2 \in \mathcal{A}$, $F(a_1) = F(a_2)$ implies $a_1 = a_2$. A function that is both surjective and injective is called *bijective*. A bijective function $F\colon \mathcal{A} \to \mathcal{A}$ is called a *permutation* of $\mathcal{A}$. Though we are able to represent functions in special cases by means of tables we usually specify functions in a more or less abbreviated way that specifies how the function values are to be determined. For example, for $n \in I\!N$, the factorial function $n!$ denotes the set of pairs $\{(n, m) \mid n \in I\!N, m = n \cdot (n - 1) \cdots 3 \cdot 2\}$. Other examples of functions are polynomials, exponential functions and logarithms.

We will say that function $f\colon I\!N \to I\!R$ is *of order* g, written $O(g)$, if there exists a constant c such that for all $k \in I\!N, f(k) \leq cg(k)$.

2.2 Problems, Algorithms, Complexity

2.2.1 Problems and their Encoding

In general, scheduling problems we will be considering belong to a broader class of combinatorial search problems. A *combinatorial search problem* Π is a set of pairs (I, A), where I is called an *instance* of a problem, i.e. a finite set of *parameters* (understood generally, e.g. numbers, sets, functions, graphs) with specified values, and A is an *answer* (*solution*) to the instance. As an example of a search problem let us consider *merging* two sorted sequences of real numbers. Any instance of this problem consists of two finite sequences of reals e and f sorted in nondecreasing order. The answer is the sequence g consisting of all the elements of e and f arranged in nondecreasing order.

Let us note that among search problems one may also distinguish two subclasses: optimization and decision problems. An *optimization problem* is defined in such a way that an answer to its instance specifies a solution for which a value of a certain objective function is at its optimum (an *optimal solution*). On the other hand, an answer to an instance of a *decision problem* may take only two values, either "yes" or "no". It is not hard to see, that for any optimization problem, there always exists a decision counterpart, in which we ask (in the case of minimization) if there exists a solution with the value of the objective function less than or equal to some additionally given threshold value y. (If in the basic problem the objective function has to be maximized, we ask if there exists a solution with the value of the objective function $\geq y$.) The following example clarifies these notions.

Example 2.2.1 Let us consider an optimization *knapsack problem*.

Knapsack

Instance: A finite set of elements $\mathcal{A} = \{a_1, a_2, \cdots, a_n\}$, each of which has an integer weight $w(a_i)$ and value $v(a_i)$, and an integer capacity b of a knapsack.

Answer: Subset $\mathcal{A}' \subseteq \mathcal{A}$ for which $\sum\limits_{a_i \in \mathcal{A}'} v(a_i)$ is at its maximum, subject to the constraint $\sum\limits_{a_i \in \mathcal{A}'} w(a_i) \leq b$ (i.e. the total value of chosen elements is at its maximum and the total weight of these elements does not exceed knapsack capacity b).

The corresponding decision problem is denoted as follows. (To distinguish optimization problems from decision problems the latter will be denoted using capital letters.)

KNAPSACK

Instance: A finite set of elements $\mathcal{A} = \{a_1, a_2, \cdots, a_n\}$, each of which has an integer weight $w(a_i)$ and value $v(a_i)$, an integer knapsack capacity b and threshold value y.

Answer: "Yes" if there exists subset $\mathcal{A}' \subseteq \mathcal{A}$ such that $\sum\limits_{a_i \in \mathcal{A}'} v(a_i) \geq y$ and $\sum\limits_{a_i \in \mathcal{A}'} w(a_i) \leq b$. Otherwise "No". □

When considering search problems, especially in the context of their solution by computer algorithms, one of the most important issues that arises is a question of data structures used to encode problems. Usually to encode instance I of problem Π (that is particular values of parameters of problem Π) one uses a finite *string* of symbols $x(I)$. These symbols belong to a predefined finite set Σ (usually called an *alphabet*) and the way of coding instances is given as a set of encoding rules (called *encoding scheme e*). By *input length (input size)* $|I|$ of instance I we mean here the length of string $x(I)$. Let us note that the requirement that an instance of a problem is encoded by a finite string of symbols is the only constraint imposed on the class of search problems which we consider here. However, it is rather a theoretical constraint, since we will try to characterize algorithms and problems from the viewpoint of the application of real computers.

Now the encoding scheme and its underlying data structure is defined in a more precise way. For representation of mathematical objects we use set Σ that contains the usual characters, i.e. capital and small Arabic letters, capital and small Greek letters, digits $(0,\cdots,9)$, symbols for mathematical operations such as $+$, $-$, $\times$, $/$, and various types of parentheses and separators. The class of mathematical objects, $\mathcal{A}$, is then mapped to the set Σ^* of words over the alphabet Σ by means of a function $\rho: \mathcal{A} \rightarrow \Sigma^*$, where Σ^* denotes the set of all finite strings (words) made up of symbols belonging to Σ. Each mathematical object $A \in \mathcal{A}$ is represented as a *structured string* in the following sense: Integers are represented by their decimal representation. A square matrix of dimension n with integer elements will be represented as a finite list whose first component represents matrix dimension n, and the following n^2 components represent the integer matrix elements in some specific order. For example, the list is a structured string of the form $(n, a(1, 1),\cdots,a(1, n), a(2, 1) ,\cdots,a(2, n) ,\cdots,a(n, n))$ where n and all the $a(i, j)$ are structured strings representing integers. The length of encoding (i.e. the complexity of storing) an integer k would then be of order $\log k$, and that of a matrix would be of order $n^2 \log k$ where k is an upper bound for the absolute value of each matrix element. Real numbers will be represented either in decimal notation (e.g. 3.14159) or in half-logarithmic representation using mantissa and exponent (e.g. $0.314159\cdot10^1$). Functions may be represented by tables which specify the function (range) value for each domain value. Representations of more complicated objects (e.g. graphs) will be introduced later, together with the definition of these types of objects.

As an example let us consider encoding of a particular instance of the knapsack problem defined in Example 2.2.1. Let the number n of elements be equal to 6 and let an encoding scheme define values of parameters in the following order: n, weights of elements, values of elements, knapsack's capacity b. A string coding an exemplary instance is : 6, 4, 2, 12, 15, 3, 7, 1, 4, 8, 12, 5, 7, 28.

The above remarks do not exclude the usage of any other *reasonable encoding scheme* which does not cause an exponential growth of the input length as compared with other encoding schemes. For this reason one has to exclude unary encoding in which each integer k is represented as a string of k 1's. We see that the length of encoding this integer would be k which is exponentially larger, as compared to the above decimal encoding.

In practice, it is worthwhile to express the input length of an instance as a function depending on the number of elements of some set whose cardinality is dominating for that instance. For the knapsack problem defined in Example 2.2.1 this would be the number of elements n, for the merging problem - the total number of elements in the two sequences, for the scheduling problem - the number of tasks. This assumption, usually made, in most cases reduces practically to the assumption that a computer word is large enough to contain any of the binary encoded numbers comprising an instance. However, in some problems, for example those in which graphs are involved, taking as input size the number of nodes may appear too great a simplification since the number of edges in a graph may be equal to $n(n-1)/2$. Nevertheless, in practice one often makes this simplification to unify computational results. Let us note that this simplification causes no exponential growth of input length.

2.2.2 Algorithms

Let us now pass to the notion of an algorithm and its complexity function. An algorithm is any procedure for solving a problem (i.e. for giving an answer). We will say that an algorithm *solves search problem* Π, if it finds a solution for any instance I of Π. In order to keep representation of algorithms easily understandable we follow a structural approach that uses language concepts known from structural programming, such as case statements, or loops of various kinds. Like functions or procedures, algorithms may also be called in an algorithm. Parameters may be used to import data to or export data from the algorithm. Besides these, we also use mathematical notations such as set-theoretic notations.

In general, an algorithm consists of two parts: a *head* and a *method*. The head starts with the keyword **Algorithm**, followed by an identifying number and, optionally, a descriptor (a name or a description of the purpose of the algorithm) and a reference to the author(s) of the algorithm. Input and output parameters are omitted in cases where they are clear from the context. In other cases, they are specified as a parameter list. In even more complex cases, two fields, *Input (Instance):* and *Output (Answer):* are used to describe parameters, and a field *Method:* is used to describe the main idea of the algorithm. The *method* part is a block of instructions. As in PASCAL, a block is embraced by **begin** and **end**. Each block is considered as a sequence of instructions. An instruction itself may again be a block, an assignment-, an else-, or a case- operation, or a loop (**for, while, repeat** ⋯ **until**, or a general **loop**), a **call** of another algorithm, or an exit instruction to terminate a loop instruction (**exit loop**, etc.) or the algorithm or procedure (just **exit**). The right hand side of an assignment operation may be any mathematical expression, or a function call. Case statements partition actions of the algorithm into several branches, depending on the value of a control variable. Loop statements may contain formulations such as: "**for all** $a \in \mathcal{M}$ **do** ⋯" or "**while** $\mathcal{M} \neq \emptyset$ **do** ⋯". If a loop is preempted by an exit statement the algorithm jumps to the first statement after the loop. Comments are started with two minus signs and are finished at the end of the line. If a comment needs more than one line, each comment line starts with '--'.

Algorithms should reflect the main idea of the method. Details like output layouts are omitted. Names for procedures, functions, variables etc. are chosen so that they reflect the semantics behind them. Sometimes a graphic notation of algorithms may be useful; we will then prefer so-called *Nassi-Shneiderman diagrams* which allow to represent structured algorithmic constructions in a better way than usual flow charts.

As an example let us consider an algorithm solving the problem of merging two sequences, defined at the beginning of this section. Nassi-Shneiderman diagrams for these algorithms can be found in Figures 2.2.1 and 2.2.2.

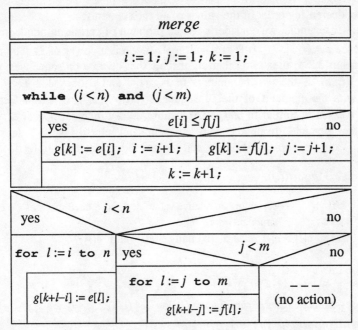

Figure 2.2.1 *Nassi-Shneiderman diagram representing Algorithm* 2.2.2.

Algorithm 2.2.2 *merge.*

Input: Two sequences of reals, $e = (e[1],\cdots,e[n])$ and $f = (f[1],\cdots,f[m])$, both sorted in nondecreasing order.

Output: Sequence $g = (g[1],\cdots,g[n+m])$ in which all elements are arranged in nondecreasing order.

```
begin
i := 1; j := 1; k := 1;        -- initialization of counters
while (i < n) and (j < m) do
            -- the while loop merges elements of sequences e and f into g;
            -- the loop is executed until all elements of one of the sequences are merged
    begin
    if e[i] ≤ f[j]
    then begin g[k] := e[i]; i := i+1; end
    else begin g[k] := f[j]; j := j+1; end;
    k := k+1;
    end;
if i < n        -- not all elements of sequence e have been merged
then for l := i to n do g[k+l-i] := e[l];
```

```
else
    if  j < m          -- not all elements of sequence f have been merged
    then for  l := j to  m  do  g[k+l−j] := f[l];
end;
```

The above algorithm returns as an answer sequence g of all the elements of e and f, sorted in nondecreasing order of the values of all the elements.

As another example, we consider a search problem of sorting in nondecreasing order a sequence $e = (e[1], \cdots, e[n])$ of $n = 2^k$ reals (i.e. n is a power of 2). The algorithm *sort* (Algorithm 2.2.4) uses two other algorithms that operate on sequences: *msort(i,j)* and *merge1(i,j,k)*. If the two parameters of *msort*, i and j, obey $1 \leq i < j \leq n$, then *msort(i,j)* sorts the elements of the subsequence $(e[i], \cdots, e[j])$ of e nondecreasingly. Algorithm *merge1* is similar to *merge* (Algorithm 2.2.2): *merge1(i,j,k)* $(1 \leq i \leq j < k \leq n)$ takes the elements from the two adjacent and already sorted subsequences $(e[i], \cdots, e[j])$ and $(e[j+1], \cdots, e[k])$ of e, and merges their elements into $(e[i], \cdots, e[k])$.

Algorithm 2.2.3 *msort(i,j)*.
```
begin
case  (i,j) of          -- depending on relative values of i and j, three subcases are considered
    i = j: exit;        -- terminate msort
    i = j−1: if  e[i] > e[j] then  Exchange  e[i]  and  e[j];
    i < j−1:
        begin
        call  msort(i,⌊(j+i)/2⌋);[1]
            -- sorts elements of subsequence (e[i],···,e[⌊(j+i)/2⌋])
        call  msort(⌊(j+i)/2⌋+1,j);
            -- sorts elements of subsequence (e[⌊(j+i)/2⌋+1],···,e[j])
        call  merge1(i,⌊(j+i)/2⌋,j);
            -- merges sorted subsequences into sequence (e[i],···,e[j])
        end;
    end;
end;
```

Algorithm 2.2.4 *sort*.
```
begin
read(n);
read((e[1],···,e[n]));
call  msort(1,n);
end;
```

Notice that in the case of an optimization problem one may also consider an *approximate (suboptimal) solution* that is *feasible* (i.e. fulfills all the conditions specified in the description of the problem) but does not extremize the objective function. It follows that one can also consider *heuristic (suboptimal)* algorithms which tend toward but do not guarantee the finding of optimal solutions for any instance of an optimization prob-

---

[1] $\lfloor x \rfloor$ denotes the largest number less than or equal to x.

lem. An algorithm which always finds an optimal solution will be called an *optimization* or *exact* algorithm.

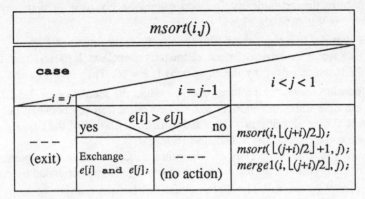

Figure 2.2.2 *Nassi-Shneiderman diagram representing Algorithm 2.2.3.*

2.2.3 Complexity

Let us turn now to the analysis of the computational complexity of algorithms. By the *time complexity function* of algorithm A solving problem Π we understand the function that maps each input length of an instance I of Π into a maximal number of elementary steps (or time units) of a computer, which are needed to solve an instance of that size by algorithm A.

It is obvious that this function will not be well defined unless the encoding scheme and the model of computation (computer model) are precisely defined. It appears, however, that the choice of a particular reasonable encoding scheme and a particular realistic computer model has no influence on the distinction between polynomial- and exponential time algorithms which are the two main types of algorithms from the computational complexity point of view [AHU74]. This is because all realistic models of computers [2] are equivalent in the sense that if a problem is solved by some computer model in time bounded from above by a polynomial in the input length (i.e. in polynomial time), then any other computer model will solve that problem in time bounded from above by a polynomial (perhaps of different degree) in the input length [AHU74]. Thus, to simplify the computation of the complexity of polynomial algorithms, we assume that, if not stated otherwise, the operation of writing a number as well as addition, subtraction and comparison of two numbers are elementary operations of a computer that need the same amount of time, if the length of a binary encoded number is bounded from above by a polynomial in the computation time of the whole algorithm. Otherwise, a logarithmic cost criterion is assumed. Now, we define the two types of algorithms.

---

[2] By "realistic" we mean here such computer models which in unit time may perform a number of elementary steps bounded from above by a polynomial in the input length. This condition is fulfilled for example by the one-tape Turing machine, the k-tape Turing machine, or the random access machine (RAM) under logarithmic cost of performing a single operation.

A *polynomial time (polynomial) algorithm* is one whose time complexity function is $O(p(k))$, where p is some polynomial and k is the input length of an instance. Each algorithm whose time complexity function cannot be bounded in that way will be called an *exponential time algorithm.*

Let us consider two algorithms with time complexity functions k and 3^k, respectively. Let us assume moreover that an elementary step lasts 1 µs and that the input length of the instance solved by the algorithms is $k = 60$. Then one may calculate that the first algorithm solves the problem in 60 µs while the second needs $1.3 \cdot 10^{13}$ centuries. This example illustrates the fact that indeed the difference between polynomial- and exponential time algorithms is large and justifies definition of the first algorithm as a "good" one and the second as a "bad" one [Edm65].

If we analyze time complexity of Algorithm 2.2.2, we see that the number of instructions being performed during execution of the algorithm is bounded by $c_1(n+m) + c_2$, where c_1 and c_2 are suitably chosen constants, i.e. the number of steps depends linearly on the total number of elements to be merged.

Now we estimate complexity of Algorithm 2.2.4. The first two *read* instructions together take $O(n)$ steps, where reading one element is assumed to take constant $(O(1))$ time. During execution of $msort(1, n)$, the sequence of elements is divided into two subsequences, each of length $n/2$; $msort$ is applied recursively on the subsequences which will thus be sorted. Then, procedure $merge1$ is applied, which combines the two sorted subsequences into one sorted sequence. Now let $T(m)$ be the number of steps $msort$ performs to sort m elements. Then, each call of $msort$ within $msort$ involves sorting of $m/2$ elements, so it takes $T(m/2)$ time. The call of $merge1$ can be performed in a number of steps proportional to $m/2 + m/2 = m$, as can easily be seen. Hence, we get the recursion

$$T(m) = 2T(m/2) + cm,$$

where c is some constant. One can easily verify that there is a constant c' such that $T(m) = c'm\log m$ [3] solves the recursion. Taking all steps of Algorithm 2.2.4 together we get the time complexity $O(\log n) + O(n) + O(n\log n) = O(n\log n)$.

Unfortunately, it is not always true that we can solve problems by algorithms of linear or polynomial time complexity. In some cases only exponential algorithms are available. We will take now a closer look to inherent complexity of some classes of search problems to explain the reasons why polynomial algorithms are unlikely to exist for these problems.

As we said before, there exist two broad subclasses of search problems, i.e. decision and optimization problems. From the computational point of view both classes may be analyzed much in the same way (strictly speaking when their computational hardness is analyzed). This is because a decision problem is computationally not harder than the corresponding optimization problem. That means that if one is able to solve an optimization problem in an "efficient" way (i.e. in polynomial time), then it will also be possible to solve a corresponding decision problem efficiently (just by comparing an optimal value of the objective function [4] to a given constant y). On the other hand, if

---

[3] We may take any fixed base for the logarithm, e.g. 2 or 10.

[4] Strictly speaking, assuming that the objective function may be calculated in polynomial time.

the decision problem is computationally "hard", then the corresponding optimization problem will also be "hard"[5].

Now, we can turn to the definition of the most important complexity classes of search problems. Basic definitions will be given for the case of decision problems since their formulation permits an easier treatment of the subject. One should, however, remember the above dependencies between decision and optimization problems. We will also point out the most important implications. In order to be independent of a particular type of a computer we have to use an abstract model of computation. From among several possibilities, we choose the *deterministic Turing machine* (*DTM*) for this purpose. Despite the fact that this choice was somehow arbitrary, our considerations are still *general* because all the realistic models of computations are polynomially related.

Class *P* consists of all decision problems that may be solved by the deterministic Turing machine in time bounded from above by a polynomial in the input length. Let us note, that the corresponding (broader) class of all search problems solvable in polynomial time, is denoted by *FP* [Joh90]. We see that both, the problem of merging two sequences and that of sorting a sequence belong to that class. In fact, class *FP* contains all the search problems which can be solved efficiently by the existing computers.

It is worth noting that there exists a large class of decision problems for which no polynomial time algorithms are known, for which, however, one can verify a positive answer in polynomial time, provided there is some additional information. If we consider for example an instance of the KNAPSACK problem defined in Example 2.2.1 and a subset $\mathcal{A}_1 \subseteq \mathcal{A}$ defining additional information, we may easily check in polynomial time whether or not the answer is "yes" in the case of this subset. This feature of polynomial time verifiability rather than solvability, is captured by a *nondeterministic Turing machine* (*NDTM*) [GJ79].

We may now define *class NP* of decision problems as consisting of all decision problems which may be solved in polynomial time by an NDTM.

It follows that $P \subseteq NP$. In order to define the most interesting class of decision problems, i.e. the class of *NP*-complete problems, one has to introduce the definition of a polynomial transformation. A *polynomial transformation* from problem Π_2 to problem Π_1 (denoted by $\Pi_2 \propto \Pi_1$) is a function f mapping the set of all instances of Π_2 into the set of instances of Π_1, that satisfies the following two conditions:

1. for each instance I_2 of Π_2 an answer is "yes" if and only if an answer for $f(I_2)$ of Π_1 is also "yes",

2. f is computable in polynomial time (depending on problem size $|I_2|$) by a DTM.

We say that decision problem Π_1 is *NP-complete* if $\Pi_1 \in NP$ and for any other problem $\Pi_2 \subset NP$, $\Pi_2 \propto \Pi_1$ [Coo71].

It follows from the above that if there existed a polynomial time algorithm for some *NP*-complete problem, then any problem from that class (and also from the *NP*

---

[5] Many decision problems and corresponding optimization problems are linked even more strictly, since it is possible to prove that a decision problem is not easier than the corresponding optimization problem [GJ79].

class of decision problems) would be solvable by a polynomial time algorithm. Since *NP*-complete problems include classical hard problems (as for example HAMILTO-NIAN CIRCUIT, TRAVELING SALESMAN, SATISFIABILITY, INTEGER PRO-GRAMMING) for which, despite many attempts, no one has yet been able to find polynomial time algorithms, probably all these problems may only be solved by the use of exponential time algorithms. This would mean that *P* is a proper subclass of *NP* and the classes *P* and *NP*-complete problems are disjoint.

Another consequence of the above definitions is that, to prove the *NP*-completeness of a given problem Π, it is sufficient to transform polynomially a known *NP*-complete problem to Π. SATISFIABILITY was the first decision problem proved to be *NP*-complete [Coo71]. The current list of *NP*-complete problems contains several thousands, from different areas. Although the choice of an *NP*-complete problem which we use to transform into a given problem in order to prove the *NP*-completeness of the latter, is theoretically arbitrary, it has an important influence on the way a polynomial transformation is constructed [Kar72]. Thus, these proofs require a good knowledge of *NP*-complete problems, especially characteristic ones in particular areas.

As was mentioned, decision problems are not computationally harder than the corresponding optimization ones. Thus, to prove that some optimization problem is computationally hard, one has to prove that the corresponding decision problem is *NP*-complete. In this case, the optimization problem belongs to the class of *NP-hard problems*, which includes computationally hard search problems. On the other hand, to prove that some optimization problem is easy, it is sufficient to construct an optimization polynomial time algorithm. The order of performing these two steps follows mainly from the intuition of the researcher, which however, is guided by several hints. In this book, by "open problems" from the computational complexity point of view we understand those problems which neither have been proved to be *NP*-complete nor solvable in polynomial time.

Despite the fact that all *NP*-complete problems are computationally hard, some of them may be solved quite efficiently in practice (as for example the KNAPSACK problem). This is because the time complexity functions of algorithms that solve these problems are bounded from above by polynomials in two variables: the input length $|I|$ and the maximal number $\max(I)$ appearing in an instance I. Since in practice $\max(I)$ is usually not very large, these algorithms have good computational properties. However, such algorithms, called *pseudopolynomial*, are not really of polynomial time complexity since in reasonable encoding schemes all numbers are encoded binary (or in another integer base greater than 2). Thus, the length of a string used to encode $\max(I)$ is $\log\max(I)$ and the time complexity function of a polynomial time algorithm would be $O(p(|I|, \log\max(I)))$ and not $O(p(|I|, \max(I)))$, for some polynomial p. It is also obvious that pseudopolynomial algorithms may perhaps be constructed for *number problems*, i.e. those problems Π for which there does not exist a polynomial p such that $\max(I) \leq p(|I|)$ for each instance I of Π. The KNAPSACK problem as well as TRAVE-LING SALESMAN and INTEGER PROGRAMMING belong to number problems; HAMILTONIAN CIRCUIT and SATISFIABILITY do not. However, there might be number problems for which pseudopolynomial algorithms cannot be constructed [GJ78].

The above reasoning leads us to a deeper characterization of a class of *NP*-complete problems by distinguishing problems which are *NP*-complete in the strong sense [GJ78, GJ79].

For a given decision problem Π and an arbitrary polynomial p, let Π_p denote the subproblem of Π which is created by restricting Π to those instances for which $\max(I) \le p(|I|)$. Thus Π_p is not a number problem.

Decision problem Π is *NP-complete in the strong sense* (*strongly NP-complete*) if $\Pi \in NP$ and there exists a polynomial p defined for integers for which Π_p is *NP*-complete.

It follows that if Π is *NP*-complete and it is not a number problem, then it is *NP*-complete in the strong sense. Moreover, if Π is *NP*-complete in the strong sense, then the existence of a pseudopolynomial algorithm for Π would be equivalent to the existence of polynomial algorithms for all *NP*-complete problems, and thus would be equivalent to the equality $P = NP$. It has been shown that TRAVELING SALESMAN and 3-PARTITION are examples of number problems that are *NP*-complete in the strong sense [GJ79].

From the above definition it follows that to prove *NP*-completeness in the strong sense for some decision problem Π, one has to find a polynomial p for which Π is *NP*-complete in the strong sense, which is usually not an easy way. To make this proof easier one may use the concept of pseudopolynomial transformation [GJ78].

To end this section, let us stress once more that the membership of a given search problem in class *FP* or in the class of *NP*-hard problems does not depend on the chosen encoding scheme if this scheme is reasonable as defined earlier. The differences in input lengths for a given instance that follow from particular encoding schemes have only influence on the complexity of the polynomial (if the problem belongs to class *FP*) or on the complexity of the exponential algorithm (if the problem is *NP*-hard). On the other hand, if numbers are written unary, then pseudopolynomial algorithms would become polynomial because of the artificial increase in input lengths. However, problems *NP*-hard in the strong sense would remain *NP*-hard even in the case of such an encoding scheme. Thus, they are also called *unary NP-hard* [LRB77].

2.3 Graphs and Networks

2.3.1 Basic Notions

A *graph* is a pair $G = (\mathcal{V}, \mathcal{E})$ where $\mathcal{V}$ is the set of *vertices* or *nodes*, and $\mathcal{E}$ is the set of *edges*. If $\mathcal{E}$ is a binary relation over $\mathcal{V}$, then G is called a *directed* graph (or *digraph*). If $\mathcal{E}$ is a set of two-element subsets of $\mathcal{V}$, i.e. $\mathcal{E} \subseteq \mathcal{P}_2(\mathcal{V})$, then G is an *undirected* graph.

A graph $G' = (\mathcal{V}', \mathcal{E}')$ is a *subgraph* of $G = (\mathcal{V}, \mathcal{E})$ (denoted by $G' \subseteq G$), if $\mathcal{V}' \subseteq \mathcal{V}$, and $\mathcal{E}'$ is the set of all edges of $\mathcal{E}$ that connect vertices of $\mathcal{V}'$.

Let $G_1 = (\mathcal{V}_1, \mathcal{E}_1)$ and $G_2 = (\mathcal{V}_2, \mathcal{E}_2)$ be graphs whose vertex sets $\mathcal{V}_1$ and $\mathcal{V}_2$ are not necessarily disjoint. Then $G_1 \cup G_2 = (\mathcal{V}_1 \cup \mathcal{V}_2, \mathcal{E}_1 \cup \mathcal{E}_2)$ is the *union* graph of G_1 and G_2, and $G_1 \cap G_2 = (\mathcal{V}_1 \cap \mathcal{V}_2, \mathcal{E}_1 \cap \mathcal{E}_2)$ is the *intersection* graph of G_1 and G_2.

Digraphs G_1 and G_2 are *isomorphic* if there is a 1–1 mapping $\chi: \mathcal{V}_1 \rightarrow \mathcal{V}_2$ such that $(v_1, v_2) \in \mathcal{E}_1$ if and only if $(\chi(v_1), \chi(v_2)) \in \mathcal{E}_2$.

A (undirected) *path* in a graph or in a digraph $G = (\mathcal{V}, \mathcal{E})$ is a sequence $i_1, \cdots, i_r$ of distinct nodes of $\mathcal{V}$ satisfying the property that either $(i_k, i_{k+1}) \in \mathcal{E}$ or $(i_{k+1}, i_k) \in \mathcal{E}$ for each $k = 1, \cdots, r-1$. A *directed path* is defined similarly, except that $(i_k, i_{k+1}) \in \mathcal{E}$ for each $k = 1, \cdots, r-1$. A (undirected) *cycle* is a path together with an edge (i_r, i_1) or (i_1, i_r). A *directed cycle* is a directed path together with the edge (i_r, i_1). We will call a graph (digraph) G *acyclic* if it contains no (directed) cycle.

Two vertices i and j of G are said to be *connected* if there is at least one undirected path between i and j. G is *connected* if all pairs of vertices are connected; otherwise it is *disconnected*.

Let v and w be vertices of the digraph $G = (\mathcal{V}, \mathcal{E})$. If there is a directed path from v to w, then w is called *successor* of v, and v is called *predecessor* of w. If $(v, w) \in \mathcal{E}$, then vertex w is called *immediate successor* of v, and v is called *immediate predecessor* of w. The set of immediate successors of vertex v is denoted by isucc(v); the sets succ(v), ipred(v), and pred(v) are defined similarly. The cardinality of ipred(v) is called *in-degree* of vertex v, whereas *out-degree* is the cardinality of isucc(v). A vertex v that has no immediate predecessor is called *initial vertex* (i.e. ipred(v) = $\varnothing$); a vertex v having no immediate successors is called *final* (i.e. isucc(v) = $\varnothing$).

Directed or undirected graphs can be represented by means of their adjacency matrix. If $\mathcal{V} = \{v_1, \cdots, v_n\}$, the *adjacency matrix* is a binary (n, n)-matrix A. In case of a directed graph, $A(i,j) = 1$ if there is an edge from v_i to v_j, and $A(i,j) = 0$ otherwise. In case of an undirected graph, $A(i,j) = 1$ if there is an edge between v_i and v_j, and $A(i,j) = 0$ otherwise. The complexity of storage (space complexity) is $O(n^2)$. If the adjacency matrix is sparse, as e.g. in case of trees, there are better ways of representation, usually based on *linked lists*. For details we refer to [AHU74].

2.3.2 Special Classes of Digraphs

A digraph $G = (\mathcal{V}, \mathcal{E})$ is called *bipartite* if its vertex set $\mathcal{V}$ can be partitioned into two subsets $\mathcal{V}_1$ and $\mathcal{V}_2$ such that for each edge $(i,j) \in \mathcal{E}$, $i \in \mathcal{V}_1$ and $j \in \mathcal{V}_2$.

If a digraph $G = (\mathcal{V}, \mathcal{E})$ contains no directed cycle it can always be enlarged to a partially ordered set (poset, see Section 2.1) by adding transitive edges, i.e. those pairs (u, w) of vertices for which there exists a directed path from u to w, and all reflexive pairs (v, v) ($v \in \mathcal{V}$) to $\mathcal{E}$. On the other hand, given a poset $(\mathcal{V}, \mathcal{R})$, where $\mathcal{R}$ is a partial order over set $\mathcal{V}$, we can always construct a "smallest" digraph $(\mathcal{V}, \mathcal{E})$ in the following way: $\mathcal{E}$ is obtained by taking those pairs of elements (u, w), $u \neq w$, for which no sequence $v_1, \cdots, v_k$ of elements with $(u, v_1) \in \mathcal{R}$, $(v_i, v_{i+1}) \in \mathcal{R}$ for $i = 1, \cdots, k-1$, $(v_k,$

$w) \in \mathcal{R}$ can be found. Such a smallest digraph without transitive edges is called *precedence graph*; it can be constructed from a given poset in $O(|\mathcal{V}|^{2.8})$ time [AHU74].

A digraph $G = (\mathcal{V}, \mathcal{E})$ is called a *chain* if in the corresponding poset $(\mathcal{V}, \mathcal{R})$ for any two vertices v and $v' \in \mathcal{V}$, $v \neq v'$, either $(v, v') \in \mathcal{R}$ or $(v', v) \in \mathcal{R}$ (such a poset is usually called a linear order). An *antichain* is a (directed) graph $(\mathcal{V}, \mathcal{E})$ where $\mathcal{E} = \varnothing$.

An *out-tree* is a precedence graph where exactly one vertex has in-degree 0, and all the other vertices have in-degree 1. If $G = (\mathcal{V}, \mathcal{E})$ is an out-tree, then graph $G' = (\mathcal{V}, \mathcal{E}^{-1})$ is called an *in-tree*. An *out-forest* [*in-forest*] is a disjoint union of out-trees [in-trees], respectively. An *opposing forest* is a disjoint union of in-trees and out-trees.

The precedence graph of a poset that is an interval order (see Section 2.1) is often called an *interval order*.

A precedence graph $(\{a, b, c, d\}, \prec)$ has *N-structure* if $a \prec c$, $b \prec c$, $b \prec d$, $a \nprec d$, $d \nprec a$, $a \nprec b$, $b \nprec a$, $c \nprec d$, and $d \nprec c$ (see also Figure 2.3.1). A precedence graph P is *N-free* if it contains no subset isomorphic to an *N*-structure.

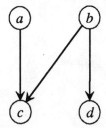

Figure 2.3.1 *N-structured precedence graph.*

Finally we introduce a class of precedence graphs that has been considered frequently in literature. Let $S = (\mathcal{V}, \prec)$ be a precedence graph, and let for each $v \in \mathcal{V}$, $P_v = (\mathcal{V}_v, \prec_v)$ be a precedence graph, where all the sets $\mathcal{V}_v$ $(v \in \mathcal{V})$ and $\mathcal{V}$ are pairwise disjoint. Let $\mathcal{U} = \bigcup_{v \in \mathcal{V}} \mathcal{V}_v$. Define $(\mathcal{U}, \prec_{\mathcal{U}})$ as the following precedence graph: for $p, q \in \mathcal{U}$, $p \prec_{\mathcal{U}} q$ if either there are $v, v' \in \mathcal{V}$ with $v \prec v'$ such that p is a final vertex in $(\mathcal{V}_v, \prec_v)$ and q is an initial vertex in $(\mathcal{V}_{v'}, \prec_{v'})$, or there is $v \in \mathcal{V}$ with $p, q \in \mathcal{V}_v$ and $p \prec_v q$. Then $(\mathcal{U}, \prec_{\mathcal{U}})$ is called the *lexicographic sum* of $(P_v)_{v \in \mathcal{V}}$ over S. Notice that each vertex v of digraph $S = (\mathcal{V}, \prec)$ is replaced by digraph $(\mathcal{V}_v, \prec_v)$, and if vertex v is connected to v' in S (i.e. $v \prec v'$), then each final vertex of $(\mathcal{V}_v, \prec_v)$ is connected to each initial vertex of $(\mathcal{V}_{v'}, \prec_{v'})$.

We need two special cases of lexicographic sums: If $S = (\mathcal{V}, \prec)$ is a chain, the lexicographic sum of $(P_v)_{v \in \mathcal{V}}$ over S is called a *linear sum*. If S is an antichain (i.e. $v_1 \prec v_2 \Rightarrow v_1 = v_2$), then the lexicographic sum of $(P_v)_{v \in \mathcal{V}}$ over S is called *disjoint sum*. A *series-parallel* precedence graph is a precedence graph that can be constructed from one-vertex precedence graphs by repeated application of the operations linear sum and disjoint sum. Opposing forests are examples of series-parallel digraphs. Another example is shown in Figure 2.3.2.

Without proof we mention some properties of series-parallel graphs. A precedence graph $G = (\mathcal{V}, \mathcal{E})$ is series-parallel if and only if it is N-free. The question if a digraph is series-parallel can be decided in $O(|\mathcal{V}| + |\mathcal{E}|)$ time [VTL82].

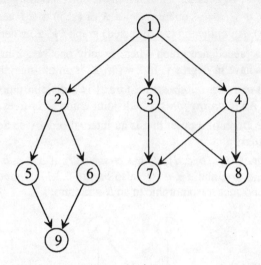

Figure 2.3.2 *Example of a series-parallel digraph.*

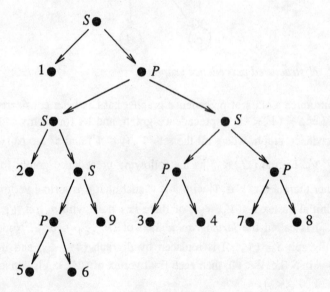

Figure 2.3.3 *Decomposition tree of the digraph of Figure 2.3.2.*

The structure of a series-parallel graph as it is obtained by successive applications of linear sum and disjoint sum operations can be displayed by a *decomposition tree*. Figure 2.3.3 shows a decomposition tree for the series-parallel graph of Figure 2.3.2. Each leaf of the decomposition tree is identified with a vertex of the series-parallel graph. An *S-node* represents an application of linear sum (series composition) to the subgraphs identified with its children; the ordering of these children is important: we adopt the convention that left precedes right. A *P-node* represents an application of the operation of disjoint sum (parallel composition) to the subgraphs identified with its children; the ordering of these children is of no relevance for the disjoint sum. The series or parallel relationship of any pair of vertices can be determined by finding their least common ancestor in the decomposition tree.

2.3.3 Networks

In this section the problem of finding a maximum flow in a network is considered. We will analyze the subject rather thoroughly because of its importance for many scheduling problems.

By a *network* we will mean a directed graph $G = (\mathcal{V}, \mathcal{E})$ without loops and parallel edges, where each edge $e \in \mathcal{E}$ is assigned a *capacity* $c(e) \in I\!R^{\geq 0}$, and sometimes a cost of a unit flow. Usually in the network two vertices s and t, called a *source* and a *sink*, respectively, are specified.

A real-valued *flow* function ρ is to be assigned to each edge such that the following conditions hold for some $F \in I\!R^{\geq 0}$:

$$0 \leq \rho(e) \leq c(e) \text{ for each } e \in \mathcal{E}, \tag{2.3.1}$$

$$\sum_{e \in IN(v)} \rho(e) - \sum_{e \in OUT(v)} \rho(e) = \begin{cases} -F & \text{for } v = s \\ 0 & \text{for } v \in \mathcal{V} - \{s, t\} \\ F & \text{for } v = t, \end{cases} \tag{2.3.2}$$

where $IN(v)$ and $OUT(v)$ are the sets of edges *incoming* to vertex v and *outgoing* from vertex v, respectively. The *total flow* (the *value of flow*) F of ρ is defined by

$$F = \sum_{e \in IN(t)} \rho(e) - \sum_{e \in OUT(t)} \rho(e). \tag{2.3.3}$$

Given a network, in the *maximum flow problem* we want to find a flow function ρ which obeys the above conditions and for which total flow F is at its maximum.

Now, some important notions will be defined and their properties will be discussed. Let S be a subset of the set of vertices $\mathcal{V}$ such that $s \in S$ and $t \notin S$, and let $\bar{S}$ be the complement of S, i.e. $\bar{S} = \mathcal{V} - S$. Let $(S, \bar{S})$ denote a set of edges of network G, each of which has its starting vertex in S and its target vertex in $\bar{S}$. Set $(\bar{S}, S)$ is defined in a similar way. Given some subset $S \subseteq \mathcal{V}$, either set, $(S, \bar{S})$ and $(\bar{S}, S)$, will be called *cut* defined by S.

Following definition (2.3.3) we see that the value of flow is measured at the sink of the network. It is however, possible to measure this value at any cut [Eve79, FF62].

Lemma 2.3.1 *For each subset of vertices* $S \subseteq \mathcal{V}$, *we have*

$$F = \sum_{e \in (S, \bar{S})} \rho(e) - \sum_{e \in (\bar{S}, S)} \rho(e). \quad \Box \tag{2.3.4}$$

Let us denote by $c(S)$ the *capacity of a cut* defined by S,

$$c(S) = \sum_{e \in (S, \bar{S})} c(e).$$ (2.3.5)

It is possible to prove the following lemma, which specifies a relation between the value of a flow and the capacity of any cut [FF62].

Lemma 2.3.2 *For any flow function* ρ *having the value F and for any cut defined by S we have*

$$F \leq c(S). \ \square$$ (2.3.6)

From the above lemma we get immediately the following corollary that specifies a relation between maximum flow and a cut of minimum capacity.

Corollary 2.3.3 *If* $F = c(S)$, *then F is at its maximum, and S defines a cut of minimum capacity.* $\square$

Let us now define, for a given flow ρ, an *augmenting path* as a path from s to t, (not necessarily directed), which can be used to increase the value of the flow. If an edge e belonging to that path is directed from s to t, then $\rho(e) < c(e)$, otherwise no increase in the flow value on that path would be possible. On the other hand, if such an edge e is directed from t to s, then $\rho(e) > 0$ must be satisfied in order to be able to increase the flow value F by decreasing $\rho(e)$.

Example 2.3.4 As an example let us consider the network given in Figure 2.3.4(a). Each edge of this network is assigned two numbers, $c(e)$ and $\rho(e)$. It is easy to check that flow ρ in this network obeys conditions (2.3.1) and (2.3.2) and its value is equal to 3. An augmenting path is shown in Figure 2.3.4(b). The flow on edge (5, 4) can be decreased by one unit. All the other edge flows on that path can be increased by one unit. The resulting network with a new flow is shown in Figure 2.3.4(c). $\square$

The first method proposed for the construction of a flow of a maximum value was given by Ford and Fulkerson [FF62]. This method consists in finding an augmenting path in a network and increasing the flow value along this path until at least one such path remains in the network. Convergence of such a general method could be proved for integer capacities only. A corresponding algorithm is of pseudopolynomial complexity [FF62, Eve79].

An important improvement of the above algorithm was made by Edmonds and Karp [EK72]. They showed that if the shortest augmenting path is chosen at every step, then the complexity of the algorithm reduces to $O(|V|^3|E|)$, no matter what are the edge capacities. Further improvements in algorithmic efficiency of network flow algorithm were made by Dinic [Din70] and Karzanov [Kar74], whose algorithms' running times are $O(|V|^2|E|)$ and $O(|V|^3)$, respectively. An algorithm proposed by Cherkassky [Che77] allows for solving the max-flow problem in time $O(|V|^2|E|^{1/2})$.

Below, Dinic's algorithm will be described, since despite its relatively high worst case complexity function, its average running time is low [Che80], and the idea behind it is quite simple. It uses the notion of a *layered network* which contains all the shortest paths in a network. This allows for a parallel increase of flows in all such paths, which is the main reason of the efficiency of the algorithm.

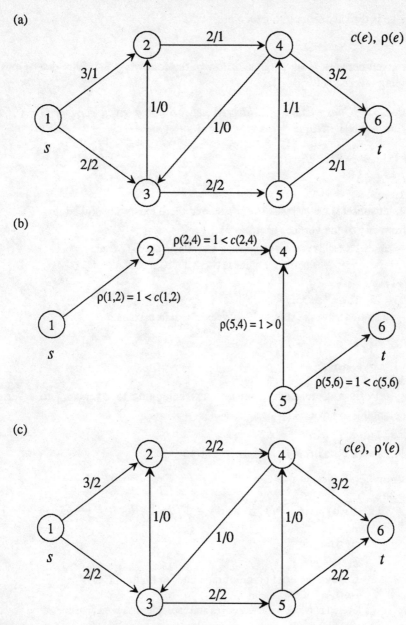

Figure 2.3.4 *A network for Example 2.3.4*
   (a) *a flow* ρ(e) *is assigned to each edge,*
   (b) *an augmenting path,*
   (c) *a new flow* ρ'(e).

In order to present this algorithm, the notion of *usefulness* of an edge for a given flow is introduced. We say that edge *e* having flow ρ(e) is *useful* from *u* to *v*, if one of the following conditions is fulfilled:

1) if the edge is directed from u to v then $\rho(e) < c(e)$;

2) otherwise, $\rho(e) > 0$.

For a given network $G = (\mathcal{V}, \mathcal{E})$ and flow ρ, the following algorithm determines a corresponding layered network.

Algorithm 2.3.5 *Construction of a layered network for a given network $G = (\mathcal{V}, \mathcal{E})$ and flow function ρ* [Din70].
```
begin
Set 𝒱₀ := {s}; 𝒯 := {s}; i := 0;
while t ∉ 𝒯 do
    begin
    Construct subset 𝒯 := {v | v ∉ 𝒱ⱼ for j ≤ i and there exists a useful edge
        from any of the vertices of 𝒱ᵢ to v};
        -- subset 𝒯 contains vertices comprising a new layer of the layered network
    𝒱ᵢ₊₁ := 𝒯;        -- a new layer of the network has been constructed
    i := i+1;
    if 𝒯 = ∅ then exit;
        -- no layered network exists, the flow value F is at its maximum
    end;
l := i; 𝒱ₗ := {t};
for j := 1 to l do
    begin
    𝐸ⱼ := {e | e is a useful edge from a vertex belonging to layer 𝒱ⱼ₋₁ to a vertex
        belonging to layer 𝒱ⱼ};
    for all e ∈ 𝐸ⱼ do
        if e = (u,v) and u ∈ 𝒱ⱼ₋₁ and v ∈ 𝒱ⱼ

        then c̃(e) := c(e)−ρ(e)
        else
            if e(v,u) and u ∈ 𝒱ⱼ₋₁ and v ∈ 𝒱ⱼ
            then
                begin
                c̃(e) := ρ(e);
                Change the orientation of the edge, so that e = (u,v);
                end;
        end;    -- a layered network with new edges and capacities has been constructed
end;
```

In such a layered network a new flow function $\tilde{\rho}$ with $\tilde{\rho} = 0$ for each e is assumed. Then a maximal flow is searched for, i.e. one such that for each path $v_0 (= s)$, v_1, $v_2, \cdots, v_{l-1}$, $v_l (= t)$, where $e_j = (v_{j-1}, v_j) \in \mathcal{E}_j$ and $v_j \in \mathcal{V}_j$, $j = 1, 2, \cdots, l$, there exists at least one edge e such that $\tilde{\rho}(e_j) = \tilde{c}(e_j)$.

Let us note, that such a maximal flow may not be of maximum value. This fact is illustrated in Figure 2.3.5 where all capacities $\tilde{c}(e) = 1$. The flow depicted in this figure is maximal and its value $F = 1$. It is not hard, however, to construct a flow of value $F = 2$.

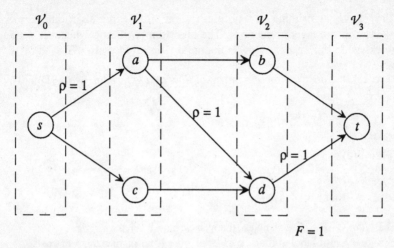

$$F = 1$$

Figure 2.3.5 *An example of a maximal flow which is not of maximum value.*

The construction of a maximal flow for a given layered network is shown below. It consists in finding augmenting paths by means of a *labeling procedure*. For this purpose a depth first search label algorithm is used, that labels all the nodes of the layered network, i.e. assigns to node u, if any, a label $lab(u)$ that corresponds to edge $e = (v, u)$ in a layered network. The algorithm uses for each node v a list isucc(v) of all immediate successors of v (i.e. all nodes u for which an arc (v, u) exists in the layered network). Let us note that, if v belongs to layer $\mathcal{V}_j$, then $u \in$ isucc(v) belongs to layer $\mathcal{V}_{j+1}$, and edge $(v, u) \in \mathcal{E}_j$. The algorithm uses recursively an algorithm $label(v)$ that labels nodes being successors of v. Boolean variable $new(v)$ is used to check whether or not a given node has been visited and consequently labeled. The algorithms are as follows.

Algorithm 2.3.6 *label(v)*.
```
begin
new(v) := false;        -- node v has been visited and labeled
for  u ∈ isucc(v)  do
if  new(u) then
    begin
```
$$lab(u) := e \ \text{if} \ e = (v, u) \in \bigcup_{j=1}^{l} \mathcal{E}_j;$$
```
    call  label(u);
    end;        -- all successors of node v have been labeled
end;
```

Algorithm 2.3.7 *label*.
```
begin
lab(s) := 0;        -- a source of layered network has been labeled
for all  v ∈ V  do  new(v) := true;        -- initialization
```

```
call label(s);
end;          -- all successors of s in the layered network are now visited and labeled
```

Using the above algorithms as subroutines the following algorithm constructs a maximal flow in the layered network. The algorithm will stop whenever no augmenting path exists; in this case the flow is maximal [Din70] (see also [Eve79]).

Algorithm 2.3.8 *Construction of a maximal flow in a layered network* [Din70].
```
begin
```
for all $e \in \bigcup_{j=1}^{l} \mathcal{E}_j$ **do**
```
    begin
```
$\qquad \rho_1(e) := \tilde{\rho}(e) := 0;$

$\qquad c_1(e) := \tilde{c}(e);$
```
    end;          -- initialization phase
loop
    call label;          -- all nodes, if any, have been labeled
    if node t is not labeled then exit;          -- no augmenting path exists
         -- a maximal flow in a layered network has been constructed
```
Find an augmenting path ap starting from node t backward and using labels;
$\Delta := \min\{c_1(e) \mid e \in ap\};$
```
    for all e ∈ ap do
        begin
```
$\qquad\quad \rho_1(e) := \Delta;$

$\qquad\quad \tilde{\rho}(e) := \tilde{\rho}(e) + \rho_1(e);$

$\qquad\quad c_1(e) := c_1(e) - \Delta;$
```
        end;          -- the value of a flow is increased along an augmenting path
    for all e with c₁(e) = 0 do Delete e from the layered network;
    repeat
        Delete all nodes which have either no incoming or no outgoing edges;
        Delete all edges incident with such nodes;
    until all such edges and nodes are deleted;
```
$\qquad$ **for all** $e \in \bigcup_{j=1}^{l} \mathcal{E}_j$ **do** $\rho_1(e) := 0;$
```
end loop;
end;
```

The flow constructed by the above algorithm is used to obtain a new flow in the original network. Next, a new layered network is created and the above procedure is repeated until no new layered network can be constructed. The obtained flow has a maximum value. This is summarized in the next algorithm.

Algorithm 2.3.9 *Construction of a flow of maximum value* [Din70].
```
begin
```
$\rho(e) := 0$ for all $e \in \mathcal{E};$
```
loop
    call Algorithm 2.3.5;
```

```
              -- a new layered network is constructed for a flow function ρ
              -- if no layered network exists, then the flow has maximum value
     call Algorithm 2.3.8;          -- a new maximal flow ρ̃ is constructed
     for all e ∈ E do
        begin
        if u ∈ 𝒱_{j-1} and v ∈ 𝒱_j and e = (u,v) ∈ E

        then ρ(e) := ρ(e) + ρ̃(e);
              -- the value of the flow increases if edge e has the same direction
              -- in the original and in the layered network
        if u ∈ 𝒱_{j-1} and v ∈ 𝒱_j and e = (v,u) ∈ E

        then ρ(e) := ρ(e) − ρ̃(e);
              -- the value of the flow decreases if edge e has opposite directions
              -- in the original and in the layered network
        end;
     -- the flow in the original network is augmented using the
     -- constructed maximal flow values
end loop;
end;
```

To analyze the complexity of the above approach let us call one loop of Algorithm 2.3.9 a *phase*. We see that one phase consists of finding a layered network, constructing a maximal flow $\tilde{\rho}$ in the latter and improving the flow in the original network. It can be proved [Din70, Eve79] that the number of phases is bounded from above by $O(|\mathcal{V}|)$. The most complex part of each phase is to find a maximal flow in a layered network. Since in Algorithm 2.3.8 a depth first search procedure has been used for visiting a network, the complexity of one phase is $O(|\mathcal{V}||E|)$. The overall complexity of Dinic's approach is thus $O(|\mathcal{V}|^2|E|)$.

Further generalizations of the subject include networks with lower bounds on edge flows, networks with linear total cost function of the flow where a flow of maximum value and of minimal total cost is looked for, and a transportation problem being a special case of the latter. All these problems can be solved in time bounded from above by a polynomial in the number of nodes and edges of the network. We refer the reader to [AMO89] or [Law76] where a detailed analysis of the subject is presented.

2.4 Enumerative Methods

In this section we describe very briefly two general methods of solving many combinatorial problems[6], namely the method of dynamic programming and the method of branch and bound. Few remarks should be made at the beginning, concerning the scope of this presentation. Firstly, we will not go into details, since both the methods are broadly treated in literature, including basic scheduling books [Bak74, Len77, Rin76], and our presentation should only fulfill the needs of this book. In particular, we will

---

[6] Dynamic programming can also be used in a wider context (see e.g. [Den82, How69, DL79]).

not perform a comparative study of the methods - an interested reader is referred to [Cof76]. We will also not present examples, since they will be given in the later chapters.

Before passing to the descripton of the methods let us mention that they are of *implicit enumeration* variety, because they consider certain solutions only indirectly, without actually evaluating them explicitly.

2.4.1 Dynamic Programming

Fundamentals of *dynamic programming* were elaborated by Bellman in the 1950's and presented in [Bel57, BD62]. The name "Dynamic Programming" is slightly misleading, but generally accepted. A better description would be "recursive" or "multistage" optimization, since it interprets optimization problems as *multistage decision processes*. It means that the problem is divided into a number of stages, and at each stage a decision is required which impacts on the decisions to be made in later stages. Now, Bellman's principle of optimality is applied to draw up a recursive equation which describes the optimal criterion value at a given stage in terms of the previously obtained one. This principle can be formulated as follows: Starting from any current stage, an optimal policy for the rest of the process, i.e. for subsequent stages, is independent of the policy adopted in the previous stages. Of course, not all optimization problems can be presented as multistage decision processes for which the above principle is true. However, the class of problems for which it works is quite large. For example, it contains problems with an additive optimality criterion, but also other problems as we will show in Sections 5.1.1 and 8.4.3.

If dynamic programming is applied to a combinatoral problem, then in order to calculate the optimal criterion value for any subset of size k, we first have to know the optimal value for each subset of size $k-1$. Thus, if our problem is characterized by a set of n elements, the number of subsets considered is 2^n. It means that dynamic programming algorithms are of exponential computational complexity. However, for problems which are *NP*-hard (but not in the strong sense) it is often possible to construct pseudopolynomial dynamic programming algorithms which are of practical value for reasonable instance sizes.

2.4.2 Branch and Bound

Suppose that given a finite [7] set S of feasible solutions and a criterion $\gamma\colon S \to I\!\!R$, we want to find $S^* \in S$ such that $\gamma(S^*) = \min_{S \in S} \gamma(S)$.

Branch and bound finds S^* by implicit enumeration of all $S \in S$ through examination of increasingly smaller subsets of S. These subsets can be treated as sets of solutions of corresponding subproblems of the original problem. This way of thinking is especially motivated if the considered problems have a clear practical interpretation. Since this is the case of this book, we will adopt this interpretation.

As its name implies, the branch and bound method consists of two fundamental procedures: branching and bounding. *Branching* is the procedure of partitioning a large

---

[7] In general, $|S|$ can be infinite (see, e.g. [Mit70]).

problem into two or more subproblems usually mutually exclusive [8]. Furthermore, the subproblems can be partioned in a similar way, etc. *Bounding* calculates a *lower bound* on the optimal solution value for each subproblem generated in the branching process. Note that the branching procedure can be conveniently represented as a *search* (or *branching*) *tree*. At level 0, this tree consists of a single node representing the original problem, and at further levels it consists of nodes representing particular subproblems of the problem at the previous level. Edges are introduced from each problem node to each of its subproblems nodes. A list of unprocessed nodes (also called active nodes) corresponding to subproblems that have not been eliminated and whose own subproblems have not yet been generated, is maintained.

Suppose that at some stage of the branch and bound process a (complete) solution S of criterion value $\gamma(S)$ has been obtained. Suppose also that a node encountered in the process has an associated lower bound $LB > \gamma(S)$. Then the node needs not be considered any further in the search for S^*, since the resulting solution can never have a value less than $\gamma(S)$. When such a node is found, it is eliminated, and its branch is said to be *fathomed*, since we do not continue the bounding process from it. The solution used for checking if a branch is fathomed is sometimes called a *trial* solution. At the beginning it may be found using a special heuristic procedure, or it can be obtained in the course of the tree search, e.g. by pursuing the tree directly to the bottom as rapidly as possible. At any later stage the best solution found so far can be chosen as a trial one. The value $\gamma(S)$ for a trial solution S is often called an *upper bound*. Let us mention that a node can be eliminated not only on the basis of lower bounds but also by means of so-called elimination criteria provided by dominance properties or feasibility conditions developed for a given problem.

The choice of a node from the set of generated nodes which have so far neither been eliminated nor led to branching is due to the chosen *search strategy*. Two search strategies are used most frequently: jumptracking and backtracking. *Jumptracking* implements a *frontier search* where a node with a minimal lower bound is selected for examination, while *backtracking* implements a *depth first search* where the descendant nodes of a parent node are examined either in an arbitrary order or in order of nondecreasing lower bounds. Thus, in the jumptracking strategy the branching process jumps from one branch of the tree to another, whereas in the backtracking strategy it first proceeds directly to the bottom along some path to find a trial solution and then retraces that path upward up to the first level with active nodes, and so on. It is easy to notice that jumptracking tends to construct a fairly large list of active nodes, while backtracking maintains relatively few nodes on the list at any time. However, an advantage of jumptracking is the quality of its trial solutions which are usually much closer to optimum than the trial solutions generated by backtracking, especially at early stages. Deeper comparative discussion of characteristcs of the search strategies can be found in [Agi66, LW66].

Summing up the above considerations we can say that in order to implement the scheme of the branch and bound method, i.e. in order to construct a branch and bound algorithm for a given problem, one must decide about

(i) the branching procedure and the search strategy,

---

[8] If this is not the case, we speak rather about a division of S instead of its partition.

(ii) the bounding procedure or elimination criteria.

Making the above decisions one should explore the problem specificity and observe the compromise between the length of the branching process and time overhead concerned with computing lower bounds or trial solutions. However, the actual computational behavior of branch and bound algorithms remains unpredictable and large computational experiments are necessary to recognize their quality. It is obvious that the computational complexity function of a branch and bound algorithm is exponential in problem size when we search for an optimal solution. However, the approach is often used for finding suboptimal solutions, and then we can obtain polynomial time complexity by stopping the branching process at a certain stage or after a certain time period elapsed.

2.5 Heuristic and Approximation Algorithms

As already mentioned, scheduling problems belong to a broad class of combinatorial optimization problems (cf. Section 2.2.1). To solve these problems one tends to use optimization algorithms which for sure always find optimal solutions. However, not for all optimization problems, polynomial time optimization algorithms can be constructed. This is because some of the problems are *NP*-hard. In such cases one often uses *heuristic (suboptimal) algorithms* which tend toward but do not guarantee the finding of optimal solutions for any instance of an optimization problem. Of course, the necessary condition for these algorithms to be applicable in practice is that their worst-case complexity function is bounded from above by a low-order polynomial in the input length. A sufficient condition follows from an evaluation of the distance between the solution value they produce and the value of an optimal solution. This evaluation may concern the worst case or a mean behavior. We will call heuristic algorithms with analytically evaluated accuracy *approximation algorithms*. To be more precise, we give here some definitions, starting with the worst case analysis [GJ79].

If Π is a minimization (maximization) problem, and I is any instance of it, we may define the ratio $R_A(I)$ for an approximation algorithm A as

$$R_A(I) = \frac{A(I)}{OPT(I)} \qquad \left(R_A(I) = \frac{OPT(I)}{A(I)} \right),$$

where $A(I)$ is the value of the solution constructed by algorithm A for instance I, and $OPT(I)$ is the value of an optimal solution for I. The *absolute performance ratio* R_A for an approximation algorithm A for problem Π is then given as

$$R_A = \inf\{r \geq 1 \mid R_A(I) \leq r \text{ for all instances of } \Pi\}.$$

The *asymptotic performance ratio* R_A^∞ for A is given as

$$R_A^\infty = \inf\{r \geq 1 \mid \text{for some positive integer } K, R_A(I) \leq r \text{ for}$$

$$\text{all instances of } \Pi \text{ satisfying } OPT(I) \geq K \}.$$

The above formulae define a measure of the "goodness" of approximation algorithms. The closer R_A^∞ is to 1, the better algorithm A performs. However, for some combinatorial problems it can be proved that there is no hope of finding an approximation algorithm of a specified accuracy, i.e. this question is as hard as finding a polynomial time algorithm for any NP-complete problem.

Analysis of the worst-case behavior of an approximation algorithm may be complemented by an analysis of its mean behavior. This can be done in two ways. The first consists in assuming that the parameters of instances of the considered problem Π are drawn from a certain distribution D and then one analyzes the *mean performance* of algorithm A.

In such an analysis it is usually assumed that all parameter values are realizations of independent probabilistic variables of the same distribution function. Then, for an instance I_n of the considered optimization problem (n being a number of generated parameters) a probabilistic value analysis is performed. The result is an asymptotic value $OPT(I_n)$ expressed in terms of problem parameters. Then, algorithm A is probabilistically evaluated by comparing solution values $A(I_n)$ it produces ($A(I_n)$ being independent probabilistic variables) with $OPT(I_n)$ [Rin87]. The two evaluation criteria used are absolute error and relative error. The *absolute error* is defined as a difference between the approximate and optimal solution values

$$a_n = A(I_n) - OPT(I_n).$$

On the other hand, the *relative error* is defined as the ratio of the absolute error and the optimal solution value

$$b_n = \frac{A(I_n) - OPT(I_n)}{OPT(I_n)}.$$

Usually, one evaluates the convergence of both errors to zero. Three types of convergence are distinguished. The strongest, i.e. *almost sure convergence* for a sequence of probabilistic variables y_n which converge to constant c is defined as

$$Pr\{\lim_{n\to\infty} y_n = c\} = 1.$$

The latter implies a weaker *convergence in probability*, which means that for every $\varepsilon > 0$,

$$\lim_{n\to\infty} Pr\{|y_n - c| > \varepsilon\} = 0.$$

The above convergence implies the first one if the following additional condition holds for every $\varepsilon > 0$:

$$\sum_{j=1}^{\infty} Pr\{|y_n - c| > \varepsilon\} < \infty.$$

Finally, the third type of convergence, *convergence in expectation* holds if

$$\lim_{n\to\infty} |E(y_n) - c| = 0,$$

where $E(y_n)$ is the mean value of y_n.

It follows from the above definitions, that an approximation algorithm A is the best from the probabilistic analysis point of view if its absolute error almost surely converges to 0. Algorithm A is then called *asymptotically optimal*.

At this point one should also mention an analysis of the *rate of convergence* of the errors of approximation algorithms which may be different for algorithms whose absolute or relative errors are the same. Of course, the higher the rate, the better the performance of the algorithm is.

It is rather obvious that the mean performance can be much better than the worst case behavior, thus justifying the use of a given approximation algorithm. A main obstacle is the difficulty of proofs of the mean performance for realistic distribution functions. Thus, the second way of evaluating the mean behavior of heuristic algorithms are computational experiments, which is still used very often. In the latter approach the values of the given criterion, constructed by the given heuristic algorithm and by an optimization algorithm are compared. This comparison should be made for a representative sample of instances. There are some practical problems which follow from the above statement and they are discussed in [SVW80].

At this point it will be worth to discuss general heuristic approaches which may be used as a framework for designing algorithms for solving particular problems. Such approaches are often called *meta-heuristics* and we will describe two recent ones: simulated annealing and tabu search.

The name *simulated annealing* [AK90, LA89] comes from the analogy between combinatorial optimization and evolution of thermal equilibrium of the solid. The base of the method is the so-called *metropolis algorithm*, which generates sequences of solid states in the following way. Given the current state of the solid, a small, randomly generated perturbation (a small displacement of randomly chosen particles) is applied. If the perturbation results in a lower energy state of the solid, then the process is continued with the new state. If energy increases, i.e. $\Delta E \geq 0$, then the new state is accepted with probability $exp(-\Delta E/(k_B T))$, where k_B is the Boltzmann constant, and T is the temperature. In the case of combinatorial optimization this idea leads to an iterative procedure where the solution plays the role of the state of the solid, and cost function γ and control parameter c_k (explained later) assume the role of energy and temperature, respectively. Being in a certain *seed solution i* simulated annealing accepts with some probability a change for an *inferior* (i.e. worse) *solution*. $AP_{ij}(k)$ represents the probability to accept an solution j inferior to seed solution i as the current seed solution at the annealing stage k. Its value is calculated as

$$AP_{ij}(k) = \min\left\{ 1, \exp(-\frac{\gamma(i) - \gamma(j)}{c_k}) \right\}.$$

Let c_k denote the value of the control parameter at stage k, and let L_k be the number of transitions performed at this stage. $\mathcal{N}_i$ denotes the *neighborhood* of seed solution i, i.e. a set of solutions close to i. The control parameter is lowered until it approaches 0. The final "frozen" configuration is taken as the solution of the problem.

Then the simulated annealing algorithm can be presented as follows.

Algorithm 2.5.1 *Simulated annealing* [AK90, LA89].
```
begin
Initialize (i_start, c_0, L_0);
k := 0;
i := i_start;
repeat
    for l := 1 to L_k do
        begin
        Generate (j from N_i);

        if γ(j) ≤ γ(i) then i := j
        else if AP_ij(k) > random[0, 1) then i := j;
        end;
    k := k + 1;
    Calculate number of transitions L_k;
    Calculate new value of control parameter c_k;
until  stop criterion;
end;
```

Note that solutions, cost function and neighborhood structure are the only prerequisities to apply simulated annealing. The initial value c_0 of the control parameter should be large enough to allow all transitions. In practice it is obtained by starting at a small positive value and multiplying it repeatedly with a constant value greater than 1, until the acceptance ratio $AP_{ij}(0)$ of the transition is close to 1.

It can be shown that under several conditions, fulfilled in practice, this method is asymptotically convergent [Haj88]. A finite-time convergence of the algorithm needs specification of several parameters combined into a so-called *cooling schedule*. These parameters are the initial value c_0, the decrement function and the final value of the control parameter, and the number L_k of the solutions visited for each value of c_k. For the most commonly used cooling schedule [KGV83] the decrement of the control parameter is given by $c_{k+1} = \alpha c_k$, where α is typically chosen from the interval [0.8, 0.99]. Execution of the algorithm is terminated if the value of the cost function remains not improved after a predefined number of consecutive reductions of c_k (stop criterion).

The number L_k of the solutions visited for each value of c_k is based on the requirement to restore quasi equilibrium state. Intuitively it is restored if a fixed number of transitions is accepted. As $c_k \rightarrow 0$ one would obtain $L_k \rightarrow \infty$. Thus, in practice, L_k is bounded by some constant to avoid long chains of trials for small values of c_k.

Simulated annealing has been successfully applied for problems like traveling salesman, graph partitioning, matching, quadratic assignment, graph coloring, scheduling, *VLSI* design, facilities layout, image processing, code design and also in biology and physics (see [AK90] for a survey).

The second method we want to describe is *tabu search* designed by F. Glover [Glo85] (cf. [HW88]). The easiest way of introducing tabu search is thinking of an iterative descent method minimizing an objective function γ. An ordinary descent method starts with an initial solution i and finds solution j in its neighborhood N_i. If $γ(j) < γ(i)$ then it moves to j and repeats the step. If no such j can be found, descent procedure stops. Tabu search, on the other hand, starts from there. From neighborhood N_i, the best solution j^* is chosen (which is not necessarily better than the best one found so far). However, such a procedure may introduce cycling. To avoid this one introduces so-called *tabu list L* as a data structure storing in a queue all the the solutions visited in the last $l = |L|$ (constant or variable) iterations. The tabu list may also hold solutions forbidden by definition of the problem at hand. Deciding that at a given step some solutions are tabu and some are not may be too restrictive. Because of this an additional feature was introduced. The tabu status of a move from solution i to solution j may be ignored if it is "sufficiently small", i.e. $\gamma(j) < a(\gamma(i))$, where $a(z)$ is the so-called *aspiration function*. Aspiration functions can be defined in many ways, one of the most common formulations is as follows. Suppose γ is integer-valued, then initially $a(z) = z$. In the course of execution of the tabu search $a(z)$ is updated so as to $a(z)$ be the smallest value reached when a move is made from a solution with the same value of γ. (In the case γ is real-valued, we consider appropriate intervals of γ values.) The search is stopped after a number of iterations without improvement. Thus, the tabu search algorithm can be presented in the following way.

Algorithm 2.5.2 *Tabu search* [Glo85, Glo89].
```
begin
Initialize (i_start, i_best, L);
i := i_start;
k := 0;
a(z) := z for each possible value of γ;
repeat
     Generate (S ⊆ N_i);        -- j ∈ S such that j is not tabu or a(γ(i)) > γ(j)
     Choose j* minimizing γ over S ;
     if  γ(j*) < a(γ(i)) then  a(γ(i)) := γ(j*)
     else
          if  γ(i) < a(γ(j)) then  a(γ(j*)) := γ(i);
     Update tabu list L;
     if  γ(j*) < γ(i_best) then
        begin
        i_best := j*;
        k := 0;
        end;
     i := j*;
     k := k+1;
until  k > nbmax;
-- the loop is repeated until a number k of iterations between two improvements of the
-- objective function does not exceed limit nbmax
end;
```

There is no widely applicable convergence theorem of this algorithm.

The length of tabu list(s) is a crucial point of the method. In practice storing solutions in tabu list could be difficult because of space limitations and time consumed to check whether solution is tabu. Often more than one tabu list is used. When one moves from solution i to j, it corresponds to a set of "independent" modifications (e.g. dimensions in a vector). Another important parameter for efficiency of the method is the number $|S|$ of solutions generated from the current neighborhood. Moreover, good definition and fast calculation of S is important. It also has been observed that formulation of the problem must be such that function γ is not too flat.

The tabu search method has been applied in graph coloring, finding independent sets in a graph, hierarchized graph representation, character recognition, scheduling, learning in neural networks, stock cutting and many more applications.

In spite of the fact that a number of studies that have been done on simulated annealing and tabu search, it is still difficult to judge these methods on their true merits. This is due to the fact that most of these papers lack appropriate depth to draw reliable conclusions. Despite this one may formulate several observations.

Simulated annealing and tabu search are meta-heuristics requiring few information on the particular problem to be implemented. The only prerequisities to apply them are a cost function and a neighborhood structure. Both methods have potential ability of avoiding being trapped in local solutions and of finding global solutions.

On the other hand, this power is also weakness because lack of the knowledge about a particular problem may reduce efficiency of implementation. Good definition of the problem and resulting from this a choice of a neighborhood structure and a cost function is significant. For example it would be a very bad choice in a graph coloring problem to treat every possible partition of the node set as a solution and a number of colors as an objective function.

Efficiency, in practice, depends also on an adequate combination of inherited ingredients of both methods. In simulated annealing it is the appropriate cooling schedule, in tabu search it is $nbmax$, $|S|$, $|L|$.

Both, simulated annealing and tabu search, compare well in many problems with some other specialized algorithms ([AK90, Glo85]). On the other hand, there are situations where simulated annealing is not very efficient (cf. [AK90]).

References

Agi66   N. Agin, Optimum seeking with branch and bound, *Management Sci.* 13, 1966, B176-185.

AHU74   A. V. Aho, J. E. Hopcroft, J. D. Ullman, *The Design and Analysis of Computer Algorithms*, Addison-Wesley, Reading, Mass., 1974.

AK90   E. Aarts, J. Korst, *Simulated Annealing and Boltzmann Machines*, John Wiley & Sons, New York, 1990.

AMO89   R. K. Ahuja, T. L. Magnanti, J. B. Orlin, Network Flows, MIT, Sloan School Working Paper No. 2059-88, 1989.

Bak74   K. Baker, *Introduction to Sequencing and Scheduling*, J. Wiley, New York, 1974.

BD62   R. Bellman, S. E. Dreyfus, Applied Dynamic Programming, Princeton University Press, Princeton, New Jersey, 1962.

Bel57   R. Bellman, Dynamic Programming, Princeton University Press, Princeton, New Jersey, 1957.

Che77   B. V. Cherkasskij, Algoritm postrojenija maksimalnogo potoka w sieti so sloznostju
         $0(V^2E^{1/2})$ operacij, *Matematiczeskije Metody Reszenija Ekonomiczeskich Problem* 7,
         1977, 117-125.

Che80   T.-Y. Cheung, Computational comparison of eight methods for the maximum network
         flow problem, *ACM Trans. Math. Software* 6, 1980, 1-16.

CHW87   M. Chams, A. Hertz, D. de Werra, Some experiments with simulated annealing for
         colouring graphs, *European J. Oper. Res.* 32, 1987, 260-266.

Cof76   E. G. Coffman, Jr. (ed.), *Scheduling in Computer and Job Shop Systems*, J. Wiley,
         New York, 1976.

Coo71   S. A. Cook, The complexity of theorem proving procedures, *Proc. 3rd ACM Sympo-
         sium on Theory of Computing*, 1971, 151-158.

Den82   E. V. Denardo, *Dynamic Programming: Models and Applications*. Prentice-Hall,
         Englewood Cliffs, New Jersey, 1982.

Din70   E. A. Dinic Algoritm reszenija zadaczi o maksimalnom potokie w sieti so stepennoj
         ocenkoj, *Dokl. Akad. Nauk SSSR* 194, 1970, 1277-1280.

DL79   S. E. Dreyfus, A. M. Law, *The Art and Theory of Dynamic Programming*, Adademic
         Press, New York, 1979.

Edm65   J. Edmonds, Paths, trees and flowers, *Canadian J. Math.* 17, 1965, 449-467.

EK72   J. Edmonds, R. M. Karp, Theoretical improvement in algorithmic efficiency for net-
         work flow problem, *J. Assoc. Comput. Mach.* 19, No.2, 1972, 248-264.

Eve79   S. Even, *Graph Algorithms*, Computer Science Press Inc., New York, 1979.

FF62   L. R. Ford, Jr., D. R. Fulkerson, *Flows in Networks*, Princeton University Press,
         Princeton, New Jersey, 1962.

GJ78   M. R. Garey, D. S. Johnson, Strong NP-completeness results: motivation, examples,
         and implications, *J. Assoc. Comput. Mach.* 25, 1978, 499-508.

GJ79   M. R. Garey, D. S. Johnson, *Computers and Intractability: A Guide to the Theory of
         NP-Completeness*, W.H. Freeman, San Francisco, 1979.

Glo85   F. Glover, Future paths for integer programming and links to artificial intelligence,
         CAAI Report 85-8, Univertisy of Colorado, Boulder, 1985.

Glo89   F. Glover, Tabu-search - Part I, *ORSA J. Comput.* 1, 1989, 190-206.

Haj88   B. Hajek, Cooling schedules for optimal annealing, *Math. Oper. Res.* 13, 1988, 311-
         329.

How69   R. A. Howard, Dynamic *Programming and Markov Processes*, MIT Press,
         Cambridge, Massachusetts, 1969.

HW88   A. Hertz, D. de Werra, The tabu search metaheuristics: How we used it, Report
         ORWP 88/13, Département de Mathématiques, Ecole Polytechnique Fédérale de
         Láusanne, 1988.

Joh90   D. S. Johnson, A Catalog of Complexity Classes, in: J. van Leeuwen (ed.), *Handbook
         of Theoretical Computer Science*, Elsevier, New York, 1990, Ch.2.

Kar72   R. M. Karp, Reducibility among combinatorial problems, in: R. E. Miller, J. W.
         Thatcher (eds.), *Complexity of Computer Computation*, Plenum Press, New York,
         1972, 85-104.

Kar74   A. W. Karzanov, Nachozdenije maksimalnogo potoka w sieti metodom predpotokow, *Dokl. Akad. Nauk SSSR* 215, 1974, 434-437.

KGV83   S. Kirkpatrick, C. D. Gelatt, M. P. Vecchi, Optimization by simulated annealing, IBM Research Report RC 9355, 1982, and *Science* 220, 1983, 671-680.

Kub87   M. Kubale, The complexity of scheduling independent two-processor tasks on dedicated processors, *Inform. Proc. Lett.* 24, 1987, 141-147.

Law76   E. L. Lawler, *Combinatorial Optimization: Networks and Matroids*, Holt, Rinehart and Winston, New York, 1976.

Len77   J. K. Lenstra, *Sequencing by Enumerative Methods*, Mathematical Centre Tracts 69, Amsterdam, 1977.

LA89   P. J. M. van Laarhoven, E. H. L. Aarts, *Simulated Annealing: Theory and Applications*, Kluwer, Dortrecht, 1989.

LRKB77   J. K. Lenstra, A. H. G. Rinnooy Kan, P. Brucker, Complexity of machine scheduling problems, *Ann. Discrete Math.* 1, 1977, 343-362.

LW66   E. L. Lawler, D. E. Wood, Branch and bound methods: a survey, *Oper. Res.* 14, 1966, 699-719.

Mit70   L. G. Mitten, Branch-and-bound methods: general formulation and properties, *Oper. Res.* 18, 1970, 24-34.

Rin76   A. H. G. Rinnooy Kan, *Machine Scheduling Problems: Classification, Complexity and Computations.* Martinus Nijhoff, The Hague, 1976.

Rin87   A. H. G. Rinnooy Kan, Probabilistic analysis of approximation algorithms, *Ann. Discrete Math.* 31, 1987, 365-384.

SVW80   E. A. Silver, R. V. Vidal, D. de Werra, A tutorial on heuristic methods, *European J. Oper. Res.* 5, 1980, 153-162.

VTL82   J. Valdes, R. E.Tarjan, E. L. Lawler, The recognition of series parallel digraphs, *SIAM J. Comput.* 11, 1982, 298-313.

3 Formulation of Scheduling Problems

3.1 Definition of Scheduling Problems

In general, scheduling problems considered in this book are characterized by three sets: set T of n *tasks* $T = \{T_1, T_2, \cdots, T_n\}$, set P of m *processors* (*machines*) $P = \{P_1, P_2, \cdots, P_m\}$ and set R of s types of *additional resources* $R = \{R_1, R_2, \cdots, R_s\}$. Scheduling, generally speaking, means to assign processors from P and (possibly) resources from R to tasks from T in order to complete all tasks under the imposed constraints. There are two general constraints in classical scheduling theory. Each task is to be processed by at most one processor at a time (plus possibly specified amounts of additional resources) and each processor is capable of processing at most one task at a time. In Sections 5.4 and 7.2 we will show some new applications in which the first constraint will be relaxed.

We will now characterize the processors. They may be either *parallel*, i.e. performing the same functions, or *dedicated* i.e. specialized for the execution of certain tasks. Three types of parallel processors are distinguished depending on their speeds. If all processors from set P have equal task processing speeds, then we call them *identical*. If the processors differ in their speeds, but the *speed* b_i of each processor is constant and does not depend on the task in T, then they are called *uniform*. Finally, if the speeds of the processors depend on the particular task processed, then they are called *unrelated*.

In case of dedicated processors there are three models of processing sets of tasks: *flow shop*, *open shop* and *job shop*. To describe these models more precisely, we assume that tasks form n subsets [1] (*chains* in case of flow- and job shops), each subset called a *job*. That is, job J_j is divided into n_j tasks, $T_{1j}, T_{2j}, \cdots, T_{n_j j}$, and two adjacent tasks are to be performed on different processors. A set of jobs will be denoted by J. In an open shop the number of tasks is the same for each job and is equal to m, i.e. $n_j = m$, $j = 1, 2, \cdots, n$. Moreover, T_{1j} should be processed on P_1, T_{2j} on P_2, and so on. A similar situation is found in flow shop, but, in addition, the processing of $T_{i-1,j}$ should precede that of T_{ij} for all $j = 1, 2, \cdots, n$ and for all $i = 1, \cdots, n_j$. In a general job shop system the number n_j is arbitrary. Usually in such systems it is assumed that buffers between processors have unlimited capacity and a job after completion on one processor may wait before its processing starts on the next one. If, however, buffers are of zero capacity, jobs cannot wait between two consecutive processors, thus, a *no-wait property* is assumed.

In general, task $T_j \in T$ is characterized by the following data.

---

[1] Thus, the number of tasks in T is assumed to be $\geq n$.

1. *Vector of processing times* $p_j = [p_{1j}, p_{2j}, \cdots, p_{mj}]^T$, where p_{ij} is the time needed by processor P_i to process T_j. In case of identical processors we have $p_{ij} = p_j$, $i = 1$, $2, \cdots, m$. If the processors in $\mathcal{P}$ are uniform then $p_{ij} = p_j/b_i$, $i = 1, 2, \cdots, m$, where p_j is the *standard processing time* (usually measured on the slowest processor) and b_i is the *processing speed factor* of processor P_i. In case of shop scheduling the vector of processing times describes the processing requirements of particular tasks comprising one job; that is, for job J_j we have $p_j = [p_{1j}, p_{2j}, \cdots, p_{n_jj}]^T$, where p_{ij} denotes the processing time of T_{ij} on the corresponding processor.

2. *Arrival time* (or *ready time*) r_j, which is the time at which task T_j is ready for processing. If the arrival times are the same for all tasks from $\mathcal{T}$, then it is assumed that $r_j = 0$ for all j.

3. *Due date* d_j, which specifies a time limit by which T_j should be completed; usually, penalty functions are defined in accordance with due dates.

4. *Deadline* $\tilde{d}_j$, which is a "hard" real time limit by which T_j must be completed.

5. *Weight* (*priority*) w_j, which expresses the relative urgency of T_j.

6. *Resource request* (if any), as defined in Chapter 7.

We assume that all these parameters, p_j, r_j, d_j, $\tilde{d}_j$, and w_j, are integers. In fact, this assumption is not very restrictive, since it is equivalent to permitting arbitrary rational values. We assume moreover, that tasks are assigned all required resources whenever they start or resume their processing and that they release all the assigned resources whenever they are completed or preempted. These assumptions imply that deadlock cannot occur.

Next, some definitions concerning task preemptions and precedence constraints among tasks are given. A schedule is called *preemptive* if each task may be preempted at any time and restarted later at no cost, perhaps on another processor. If preemption of all the tasks is not allowed we will call the schedule *nonpreemptive*.

In set $\mathcal{T}$ *precedence constraints* among tasks may be defined. $T_i \prec T_j$ means that the processing of T_i must be completed before T_j can be started. In other words, set $\mathcal{T}$ is partially ordered by a precedence relation $\prec$. The tasks in set $\mathcal{T}$ are called *dependent* if the order of execution of at least two tasks in $\mathcal{T}$ is restricted by this relation. Otherwise, the tasks are called *independent*. A task set ordered by the precedence relation is usually represented as a directed graph (a digraph) in which nodes correspond to tasks and arcs to precedence constraints (a *task-on-node graph*). It is assumed that no transitive arcs exist in precedence graphs. An example of a set of dependent tasks is shown in Figure 3.1.1(a) (nodes are denoted by T_j/p_j). Several special types of precedence graphs have already been described in Section 2.3.2. Let us notice that in the case of dedicated processors (except in open shop systems) tasks that constitute a job are always dependent, but the jobs themselves can be either independent or dependent. There is another way of representing task dependencies which is useful in certain circumstances. In this so-called *activity network* precedence constraints are represented as a *task-on-arc graph*, where arcs represent tasks and nodes time events. Let us mention here a special graph of this type called *uniconnected activity network* (*uan*), which is defined as a graph in which any two nodes are connected by a directed path in one direction only. Thus, all nodes are uniquely ordered. For every precedence graph one can construct a corresponding activity network (and vice versa), perhaps using dummy tasks of zero length. The corresponding acitvity network for the precedence graph from Figure 3.1.1(a) is shown in Figure 3.1.1(b).

Task T_j will be called *available* at time t if $r_j \leq t$ and all its predecessors (with respect to the precedence constraints) have been completed by time t.

Now we will give the definitions concerning schedules and optimality criteria. A *schedule* is an assignment of processors from set $\mathcal{P}$ (and possibly resources from set $\mathcal{R}$) to tasks from set $\mathcal{T}$ in time such that the following conditions are satisfied:

- at every moment each processor is assigned to at most one task and each task is processed by at most one processor[2],

- task T_j is processed in time interval $[r_j, \infty)$,

- all tasks are completed,

- if tasks T_i, T_j are in relation $T_i \prec T_j$, the processing of T_j is not started before T_i is completed,

- in the case of nonpreemptive scheduling no task is preempted (then the schedule is called *nonpreemptive*), otherwise the number of preemptions of each task is finite[3] (then the schedule is called *preemptive*),

- resource constraints, if any, are satisfied.

To represent schedules we will use so-called *Gantt charts*. An example schedule for the task set of Figure 3.1.1 on three parallel, identical processors is shown in Figure 3.1.2. The following parameters can be calculated for each task T_j, $j = 1, 2, \cdots, n$, processed in a given schedule:

> *completion time* C_j;
>
> *flow time* F_j, being the sum of waiting and processing times, $F_j = C_j - r_j$;
>
> *lateness* L_j, $L_j = C_j - d_j$;
>
> *tardiness* D_j, $D_j = \max\{C_j - d_j, 0\}$.

For the schedule given in Figure 3.1.2 one can easily calculate the two first parameters. In vector notation these are $C = [3, 4, 5, 6, 1, 8, 8, 8]$ and $F = C$. The other two parameters could be calculated, if due dates would be defined. Suppose that due dates are given by the vector $d = [5, 4, 5, 3, 7, 6, 9, 12]$. Then the latenesses and tardinesses for the tasks in the schedule are: $L = [-2, 0, 0, 3, -6, 2, -1, -4]$, $D = [0, 0, 0, 3, 0, 2, 0, 0]$.

To evaluate schedules we will use three main *performance measures* or *optimality criteria*:

---

[2] As we mentioned, this assumption can be relaxed.
[3] This condition is imposed by practical considerations only.

Schedule length (makespan) $C_{max} = \max\{C_j\}$,

mean flow time $\bar{F} = \frac{1}{n}\sum_{j=1}^{n}F_j$,

or *mean weighted flow time* $\bar{F}_w = \sum_{j=1}^{n}w_j F_j / \sum_{j=1}^{n}w_j$,

maximum lateness $L_{max} = \max\{L_j\}$.

(a)

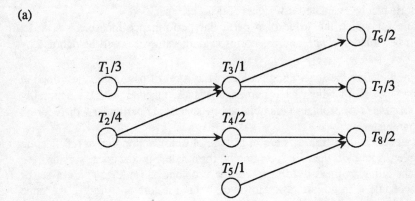

(b)

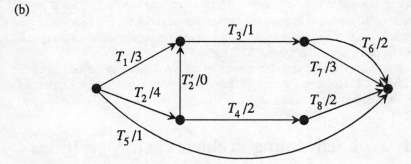

Figure 3.1.1 *An example task set*

    (a) *task-on-node representation,*

    (b) *task-on-arc representation (dumy tasks are primed).*

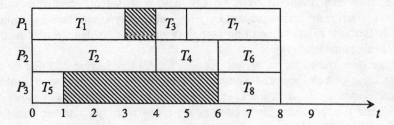

Figure 3.1.2 *A schedule for the task set given in Figure* 3.1.1.

In some applications, other related criteria may be used, as for example: *mean tardiness* $\bar{D} = \frac{1}{n}\sum_{j=1}^{n}D_j$, *mean weighted tardiness* $\bar{D}_w = \sum_{j=1}^{n}w_j D_j / \sum_{j=1}^{n}w_j$, *number of tardy tasks* $U = \sum_{j=1}^{n}U_j$, where $U_j = 1$, if $C_j > d_j$, and 0 otherwise, or *weighted number of tardy tasks* $U_w = \sum_{j=1}^{n}w_j U_j$. Again, let us calculate values of particular criteria for the schedule in Figure 3.1.2. They are: schedule length $C_{max} = 8$, mean flow time $\bar{F} = 43/8$, maximum lateness $L_{max} = 3$, mean tardiness $\bar{D} = 5/8$, and number of tardy jobs $U = 2$. The other criteria can be evaluated if weights of tasks are specified.

A schedule for which the value of a particular performance measure γ is at its minimum will be called *optimal*, and the corresponding value of γ will be denoted by γ^*.

We may now define the *scheduling problem* Π as a set of parameters described in this subsection[4] not all of which have numerical values, together with an optimality criterion. An *instance I* of problem Π is obtained by specifying particular values for all the problem parameters.

We see that scheduling problems are in general of optimization nature (cf. Section 2.2.1). However, some of them are originally formulated in decision version. An example is scheduling to meet deadlines, i.e. the problem of finding, given a set of deadlines, a schedule with no late task. However, both cases are analyzed in the same way when complexity issues are considered.

A *scheduling algorithm* is an algorithm which constructs a schedule for a given problem Π. In general, we are interested in optimization algorithms, but because of the inherent complexity of many problems of that type, approximation or heuristic algorithms will be discussed (cf. Sections 2.2.2 and 2.5).

Scheduling problems, as defined above, may be analyzed much in the same way as discussed in Chapter 2. However, their specifity raises some more detailed questions which will be discussed in the next section.

3.2 Analysis of Scheduling Problems and Algorithms

Deterministic scheduling problems are a part of a much broader class of combinatorial optimization problems. Thus, the general approach to the analysis of these problems can follow similar lines, but one should take into account their peculiarities. It is rather obvious that very often the time we can devote to solving particular scheduling problems is seriously limited so that only low order polynomial time algorithms may be used. Thus, the examination of the complexity of these problems should be the basis of any further analysis.

It has been known for some time [Coo71, Kar72] (cf. Section 2.2) that there exists a large class of combinatorial optimization problems for which most probably no *efficient optimization* algorithms exist. These are the problems whose decision counterparts (i.e. problems formulated as questions with "yes" or "no" answers) are

---

[4] Parameters are understood generally, including e.g. relation $\prec$

NP-complete. The optimization problems are called *NP-hard* in this case. We refer the reader to [GJ79] and to Section 2.2 for a comprehensive treatment of the *NP*-completeness theory, and in the following we assume knowledge of its basic concepts like *NP*-completeness, *NP*-hardness, polynomial time transformation, etc. It follows that the complexity analysis answers the question whether or not an analyzed scheduling problem may be solved (i.e. an optimal schedule found) in time bounded from above by a polynomial in the input length of the problem (i.e. in polynomial time). If the answer is positive, then an optimization polynomial time algorithm must have been found. Its usefulness depends on the order of its worst-case complexity function and on the particular application. Sometimes, when the worst-case complexity function is not low enough, although still polynomial, a mean complexity function of the algorithm may be sufficient. This issue is discussed in detail in [AHU74]. On the other hand, if the answer is negative, i.e. when the decision version of the analyzed problem is *NP*-complete, then there are several other ways of further analysis.

Firstly, one may try to relax some constraints imposed on the original problem and then solve the relaxed problem. The solution of the latter may be a good approximation to the solution of the original problem. In the case of scheduling problems such a relaxation may consist of

- allowing preemptions, even if the original problem dealt with nonpreemptive schedules,

- assuming unit-length tasks, when arbitrary-length tasks were considered in the original problem,

- assuming certain types of precedence graphs, e.g. trees or chains, when arbitrary graphs were considered in the original problem, etc.

Considering computer applications, especially the first relaxation can be justified in the case when parallel processors share a common primary memory. Moreover, such a relaxation is also advantageous from the viewpoint of certain optimality criteria.

Secondly, when trying to solve *NP*-hard scheduling problems one often uses approximation algorithms which tend to find an optimal schedule but do not always succeed. Of course, the necessary condition for these algorithms to be applicable in practice is that their worst-case complexity function is bounded from above by a low-order polynomial in the input length. Their sufficiency follows from an evaluation of the difference between the value of a solution they produce and the value of an optimal solution. This evaluation may concern the worst case or a mean behavior. To be more precise, we use here notions that have been introduced in Section 2.5, i.e. absolute performance ratio R_A and asymptotic performance ratio R_A^∞ of an approximation algorithm A.

These notions define a measure of "goodness" of approximation algorithms; the closer R_A^∞ is to 1, the better algorithm A performs. However, for some combinatorial problems it can be proved that there is no hope of finding an approximation algorithm of a certain accuracy, i.e. this question is as hard as finding a polynomial time algorithm for any *NP*-complete problem.

Analysis of the worst-case behavior of an approximation algorithm may be complemented by an analysis of its mean behavior. This can be done in two ways. The first consists in assuming that the parameters of instances of the considered problem Π

are drawn from a certain distribution, and then the *mean performance* of algorithm *A* is analyzed. One may distinguish between the *absolute error* of an approximation algorithm, which is the difference between the approximate and optimal values and the *relative error*, which is the ratio of these two (cf. Section 2.5). Asymptotic optimality results in the stronger (absolute) sense are quite rare. On the other hand, asymptotic optimality in the relative sense is often easier to establish. It is rather obvious that the mean performance can be much better than the worst case behavior, thus justifying the use of a given approximation algorithm. A main obstacle is the difficulty of proofs of the mean performance for realistic distribution functions. Thus, the second way of evaluating the mean behavior of approximation algorithms, consisting of experimental studies, is still used very often. In the latter approach one compares solutions, in the sense of the values of an optimality criterion, constructed by a given approximation algorithm and by an optimization algorithm. This comparison should be made for a large representative sample of instances.

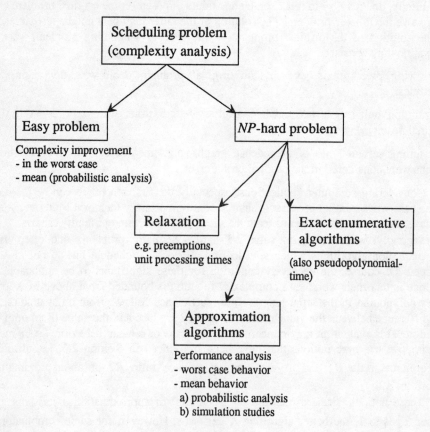

Figure 3.2.1 *An analysis of a scheduling problem - schematic view.*

In this context let us mention the most often used approximation scheduling algorithm which is the so-called *list scheduling algorithm* (which is in fact a general approach). In this algorithm a certain list of tasks is given and at each step the first available processor is selected to process the first available task on the list. The accuracy of a particular list scheduling algorithm depends on the given optimality criterion and the way the list has been constructed.

The third and last way of dealing with hard scheduling problems is to use exact enumerative algorithms whose worst-case complexity function is exponential in the input length. However, sometimes, when the analyzed problem is not *NP*-hard in the strong sense, it is possible to solve it by a pseudopolynomial optimization algorithm whose worst-case complexity function is bounded from above by a polynomial in the input length and in the maximum number appearing in the instance of the problem. For reasonably small numbers such an algorithm may behave quite well in practice and it can be used even in computer applications. On the other hand, "pure" exponential algorithms have probably to be excluded from this application, but they may be used sometimes for other scheduling problems which can be solved by off-line algorithms.

The above discussion is summarized in a schematic way in Figure 3.2.1. In the following chapters we will use the above scheme when analyzing scheduling problems.

3.3 Motivations for Deterministic Scheduling Problems

In this section, an interpretation of the assumptions and results in deterministic scheduling theory which motivate and justify the use of this model, is presented. We will underline especially computer applications, but we will also refer to manufacturing systems, even if the practical interpretation of the model is not for this application area. In a manufacturing environment deterministic scheduling is also known as *predictive*. Its complement is *reactive scheduling*, which can also be regarded as deterministic scheduling with a shorter planning horizon.

Let us begin with an analysis of processors (machines). *Parallel processors* may be interpreted as central processors which are able to process every task (i.e. every program). *Uniform processors* differ from each other by their speeds, but they do not prefer any type of tasks. Unrelated processors, on the contrary, are specialized in the sense that they prefer certain types of tasks, for example numerical computations, logical programs, or simulation procedures. The processors may have different instruction sets, but they are still of comparable processing capacity so they can process tasks of any type, only processing times may be different. In manufacturing systems, pools of machines exist where all the machines have the same capability (except possibly speed) to process tasks.

Completely different from the above are *dedicated* processors (dedicated machines) which may process only certain types of tasks. The interpretation of this model for manufacturing systems is straightforward but it can also be applied to computer systems. As an example let us consider a computer system consisting of an input processor, a central processor and an output processor. It is not difficult to see that such a system corresponds to a flow shop with $m = 3$. On the other hand, a situation in which each task is to be processed by an input/output processor, then by a central processor and at the end again by the input/output processor, can easily be modelled by a job shop system with $m = 2$. As far as an open shop is concerned, there is no obvious computer interpretation. But this case, like the other shop scheduling problems, has great significance in other applications, especially in an industrial environment.

By an *additional resource* we understand in this book a "facility" besides processors the tasks to be performed compete for. The competition aspect in this definition should be stressed, since "facilities" dedicated to only one task will not be treated as resources in this book. In computer systems, for example, messages sent from one task to another specified task will not be considered as resources. In manufacturing environments tools, material, transport facilities, etc. can be treated as additional resources.

Let us now consider the assumptions associated with the task set. As mentioned in Section 3.1, in deterministic scheduling theory a priori knowledge of ready times and processing times of tasks is usually assumed. As opposed to other practical applications, the question of a priori knowledge of these parameters in computer systems needs a thorough comment.

Ready times are obviously known in systems working in an off-line mode and in control systems in which measurement samples are taken from sensing devices at fixed time moments.

As far as *processing times* are concerned, they are usually not known a priori in computer systems. Despite this fact the solution of a deterministic scheduling problem may also have an important interpretation in these systems. Firstly, when scheduling tasks to meet deadlines, the only approach (when the task processing times are not known) is to solve the problem with assumed upper bounds on the processing times. Such a bound for a given task may be implied by the worst case complexity function of an algorithm connected with that task. Then, if all deadlines are met with respect to the upper bounds, no deadline will be exceeded for the real task processing times [5]. This approach is often used in a broad class of computer control systems working in a hard real time environment, where a certain set of control programs must be processed before taking the next sample from the same sensing device.

Secondly, instead of exact values of processing times one can take their mean values and, using the procedure described by Coffman and Denning in [CD73], calculate an optimistic estimate of the mean value of the schedule length.

Thirdly, one can measure the processing times of tasks *after* processing a task set scheduled according to a certain algorithm A. Taking these values as an input in the deterministic scheduling problem, one may construct an optimal schedule and compare it with the one produced by algorithm A, thus evaluating the latter.

Apart from the above, optimization algorithms for deterministic scheduling problems give some indications for the construction of heuristics under weaker assumptions than those made in stochastic scheduling problems, cf. [BCSW86].

The existence of *precedence constraints* in computer systems also requires an explanation. In the simplest case the results of certain programs may be the input data for others. Moreover, precedence constraints may also concern parts of the same program. A conventional serially written program may be analyzed by a special procedure looking for parallel parts in it (see for example [RG69, Rus69], or [Vol70]). These parts may also be defined by the programmer who can use special programming languages supporting parallel concepts. Apart from this, a solution of certain reliability problems in operating systems, as for example the *determinacy problem* (see [ACM70, Bae73, Ber66]), requires an introduction of additional precedence constraints.

---

[5] However, one has to take into account list scheduling anomalies which will be explained in Section 5.1.

We will now discuss particular *optimality criteria* for scheduling problems from their practical significance point of view. Minimizing *schedule length* is important from the viewpoint of the owner of a set of processors (machines), since it leads to both, the maximization of the processor utilization factor (within schedule length C_{max}), and the minimization of the maximum in-process time of the scheduled set of tasks. This criterion may also be of importance in a computer control system in which a task set arrives periodically and is to be processed in the shortest time.

The *mean flow time* criterion is important from the user's viewpoint since its minimization yields a minimization of the mean response time and the mean in-process time of the scheduled task set.

Due date involving criteria are of great importance in manufacturing systems, especially in those that produce to specific customer orders. Moreover, the *maximum lateness* criterion is of great significance in computer control systems working in the hard real time environment since its minimization leads to the construction of a schedule with no task late whenever such schedules exist (i.e. when $L_{max}^* \leq 0$ for an optimal schedule).

The criteria mentioned above are basic in the sense that they require specific approaches to the construction of schedules.

3.4 Classification of Deterministic Scheduling Problems

The great variety of scheduling problems we have seen from the preceeding section motivates the introduction of a systematic notation that could serve as a basis for a classification scheme. Such a notation of problem types would greatly facilitate the presentation and discussion of scheduling problems. A notation proposed by Graham et al. [GLLR79] and Błażewicz et al. [BLRK83] will be presented next and then used throughout the book.

The notation is composed of three fields $\alpha \mid \beta \mid \gamma$. They have the following meaning. The first field $\alpha = \alpha_1 \alpha_2$ describes the processor environment. Parameter $\alpha_1 \in \{\emptyset, P, Q, R, O, F, J\}$ characterizes the type of processor used:

$\alpha_1 = \emptyset$: one processor [6],

$\alpha_1 = P$: identical processors,

$\alpha_1 = Q$: uniform processors,

$\alpha_1 = R$: unrelated processors,

$\alpha_1 = O$: dedicated processors: open shop system,

$\alpha_1 = F$: dedicated processors: flow shop system,

$\alpha_1 = J$: dedicated processors: job shop system.

Parameter $\alpha_2 \in \{\emptyset, k\}$ denotes the number of processors in the problem:

$\alpha_2 = \emptyset$: the number of processors is assumed to be variable,

$\alpha_2 = k$: the number of processors is equal to k (k is a positive integer).

---

[6] In this notation $\emptyset$ denotes an empty symbol which will be omitted in presenting problems.

The second field $\beta = \beta_1, \beta_2, \beta_3, \beta_4, \beta_5, \beta_6, \beta_7, \beta_8$ describes task and resource characteristics. Parameter $\beta_1 \in \{\varnothing, pmtn\}$ indicates the possibility of task preemption:

$\beta_1 = \varnothing$: no preemption is allowed,

$\beta_1 = pmtn$: preemptions are allowed.

Parameter $\beta_2 \in \{\varnothing, res\}$ characterizes additional resources:

$\beta_2 = \varnothing$: no additional resources exist,

$\beta_2 = res$: there are specified resource constraints; they will be described in detail in Chapter 7.

Parameter $\beta_3 \in \{\varnothing, prec, uan, tree, chains\}$ reflects the precedence constraints:

$\beta_3 = \varnothing, prec, uan, tree, chains$: denotes respectively independent tasks, general precedence constraints, unconnected activity networks, precedence constraints forming a tree or a set of chains.

Parameter $\beta_4 \in \{\varnothing, r_j\}$ describes ready times:

$\beta_4 = \varnothing$: all ready times are zero,

$\beta_4 = r_j$: ready times differ per task.

Parameter $\beta_5 \in \{\varnothing, p_j = p, \underline{p} \le p_j \le \bar{p}\}$ describes task processing times:

$\beta_5 = \varnothing$: tasks have arbitrary processing times,

$\beta_5 = (p_j = p)$: all tasks have processing times equal to p units,

$\beta_5 = (\underline{p} \le p_j \le \bar{p})$: no p_j is less than $\underline{p}$ or greater than $\bar{p}$.

Parameter $\beta_6 \in \{\varnothing, \tilde{d}\}$ describes deadlines:

$\beta_6 = \varnothing$: no deadlines are assumed in the system (however, due dates may be defined if a due date involving criterion is used to evaluate schedules),

$\beta_6 = \tilde{d}$: deadlines are imposed on the performance of a task set.

Parameter $\beta_7 \in \{\varnothing, n_j \le k\}$ describes the maximal number of tasks constituting a job in case of job shop systems:

$\beta_7 = \varnothing$: the above number is arbitrary or the scheduling problem is not a job shop problem,

$\beta_7 = (n_j \le k)$: the number of tasks for each job is not greater than k.

Parameter $\beta_8 \in \{\varnothing, no\text{-}wait\}$ describes a no-wait property in the case of scheduling on dedicated processors:

$\beta_8 = \varnothing$: buffers of unlimited capacity are assumed,

$\beta_8 = no\text{-}wait$: buffers among processors are of zero capacity and a job after finishing its processing on one processor must immediately start on the consecutive processor.

The third field, γ, denotes an optimality criterion (performance measure), i.e. $\gamma \in \{C_{max}, \Sigma C_j, \Sigma w_j C_j, L_{max}, \Sigma D_j, \Sigma w_j D_j, \Sigma U_j, \Sigma w_j U_j, -\}$, where $\Sigma C_j = \bar{F}$, $\Sigma w_j C_j = \bar{F}_w$, $\Sigma D_j = \bar{D}$, $\Sigma w_j D_j = \bar{D}_w$, $\Sigma U_j = U$ and $\Sigma w_j U_j = U_w$, and "$-$" means testing for feasibility whenever scheduling to meet deadlines is considered.

The use of this notation is illustrated by Example 3.4.1.

Example 3.4.1

(a) Problem $P||C_{max}$ reads as follows: *Scheduling of nonpreemptable and independent tasks of arbitrary processing times (lengths), arriving to the system at time 0, on parallel, identical processors in order to minimize schedule length.*

(b) $O|pmtn, r_j|\Sigma C_j$ stands for : *Preemptive scheduling of arbitrary length tasks in three machine open shop where operations arrive at different time moments, and the objective is to minimize mean flow time.* $\square$

At this point it is worth mentioning that scheduling problems are closely related in the sense of polynomial transformation[7]. Some basic polynomial transformations between scheduling problems are shown in Figure 3.4.1. For each graph in the figure, the presented problems differ only by one parameter (e.g. by type and number as in Figure 3.4.1(a)) and the arrows indicate the direction of the polynomial transformation. These simple transformations are very useful in many situations when analyzing new scheduling problems. Thus, many of the results presented in this book can immediately be extended to cover a broader class of scheduling problems.

(a)

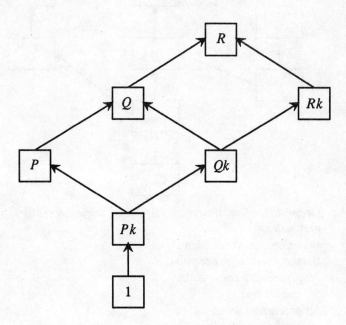

---

[7] This term has been explained in Section 2.2

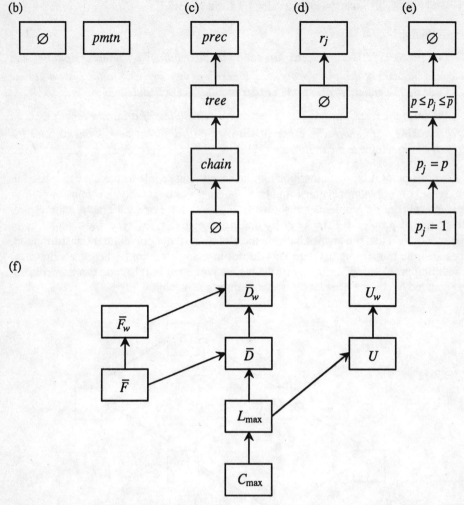

Figure 3.4.1 *Graphs showing interrelations among different values of particular parameters*
(a) *processor environment,*
(b) *possibility of preemption,*
(c) *precedence constraints,*
(d) *ready times,*
(e) *processing times,*
(f) *optimality criteria.*

References

ACM70   ACM Record of the project MAC conference on concurrent system and parallel computation, Wood's Hole, Mass, 1970.

AHU74   A. V. Aho, J. E. Hopcroft, J. D. Ullman, *The Design and Analysis of Computer Algorithms*, Addison-Wesley, Reading, Mass., 1974.

Bae73   J. L. Baer, Optimal scheduling on two processors of different speeds, in: E. Gelenbe, R. Mahl (eds.), *Computer Architecture and Networks*, North Holland, Amsterdam, 1974.

BCSW86   J. Błażewicz, W. Cellary, R. Słowiński, J. Węglarz, *Scheduling under Resource Constraints: Deterministic Models*, J. C. Baltzer, Basel, 1986.

Ber66   A. J. Bernstein, Analysis of programs for parallel programming, *IEEE Trans. Comput.* EC-15, 1966. 757-762.

BLRK83   J. Błażewicz, J. K. Lenstra, A. H. G. Rinnooy Kan, Scheduling subject to resource constraints: classification and complexity, *Discrete Appl. Math.* 5, 1983, 11-24.

CD73   E. G. Coffman, Jr., P. J. Denning, *Operating Systems Theory*, Prentice-Hall, Englewood Cliffs, N.J., 1973.

Coo71   S. A. Cook, The complexity of theorem proving procedures, *Proc. 3rd ACM Symposium on Theory of Computing,* 1971, 151-158.

GJ79   M. R. Garey, D. S. Johnson, *Computers and Intractability: A Guide to the Theory of NP-Completeness.* W. H. Freeman, San Francisco, 1979.

GLLRK79   R. L. Graham, E. L. Lawler, J. K. Lenstra, A. H. G. Rinnooy Kan, Optimization and approximation in deterministic sequencing and scheduling theory: a survey, *Ann. Discrete Math.* 5, 1979, 287-326.

Kar72   R. M. Karp, Reducibility among combinatorial problems, in: R. E. Miller, J. W. Thatcher (eds.), *Complexity of Computer Computations*, Plenum Press, New York, 1972, 85-104.

RG69   C. V. Ramamoorthy, M. J. Gonzalez, A survey of techniques for recognizinmg parallel processable streams in computer programs, *AFIPS Conference Proceedings, Fall Joint Computer Conference,* 1969, 1-15.

Rus69   E. C. Russel, Automatic program analysis, Ph.D. thesis, Dept. of Eng. University of California, Los Angeles, 1969.

Vol70   S. Volansky, Graph model analysis and implementation of computational sequences Ph.D.thesis, Rep. No.UCLA-ENG-7048, School of Engineering Applied Sciences, University of California, Los Angeles, 1970.

4 Single Processor Scheduling

Single machine scheduling (SMS) problems seem to have received substantial attention because of several reasons. These type of problems are important both because of their own intrinsic value, as well as their role as building blocks for more generalized and complex problems. In a multi-processor environment single processor schedules may be used in bottlenecks, or to organize task assignment to an expensive processor; sometimes an entire production line may be treated as a single processor for scheduling purposes. Also, compared to multiple processor scheduling, SMS problems are mathematically more tractable. Hence more problem classes can be solved in polynomial time, and a larger variety of model parameters, such as various types of cost functions, or an introduction of change-over cost, can be analyzed. Single processor problems are thus of rather fundamental character and allow for some insight and development of ideas when treating more general scheduling problems.

The relative simplicity of the single-processor scheduling on one hand, and its fundamental character also for multiprocessor scheduling problems on the other hand motivate to dicuss the single processor case to a wider extent. In the next five sections we will study scheduling problems on one processor with the objective to minimize the following criteria: schedule length, mean (and mean weighted) flow time, due date involving criteria such as different lateness or tardiness functions, change-over cost and different maximum and mean cost functions.

4.1 Minimizing Schedule Length

One of the simplest type of scheduling problems considered here is the problem $1 \mid prec \mid C_{max}$, i.e. one in which all tasks are assumed to be nonpreemptable, ordered by some precedence relation, and available at time $t = 0$. It is trivial to observe that in whatever order in accordance with the precedence relation the tasks are assigned to the processor, the schedule length is $C_{max} = \sum_{j=1}^{n} p_j$. If each task has a given release time (ready time), an optimal schedule can easily be obtained by a polynomial time algorithm where tasks are scheduled in the order of nondecreasing release times. Similarly, if each task has a given deadline, the earliest deadline scheduling rule would produce an optimal solution provided there exists a schedule that meets all the deadlines. Thus in fact, problems $1 \mid r_j \mid C_{max}$ and $1 \mid \mid L_{max}$ are equivalent as far as their complexities and solution techniques are concerned. The situation becomes considerably more complex from the algorithmic complexity point of view if both, release times and deadlines restrict task processing.

In the following section, for each task there is specified a release time and a deadline by which the task is to be completed. The aim is then to find a schedule that meets all the given deadlines and, in addition, minimizes C_{max}.

4.1.1 Scheduling with Release Times and Deadlines

Problem $1 \mid r_j, \tilde{d}_j \mid C_{\max}$

In case of problem $1 \mid r_j, \tilde{d}_j \mid C_{\max}$, i.e. if the tasks are allowed to have unequal processing times, a transformation from the 3-PARTITION problem [1] shows that the problem is *NP*-hard in the strong sense, even for integer release times and deadlines [LRKB77]. Only if all tasks have unit processing times, an optimization algorithm of polynomial time complexity is available.

The general problem can be solved by applying a branch and bound algorithm. Bratley et al. [BFR71] proposed an algorithm which is shortly described below.

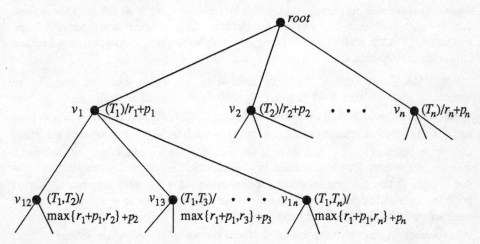

Figure 4.1.1 *Search tree in the branch and bound algorithm of Bratley et al.* [BFR71].

All possible task schedules are implicitly enumerated by a search tree construction, as shown in Figure 4.1.1. From the root node of the tree we branch to n new nodes at the first level of descendant nodes. The ith of these nodes, v_i, represents the assignment of task T_i to be the first in the schedule, $i = 1, \cdots, n$. Associated with each node is the completion time of the corresponding task, i.e. $r_i + p_i$ for node v_i. Next we branch from each node on the first level to $n - 1$ nodes on the second level. Each of these represents the assignment of one of the $n - 1$ unassigned tasks to be the second in the schedule. Again, the completion time is associated with each of the second level nodes. If v_{ij} is the successor node of v_i to which task T_j is assigned, the associated completion time

---

[1] The 3-PARTITION problem is defined as follows (see [GJ79]).

Instance: A finite set $\mathcal{A}$ of $3m$ elements, a bound $B \in Z^+$, and a "size" $s(a) \in Z^+$ for each $a \in \mathcal{A}$, such that each $s(a)$ satisfies $B/4 < s(a) < B/2$ and such that $\sum_{a \in S_i} s(a) = mB$.

Answer: "Yes" if $\mathcal{A}$ can be partitioned into m disjoint sets $S_1, S_2, \cdots, S_m$ such that, for $1 \le i \le m$, $\sum_{a \in S_i} s(a) = B$. Otherwise "No".

would be $\max\{r_i+p_i, r_j\} + p_j$. This value represents the completion time of the partial schedule (T_i, T_j). Continuing that way, on level k, $1 \le k \le n$, there are $n-k+1$ new nodes generated from each node of the preceding level. It is evident that all the $n!$ possible different schedules will be enumerated that way.

The order in which the nodes of the tree are examined is based on a backtracking search strategy. However, the algorithm uses two criteria to reduce the number of search steps.

(i) *Exceeding deadlines*. Consider node v at level $k-1$, and its $n-k+1$ immediate successors on level k of the tree. If the completion time associated with at least one of these nodes exceeds the deadline of the task added at level k, then all $n-k+1$ nodes may be excluded from further consideration. This follows from the fact that if any of these tasks exceeds its deadline at level k (i.e. this task is at k^{th} position in the schedule), it will certainly exceed its deadline if scheduled later. Since all the successors of node v represent orderings in which the task in question is scheduled later, they may be omitted.

(ii) *Problem decomposition*. Consider level k of the search tree and suppose we generate a node on that level for task T_i. This is equivalent to assigning task T_i in position k of the schedule. If the completion time C_i of T_i in this position is less than or equal to the smallest release time r_{min} among the yet unscheduled tasks, then the problem decomposes at level k, and there is no need to enter another branch of the search tree, i.e. one doesn't need to backtrack beyond level k. The reason for this strong exclusion feature is that the best schedule for the remaining $n-k$ tasks may not be started prior to the smallest release time among these tasks, and hence not earlier than the completion time C_i of the first k tasks.

To recognize an optimal solution we focus our attention on certain groups of tasks in a given feasible schedule. A *block* is a group of tasks such that the first task starts at its release time and all the following tasks to the end of the schedule are processed without idle times. Thus the length of a block is the sum of processing times of the tasks in the block. If a block has the property that the release times of all the tasks in the block are greater than or equal to the release time of the first task in the block (in that case we will say that "the block satisfies the *release time property*"), then the schedule found for this block is clearly optimal.

A block satisfying the release time property may be found by scanning the given schedule, starting from the last task and attempting to find a group of tasks of the described property. In particular, if T_{α_n} is the last task in the schedule, and $C_{max} = r_{\alpha_n}+p_{\alpha_n}$, then $\{T_{\alpha_n}\}$ is a block that satisfies the release time property. Another example is a schedule $(T_{\alpha_1},\cdots,T_{\alpha_n})$ whose length is $\min_j\{r_j\} + \sum_{i=1}^{n} p_i$; in this case the block consists of all the tasks to be performed.

Lemma 4.1.1 *A schedule for problem $1\,|\,r_j\,|\,C_{max}$ is optimal if and only if it contains a block that satisfies the release time property.*

Proof. The "if-part" is clear from the definition of block and release time property. To prove necessity, suppose the schedule $(T_{\alpha_1},\cdots,T_{\alpha_n})$ is optimal. If T_{α_n} is started at its release time r_{α_n}, then $\{T_{\alpha_n}\}$ is a block that satisfies the release time property. Consider $(T_{\alpha_l}, \cdots, T_{\alpha_n})$ such that the schedule has no idle times between the tasks $T_{\alpha_l}, \cdots, T_{\alpha_n}$, but there is an idle interval immediatley before T_{α_l}, $1 \le l < n$. Then, because of the optimality of the schedule, T_{α_l} or a task following T_{α_l} must start at its release time, and hence a block with release time property exists. $\square$

Lemma 4.1.1 can be used to prove optimality of a schedule for problem $1 \mid r_j, \tilde{d}_j \mid C_{max}$. On the other hand, it may happen that a schedule constructed in the branch and bound procedure cannot be proved to be optimal by this lemma, because no block satisfying the release time property could be found. Then the completion time C of the schedule can still be used for bounding further solutions. This can be done by reducing all deadlines $\tilde{d}_j$ to be at most $C-1$, which ensures that if other feasible schedules exist, only those that are better than the solution at hand are generated.

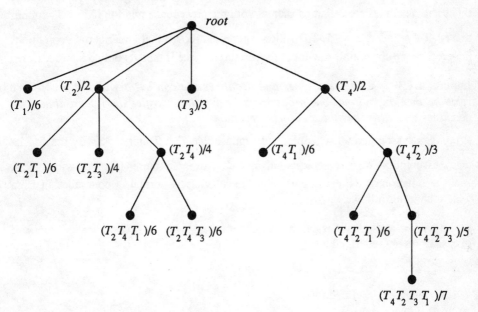

Figure 4.1.2 *Complete search tree of the sample problem of Example* 4.1.2.

Example 4.1.2 To demonstrate the idea of the branch and bound algorithm described above consider the following sample problem of four tasks and vectors describing respectively task release times, processing times, and deadlines, $r = [4, 1, 1, 0]$, $p = [2, 1, 2, 2]$, and $d = [7, 5, 6, 4]$. The branch and bound algorithm would scan the nodes of the search tree shown in Figure 4.1.2 in some order that depends on the implementation of the algorithm. At each node the above criteria (i) and (ii) will be checked. When a schedule is obtained, its optimality will be checked by means of Lemma 4.1.1. We see that schedule (T_4, T_2, T_3, T_1), when started at time 0, obeys all release times and deadlines, and is of minimum length. $\square$

If task preemption is allowed, the problem $1 \mid pmtn, r_j, \tilde{d}_j \mid C_{\max}$ can be formulated as a maximum flow problem and can thus be solved in polynomial time [BFR71].

Problem $1 \mid prec, r_j, \tilde{d}_j \mid C_{\max}$

Problem $1 \mid prec, r_j, \tilde{d}_j \mid C_{\max}$ is *NP*-hard in the strong sense because problem $1 \mid r_j, \tilde{d}_j \mid C_{\max}$ already is. However, if all tasks have unit processing times (i.e. for the problem $1 \mid prec, r_j, p_j = 1, \tilde{d}_j \mid C_{\max}$), and if all release times and deadlines are integer multiples of a given unit of time, a modification of the earliest deadline scheduling rule solves the problem optimally in polynomial time. We will describe this approach below.

Given schedule S, let s_i be the starting time of task T_i, $i = 1, \cdots, n$. A schedule is called *normal* if, for any two tasks T_i and T_j, $s_i < s_j$ implies that $\tilde{d}_i \leq \tilde{d}_j$ or $r_j > s_i$. Release times and deadlines are called *consistent* with the precedence relation if $T_i < T_j$ implies that $r_i + 1 \leq r_j$ and $\tilde{d}_i \leq \tilde{d}_j - 1$. The following lemma proves that under certain conditions the precedence constraints are not of essential relevance if there is only one processor.

Lemma 4.1.3 *If the release times and deadlines are consistent with the precedence relation, then any normal one-processor schedule that satisfies the release times and deadlines must also obey the precedence relation.*

Proof. Consider a normal schedule, and suppose that $T_i < T_j$ but $s_i > s_j$. By the consistency assumption we have $r_i < r_j$ and $\tilde{d}_i < \tilde{d}_j$. However, these, together with $r_j \leq s_j$, cause a violation of the assumption that the schedule is normal, a contradiction from which the result follows. $\square$

Release times and deadlines can be made consistent with the precedence relation $<$ if release times are redefined by

$$r'_{\alpha_j} = \max \left(\{ r_{\alpha_j} \} \cup \{ r_{\alpha_i} + 1 \mid T_{\alpha_i} < T_{\alpha_j} \} \right),$$

and deadlines are redefined by by

$$d'_{\alpha_j} = \min \left(\{ d_{\alpha_j} \} \cup \{ d_{\alpha_i} - 1 \mid T_{\alpha_i} < T_{\alpha_j} \} \right).$$

These changes obviously do not alter the feasibility of any schedule. Furthermore, it follows from Lemma 4.1.3 that a precedence relation is essentially irrelevant when scheduling on one processor. Henceforth we will assume that no precedence relation is imposed, and we will consider only normal schedules.

As already mentioned, if all release times are zero, the earliest deadline algorithm would be exact. Now, in the case of unequal release times, it may happen that task T_i, though available for processing, must give preference to another task T_j with larger release time, because $\tilde{d}_j < \tilde{d}_i$. Hence, in such a situation some idle interval should be introduced in the schedule in order to gain feasibility. These idle intervals are called *forbidden regions* [GJST81]. A forbidden region is an interval (f_1, f_2) of time (open both on the left and right) during which no task is allowed to start if the schedule is to be feasible. Notice that we do not forbid execution of a task during (f_1, f_2) that had been started at time f_1 or earlier. Algorithm 4.1.4 will show how forbidden regions are used. How forbidden regions are found systematically will be described in Algorithm 4.1.6. Let us assume for the moment that we have found a finite set of forbidden regions $F_1, \cdots, F_m$.

The following algorithm represents the basic way of how a feasible schedule will be generated. The algorithm schedules k unit time tasks, all of which must be completed by some time $\tilde{d}$. Release times are of no concern, but no task is allowed to start within one of given forbidden regions $F_1, \cdots, F_m$. The algorithm finds the latest possible time by which the first task must start if all of them are to be completed by time $\tilde{d}$, without starting any task in a forbidden region.

Algorithm 4.1.4 *Backscheduling of a set of unit time tasks* $\{T_1, \cdots, T_k\}$ *with no release times and common deadline* $\tilde{d}$, *considering a set of forbidden regions* [GJST 81].
begin
Order the tasks arbitrarily as $T_1, \cdots, T_k$;
for $i := k$ **downto** 1 **do**

Start T_i at the latest time $s_i \leq s_{i+1} - 1$ (or $\tilde{d} - 1$, if $i = k$) which does not fall into a
forbidden region;
end;

Lemma 4.1.5 *The starting time* s_1 *found for* T_1 *by Algorithm 4.1.4 is such that, if all the given tasks (including* T_1*) were to start at times strictly greater than* s_1, *with none of them starting in one of the given forbidden regions, then at least one task would not be completed by time* $\tilde{d}$.

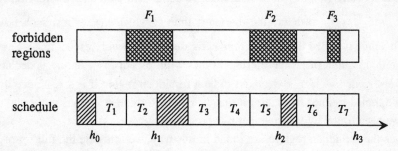

Figure 4.1.3 *A schedule with forbidden regions and idle periods.*

Proof. Consider a schedule found by Algorithm 4.1.4. Let $h_0 = s_1$, let $h_1, \cdots, h_j$ be the starting times of the idle periods (if any) in the schedule, and let $h_{j+1} = \tilde{d}$ (see Figure 4.1.3). Notice that whenever (t_1, t_2) is an idle period, it must be the case that $(t_1 - 1, t_2 - 1]$ is part of some forbidden region, for otherwise Algorithm 4.1.4 would have scheduled some task to overlap or finish during $(t_1, t_2]$. Now consider any interval $(h_i,$

$h_{i+1}]$, $0 \le i \le j$. By definition of the times h_i, the tasks that are finished in the interval are scheduled with no idle periods separating them and with the rightmost one finishing at time h_{i+1}. It follows that Algorithm 4.1.4 processes the maximum possible number of tasks in each interval $(h_i, h_{i+1}]$. Any other schedule that started all the tasks later than time s_1 and finished them all by time $\tilde{d}$ would have to exceed this maximum number of tasks in some interval $(h_i, h_{i+1}]$, $1 \le i \le j$, a contradiction. $\square$

We will use Algorithm 4.1.4 as follows. Consider any two tasks T_i and T_j such that $\tilde{d}_i \le \tilde{d}_j$. We focus our interest on the interval $[r_i, \tilde{d}_j]$, and assume that we have already found a set of forbidden regions in this interval. We then apply Algorithm 4.1.4, with $\tilde{d} = \tilde{d}_j$ and with these forbidden regions, to the set of all tasks T_k satisfying $r_i \le r_k \le \tilde{d}_k \le \tilde{d}_j$. Let s be the latest possible start time found by Algorithm 4.1.4 in this case. There are two possibilities which are of interest. If $s < r_i$, then we know from Lemma 4.1.5 that there can be no feasible schedule since all these tasks must be completed by time $\tilde{d}$, none of them can be started before r_i, but at least one must be started by time $s < r_i$ if all are to be completed by $\tilde{d}$. If $r_i \le s < r_i + 1$, then we know that $(s-1, r_i)$ can be declared to be a forbidden region, since any task started in that region would not belong to our set (its release time is less than r_i) and it would force the first task of our set to be started later than s, thus preventing these tasks from being completed by $\tilde{d}$.

The algorithm presented next essentially applies Algorithm 4.1.4 to all such pairs of release times and deadlines in such a manner as to find forbidden regions from right to left. This is done by "considering the release times" in order from largest to smallest. To process a release time r_i, for each deadline $\tilde{d}_j \ge \tilde{d}_i$ the number of tasks is determined which cannot start before r_i and which must be completed by $\tilde{d}_j$. Then Algorithm 4.1.4 is used (with $\tilde{d} = \tilde{d}_j$) to determine the latest time at which the earliest such task can start. This time is called the *critical time* e_j for deadline $\tilde{d}_j$ (with respect to r_i). Letting e denote the minimum of all these critical times with respect to r_i, failure is declared in case of $e < r_i$, or $(e-1, r_i)$ is declared to be a forbidden region if $r_i \le e$. Notice that by processing release times from largest to smallest, all forbidden regions to the right of r_i will have been found by the time that r_i is processed.

Once the forbidden regions are found in this way, we schedule the full set of tasks forward from time 0 using the *earliest deadline rule*. This proceeds by initially setting t to the least nonnegative time not in a forbidden region and then assigning start time t to a task with lowest deadline among those ready at t. At each subsequent step, we first update t to the least time which is greater than or equal to the finishing time of the last scheduled task, and greater than or equal to the earliest ready time of an unscheduled task, and which does not fall into a forbidden region. Then we assign start time t to a task with lowest deadline among those ready (but not previously scheduled) at t.

Algorithm 4.1.6 *for problem* $1 \mid prec, r_j, p_j{=}1, \tilde{d}_j \mid C_{\max}$ [GJST81].
```
begin
```
Order tasks so that $r_1 \le r_2 \le \cdots \le r_n$;

$\mathcal{F} := \varnothing;$ -- the set of forbidden intervals is initially empty

```
for i := n downto 1 do
    begin
```
  ```for each``` task T_j ```with``` $\tilde{d}_j \ge \tilde{d}_i$ ```do```
   ```begin```
    ```if``` e_j is undefined ```then``` $e_j := \tilde{d}_j - 1$ ```else``` $e_j := e_j - 1$;
    ```while``` $e_j \in F$ for some forbidden region $F = (f_1, f_2) \in \mathcal{F}$, ```do``` $e_j := f_1$;
   ```end;```
  ```end;```
```
    if i = 1 or``` $r_{i-1} < r_i$
```
    then
        begin
```
  $e := \min\{e_j \mid e_j \text{ is defined}\};$
  ```if``` $e < r_i$ ```then begin``` write('No feasible schedule exists'); exit; ```end;```
  ```if``` $r_i \le e < r_i + 1$ ```then``` $\mathcal{F} := \mathcal{F} \cup \{(e-1, r_i)\};$
  ```end;```
  $t := 0;$
```
    while``` $\mathcal{T} \ne \varnothing$ ```do
        begin
```
  ```if``` $r_i > t$ ```for all``` $T_i \in \mathcal{T}$ ```then``` $t := \min\limits_{T_i \in \mathcal{T}}\{r_i\};$
  ```while``` $t \in F$ for some forbidden region $F = (f_1, f_2) \in \mathcal{F}$, ```do``` $t := f_2;$

  Choose $T_i \in \{T_i \mid T_i \in \mathcal{T}$ such that $\tilde{d}_i = \min\{\tilde{d}_k\}$ and $r_i \le t\}\};$
  $t := t + 1;$
  ```end;```
```
end;
```

The following facts concerning Algorithm 4.1.6 can easily be proved [GJST81].

(i)   If the algorithm exits with failure, then there is no feasible schedule.

(ii)  If the algorithm does not declare failure, then it finds a feasible schedule; this schedule has minimum makespan among all feasible schedules.

(iii) The time complexity of the algorithm is $O(n^2)$.

In [GJST81], there is also presented an improved version of Algorithm 4.1.6 which runs in time $O(n\log n)$.

## 4.1.2  Scheduling with Release Times and Delivery Times

In this type of problems, task $T_j$ is available for processing at time $r_j$, needs processing time $p_j$, and, finally, has to spend some "delivery" time $q_j$ in the system after its
```

processing. We will generalize the notation introduced in Section 3.4 and write $1 \mid r_j,$ *delivery times* $\mid C_{\max}$ for this type of problems. The aim is to find a schedule for tasks $T_1, \cdots, T_n$ such that the final completion time is minimal.

One may think of a production process consisting of two stages where the first stage is processed on a single processor, and in the second stage some finishing operations are performed which are not restricted by the bottleneck processor. We will see in Section 4.3.1 that maximum lateness problems are very closely related to the problem considered here. Numerous authors, e.g. [BS74, BFR73, FTM71, Pot80a, Pot80b, LLRK76, and Car82], studied this type of scheduling problems. Garey and Johnson [GJ79] proved the problem to be *NP*-hard in the strong sense.

Problem $1 \mid r_j,$ *delivery times* $\mid C_{\max}$

Schrage [Sch71] presented a heuristic algorithm which follows the idea that a task of maximal delivery time among those of earliest release time is chosen. The algorithm can be implemented with time complexity $O(n\log n)$.

Algorithm 4.1.7 *Schrage's algorithm for* $1 \mid r_j,$ *delivery times* $\mid C_{\max}$ [Car82].
```
begin
```
$t := \min_{T_j \in \mathcal{T}} \{r_j\};$
```
while  T ≠ ∅  do
      begin
```
$\mathcal{T}' := \{T_j \mid T_j \in \mathcal{T}, \text{ and } r_j \leq t\};$

Choose $T_j \in \mathcal{T}'$ such that $p_j = \max_{T_k \in \mathcal{T}'} \{p_k \mid q_k = \max_{T_l \in \mathcal{T}'} \{q_l\}\};$

Schedule T_j at time t;

$\mathcal{T} := \mathcal{T} - \{T_j\};$

$t := \max\{t + p_j, \min_{T_l \in \mathcal{T}} \{q_l\}\};$
```
      end;
end;
```

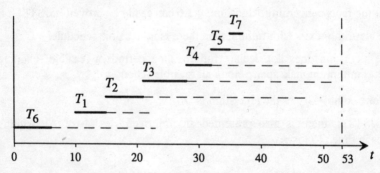

Figure 4.1.4 *A schedule generated by Schrage's algorithm for Example* 4.1.8.

Example 4.1.8 [Car82] Consider seven tasks with release times $r = [10, 13, 11, 20, 30, 0, 30]$, processing times $p = [5, 6, 7, 4, 3, 6, 2]$, and delivery times $q = [7, 26, 24, 21, 8,$

17, 0]. Schrage's algorithm determines the schedule $(T_6, T_1, T_2, T_3, T_4, T_5, T_7)$ of length 53, which is shown in Figure 4.1.4. Execution on the single processor is represented by solid lines, and delivery times are represented by dashed lines. An optimal schedule, however, would be $(T_6, T_3, T_2, T_4, T_1, T_5, T_7)$, and its total length is 50. $\square$

Carlier [Car82] improved the performance of Schrage's algorithm. Furthermore, he presented a branch and bound algorithm for the problem.

Problem $1 \mid pmtn, r_j, delivery\ times \mid C_{max}$

If task execution is allowed to be preempted, an optimal schedule can be constructed in $O(n\log n)$ time. We simply modify the **while**-loop in Schrage's algorithm such that processing of a task is preempted as soon as a task with a higher priority becomes available ("preemptive version" of Schrage's algorithm). The following result is mentioned without a proof (cf. [Car82]).

Theorem 4.1.9 *The preemptive version of Schrage's algorithm generates optimal preemptive schedules in $O(n\log n)$ time. The number of preemptions is not greater than $n-1$.* $\square$

4.2 Minimizing Mean Weighted Flow Time

This section deals with scheduling problems subject to minimizing $\Sigma w_j C_j$. The problem $1 \mid\mid \Sigma w_j C_j$, i.e. scheduling a set of n tasks in such a way that the weighted sum of completion times is minimal, can be optimally solved by scheduling the tasks in order of nondecreasing ratios of processing times and weights, p_j/w_j. In the special case $1 \mid\mid \Sigma C_j$ (all weights are equal to 1), this reduces to the *shortest processing time (SPT)* rule.

The problem of minimizing the sum of weighted completion times subject to release dates is strongly *NP*-hard, even if all weights are 1 [LRKB77]. In the preemptive case, $1 \mid pmtn, r_j \mid \Sigma C_j$ can be solved optimally by a simple extension of the SPT rule [Smi56], whereas $1 \mid pmtn, r_j \mid \Sigma w_j C_j$ turns out to be strongly *NP*-hard [LLLRK84].

If deadlines are introduced, the situation is similar: $1 \mid \tilde{d}_j \mid \Sigma C_j$ can be solved optimally by another simple extension of the SPT rule, but the weighted case $1 \mid \tilde{d}_j \mid \Sigma w_j C_j$ is strongly *NP*-hard. Several elimination criteria and branch and bound algorithms have been proposed for this problem.

If the order of task execution is restricted by arbitrary precedence constraints, the problem $1 \mid prec \mid \Sigma w_j C_j$ becomes *NP*-hard [LRK78]. This remains true, even if all processing times p_j are 1 or all weights w_j are 1. For special classes of precedence constraints such as tree-like and series-parallel, however, polynomial time optimization algorithms are known.

Problem $1 \mid \mid \Sigma w_j C_j$

Suppose each task $T_j \in \mathcal{T}$ has a specified processing time p_j and weight w_j; the problem of determining a schedule with minimal weighted sum of task completion times, i.e. for which $\Sigma w_j C_j$ is minimal, can be optimally solved by means of Smith's "ratio rule" [Smi56], also known as Smith's *weighted shortest processing time (WSPT)* rule: Any schedule is optimal that puts the tasks in order of nondecreasing ratios p_j/w_j. In the special case that all tasks have equal weights, any schedule is optimal which places the tasks according to *SPT* rule, i.e. in nondecreasing order of processing times.

In order to prove the optimality of the WSPT rule for $1 \mid \mid \Sigma w_j C_j$, we present a far more general result due to Lawler [Law83] that includes $1 \mid \mid \Sigma w_j C_j$ as a special case: Given a set $\mathcal{T}$ of n tasks and a real-valued function γ which assigns value $\gamma(\pi)$ to each permutation π of tasks, find permutation π^* such that

$$\gamma(\pi^*) = \min\{\gamma(\pi) \mid \pi \text{ is a permutation of task set } \mathcal{T}\}.$$

If we know nothing about the structure of function γ, there is clearly nothing to be done except evaluating $\gamma(\pi)$ for each of the $n!$ possible different permutations of the task set.

But for a given function γ we can sometimes find a transitive and complete relation $\precsim$ on the set of tasks with the property that for any two tasks T_i, T_k, and for any permutation of the form $\alpha T_i T_k \delta$ we have

$$T_i \precsim T_k \Rightarrow \gamma(\alpha T_i T_k \delta) \leq \gamma(\alpha T_k T_i \delta). \tag{4.2.1}$$

If such a relation exists for a given function γ, we say: "γ *admits the relation* $\precsim$", or: "$\precsim$ *is a task interchange relation for* γ". This means that whenever T_i and T_k occur as adjacent tasks with T_k before T_i in a schedule, we are at least as well off to interchange their order. This relation is also referred to as the *adjacent pairwise interchange property*. Hence we have the following theorem:

Theorem 4.2.1 *If γ admits a task interchange relation $\precsim$, then an optimal permutation π^* can be found by ordering the tasks according to $\precsim$.* $\square$

Consider, for example, *Smith's WSPT rule*,

$$T_i \precsim T_k \Leftrightarrow p_i/w_i \leq p_k/w_k. \tag{4.2.2}$$

If the last task in the subsequence α in (4.2.1) finishes at time t, the cost $\Sigma w_j C_j$ of $\alpha T_i T_k \delta$ will be $w_i(t+p_i) + w_k(t+p_i+p_k) + C$ where C considers all the costs of tasks in the subsequences α and δ. If T_i and T_k are interchanged, the cost of $\alpha T_k T_i \delta$ will be $w_k(t+p_k) + w_i(t+p_k+p_i) + C$. Clearly, because of (4.2.2), the first sequence is of smaller cost than the second. As a consequence, the function $\Sigma w_j C_j$ admits Smith's *WSPT* rule, hence, by Theorem 4.2.1, this rule solves $1 \mid \mid \Sigma w_j C_j$ optimally.

Example 4.2.2 Let $T = \{T_1, \cdots, T_{10}\}$, with processing times and weights given by vectors $p = [16, 12, 19, 4, 7, 11, 12, 10, 6, 8]$ and $w = [2, 4, 3, 2, 5, 5, 1, 3, 6, 2]$. The optimal schedule is obtained by sorting the tasks in order of nondecreasing values of p_j/w_j, i.e. we get the task list $(T_9, T_5, T_4, T_6, T_2, T_8, T_{10}, T_3, T_1, T_7)$. The weighted sum of completion times is $6 \cdot 6 + 13 \cdot 5 + 17 \cdot 2 + 28 \cdot 5 + 40 \cdot 4 + 50 \cdot 3 + 58 \cdot 2 + 79 \cdot 3 + 95 \cdot 2 + 105 \cdot 1 = 1233$. Note that interchanging any two tasks in the schedule causes an increase of $\Sigma w_j C_j$. $\square$

Problem $1 | r_j | \Sigma w_j C_j$

If the task ready times are not identical, the problem has been proved to be *NP*-hard even in the case that all weights are 1 [LRKB77]. We will first present two heuristic algorithms for scheduling the tasks, where each rule specifies priority criteria for adding a task to an existing partial schedule, $S_{\mathcal{U}}$ of already scheduled tasks $\mathcal{U} \subseteq T$, starting with $\mathcal{U} = \varnothing$.

Suppose that the schedule is constructed by adding one task at a time, starting from the empty schedule. At any point, we have a partial schedule $S_{\mathcal{U}}$ of task set $\mathcal{U} \subseteq T$, $S_{\mathcal{U}} = (T_{\alpha_1}, \cdots, T_{\alpha_{|\mathcal{U}|}})$. The earliest start time of task $T_j \in \mathcal{U}$, s_j, and its completion time, C_j, are given by

$$s_i = \begin{cases} r_i & \text{if } i = \alpha_1 \\ \max\{r_i, C_{\alpha_{j-1}}\} & \text{if } i = \alpha_j, i \neq 1, \\ \max\{r_i, C_{\alpha_{|\mathcal{U}|}}\} & \text{if } T_i \in T - \mathcal{U}; \end{cases} \qquad (4.2.3)$$

$$C_i = s_i + p_i. \qquad (4.2.4)$$

The two heuristics are as follows.

A. *The earliest completion time (ECT) rule*: Select task T_i with $\min\{C_i | T_i \in T - \mathcal{U}\}$. Break ties by choosing T_i with $\max_i\{s_i\}$, and further ties by choosing T_i with minimum index i. Update s_i and C_i using (4.2.3) and (4.2.4).

B. *The earliest start time (EST) rule*: Select task T_i with $\min\{s_i | T_i \in T - \mathcal{U}\}$. Break ties by choosing T_i with $\min\{C_i\}$, and further ties by choosing T_i with $\min\{i\}$. Update s_i and C_i using (4.2.3) and (4.2.4).

For these two heuristics, no accuracy bounds are known. The main difficulty arises from the fact that, since $r_j \geq 0$, idle times may be inserted in the optimal schedule. Consider the following example.

Example 4.2.3 Let $T = \{T_1, \cdots, T_5\}$ with processing times $p = [3, 18, 17, 21, 25]$ and ready times $r = [35, 22, 34, 37, 66]$. The *ECT* rule results in the schedule $(T_1, T_3, T_2, T_4, T_5)$. The final values of the earliest start time s_j and the completion times C_j are given by the vectors $s = [35, 55, 38, 73, 94]$ and $C = [38, 73, 55, 94, 119]$, respectively, and the sum of completion times is 379. An optimal schedule, however, would be $(T_2, T_1, T_3, T_5, T_4)$ whose sum of completion times is 334. □

For the case of *equal weights*, an enumerative algorithm for solving the problem optimally was presented by Dessouky and Deogun [DD81]. This is a branch and bound algorithm using a search tree in which a node at level k represents a partial schedule. If $S_{\mathcal{U}}$ is such a partial schedule for a subset $\mathcal{U}$ of k tasks, then let $C^*_{S_{\mathcal{U}}}$ denote the minimal total completion time of any schedule starting with $S_{\mathcal{U}}$. For each node at level k, if $S_{\mathcal{U}} = (T_{\alpha_1}, \cdots, T_{\alpha_k})$ is the corresponding partial schedule, a lower bound $\underline{C}_{S_{\mathcal{U}}}$ and an upper bound $\overline{C}_{S_{\mathcal{U}}}$ on $C^*_{S_{\mathcal{U}}}$ are computed. A successor node at level $k+1$ is obtained by selecting a task $T_i \in \mathcal{T} - \mathcal{U}$ and adding it to $S_{\mathcal{U}}$ in position $k+1$ to form partial schedule $(T_{\alpha_1}, \cdots, T_{\alpha_k}, T_i)$.

At any iteration, the branch and bound search chooses for branching a node that has currently the lowest lower bound $\underline{C}_{S_{\mathcal{U}}}$. Among the nodes generated from the same parent node, dominance is tested. A partial schedule $S_i = (T_{\alpha_1}, \cdots, T_{\alpha_k}, T_i)$ is *dominated* if another partial schedule $S_j = (T_{\alpha_1}, \cdots, T_{\alpha_k}, T_j)$ exists, and $C^*_{S_i} \geq C^*_{S_j}$. A node whose partial schedule has been found dominated by that of another node is eliminated from further consideration.

The crucial steps are indeed those where lower and upper bounds for the total completion time are estimated. For this, a number of tests are available (see [DD81]).

An extension of this branch and bound algorithm to the case of unequal weights is presented in [BR82].

The case in which the tasks have unit processing times can be solved in polynomial time [LRK80]. The preemptive case, $1\,|\,pmtn, r_j|\,\Sigma C_j$, can be solved optimally by a simple modification of Smith's *WSPT* rule [Smi56], whereas $1\,|\,pmtn, r_j|\,\Sigma w_j C_j$ turns out to be strongly *NP*-hard [LLLRK84].

Problem $1|\tilde{d}_j|\Sigma w_j C_j$

Each task T_j becomes available for processing at time zero, has processing time p_j, a deadline $\tilde{d}_j$ by which it must be completed (i.e. $C_j \leq \tilde{d}_j$, $j = 1, \cdots, n$), and has a positive weight w_j. The tasks are to be processed without preemption. The objective is to find a schedule of the tasks which minimizes the sum of weighted completion times $\Sigma w_j C_j$, subject to meeting all deadlines. This problem was first studied by Smith, who found a simple solution procedure both for situations with no deadlines, and for situations with deadlines, but with equal weights. Emmons [Emm75] showed that Smith's procedure does not extend to the case of unequal weights, and from Lenstra [Len77] we know that problem $1|\tilde{d}_j|\Sigma w_j C_j$ is *NP*-hard. Burns [Bur76] constructed a pairwise interchange heuristic for the problem that was improved by Miyazaki [Miy81]. Bansal [Ban80] developed an optimization algorithm based on a branch and bound approach and dominance criteria, and used Smith's *WSPT* rule to calculate lower bounds. Potts and van Wassenhove [PW83] presented a branch and bound algorithm based on a Lagrangian relaxation of the problem and found additional dominance criteria. Similar improvements have been presented by Kalra and Khurana [KK83], Posner [Pos85] and Bagchi and Ahmadi [BA87]. The latter used a task-splitting procedure to compute lower bounds for the weighted sum of completion times.

In the following we will assume that at least one feasible schedule exists for the given problem; this is easily checked by ordering the tasks in nondecreasing order of deadlines. If any of the tasks in this sequence is completed after its deadline, then no feasible schedule exists. It can be shown that if tasks have agreeable deadlines, i.e. $p_j/w_j \leq p_k/w_k$ implies $\tilde{d}_j \leq \tilde{d}_k$ for all tasks T_j and T_k, then an optimal solution is obtained by ordering the tasks in nondecreasing order of their deadlines.

Another interesting heuristic algorithm for $1|\tilde{d}_j|\Sigma w_j C_j$ is *Smith's backward scheduling rule* [Smi56]. Provided there exists a schedule in which all tasks meet their deadlines, the algorithm chooses one task of largest processing time among all tasks T_j with $\tilde{d}_j \geq p_1 + \cdots + p_n$, and schedules the selected task last. It then continues by choosing an element of largest processing time among the remaining $n-1$ tasks and placing it in front of the already scheduled tasks, etc.

Algorithm 4.2.4 *Smith's backward scheduling rule for* $1|\tilde{d}_j|\Sigma w_j C_j$ *[Smi56].*
```
begin
```
$p := \sum_{j=1}^{n} \{p_j\};$
```
while T ≠ ∅ do
    begin
```
$\quad T_p := \{T_j | T_j \in T, \tilde{d}_j \geq p\};$
$\quad$ Choose task $T_j \in T_p$ such that p_j/w_j is maximal;
$\quad$ Schedule T_j in position n;
$\quad n := n-1;$
$\quad T := T - \{T_j\};$
$\quad p := p - p_j;$
```
    end;
end;
```

This algorithm can be implemented to run in $O(n\log n)$ time. We also know that the algorithm is exact in the following cases (cf. [PW83]):

(i) Unit processing times, i.e. for the problem $1|p_j-1, \tilde{d}_j|\Sigma w_j C_j$,

(ii) unit weights, i.e. for problem $1|\tilde{d}_j|\Sigma C_j$,

(iii) agreeable weights, i.e. for problems where $p_i \leq p_j$ implies $w_i \geq w_j$ for $i, j = 1, \cdots, n$.

However, in case of arbitrary weights, simple examples show that this algorithm is not exact.

We will present a branch and bound algorithm for $1 \mid \tilde{d}_j \mid \Sigma w_j C_j$. In order to reduce the search for an optimal solution dominance conditions are useful. Dominace theorems usually specify that if certain conditions are satisfied, then task T_i precedes task T_j in at least one optimal schedule. When such conditions are satisfied, we say that task T_i is a *predecessor* of task T_j, and T_j is *successor* of T_i. In that way, dominance theorems result in a set of precedence constraints between pairs of tasks. It is clear that any enumerative algorithm can restrict its search to schedules obeying these precedence constraints. Hence, if many precedence constraints are found, the number of schedules to be investigated can be considerably reduced. Following [PW83], we formulate without proof three examples of such constraints.

Lemma 4.2.5 *Let $T' \subseteq T$ be a subset of tasks chosen such that for any $T_i \in T - T'$ and for any T_j, $T_k \in T'$ with $\tilde{d}_j \leq \tilde{d}_k$, $p_i/w_i \leq p_j/w_j \leq p_k/w_k$ holds. Then for any pair of tasks $T_i \in T$ and $T_j \in T'$ with $\tilde{d}_i \leq \tilde{d}_j$, there exists an optimal schedule in which task T_i appears before task T_j.* $\square$

For the next lemma, let $\mathcal{A}_i$ denote the set of tasks which, according to the precedence condition of Lemma 4.2.5, are successors of task T_i $(i = 1, \cdots, n)$.

Lemma 4.2.6 *If $p_i \leq p_j$, $w_i \geq w_j$ and $\min\{\tilde{d}_i, \sum_{T_k \in T - \mathcal{A}_i} \{p_k\}\} \leq \tilde{d}_j$, then there exists an optimal schedule in which task T_i is processed before task T_j.* $\square$

Lemma 4.2.7 *If the tasks are renumbered so that $\tilde{d}_i \leq \cdots \leq \tilde{d}_n$, and if $\sum_{k=1}^{i} \{p_k\} + p_j > \tilde{d}_i$ for some j with $1 \leq i \leq j \leq n$, then tasks $T_1, \cdots, T_i$ are scheduled before task T_j in any feasible schedule.* $\square$

Obviously, each deadline that exceeds the total processing time $p = \Sigma p_i$ can be replaced by p without any changes of the resulting schedule. In addition, after some precedence conditions have been derived, the deadline of each task T_i can be reset to $\tilde{d}_i = \min\{\tilde{d}_i, p - \sum_{T_k \in T - \mathcal{A}_i} p_k\}$ $(i = 1, \cdots, n)$ where $\mathcal{A}_i$ is the set of successors of task T_i. Furthermore, the deadline of any task T_i which is predecessor of another task T_j is reset using $\tilde{d}_i = \min\{\tilde{d}_i, \tilde{d}_j - p_j - \sum_{T_k \in \mathcal{A}_i \cap \mathcal{B}_j} p_k\}$, where $\mathcal{B}_j$ is the set of predecessors of task T_j.

Reducing deadlines that way may induce additional precedence conditions between tasks. Lemmas 4.2.6 and 4.2.7 are applied repeatedly until no additional precedences can be found. It is indeed our aim to find as many precedences as possible because they allow to reduce the deadlines, and thus decrease the number of potential schedules in the branch and bound algorithm.

Scheduling a set of tasks according to Smith's backward scheduling rule allows to partition the task set T into *blocks* $T_1, \cdots, T_k$. Assume that the tasks have been renumbered so that the schedule generated by Algorithm 4.2.4 is $(T_1, \cdots, T_n)$. A task $T_{l'}$ is called *final* if $\tilde{d}_i \le C_{l'}$ for $i = 1, \cdots, l'$ (implying $C_{l'} = \tilde{d}_{l'}$). The reasoning behind this definition is that tasks $T_1, \cdots, T_{l'}$ must be scheduled before all other tasks in any feasible schedule. A set of tasks $T_i = \{T_{\alpha_i}, \cdots, T_{\beta_i}\}$ forms a *block* if the following conditions are satisfied:

(i) $\alpha_i = 1$, or task T_{α_i-1} is final,

(ii) task T_i is not final for $i = \alpha_i, \cdots, \beta_i - 1$,

(iii) T_{β_i} is final.

If the deadlines force tasks $T_1, \cdots, T_{\beta_i}$ to be scheduled before all other tasks, then the previous deadline adjustment procedures will ensure that $\tilde{d}_j \le C_j$ for $j = 1, \cdots, \beta_i$, and $C_{\beta_i} = \tilde{d}_{\beta_i}$; thus, T_{β_i} will be the last task in a block.

The following theorem gives a sufficient condition for a schedule generated by Smith's backward scheduling rule to be exact.

Theorem 4.2.8 *A schedule generated by Smith's backward scheduling rule is optimal if there is a block partition (in the above sense) of the given task set, the tasks within each block being scheduled in nondecreasing order of p_j/w_j.*

Proof. Suppose that the construction of blocks results in k blocks $T_1, \cdots, T_k$. It is clear that all tasks in block T_j must precede all tasks in block T_{j+1}, $j = 1, \cdots, k-1$ in any feasible schedule. Therefore, the problem decomposes into subproblems each of which involves scheduling tasks within a block. From Smith's backward scheduling rule we know that if the tasks within a block are scheduled in nondecreasing order of p_j/w_j, then that schedule is optimal. $\square$

Example 4.2.9 Let $T = \{T_1, \cdots, T_8\}$ with processing times, deadlines and weights as follows: $p = [4, 3, 8, 2, 4, 7, 5, 4]$, $\tilde{d} = [13, 8, 38, 14, 9, 40, 25, 22]$, $w = [2, 6, 3, 3, 4, 2, 9, 2]$. A feasible schedule is $(T_2, T_5, T_1, T_4, T_8, T_7, T_3, T_6)$. Applying Lemmas 4.2.5-4.2.7 allows to reduce the deadlines to $\tilde{d} = [13, 8, 37, 13, 9, 37, 22, 22]$, and Algorithm 4.2.4 defines the heuristic schedule $(T_2, T_4, T_5, T_1, T_7, T_8, T_3, T_6)$. We see that tasks T_1 and T_6 are final, hence both, the first four and the last four tasks define a partial schedule. As within the partial schedules the values of p_j/w_j are nondecreasing, both partial schedules are optimal; hence the total schedule is optimal. $\square$

In general we will not be able to partition the given set of tasks into blocks. Algorithm 4.2.4 will then produce a schedule S that is not necessarily optimal. However, as this schedule may be considered as an approximate solution, its value $\gamma_S = \Sigma w_j C_j$ serves as an upper bound for the value of an optimal schedule.

A branch and bound method can now be applied in the following way: a node at level l of the search tree corresponds to a final partial schedule in which tasks are scheduled in the last l positions. The value of the partial schedule represents a lower bound for the schedule that can be obtained by descending from that node. Hence, if the lower bound is greater than or equal to any upper bound γ_S, the node can be discarded from further consideration.

An interesting modification of the problem is to allow tasks to be tardy up to a given *maximum allowable tardiness* $D \geq 0$, i.e. the objective is to minimize $\Sigma w_j C_j$ subject to $C_j - \tilde{d}_j \leq D$ for $j = 1, \cdots, n$. This problem is called *constrained weighted completion time (CWCT) problem* [CS86]. This has been shown to be *NP*-hard by Lenstra et al. [LRKB77]. From Chand and Schneeberger [CS86] we know that the CWCT problem can be solved optimally, e.g. in the case that the weight w_j of each task is a nonincreasing function of the procesing time p_j. Furthermore they discussed a worst-case analysis of the *WSPT* heusistic and showed that the accuracy performance ratio can become arbitrarily large in the worst case.

The case in which tasks have unit processing times and both, release times and deadlines, is solvable as a linear assignment problem in $O(n^3)$ time [LRK80]. As can easily be shown there is no advantage to preempt task execution, as any solution that is optimal for $1 \mid \tilde{d}_j \mid \Sigma w_j C_j$ is also optimal for $1 \mid pmtn, \tilde{d}_j \mid \Sigma w_j C_j$. Consequently $1 \mid pmtn, \tilde{d}_j \mid \Sigma C_j$ can be solved in polynomial time. On the other hand, the problems $1 \mid pmtn, \tilde{d}_j \mid \Sigma w_j C_j$ and $1 \mid pmtn, r_j, \tilde{d}_j \mid \Sigma w_j C_j$ are *NP*-hard.

Problem $1 \mid prec \mid \Sigma w_j C_j$

For general precedence constraints, Lawler [Law78] and Lenstra and Rinnooy Kan [LRK78] showed that the problem is *NP*-hard. Sidney [Sid75] presented a decomposition approach which produces an optimal schedule. Among others, Potts [Pot85] presented an especially interesting branch and bound algorithm where lower bounds are derived using a Lagrangian relaxation technique in which the multipliers are determined by the cost reduction method. Optimization scheduling algorithms running in polynomial time have been presented for tree-like precedences [Hor72, AH73], for series-parallel precedences [Sid75, IIN81], and for more general precedence relations [BM83, MS89].

Following [Sid75], a subset $\mathcal{U} \subset \mathcal{T}$ is said to have *precedence* over subset $\mathcal{V} \subset \mathcal{T}$ if there exist tasks $T_i \in \mathcal{U}$ and $T_j \in \mathcal{V}$ such that $T_j \in \text{succ}(T_i)$. If this is the case we will write $\mathcal{U} \rightarrow \mathcal{V}$. A set $\mathcal{U} \subset \mathcal{T}$ is said to be *initial* in $(\mathcal{T}, \prec)$ if $(\mathcal{T} - \mathcal{U}) \nrightarrow \mathcal{U}$, i.e. if $(\mathcal{T} - \mathcal{U}) \rightarrow \mathcal{U}$ is not true. In effect, no task from $\mathcal{T} - \mathcal{U}$ has a successor in $\mathcal{U}$, or, in other words, for each task in $\mathcal{U}$, all its predecessors are in $\mathcal{U}$, too. Obviously, there exists a feasible task order in which the elements of set $\mathcal{U}$ are arranged before that of $\mathcal{T} - \mathcal{U}$.

For a nonempty set $\mathcal{U} \subset \mathcal{T}$, define $p(\mathcal{U}) = \sum\limits_{T_i \in \mathcal{U}} p_i$, $w(\mathcal{U}) = \sum\limits_{T_i \in \mathcal{U}} w_i$, and $\rho(\mathcal{U}) = p(\mathcal{U})/w(\mathcal{U})$. We are interested in initial task sets that have some minimality property. Set $\mathcal{U} \subset \mathcal{T}$ is said to be ρ^*-*minimal* for $(\mathcal{T}, \prec)$ if

(i) $\mathcal{U}$ is initial in $(\mathcal{T}, \prec)$,

(ii) $\rho(\mathcal{U}) \leq \rho(\mathcal{V})$ for any $\mathcal{V}$ which is initial in $(\mathcal{T}, \prec)$, and

(iii) $\rho(\mathcal{U}) < \rho(\mathcal{V})$ for each proper initial subset $\mathcal{V} \subset \mathcal{U}$.

With this notations we are able to formulate the following algorithm.

Algorithm 4.2.10 *Sidney's decomposition algorithm for* $1 \mid prec \mid \Sigma w_j C_j$ [Sid75, IIN81].

```
begin
while T ≠ ∅ do
    begin
    Determine task set U that is ρ*-minimal for (T, <);
    Schedule the members of task set U optimally;
    T := T - U;
    end;
end;
```

From Sidney [Sid75] we know that a schedule is optimal if and only if it can be generated by this algorithm. Instead of proving this fact, we give an intuitive explanation why the algorithm works. Observe that at each step of the iteration, the next subset added to the current schedule is an available subset (i.e. an initial subset) that minimizes $\rho(\mathcal{U}) = p(\mathcal{U})/w(\mathcal{U})$. Thus, subsets containing tasks with small processing times will be favored, which is consistent with the fact that such tasks delay future tasks by relatively little amounts of time. Also, subsets containing tasks with high deferral rates are favored, as we would expect from the fact that it is costly to delay such tasks.

For implementing the first instruction of the **while**-loop, Ichimori et al. [IIN81] gave an algorithm of time complexity $O(n^4)$. Consequently, because of the *NP*-hardness of the problem, the second step of Algorithm 4.2.10 must be of exponentioal time complexity. Only for special types of precedence graphs such as series parallel graphs, the second step of the Algorithm 4.2.10 can be implemented to run in time polynomial in the number of tasks.

Note that in the special case for which there are no precedence constraints (i.e. < is empty), Algorithm 4.2.10 reduces to the Smith's ratio rule introduced in (4.2.2).

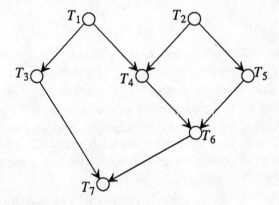

Figure 4.2.1 *A precedence graph for Example 4.2.11.*

Example 4.2.11 [Sid75] Let $T = \{T_1, \cdots, T_7\}$, and let the processing times and weights given by the vectors $p = [5, 8, 3, 5, 3, 7, 6]$ and $w = [1, 1, 1, 1, 1, 1, 1]$. The precedence constraints are shown in Figure 4.2.1. The subset $U = \{T_1, T_3\}$ is initial, and $p(U) = 8$, $w(U) = 2$, $\rho(U) = 4$. I is easy to verify that there is no other initial subset V with the property $\rho(V) < \rho(U)$. Furthermore, the only proper subset of U that is initial in $(T, \prec)$ is $\{T_1\}$, with $\rho(T_1) = p_1 = 5 > \rho(U)$. Hence U is ρ^*-minimal.

If U is the first subset selected in the **while**-loop of Algorithm 4.2.10, the schedule will start with tasks T_1 and T_3, and the algorithm proceeds with task set $\{T_2, T_4, T_5, T_6, T_7\}$. Next the ρ^*-minimal subset $\{T_2, T_4, T_5\}$ could be chosen, thus giving the partial schedule $(T_1, T_3, T_2, T_5, T_4)$, etc. $\square$

A series of branch and bound algorithms have been developed for problem $1 \mid prec \mid \Sigma w_j C_j$ during the last decades. A more recent algorithm was presented by Potts [Pot85] where lower bounds are derived using a Lagrangian relaxation technique in which the multipliers are determined by a cost reduction method. A zero-one programming formulation of the problem uses variables x_{ij} $(i, j = 1, \cdots, n)$ defined by

$$x_{ij} = \begin{cases} 0 & \text{if task } T_i \text{ is scheduled before task } T_j, \text{ or } i = j, \\ 1 & \text{otherwise.} \end{cases}$$

The values of some x_{ij} are implied by the precedence constraints, while others need to be determined. Let $e_{ij} = 1$ when the precedence constraints specify that task T_i is a predecessor of task T_j and let $e_{ij} = 0$ otherwise. Now, since the completion of task T_j occurs at time $\sum_i p_i x_{ij} + p_j$, the problem can be written as

$$minimize \quad \sum_i \sum_j p_i x_{ij} w_j \tag{4.2.5}$$

$$subject\ to \quad x_{ij} \ge e_{ij}, \qquad (i, j = 1, \cdots, n), \tag{4.2.6}$$

$$x_{ij} + x_{ji} = 1, \qquad (i, j = 1, \cdots, n,\ i \ne j), \tag{4.2.7}$$

$$x_{ij} + x_{jk} + x_{ki} \ge 1, \qquad (i, j, k = 1, \cdots, n,\ i \ne j,\ i \ne k,\ j \ne k), \tag{4.2.8}$$

$$x_{ij} \in \{0, 1\}, \qquad (i, j = 1, \cdots, n), \tag{4.2.9}$$

$$x_{ii} = 0 \qquad (i = 1, \cdots, n). \tag{4.2.10}$$

The constraints (4.2.6) ensure that $x_{ij} = 1$ whenever the precedence constraints specify that task T_i is a predecessor of task T_j. The fact that any task T_i is to be scheduled either before or after any other task T_j is presented by (4.2.7). The matrix $X = [x_{ij}]$ may be regarded as the adjacency matrix of a complete directed graph G_X of which G is a subgraph. If any complete directed graph contains a cycle, then it contains a cycle with three edges. Thus the constraints (4.2.7) and (4.2.8) ensure that G_X contains no cycles. When all constraints are satisfied, G_X defines a complete ordering of the tasks in which case G_X is called the *order graph* of X.

Using (4.2.7) and (4.2.8), it is possible to derive more general cycle elimination constraints involving r edges. They are of the form

$$\sum_{h=1}^{r} x_{i_h\, i_{h+1}} \geq 1,\qquad\qquad\qquad\qquad\qquad\qquad (4.2.11)$$

where $i_1,\cdots,i_r$ correspond to r different tasks and where $i_{r+1} = i_1$. For example, adding the constraints $x_{hi}+x_{ij}+x_{jk} \geq 1$ and $x_{hj}+x_{jk}+x_{kh} \geq 1$ and using $x_{jh}+x_{hj} = 1$ yields $x_{hi}+ x_{ij}+x_{jk}+x_{kh} \geq 1$.

The coefficient $p_i w_j$ of x_{ij} in (4.2.5) may be regarded as the cost of scheduling task T_i before T_j. It is convenient to define the cost matrix $C = [c_{ij}]$, where the cost of scheduling task T_i before task T_j is

$$c_{ij} = \begin{cases} p_i w_j & \text{if } e_{ji} = 0 \\ \infty & \text{if } e_{ji} = 1 \end{cases} \qquad (i, j = 1,\cdots,n,\ i \neq j). \qquad (4.2.12)$$

Whenever the precedence constraints specify that task T_j is a predecessor of task T_i, we have $c_{ij} = \infty$ which ensures that constraints (4.2.6) are satisfied without applying them explicitly. The problem can now be written as

minimize $\sum_i \sum_j c_{ij} x_{ij}$

subject to (4.2.7) - (4.2.10).

For special classes of precedence constraints optimization scheduling algorithms running in polynomial time are known. Horn [Hor72] and Adolphson and Hu [AH73] discussed the problem for tree-like precedence graphs. For series-parallel precedence graphs, Lawler [Law78] presented an $O(n\log n)$ time algorithm where an interchange relation similar to that presented in (4.2.1) is applied. Ichimori et al. [IIN81] considered classes of graphs for which Algorithm 4.2.10 has polynomial time complexity. They showed that if the precedence constraints $<$ are such that the ρ^*-minimal subsets for $(\mathcal{T}, <)$ are series-parallel, Algorithm 4.2.10 can be implemented to run in $O(n^5)$ time. In fact, Lawler [Law78] was able to prove the existence of exact algorithms for scheduling problems with far more general optimization criteria than $\Sigma w_j C_j$. Let again γ be a real-valued function of permutations. Note that a schedule for one processor is defined by a permutation of the given task set, hence, as the order of task execution is restricted by the given precedence constraints, only "feasible" permutations are allowed. A permutation π is called *feasible* if $T_i < T_k$ implies that task T_i precedes task T_k under π. The objective is to find a feasible permutation π^* such that

$$\gamma(\pi^*) = \min\{\gamma(\pi) \mid \pi \text{ feasible}\} .$$

Unfortunately, the task interchange relation introduced in (4.2.1) is not general enough to solve this problem. Instead considering pairs of tasks, we should rather deal with pairs of strings of tasks: A *string interchange relation* is a transitive and complete relation $\lesssim$ on strings with the property that for any two disjoint strings δ and δ' of tasks, and any permutation of the form $\alpha\delta\delta'\beta$ we have

$$\delta \lesssim \delta' \implies \gamma(\alpha\delta\delta'\beta) \leq \gamma(\alpha\delta'\delta\beta) .$$

Smith's *WSPT* rule can again be used to define a string interchange relation: for any string δ, define $\rho_\delta = \sum_{T_j \in \delta} p_j / \sum_{T_j \in \delta} w_j$, and $\delta \lesssim \delta' \Leftrightarrow \rho_\delta \leq \rho_{\delta'}$. A reasoning similar to that following eq. (4.2.2) proves that the function $\Sigma w_j C_j$ admits this string interchange relation $\lesssim$.

Clearly, a string interchange relation implies a task interchange relation; but it is not true in general that every function γ which admits a task interchange relation also has a string interchange relation. Lawler's result is the following.

Theorem 4.2.12 [Law78] *If γ admits a string interchange relation $\lesssim$ and if the precedence constraints $<$ are series-parallel, then an optimal permutation π^* can be found by an algorithm which requires $O(n \log n)$ comparisons of strings with respect to $\lesssim$.* $\square$

We can solve the scheduling problem for series-parallel posets; recall from Section 2.3 that these can be described by means of a decomposition tree (see for example Figure 2.3.3). Working from the bottom of the tree upward, we can compute a set of strings of tasks for each node of the tree from the sets of strings obtained for its children. The objective is to obtain a set of strings at the root such that concatinating these strings in order according to $\lesssim$ yields an optimal feasible schedule. We will accomplish this objective if the sets S of strings we obtain satisfy two conditions.

(i) Any concatenation of the strings in a set S in order according to $\lesssim$ does not contradict the order given by the precedence constraint $<$, and

(ii) At any point in the computation, let $S_1, \cdots, S_k$ be the sets of strings computed for nodes such that sets have not yet been computed for their parents. Then some ordering of the strings in the set $S_1 \cup \cdots \cup S_k$ yields an optimal feasible subschedule.

If the strings computed at the root are concatenated in order according to $\lesssim$, then condition (i) ensures that the resulting schedule is feasible, and condition (ii) ensures that it is optimal.

We give an informal description of the algorithm. For each leaf of the decomposition tree, let $S = \{(T_j)\}$, where T_j is the task identified with the leaf. Then, condition (i) is satisfied trivially, and condition (ii) is clearly satisfied for the union of the leaf-sets. Suppose S_1 and S_2 have been obtained for the children of a P-node in the tree. As there are no precedence constraints between the strings in S_1 and the strings in S_2, conditions (i) and (ii) remain satisfied if we take $S = S_1 \cup S_2$ for the P-node. Suppose S_1 and S_2 have been obtained for the left child and the right child of an S-node, respectively. Let $\sigma_1 = \max_{\lesssim} S_1$, i.e. σ_1 is a task string of S_1 that represents a subschedule of maximum γ-value, and let $\sigma_2 = \min_{\lesssim} S_2$ be a task string of S_2 representing a subschedule of minimum γ-value. If $\sigma_2 \not\lesssim \sigma_1$, then conditions (i) and (ii) are still satisfied if we take $S = S_1 \cup S_2$ for the S-node. Otherwise, if $\sigma_2 \lesssim \sigma_1$, we assert that there exists an optimal feasible subschedule in which σ_1 and σ_2 are replaced by their concatenation $\sigma_1 \oplus \sigma_2$ (this follows from simple interchange arguments, cf. Lawler [Law78]). This suggests the following procedure for S-nodes:

```
begin
σ₁ := maxₖ S₁; σ₂ := minₖ S₂;     -- if S₁ = ∅ then σ₁ := ε (empty string)
if σ₁ ⊀ σ₂
then S := S₁ ∪ S₂
else
    begin
    σ := σ₁σ₂;
    S₁ := S₁ - {σ₁}; σ₁ := maxₖ S₁;
    S₂ := S₂ - {σ₂}; σ₂ := maxₖ S₂;
    while (σ ≺ σ₁) or (σ₂ ≺ σ) do
        if σ ≺ σ₁
        then begin σ := σ₁ ⊕ σ; S₁ := S₁ - {σ₁}; σ₁ := maxₖ S₁; end
        else begin σ := σ ⊕ σ₂; S₂ := S₂ - {σ₂}; σ ⊕ σ₂ := minₖ S₂; end;
    S := S₁ ∪ {σ} ∪ S₂;
    end;
end;
```

It is not difficult to verify that the previous conditions (i) and (ii) remain satisfied if for an S-node we compute a set of strings according to this procedure.

The entire algorithm can be implemented so as to require $O(n\log n)$ time plus the time for the $O(n\log n)$ comparisons with respect to $\precsim$.

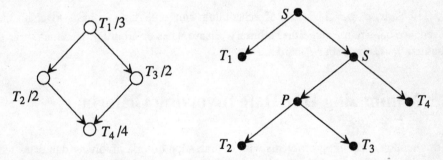

Figure 4.2.2 *Series-parallel task graph and its decomposition tree for Example 4.2.13.*

Example 4.2.13 Let $T = \{T_1, \cdots, T_4\}$, and series-parallel precedence constraints and processing times as shown in Figure 4.2.2 (left). Take minimization of $\Sigma w_j C_j$ as scheduling objective, where all weights w_j are 1. For the P-node (see Figure 4.2.2, right) we recognize that the sets of task strings of the successor vertices are $S_1 = \{(T_2)\}$ and $S_2 = \{(T_3)\}$, hence we get $S = \{(T_2), (T_3)\}$ for the P-node. Continuing bottom-up, the input sets of task strings S_1 and S_2 for the S-node are $S_1 = \{(T_2), (T_3)\}$ and $S_2 = \{(T_4)\}$. Applying the above procedure we get $S = \{(T_2), (T_3, T_4)\}$. Finally, for the root vertex we get $S = \{(T_1, T_2, T_3, T_4)\}$, hence the schedule (T_1, T_2, T_3, T_4) is optimal, i.e. it minimizes $\Sigma w_j C_j$. □

There is another class of promising scheduling algorithms. These algorithms obtain optimal schedules by finding optimal subschedules for progressively larger *modules* of tasks until all tasks are scheduled. This idea can be, for example, applied to series-parallel graphs which can be built up recursively from modules as specified by the decomposition tree (see Section 2.3.2). Möhring and Radermacher [MR85] generalized the notion of a decomposition tree to arbitrary precedence graphs. For the class of all precedence graphs built up by substitution from *prime* (indecomposable) *modules* of size $\leq k$, k arbitrary, there is an optimization algorithm of complexity $O(n^{(k^2)})$ to minimize $\Sigma w_j C_j$. Sidney and Steiner [SS86] improved this algorithm to run in $O(n^{w+1})$ time, where w denotes the maximum width of a prime module.

The idea of decomposing posets into prime modules can also be applied to optimization criteria other than $\Sigma w_j C_j$, as for example for the exponential cost function criterion (see Section 4.4.2). Monma and Sidney [MS87] proved that if the objective function obeys certain interchange properties then the so-called *job module property* is satisfied. The job module property says that any optimal solution to a subproblem defined by a task module is consistent with at least one optimal schedule for the entire problem.

Problems $1 | prec, r_j | \Sigma w_j C_j$ *and* $1 | prec, \tilde{d}_j | \Sigma w_j C_j$

Lenstra and Rinnoy Kan [LRK80] proved that the problems $1 | chains, r_j, p_j = 1 | \Sigma w_j C_j$ and $1 | chains, \tilde{d}_j, p_j = 1 | \Sigma w_j C_j$ of scheduling unit time tasks subject to chain-like precedence constraints and either arbitrary release dates or arbitrary deadlines so as to minimize $\Sigma w_j C_j$ are both *NP*-hard.

4.3 Minimizing Due Date Involving Criteria

In this section scheduling problems with optimization criteria involving due dates will be considered. These include: maximum lateness L_{max}, weighted number of tardy tasks $\Sigma w_j U_j$, mean weighted tardiness $\Sigma w_j D_j$, and a combination of earliness-tardiness criteria.

4.3.1 Maximum Lateness

Recall from Chapter 3 that, given a schedule S for a task set $\mathcal{T}$, the lateness of a task $T_j \in \mathcal{T}$ is defined as $L_j = C_j - d_j$. The objective is to minimize the maximum lateness among all the scheduled tasks. Whereas the problem $1 || L_{max}$ can easily be solved in polynomial time by Jackson's earliest due date algorithm, other cases turn out to be more complex. The problem $1 | r_j | L_{max}$ is strongly *NP*-hard [LLRKB77]. For this, and for $1 | prec, r_j | L_{max}$ as well, solution methods based on branch and bound are known. If tasks are preemptable or have unit processing time, the problem is easy, even if the order of task execution in constrained by a precedence relation [Sid78, Mon82].

Problem $1 || L_{max}$

The *earliest due date algorithm* (*EDD* rule) of Jackson [Jac55] provides a simple and elegant solution to this problem. In this algorithm, tasks are scheduled in order of non-decreasing due dates. The optimality of this rule can be proved by a simple interchange argument. Let S be any schedule and S^* be an *EDD* schedule. If $S \neq S^*$ then there exist two tasks T_j and T_k with $d_k \leq d_j$, such that T_j immediately precedes T_k in S, but T_k precedes T_j in S^*. Since $d_k \leq d_j$, interchanging the positions of T_j and T_k in S cannot increase the value of L_{max}. A finite number of such changes transforms S into S^*, showing that S^* is optimal. The *EDD* rule minimizes maximum lateness and maximum tardiness as well.

Problem $1 | r_j | L_{max}$

The problem $1 | r_j | L_{max}$ is known to be *NP*-hard in the strong sense [LRKB77]. Many exact algorithms have been proposed for this problem, but they are all based on enumerative methods and their computation time grows exponentially with the size of the problem. Research on this problem has focused on reducing the computational time for scheduling large task sets. Achieving this goal will also improve the efficiency of algorithms used to solve the more difficult $Pm | r_j | L_{max}$ problem by using the optimal solutions to the $1 | r_j | L_{max}$ problem [LLRK76].

There is a certain symmetry inherent in the problem which becomes apparent if the model is presented in an alternative way. In this *delivery time model*, there are three processors, P_1, P_2, and P_3, where P_1 and P_3 are assumed to be *non-bottleneck processors* of infinite capacity, and P_2 is a *bottleneck processor* of capacity 1 (i.e. only one task can be processed at a time). Each task T_j has to visit P_1, P_2, P_3 in that order and has to spend

- a *head* $T_j^{(1)}$ on P_1 during time interval $[0, r_j)$,
- a *body* $T_j^{(2)}$ on P_2 from time $s_j \geq r_j$ to $C_j = s_j + p_j$,
- a *tail* $T_j^{(3)}$ on P_3 from time C_j to $L_j' = C_j + q_j$,

where the processing time q_j of tail $T_j^{(3)}$ is assumed to be $K - d_j$ for some constant $K \geq \max_i \{d_i\}$. The objective is to minimize the maximum completion time $L_{max}' = \max_i \{L_i'\} = L_{max} + K$. Notice that this model is exactly the same as the *delivery time model* discussed in Section 4.1.2. Whereas the head part of a task simply realizes the release time, the body part corresponds to the actual task to be processed on the single processor, and the tail part represents the delivery time of the task.

We will refer to the delivery time model as (r, p, q) where r, p, q are vectors of dimension n specifying release times (heads), processing times (bodies), and tails, respectively, for the tasks. It is interesting to note that problem (r, p, q) can be reversed: the inverse problem is defined by (q, p, r), and an optimal schedule for (q, p, r) can be reversed to obtain an optimal schedule for (r, p, q), with the same value of L_{max}.

Of particular importance are the algorithms of Bratley et al. [BFR73], Baker and Su [BS74], and McMahon and Florian [MF75]. The algorithm of McMahon and

Florian (in the following referred to as *MF* algorithm) follows a novel approach in the way it applies the branch and bound method to scheduling problems. It searches for an optimal schedule over a tree of all possible schedules. Unlike other branch and bound algorithms in which most nodes in the tree represent partial schedules, the *MF* tree defines a complete schedule on each node. The schedule is used to derive a lower bound (*LB*) and an upper bound (*UB*) on the optimal solution at that node. In addition, the value of the maximum lateness of all tasks (L_{max}) in the schedule is computed. The search strategy is of the *jumptracking* type and follows always the node with the current lowest *LB* (the current node). From that node, only schedules which can potentially reduce the value of L_{max} are generated. The current lowest upper bound (*LUB*) is continually updated, and a node is eliminated if its $LB \geq LUB$. The search stops when the current node passes an optimality test. The algorithm derives its efficiency from the procedures which perform the following functions:

(1) construct a complete schedule at each node, including the initial schedule;

(2) test each schedule for optimality and compute the lower bound if the current solution is not proven optimal;

(3) generate successor of a node.

The *MF* algorithm can be characterized as a forward scheduling procedure since it starts by placing a task in the first position and continues to place tasks in succeeding positions until it reaches the task in the last position. It turns out that the *MF* algorithm tends to be inefficient when the problem (r, p, q) has a particular structure, for example when the range of ready times is less than that of due dates. Recognizing this difficulty, Lenstra [Len77] reversed the problem to (q, p, r). Since the ready times (r_j) are exchanged with the values q_j, the ranges of ready times and due dates are exchanged, too. As a consequence, the performance of the *MF* algorithm was improved considerably.

Erschler et al. [EFMR83] introduced a new *dominace concept* which permits a restricted set of schedules (the "most feasible ones") to be established on the basis of the ordering of ready times and due dates only. In particular, this dominance property is independent of task processing times, which is especially attractive if the data are not reliable. Carlier [Car82] and Larson et al. [LDD85] improved the previous algorithms with approaches following the *MF* algorithm, where the principles of branching are quite different and fully exploiting the problems' symmetrical features.

Compared to the branch and bound algorithms known for the problem in question, heuristic algorithms such as special list scheduling algorithms can be extremely efficient and often provide solutions adequate for practical applications. They can also be used to to provide upper bounds on the criterion values of optimal schedules. This practical and theoretical importance of the problem motivates the search for efficient approximation algorithms with guaranteed accuracies. Larson and Dessouky [LD78] considered eleven heuristic algorithms and compared them experimentally. Kise et al [KIM79] discussed several heuristic strategies from a more theoretical point of view. Among them are simple heuristics such as Jackson's *EDD* rule, or an algorithm where tasks are scheduled in order of their ready times, or combinations of these two strategies. The main result of [KIM79] is that the relative deviation L_{max} / L_{max}^{*} of the approximate solutions is not larger than $2 - 2/p$ where p is the sum of processing times of the tasks. For an iterative version of Jackson's rule (IJ) Potts [Pot80b] was able to prove

$$L_{max}(IJ)/L_{max}^* \leq 3/2.$$

Hall & Shmoys [HS88] proved that a modification of IJ, MIJ, where the roles of release times and delivery times are interchanged, guarantees

$$L_{max}(MIJ)/L_{max}^* \leq 4/3.$$

In the same paper, the authors also presented two algorithms A_{1k} and A_{2k} that guarantee

$$L_{max}(A_{ik})/L_{max}^* \leq 1 + 1/k \text{ for } i = 1, 2 \text{ and natural } k.$$

A_{1k} runs in $O(n\log n + nk^{16k^2+8k})$ time, whereas A_{2k} runs in $O(2^{4k}(nk)^{4k+3})$ time.

The case of equal due dates is equivalent to $1 \mid r_j \mid C_{max}$ which can be solved optimally by scheduling the tasks in order of nondecreasing release dates (see Section 4.1).

If all execution times p_j are equal, such a simple solution method is not available, unless $p_j = 1$ for all tasks T_j. If all the tasks have unit execution time $(1 \mid r_j, p_j = 1 \mid L_{max})$, an optimal schedule is generated in polynomial time by involving repeated application of Jackson's EDD rule.

Algorithm 4.3.1 *Modification of EDD rule for* $1 \mid r_j, p_j = 1 \mid L_{max}$ [BS74].
```
begin
t := 0;
while T ≠ ∅ do
   begin
   t := max{t, min {r_j}};
           T_j∈T
   T' := {T_j|T_j ∈ T, r_j ≤ t};
   Choose T_i ∈ {T_j|T_j ∈ T', d_j = min{d_k|T_k ∈ T'}};
   T := T - {T_i};
   Schedule T_i at time t;
   t := t + 1;
   end;
end;
```

The proof of this result is straightforward and depends on the fact that no task can become available during the processing of another one, so that it is never advantageous to postpone processing the selected task T_i.

If $p_j = p$, where p is an arbitrary integer, Algorithm 4.3.1 is not exact if p does not divide all r_j. For example, if $n = p = 2$, $r_1 = 0$, $r_2 = 1$, $d_1 = 7$, $d_2 = 5$, postponing T_1 is clearly advantageous. Simons [Sim78] presented a more sophisticated approach to solve the problem $1 \mid r_j, p_j = p \mid L_{max}$, where p is an arbitrary integer.

Problem $1 | pmtn, r_j | L_{max}$

For the preemptive case, $1 | pmtn, r_j | L_{max}$, a modification of Jackson's rule due to Horn [Hor74] solves the problem optimally in polynomial time.

Algorithm 4.3.2 *for problem* $1 | pmtn, r_j | L_{max}$ [Hor74].
```
begin
repeat
    ρ₁ := min {rⱼ};
          Tⱼ∈T
    if all tasks are available at time ρ₁
    then ρ₂ := ∞
    else ρ₂ := min{rⱼ|rⱼ ≠ ρ₁};
    E := {Tⱼ|rⱼ = ρ₁};
    Choose Tₖ ∈ E such that dₖ = min {dⱼ};
                                  Tⱼ∈E
    l := min{pₖ, ρ₂−ρ₁};
    Assign Tₖ to the interval [ρ₁,ρ₁ + l);
    if pₖ ≤ l
    then T := T − {Tₖ}
    else
        begin
        pₖ := pₖ−l;
        for all Tⱼ∈ E do rⱼ := ρ₁+l;
        end;
until T = ∅;
end;
```

Problem $1 | prec, r_j | L_{max}$

We first emphasize that the considerations concerning symmetry of problems $1 | r_j | L_{max}$ can be generalized to the case of precedence constraints. If a problem is specified by a triple of vectors (r, p, q) and - in addition - a precedence relation $\prec$, this is clearly equivalent to the inverse problem defined by (q, p, r) and $\prec'$ with $T_i \prec' T_j$ if $T_j \prec T_i$. Again, an optimal schedule for a problem can be reversed to obtain an optimal schedule for the original problem, with the same criterion value.

Let us now examine the introduction of precedence constraints in the problem in detail. As a general principle, release times r_j and tails q_j may be replaced by

$$r_j = \max \{r_j, \max\{r_i + p_i \mid T_i \prec T_j\}\}$$

$$q_j = \min \{q_j, \max\{p_i + q_i \mid T_j \prec T_i\}\},$$

because in every feasible schedule $s_i \geq C_j \geq r_j + p_j$ for all T_j with $T_i \prec T_j$ and $L'_i \geq C_i + p_j - q_j$ for all T_j with $T_j \prec T_i$. Hence, if $T_i \prec T_j$, we may assume that $r_i + p_i \leq r_j$ and $q_i \leq q_j + p_j > q_j$.

It follows that the case in which all d_j are equal is again solved by ordering the tasks according to nondecreasing r_j. Such an ordering will respect all precedence constraints in view of the preceding argument. If we apply this method to the problem in which all r_j are equal, i.e. for $1 \mid prec \mid L_{max}$, the resulting algorithm can be interpreted as a special case of Lawler's more general algorithm to minimize $\max_j \{G_j(C_j)\}$ for arbitrary nondecreasing cost functions G_j (cf. Section 4.4). A similar observation can be made with respect to the case $p_j = 1$ for all j, where Algorithm 4.3.1 will produce a schedule respecting the precedence constraints.

In the general case, however, the precedence constraints are not respected automatically. Consider for example five tasks with release times $r = [0, 2, 3, 0, 7]$, processing times $p = [2, 1, 2, 2, 2]$, and tales $q = [5, 2, 6, 3, 2]$, and the precedence constraint $T_4 \prec T_2$ (cf. [LRK73]); note that $r_4 + p_4 \leq r_2$ and $q_4 \geq p_2 + q_2$. If the constraint $T_4 \prec T_2$ is ignored, the unique optimal schedule is given by $(T_1, T_2, T_3, T_4, T_5)$ with value $L_{max}^* = 11$. Explicit inclusion of this constraint leads to $L_{max}^* = 12$.

The *MF* algorithm introduced by McMahon and Florian [MF75] can easily be adapted to deal with given precedence constraints. Since we may assume that $r_i < r_j$ and $q_i > q_j$ if $T_i \prec T_j$, they are respected by the *MF* algorithm, and obviously, the lower bound remains valid.

Problem $1 \mid pmtn, prec, r_j \mid L_{max}$

This problem can be solved in $O(n^2)$ time by an application of the algorithm given in [Bla76], which combines the ideas of Lawler's approach to the solution of problem $1 \mid prec \mid L_{max}$ and these of Algorithm 4.3.2. We mention here that in fact the much larger class of problems $1 \mid pmtn, prec, r_j \mid G_{max}$, where quite arbitrary cost functions are assigned to the tasks and maximum cost is to be minimized, can be optimally solved in time $O(n^2)$ by a modification of Lawler's minimax algorithm. This will be discussed in Section 4.4.

Minimizing lateness range

The usual type of scheduling problems considered in literature involves penalty functions which are nondecreasing in task completion times. Conway et al. [CMM67] refer to such functions as *regular performance criteria*. There are, however, many applications in which *nonregular criteria* are appropriate. One of them is the problem of minimizing the difference between maximum and minimum task lateness which is important in real life whenever it is desirable to give equal treatment to all customers (tasks). That is, the delays in filling the customer orders should be as nearly equal as possible for all customers. Another example are file organization problems the objective is to minimize the variance of retrieval times for records in a file.

In spite of the importance of nonregular performance measures, very little analytical work has been done in this area. Gupta and Sen [GS84] studied the problem $1 \mid \mid L_{max} - L_{min}$ where the tasks are pairwise independent, ready at time zero, each having a due date d_j and processing time p_j. They used a heuristic rule in which tasks are ordered according to nondecreasing values of $d_j - p_j$ (*minimum slack time rule, MST*), and ties are broken according to earliest due dates. This heuristic allows to compute lower bounds for $L_{max} - L_{min}$ which are then used in a branch and bound algorithm to eliminate nodes from further consideration.

A more general objective function has been considered by Raiszadeh et al. [RDS87]. There aim was to minimize the convex combination $Z = \lambda(L_{max} - L_{min}) + (1 - \lambda)L_{max}$, $0 \le \lambda \le 1$, of range of lateness and maximum lateness.

Let all the tasks be arranged in the earliest due date order (*EDD*) and indexed accordingly $(T_1, \cdots, T_n)$. Thus for any two tasks T_i, $T_j \in \mathcal{T}$, if $d_i < d_j$, we must have $i < j$. Ties are broken such that $d_i - p_i \le d_j - p_j$, i.e. in the minimum slack time (*MST*) order. If there is still a tie, it can be broken arbitrarily.

Let S be a schedule in which task T_i immediately precedes task T_j, and let S' be constructed from S by interchanging tasks T_i and T_j without changing the position of any other task in S. Then, due to [RDS87], we have the following result for the values Z of S and S'.

Lemma 4.3.3 (a) If $d_i - p_i \le d_j - p_j$, then $Z(S) \le Z(S')$.
(b) *If* $d_i - p_i > d_j - p_j$, *then* $Z(S) - Z(S') \le \lambda((d_i - p_i) - (d_j - p_j))$. $\square$

Lemma 4.3.3 can be used to find lower bounds for an optimal solution. This computation is illustrated in the following example.

Example 4.3.4 [RDS87] Consider $n = 4$ tasks with processing times and due dates given by $p = [6, 9, 11, 10]$ and $d = [17, 18, 19, 20]$, respectively. For the *EDD* ordering $S = (T_1, T_2, T_3, T_4)$, the value of the optimization criterion is $Z(S) = 16 + 11\lambda$. Call this ordering "primary". A "secondary" ordering (this notation is due to Townsend [Tow78]) is obtained by repeatedly interchanging neighboring tasks T_i, T_j with $d_i - p_i > d_j - p_j$, until tasks are in *MST* order. From Lemma 4.3.3(b) we see that such an exchange operation will improve the criterion value of the schedule by at most $\lambda((d_i - p_i) - (d_j - p_j))$. For each interchange operation the maximum potential reduction (*MPR*) of the objective function is given in Table 4.3.1. Obviously, the value $Z(S)$ of the primary order can never be improved by more than 7λ, hence $Z(S) - 7\lambda = 16 + 4\lambda$ is a lower bound on the optimal solution. $\square$

This bounding procedure is used in a branch and bound algorithm where a search tree is constructed according to the following scheme. A node at the rth level of the tree corresponds to a particular schedule with the task arrangement of the first r positions fixed. One of the remaining $n - r$ tasks is then selected for the $(r + 1)^{st}$ position. The lower bound for the node is then computed as discussed above. For this purpose the primary ordering will have the first $r + 1$ positions fixed and the remaining $n - r - 1$ positions in the MST order. Pairwise interchanges of tasks are executed among the last $n - r - 1$ positions. At each step the branching is done from a node having the least lower bound.

Original Schedule	Interchange	Changed Schedule	MPR
(T_1, T_2, T_3, T_4)	T_1 and T_2	(T_2, T_1, T_3, T_4)	2λ
(T_2, T_1, T_3, T_4)	T_1 and T_3	(T_2, T_3, T_1, T_4)	3λ
(T_2, T_3, T_1, T_4)	T_1 and T_4	(T_2, T_3, T_4, T_1)	1λ
(T_2, T_3, T_4, T_1)	T_2 and T_3	(T_3, T_2, T_4, T_1)	1λ

total 7λ

Table 4.3.1

A performance measure similar to the one considered above is the average deviation of task completion times. Under the restriction that tasks have a common due date d, a schedule which minimizes $\sum_{j=1}^{n} |C_j - d|$ has to be constructed. This type of criterion has applications e.g. in industrial situations involving scheduling, where the completion of a task either before or after its due date is costly. It is widely recognized that completion after a due date is likely to incur costs in the loss of the order and of customer goodwill. On the other hand, completion before the due date may lead to higher inventory costs and, if goods are perishable, potential losses.

Raghavachari [Rag86] proved that optimal schedules are "V-shaped". Let T_k be a task with the smallest processing time among all the tasks to be scheduled. A schedule is *V-shaped* if all tasks placed before task T_k are in descending order of processing time and the tasks placed after T_k are in ascending order of processing time. For the special case of $d = \sum_{j=1}^{n} p_j$, an optimal schedule for $1 \,||\, \Sigma |C_j - d|$ can be obtained in the following way.

Algorithm 4.3.5 *for problem* $1 \,||\, \Sigma |C_j - d|$ [Kan81].

Method: The algorithm determines two schedules, $S^\leq$ and $S^>$. The tasks of $S^\leq$ are processed without idle times, starting at time $d - \sum_{T_j \in S^\leq} \{p_j\}$, the tasks of $S^>$ are processed without idle times, starting at time d.

```
begin
S≤ := ∅; S> := ∅;        -- initialization: empty schedules
while T ≠ ∅ do
    begin
    Choose Tₗ ∈ T such that pₗ = max {pⱼ | Tⱼ ∈ T};
                                   j

    T := T - {Tₗ};  S≤ := S≤ ⊕ (Tₗ);
        -- Task Tₗ is inserted into the last position in subschedule S≤
    if T ≠ ∅ do
        begin
        Choose Tₗ ∈ T such that pₗ = max {pⱼ | Tⱼ ∈ T};
                                       j
```

$$\mathcal{T} := \mathcal{T} - \{T_l\}; \quad S^> := (T_l) \oplus S^>;$$

-- Task T_l is inserted before the first task of subschedule $S^\leq$

    end;
  end;
end;

Baghi et al. [BSC86] generalized this algorithm to the case

$$d \geq \begin{cases} p_1 + p_3 + \cdots + p_{n-1} + p_n & \text{if } n \text{ is even} \\ p_2 + p_4 + \cdots + p_{n-1} + p_n & \text{if } n \text{ is odd,} \end{cases}$$

where tasks are numbered in nondecreasing order of processing times, $p_1 \leq p_2 \leq \cdots \leq p_n$.

4.3.2 Number of Tardy Tasks

Another possibility of evaluating task schedules where due dates are involved is to count the number of tasks exceeding their due dates. Let us recall that for each task T_j, the function U_j is defined as

$$U_j = \begin{cases} 0 & \text{if } C_j \leq d_j \\ 1 & \text{otherwise.} \end{cases}$$

Hence, task T_j is tardy iff $U_j = 1$.

The problem of finding a schedule that minimizes the weighted number $\Sigma w_j U_j$ of tardy tasks is *NP*-hard [Kar72]. Villarreal et al. [VB83] presented a branch and bound algorithm for $1 \mid\mid \Sigma w_j U_j$. For the (simpler) case of minimizing the unweighted number of tardy tasks, Moore [Moo68] published an optimization algorithm that solves the problem in polynomial time. A generalization of this algorithm to the case that only certain specified tasks have to be finished within their due dates was discussed by Sidney [Sid73]. If there are certain relationships between the task procesing times and the task weights, then the problem can be solved optimally in polynomial time [Law76].

Given arbitrary ready times, i.e. in the case $1 \mid r_j \mid \Sigma U_j$, the problem is strongly *NP*-hard, as was proved by Lenstra et al. [LRKB77]. For the special case that there are certain dependencies between ready times and due dates, however, optimal schedules can be constructed in polynomial time [KIM78]. Lawler [Law82] proved that a variant of the Moore-Hodgson algorithm solves this problem optimally in $O(n\log n)$ time.

If precedence constraints are introduced between tasks then the problem is *NP*-hard, even in the special case of equal processing times and chain-like precedence constraints. In [IK78], a heuristic algorithm for problem $1 \mid tree, p_j = 1 \mid \Sigma U_j$ is presented. We start our discussion with the simplest cases.

Problem $1 \mid\mid \Sigma U_j$

Several special cases do admit exact polynomial time algorithms. The most common special case occurs when all weights are equal. Moore [Moo68] published an optimization algorithm that solves the problem in polynomial time. This algorithm sorts the tasks according to *EDD* rule (tasks with earlier due dates first, also known as *Hodgson's algorithm*).

Algorithm 4.3.6 *Hodgson's algorithm for* $1||\Sigma U_j$ [Law82].

Input: Task set $T = \{T_1,\cdots,T_n\}$; processing time of T_j is p_j; due date of T_j is d_j.

Method: The algorithm operates in two steps: first, the subset $T^\leq$ of tasks of T that can be processed on time is determined; then a schedule is determined from the subsets $T^\leq$ and $T - T^\leq$.

```
begin
Sort tasks in EDD order;        -- w.l.o.g. assume that  d₁ ≤ d₂ ≤···≤ dₙ
T^≤ := ∅;
p := 0;       -- p keeps track of the execution time of tasks of  T^≤
for j := 1 to n do
   begin
   T^≤ := T^≤ ∪ {Tⱼ};
   p := p + pⱼ;
   if p > dⱼ       -- i.e. task Tⱼ doesn't meet its due date
   then
      begin
      Let Tₖ be a task in T^≤ with maximal processing time,
          i.e. pₖ = max{pᵢ|Tᵢ ∈ T^≤};
      p := p - pₖ;
      T^≤ := T^≤ - {Tₖ};
      end;
   end;
Schedule the tasks of T^≤ according to EDD rule;
Schedule the remaining tasks (T - T^≤) in an arbitrary order;
end;
```

Without proof we mention that this algorithm generates a schedule with the minimal number of tardy tasks. The algorithm can easily be implemented to run in $O(n\log n)$ time.

Example 4.3.7 Suppose there are tasks T_i, $i = 1,\cdots,8$, with processing times $p = [10, 6, 3, 1, 4, 8, 7, 6]$ and due dates $d = [5, 29, 11, 8, 6, 25, 28, 9]$. Set $T^\leq$ will be $\{T_4, T_3, T_5, T_2, T_7, T_1\}$, and the schedule is $(T_5, T_4, T_3, T_2, T_7, T_1, T_6, T_8)$. The next table compares the due dates and completion times; note that the due dates of the last two tasks are violated. □

	T_5	T_4	T_3	T_2	T_7	T_1	T_6	T_8
Due date d_j	6	8	11	20	28	35	25	9
Completion time C_j	4	5	8	14	21	31	39	45

Table 4.3.2

Problem $1 \| \Sigma w_j U_j$

Karp [Kar72] included the decision version of minimizing the weighted sum of tardy tasks in his list of 21 *NP*-complete problems. Even if all the due dates d_j are equal, the problem is *NP*-hard; in fact, this problem is equivalent to the knapsack problem. An optimal solution for $1 \| \Sigma w_j U_j$ can be specified by a partition of the task set $\mathcal{T}$ into two subsets, say $\mathcal{T}^\leq$ and $\mathcal{T}^>$. The set $\mathcal{T}^\leq$, also called feasible on-time set, represents those tasks that are completed before their due dates while the set $\mathcal{T}^>$ represents the tasks that are tardy. A schedule is found by placing the tasks in $\mathcal{T}^\leq$ in *EDD* order followed by the tasks in $\mathcal{T}^>$ in arbitrary order. Thus it suffices to find an optimal partition of the task set $\mathcal{T}$.

Sahni [Sah76] developed an exact pseudopolynomial time algorithm for $1 \| \Sigma w_j U_j$ which is based on dynamic programming and requires $O(n\Sigma w_j)$ time. Using digit truncation, depending from which digit on the weights are truncated, a series of approximation algorithms $A_1, \cdots, A_k$ (i.e. a so-called *approximation scheme*) with $O(n^3 k)$ running time can be derived such that

$$\Sigma(w_j \overline{U}_j(A_k)) / \overline{U}_w^* \geq 1 - 1/k,$$

where $\overline{U}_j = 1 - U_j$. Note that $\Sigma w_j \overline{U}_j$ is the weighted sum of on-time tasks. It is possible to decide in polynomial time whether $\Sigma w_j U_j^* = 0$. Gens and Levner [GL78] developed an algorithm B_k with running time $O(n^3)$ such that

$$U_w^{B_k} / U_w^* \leq 1 + 1/k.$$

The same authors improved the implementation of algorithm B_k to run in $O(n^2 \log n + n^2 k)$ time [GL81].

When all processing times are equal, the problem $1 \mid p_j = 1 \mid \Sigma w_j U_j$ can easily be solved. For the more general case of $1 \| \Sigma w_j U_j$ where processing times and weights are *agreeable*, i.e. $p_i < p_j$ implies $w_i \geq w_j$, an exact $O(n \log n)$ time algorithm can be obtained by a simple modification of the Hodgson's algorithm [Law76]. We will present this algorithm below.

Suppose tasks are placed and indexed in *EDD* order. Let again $\mathcal{T}^\leq$ be a subset of tasks, all of which can be completed on time when processed in nondecreasing due date order. $\mathcal{T}^\leq$ is said to be *j-optimal* if $\mathcal{T}^\leq \subseteq \{T_1, \cdots, T_j\}$ and the sum of weights of tasks in $\mathcal{T}^\leq$ is maximal with respect to all feasible sets having that property. Thus, an optimal solution is obtained from an *n*-optimal set $\mathcal{T}^\leq$ processed in nondecreasing due date order, and then executing the tasks of $T - T^S$ in any order. Lawler's algorithm is a variation of Algorithm 4.3.6 for the construction of j-optimal sets. The following algorithm uses a linear ordering $\lesssim$ induced on tasks by their *relative desirability*, for inclusion in an on-time set, i.e.:

$T_i \lesssim T_j$ if and only if $\quad p_i > p_j$,
$\qquad\qquad\qquad\qquad$ or if $p_i = p_j$ and $w_i < w_j$,
$\qquad\qquad\qquad\qquad$ or if $p_i = p_j$ and $w_i = w_j$ and $i < j$.

Algorithm 4.3.8 *for problem* $1 || \Sigma w_j U_j$ *with agreeable weights* [Law76].
begin
Sort tasks according to *EDD* rule; $\quad$ -- w.l.o.g. assume that $d_1 \le d_2 \le \cdots \le d_n$
$T^0 := \varnothing$;
for $j := 1$ **to** n **do**
$\quad$ **if** $p(T^j) + p_{j+1} \le d_{j+1}$ $\quad$ -- $p(T^j)$ denotes the sum of processing times of tasks in T^j
$\quad$ **then** $T^{j+1} := T^j \cup \{T_{j+1}\}$
$\quad$ **else**
$\quad\quad$ **begin**
$\quad\quad\quad$ Choose $T_l \in T^j \cup \{T_{j+1}\}$ minimal with respect to $\lesssim$;
$\quad\quad\quad$ $T^{j+1} := (T^j \cup \{T_{j+1}\}) - \{T_l\}$;
$\quad\quad$ **end**;
end;

It is easy to prove that for all j, T^j is a j-optimal set. Hence, T^n presents an exact solution in the sense that all tasks of T^n are completed on time, and the tasks of $T - T^n$ are tardy.

Another special case considered by Sidney [Sid73] assumes that the tasks of a given subset $T' \subseteq T$ must be completed on time. This problem can be formulated as $1 || \Sigma w_j U_j$ where the weights w_j are 0 or 1. Sidney presented two algorithms of polynomial time complexity which generalize the Hodgson's algorithm and solve the problem optimally.

Problem $1 | r_j | \Sigma w_j U_j$

From Lenstra et al. [LRKB77] this scheduling problem is known to be *NP*-hard in the strong sense. If, however, all weights are 1 and there are certain dependencies between ready times and due dates, optimal schedules can be constructed in polynomial time. Kise et al. [KIM78] used a variation of the Lawler's Algorithm 4.3.8, and Lawler [Law82] proved that the algorithm can be improved to run in $O(n \log n)$ time. For a given set of tasks, the release times and due dates are called *consistent*, if $r_i < r_j$ implies $d_i \le d_j$ for all tasks T_i, T_j. We start with ordering tasks according to both, nondecreasing ready times and nondecreasing due dates. Without loss of generality we may assume that the tasks are already indexed appropriately, i.e. $r_1 \le r_2 \le \cdots \le r_n$ and $d_1 \le d_2 \le \cdots \le$

d_n. Any schedule S can again be described by a partition of task set $\mathcal{T}$ into on-time set $\mathcal{T}^{\leq}$ and tardy set $\mathcal{T}^{>}$. Tasks of $\mathcal{T}^{\leq}$ are processed in *EDD* order, so they are ordered according to their indices. Let $\mathcal{T}^{\leq} = \{T_{k_1}, \cdots, T_{k_m}\}$, $k_1 < \cdots < k_m$. The completion time C_{k_i} of task T_{k_i} in this schedule is given by

$$C_{k_1} = r_{k_1} + p_{k_1}$$

$$C_{k_i} = \max\{C_{k_{i-1}}, r_{k_i}\} + p_{k_i} \ (i = 2, \cdots, m).$$

Then the last task of $\mathcal{T}^{\leq}$ is completed at time $C(\mathcal{T}^{\leq}) = C_{k_m}$.

The following algorithm generates optimal schedules for the subsets $\{T_1, \cdots, T_i\}$ in the order of $i = 1, \cdots, n$. Let an optimal schedule for $\{T_1, \cdots, T_i\}$ be specified by the subset $\mathcal{E}_i \subseteq \{T_1, \cdots, T_i\}$ of on-time tasks. Then, set $\mathcal{E}_n$ will yield an optimal schedule for $\mathcal{T}$.

Algorithm 4.3.9 *for computing* $\mathcal{E}_n$ [KIM78].
```
begin
```
Order tasks according to both, nondecreasing ready times and nondecreasing due dates;
$$\mathcal{E}_0 := \varnothing;$$
```
for j := 1 to n do
    begin
```
$$\mathcal{E}_j := \mathcal{E}_{j-1} \cup \{T_j\};$$
-- a subschedule $S(\mathcal{E}_j)$ is obtained by sequencing the tasks of $\mathcal{E}_j$ in EDD order
```
    if
```
$C(\mathcal{E}_j) > d_j$
-- $C(\mathcal{E}_j)$ denotes the completion time of the last task in $S(\mathcal{E}_j)$
```
    then
        begin
```
Choose $T_k \in \mathcal{E}_j$ such that the subschedule obtained for $\mathcal{E}_j - \{T_k\}$ in EDD order is of minimal length;
$$\mathcal{E}_j := \mathcal{E}_j - \{T_k\};$$
```
        end;
    end;
end;
```

We mention that, under the condition of consistent release times and due dates, Algorithm 4.3.9 determines an optimal schedule for problem $1 \,|\, r_j \,|\, \Sigma U_j$ in $O(n^2)$ time.

Example 4.3.10 Let 6 tasks already be ordered according to increasing ready times, $p = [4, 3, 3, 7, 7, 4]$, $r = [0, 0, 4, 4, 5, 8]$, $d = [4, 5, 7, 11, 14, 15]$. Algorithm 4.3.9 determines set $\mathcal{E}_n$ to be $\mathcal{E}_n = \{T_2, T_3, T_6\}$, and the corresponding optimal schedule is $(T_2, T_3, T_6, T_1, T_4, T_5)$ where the last three tasks are tardy. □

If task preemptions are allowed, dynamic programming algorithms can be applied to solve $1 | pmtn, r_j | \Sigma U_j$ in $O(n^5)$ time, and $1 | pmtn, r_j | \Sigma w_j U_j$ in $O(n^3 (\Sigma w_j)^2)$ time. We refer the interested reader to [Law82].

Problem $1|prec|\Sigma w_j U_j$

Lenstra and Rinnooy Kan [LRK80] proved that the 3-PARTITION problem (see Section 4.1.1) is reducible to the problem $1 | chains, p_j = 1 | \Sigma U_j$. Hence, scheduling unit time tasks on a single processor subject to chain-like precedence constraints so as to minimize the unweighted number of late tasks is *NP*-hard in the strong sense. For $1 | forest | \Sigma w_j U_j$, Ibarra and Kim [IK78] discussed an algorithm that finds for any positive integer k an approximate schedule S^k such that

$$U_w^k / U_w^* < 1 + \frac{1}{k+1}.$$

The approximate solution is found in $O(kn^{k+2})$ time. They give also examples showing that the algorithm is not applicable to tasks forming an arbitrary precedence graph.

4.3.3 Tardiness Problems

In this section we will consider problems concerned with the minimization of mean or mean weighted tardiness.

Problem $1||\Sigma w_j D_j$

McNaughton [McN59] has shown that preemption cannot reduce mean weighted tardiness for any given set of tasks. Thus, an optimal preemptive schedule has the same value of mean weighted tardiness as an optimal, nonpreemptive schedule. It has been shown by Lawler [Law77] and by Lenstra et al. [LRKB77] that the problem of minimizing mean weighted tardiness is *NP*-hard in the strong sense. If all weights are equal, the problem is still *NP*-hard in the ordinary sense [DL90]. If unit processing times are assumed, the problem of scheduling independent tasks can be formulated as a linear assignment problem, and hence it can be solved in time $O(n^3)$ time [GLLRK79]. If in addition all tasks have unit weights, simply sequencing tasks in nondecreasing order of their due dates minimizes the total tardiness, and hence this special problem can be solved in $O(n\log n)$ time.

In more detail we will consider another special problem of type $1 || \Sigma w_j D_j$ where weights of tasks are *agreeable* (see Section 4.3.2) and processing times are integer. Lawler [Law77] presented a pseudopolynomial dynamic programming algorithm of the worst-case running time $O(n^4 p)$ or $O(n^5 p_{max})$, if $p = \sum_{j=1}^{n} p_j$, and $p_{max} = \max\{p_j\}$, respectively. The algorithm is pseudopolynomial because its time complexity is polynomial only with respect to an encoding in which p_j values are expressed in unary notation (see Section 2.2). We are going to present this algorithm because of its interesting approach.

Recall from Section 4.3.2 that weights of tasks of a set $\{T_1, \cdots, T_n\}$ are called *agreeable* iff $p_i < p_j$ implies $w_i \geq w_j$. Suppose we wish to find an optimal schedule, where processing of the first task is to begin at time $t = 0$. The algorithm to be presented is based on the following theorem which claims an important property of an optimal schedule for $1 \| \Sigma w_j D_j$.

Theorem 4.3.11 [Law77] *Suppose the tasks are agreeably weighted and numbered in nondecreasing due date order, i.e. $d_1 \leq d_2 \leq \cdots \leq d_n$. Let task T_k be such that $p_k = \max\{p_j \mid j = 1, \cdots, n\}$. Then there is some index σ, $k \leq \sigma \leq n$, such that there exists an optimal schedule S in which T_k is preceded by all tasks T_j with $j \leq \sigma$ and $j \neq k$, and followed by all tasks T_j such that $j > \sigma$. $\square$*

So, if T_k is the task with largest processing time, we know from Theorem 4.3.11 that, for some task T_σ, $k \leq \sigma \leq n$, there exists an optimal schedule where (see Figure 4.3.1)

(i) tasks $T_1, T_2, \cdots, T_{k-1}, T_{k+1}, \cdots, T_\sigma$, arranged in some schedule and starting at time 0, followed by

(ii) task T_k, with completion time $C_\sigma = \sum_{j \leq \sigma} p_j$, followed by

(iii) tasks $T_{\sigma+1}, T_{\sigma+2}, \cdots, T_n$, arranged in some order and starting at time C_σ.

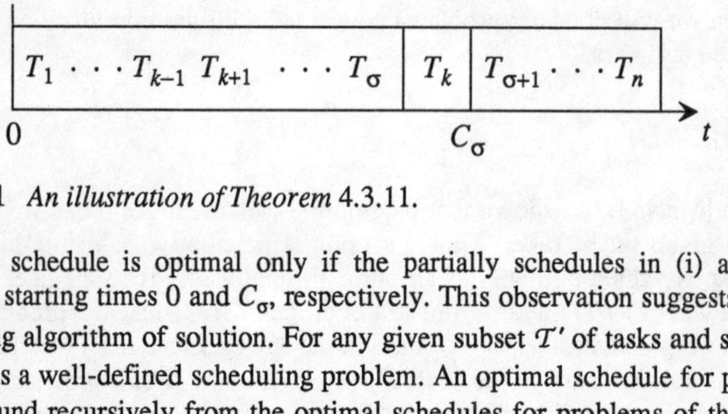

Figure 4.3.1 *An illustration of Theorem 4.3.11.*

The overall schedule is optimal only if the partially schedules in (i) and (iii) are optimal, for starting times 0 and C_σ, respectively. This observation suggests a dynamic programming algorithm of solution. For any given subset $\mathcal{T}'$ of tasks and starting time $t \geq 0$, there is a well-defined scheduling problem. An optimal schedule for problem $(\mathcal{T}, t)$ can be found recursively from the optimal schedules for problems of the form $(\mathcal{T}', t')$, where $\mathcal{T}'$ is a proper subset of $\mathcal{T}$, and $t' \geq t$.

Algorithm 4.3.12 *for problem $1 \| \Sigma w_j D_j$* [Law77].
Method: The algorithm calls the recursive procedure *sequence* with parameters t, a start time of the subschedule to be determined, $\mathcal{T}'$ a subset of tasks numbered in nondecreasing due date order, and S', being an optimal schedule for the tasks in $\mathcal{T}'$.

procedure *sequence*$(t, \mathcal{T}'; $ **var** $S')$;
begin
if $\mathcal{T}' = \emptyset$ **then** S' is the empty schedule
else
    begin
      Let $T_1, \cdots, T_m$ be the tasks of $\mathcal{T}'$, and $d_1 \leq d_2 \leq \cdots \leq d_m$;

Choose T_k with maximum processing time among the tasks of $\mathcal{T}'$;

for $\sigma := k$ **to** m **do**
    begin
        Let $\mathcal{T}^{\leq\sigma}$ be the subset $\{T_j \mid j \leq \sigma, j \neq k\}$ of $\mathcal{T}'$ tasks;
        Let $\mathcal{T}^{>\sigma}$ be the subset $\{T_j \mid j > \sigma\}$ of $\mathcal{T}'$ tasks;
        Call $sequence(t, \mathcal{T}^{\leq\sigma}, S^{\leq\sigma})$;
        $C_\sigma := t + \sum_{j \leq \sigma} p_j$;
        Call $sequence(C_\sigma, \mathcal{T}^{>\sigma}, S^{>\sigma})$;
        -- optimal subschedules for $\mathcal{T}^{\leq\sigma}$ and $\mathcal{T}^{>\sigma}$ are created
        $S_\sigma := S^{\leq\sigma} \oplus (T_k) \oplus S^{>\sigma}$; -- concatenation of subschedules and task T_k is constructed
        Compute value $\bar{D}_w^\sigma = \Sigma w_j D_j$ of subschedule S_σ;
    end;

    Choose S with minimum value $\bar{D}_w^\sigma$ among the schedules S_σ, $k \leq \sigma \leq m$;
    end;
end;

begin
Order (and index) tasks of $\mathcal{T}$ in nondecreasing due date order;
$\mathcal{T} := (T_1, \cdots, T_n)$;
Call $sequence(0, \mathcal{T}, S)$;
    -- This call generates an optimal schedule S for $\mathcal{T}$, starting at time 0
end;

It is easy to establish an upper bound on the worst-case running time required to compute an optimal schedule for the complete set of n tasks. The subsets $\mathcal{T}'$ which enter into the recursion are of a very restricted type. Each subset consists of tasks whose subscripts are indexed consecutively, say from i to j, where possibly one of the indices, k, is missing, and where the processing times $p_i, \cdots, p_j$ of the tasks $T_i, \cdots, T_j$ are less than or equal to p_k. There are no more than $O(n^3)$ such subsets $\mathcal{T}'$, because there are no more than n values for each of the indices, i, j, k; moreover, several distinct choices of the indices may specify the same subset of tasks. There are surely no more than $p = \sum_{j=1}^{n} p_j \leq np_{max}$ possible values of t. Hence there are no more than $O(n^3 p)$ or $O(n^4 p_{max})$ different calls of procedure $sequence$ in Algorithm 4.3.12. Each call of $sequence$ requires minimization over at most n alternatives, i.e. in addition $O(n)$ running time. Therefore the overall running time is bounded by $O(n^3 p)$ or $O(n^4 p_{max})$.

Example 4.3.13 [Law77] The following example illustrates performance of the algorithm. Let $\mathcal{T} = \{T_1, \cdots, T_8\}$, and processing times, due dates and weights are given by $p = [121, 79, 147, 83, 130, 102, 96, 88]$, $d = [260, 266, 269, 336, 337, 400, 683, 719]$ and $w = [3, 8, 1, 6, 3, 3, 5, 6]$, respectively. Notice that task weights are agreeable. Algorithm 4.3.12 calls procedure $sequence$ with $\mathcal{T} = (T_1, \cdots, T_8)$; T_3 is the task with largest processing time, so in the **for**-loop procedure $sequence$ will be called again for $\sigma =$

$3, \cdots, 8$. Table 4.3.3 shows the respective optimal schedules if task T_3 is placed in positions $\sigma = 3, \cdots, 8$. $\square$

σ	$sequence(C_\sigma, \mathcal{T}', S')$	optimal schedule	value $\overline{D}$
3	$sequence(0, \{T_1, T_2\}, S^{\leq 3})$ $sequence(347, \{T_4, T_5, T_6, T_7, T_8\}, S^{>3})$	$(T_1, T_2, T_3, T_4, T_6, T_7, T_8, T_5)$	2565
4	$sequence(0, \{T_1, T_2, T_4\}, S^{\leq 4})$ $sequence(430, \{T_5, T_6, T_7, T_8\}, S^{>4})$	$(T_1, T_2, T_4, T_3, T_6, T_7, T_8, T_5)$	2084
5	$sequence(0, \{T_1, T_2, T_4, T_5\}, S^{\leq 5})$ $sequence(560, \{T_6, T_7, T_8\}, S^{>5})$	$(T_1, T_2, T_4, T_5, T_3, T_7, T_8, T_6)$	2007
6	$sequence(0, \{T_1, T_2, T_4, T_5, T_6\}, S^{\leq 6})$ $sequence(662, \{T_7, T_8\}, S^{>6})$	$(T_1, T_2, T_4, T_6, T_5, T_3, T_7, T_8)$	1928
7	$sequence(0, \{T_1, T_2, T_4, T_5, T_6, T_7\}, S^{\leq 7})$ $sequence(758, \{T_8\}, S^{>7})$	$(T_1, T_2, T_4, T_6, T_5, T_7, T_3, T_8)$	1785
8	$sequence(0, \{T_1, T_2, T_4, T_5, T_6, T_7, T_8\}, S^{\leq 8})$ $sequence(840, \varnothing, S^{>8})$	$(T_1, T_2, T_4, T_6, T_5, T_7, T_8, T_3)$	1111

Table 4.3.3   *Calls of procedure sequence in Example* 4.3.13.

Problem $1|prec|\Sigma w_j D_j$

Lenstra and Rinooy Kan [LRK78] studied the complexity of the mean tardiness problem when precedence constraints are introduced. They showed that $1|prec, p_j = 1|\Sigma D_j$ is *NP*-hard in the strong sense. For chain-like precedence constraints, they proved problem $1|chains, p_j = 1|\Sigma w_j D_j$ to be *NP*-hard, but Leung and Young [LY90] were able to prove that the problem remains *NP*-hard even in the case of equal weights.

4.3.4 Earliness and Lateness Problems

As in the case of tardiness, we are given n tasks $\mathcal{T} = \{T_1, \cdots, T_n\}$, each task T_j having a processing time p_j, and a due date d_j. The *earliness* E_j of a task T_j in schedule S is defined as $\max\{0, d_j - C_j\}$. The objective is to find a schedule S such that the *mean earliness* $\overline{E} = \frac{1}{n}\sum_{j=1}^{n} E_j$ of S is minimized. It was pointed out by [DL90] that this problem is equivalent to the mean tardiness problem. To see this, we replace the given mean earliness problem by an equivalent mean tardiness scheduling problem.

Let $C = \sum_{j=1}^{n} p_j$. We construct an instance $\mathcal{T}' = \{T_1', \cdots, T_n'\}$ of the mean tardiness problem, where $p_j' = p_j$ for $j = 1, \cdots, n$, and where the due dates are defined by $d_j' = C - d_j + p_j$. Suppose S is an optimal schedule for $\mathcal{T}$. We define a schedule S' for $\mathcal{T}'$ as follows. If T_j is the kth task scheduled in S, then T_j' will be the $(n-k+1)^{th}$ task scheduled in S'. Clearly, we have $C_j' = C - C_j + p_j$, and hence

$$D_j' = \max\{0, C_j' - d_j'\}$$
$$= \max\{0, (C - C_j + p_j) - (C - d_j + p_j)\}$$
$$= \max\{0, d_j - C_j\} = E_j.$$

Thus, $\bar{E} = \bar{D}'$. Similarly, if S' is a schedule for $\mathcal{T}'$ such that $\bar{D}'$ is minimum we can construct a schedule S for $\mathcal{T}$ such that $\bar{E} = \bar{D}'$. Therefore, the minimum mean earliness of $\mathcal{T}$ is the same as the minimum mean tardiness for $\mathcal{T}'$. Hence, as we know that the mean tardiness problem on one processor is NP-hard, the mean earliness problem must also be NP-hard.

4.4 Other Criteria

In this section we are concerned with single processor scheduling problems where each task T_j of the given task set $\mathcal{T} = \{T_1, \cdots, T_n\}$ is assigned a nondecreasing cost function G_j. Instead of a due date, function G_j specifies the cost $G_j(C_j)$ that is incurred by the completion of task T_j at time C_j. We will discuss two objective functions, minimization of maximum cost G_{max} that is incurred by the completion of the tasks, and minimization of sum $\Sigma G_j(C_j)$ of functions of completion times of the tasks.

4.4.1 Minimizing Maximum Cost

First we consider the problem of minimizing the maximum cost that is incurred by the completion of the tasks. We already know that the problem $1 \mid r_j \mid G_{max}$ with $G_j(C_j) = L_j = C_j - d_j$ for given due dates d_j for the tasks, is NP-hard in the strong sense (cf. Section 4.3.1). On the other hand, if task preemptions are allowed, the problem becomes easy if the cost functions depend nondecreasingly on the task completion times. Also, the cases $1 \mid prec \mid G_{max}$ and $1 \mid pmtn, prec, r_j \mid G_{max}$ are solvable in polynomial time.

Problem $1 \mid pmtn, r_j \mid G_{max}$

Consider the case where task preemptions are allowed. Since cost functions are nondecreasing, it is never advantageous to leave the processor idle when unscheduled tasks are available. Hence, the time at which all tasks will be completed can be determined in advance by scheduling the tasks in order of nondecreasing release times r_j. This schedule naturally decomposes into blocks, where a block $\mathcal{B} \subseteq \mathcal{T}$ is defined as the minimal set of tasks processed without idle time from time $r(\mathcal{B}) = \min \{r_j \mid T_j \in \mathcal{B}\}$ until $C(\mathcal{B}) = r(\mathcal{B}) + \sum_{T_j \in \mathcal{B}} p_j$, such that each task $T_k \notin \mathcal{B}$ is either completed not later than $r(\mathcal{B})$ (i.e. $C_k \leq r(\mathcal{B})$) or not released before $C(\mathcal{B})$ (i.e. $r_k \geq C(\mathcal{B})$).

It is easily seen that, when minimizing G_{max}, we can consider each block $\mathcal{B}$ separately. Let $G_{max}^*(\mathcal{B})$ be the value of G_{max} in an optimal schedule for the tasks in block $\mathcal{B}$. Then $G_{max}^*(\mathcal{B})$ satisfies the following inequalities:

$$G_{max}^*(\mathcal{B}) \geq \min_{T_j \in \mathcal{B}} \{G_j(C(\mathcal{B}))\},$$

and

$$G_{max}^*(\mathcal{B}) \geq G_{max}^*(\mathcal{B} - \{T_j\}) \text{ for all } T_j \in \mathcal{B}.$$

Let task $T_l \in \mathcal{B}$ be such that

$$G_l(C(\mathcal{B})) = \min_{T_j \in \mathcal{B}} \{G_j(C(\mathcal{B}))\}. \tag{4.4.1}$$

Consider a schedule for block $\mathcal{B}$ which is optimal subject to the condition that task T_l is processed only if no other task is available. This schedule consists of two complementary parts:

(i) An optimal schedule for the set $\mathcal{B} - \{T_l\}$, which decomposes into a number of subblocks $\mathcal{B}_1, \cdots, \mathcal{B}_b$;

(ii) A schedule for task T_l, where T_l is preemptively scheduled during the difference of time intervals given by $[r(\mathcal{B}), C(\mathcal{B})) - \bigcup_{j=1}^{b} [r(\mathcal{B}_j), C(\mathcal{B}_j))$.

For any such schedule we have $G_{max}(\mathcal{B}) = \max\{G_l(C(\mathcal{B})), G_{max}^*(\mathcal{B} - \{T_l\})\} \leq G_{max}^*(\mathcal{B})$. It hence follows that there is an optimal schedule in which task T_l is scheduled as described above.

The problem can now be solved in the following way. First, order the tasks according to nondecreasing r_j. Next, determine the initial block structure by scheduling the tasks in order of nondecreasing r_j. For each block $\mathcal{B}$, select task $T_l \in \mathcal{B}$ subject to (4.4.1). Determine the block structure for the set $\mathcal{B} - \{T_l\}$ by scheduling the tasks in this set in order of nondecreasing r_j, and construct the schedule for task T_l as described above. By repeated application of this procedure to each of the subblocks one obtains an optimal schedule. The algorithm is as follows.

Algorithm 4.4.1 *for solving problem* $1 \mid pmtn, r_j \mid G_{max}$ [BLLRK83].
Method: The algorithm recursively uses procedure *oneblock* which is applied to blocks of tasks as described in the preceding text.

Procedure *oneblock*($\mathcal{B} \subseteq \mathcal{T}$);
begin
Select task $T_l \in \mathcal{B}$ such that $G_l(C(\mathcal{B})) = \min_{T_j \in \mathcal{B}} \{G_j(C(\mathcal{B}))\}$;

Determine subblocks $\mathcal{B}_1, \cdots, \mathcal{B}_b$ of the set $\mathcal{B} - \{T_l\}$;

Schedule task T_l in the intervals $[r(\mathcal{B}), C(\mathcal{B})) - \bigcup_{j=1}^{b} [r(\mathcal{B}_j), C(\mathcal{B}_j))$;

for $j := 1$ **to** b **do call** *oneblock*($\mathcal{B}_j$);
end;

```
begin
```
Order tasks so that $r_1 \le r_2 \le \cdots \le r_n$;

oneblock($\mathcal{T}$);

```
end;
```

We just mention that the time complexity of Algorithm 4.4.1 can be proved to be $O(n^2)$. Another fact is that the algorithm generates at most $n-1$ preemptions. This is easily proved by induction: It is obviously true for $n = 1$. Suppose it is true for blocks of size smaller than $|\mathcal{B}|$. The schedule for block $\mathcal{B}$ contains at most $|\mathcal{B}_i|-1$ preemptions for each subblock $\mathcal{B}_i$, $i = 1, \cdots, b$, and at most b preemptions for the selected tasks T_l. Hence, and also considering the fact that $T_l \notin \bigcup_{i=1}^{b} \mathcal{B}_i$, we see that the total number of preemptions is no more than $\sum_{i=1}^{b}(|\mathcal{B}_i|-1) + b = |\mathcal{B}|-1$. This bound on the number of preemptions is best possible. It is achieved by the class of problem instances defined by $r_j = j$, $p_j = 2$, $G_j(t) = 0$ if $t \le 2n-j$, and $G_j(t) = 1$ otherwise ($j = 1, \cdots, n$). The only way to incur zero cost is to schedule task T_j in the intervals $[j, j+1)$ and $[2n-j, 2n-j+1)$, $j = 1, \cdots, n$. This uniquely optimal schedule contains $n-1$ preemptions.

Note that the use of preemptions is essential in the algorithm. If no preemption is allowed, it is not possible to determine the block structure of an optimal schedule in advance.

Problem $1|prec|G_{\max}$

Suppose now that the order of task execution is restricted by given precedence constraints $\prec$, and tasks are processed without preemption. Problems of this type can be optimally solved by an algorithm presented by Lawler [Law73]. The basic idea of the algorithm is as follows: From among all tasks that are eligible to be scheduled last, i.e. that without successors under the precedence relation $\prec$, put that task last that will incur the smallest cost in that position. Then repeat this procedure on the set of $n-1$ remaining tasks, etc. This rule is justified as follows: Let $\mathcal{T} = \{T_1, \cdots, T_n\}$ be the set of all tasks, and let $L \subseteq \mathcal{T}$ be the subset of tasks without successors. For any $\mathcal{T}' \in \mathcal{T}$ let $G^*(\mathcal{T}')$ be the maximum task completion cost in an optimal schedule for $\mathcal{T}'$. If p denotes the completion time of the last task, i.e. $p = p_1 + p_2 + \cdots + p_n$, task $T_l \in L$ is chosen such that $G_l(p) = \min_{T_j \in L} \{G_j(p)\}$. Then the optimal value of a schedule subject to the condition that task T_l is processed last is given by $\max\{G^*(L - \{T_l\}), G_l(p)\}$. Since both, $G^*(L - \{T_l\}) \le G^*(L)$ and $G_l(p) \le G^*(L)$, the rule is proved.

The following algorithm finds a task that can be placed last in schedule S. Then, having this task removed from the problem, the algorithm determines a task that can be placed last among the remaining $n-1$ tasks and second-to-last in the complete schedule, and so on.

Algorithm 4.4.2   *for problem* $1 \mid prec \mid G_{max}$ *with nondecreasing cost functions* [Law73].
begin
Let S be the empty schedule;
while $\mathcal{T} \neq \emptyset$ **do**
   begin
   $p := \sum_{T_j \in \mathcal{T}} p_j;$

   Let $L \subseteq \mathcal{T}$ be the subset of tasks with no successors;
   Choose task $T_k \in L$ such that $G_k(p) = \min_{T_j \in L} \{G_j(p)\};$

   $S := T_k \oplus S;$ -- task T_k is placed in front of the first element of schedule S
   $\mathcal{T} := \mathcal{T} - \{T_k\};$
   end;
end;

Notice that this algorithm requires $O(n^2)$ steps, where n is the number of tasks.

(a)

(b)

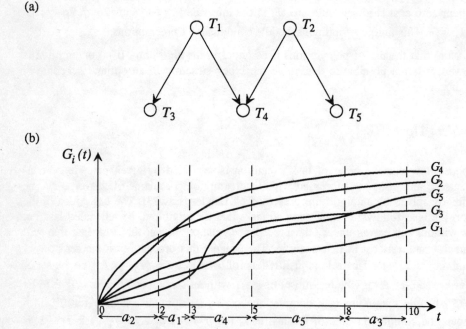

Figure 4.4.1   *An example problem for Algorithm* 4.4.2
         (a) *task set with precedence constraints,*
         (b) *cost functions specifying penalties associated with task completion times.*

Example 4.4.3   Suppose there are five tasks $\{T_1, \cdots, T_5\}$ with processing times $p = [1, 2, 2, 2, 3]$ and precedence constraints as shown in Figure 4.4.1(a), and cost functions as indicated in Figure 4.4.1(b). The last task in a schedule for this problem will finish at time p = 10. Among the tasks having no successors the algorithm chooses T_3 to be placed last because $G_3(10)$ is minimum. Note that in the final schedule, T_3 will be started at time 8. Among the remaining tasks, $\{T_1, T_2, T_4, T_5\}$, T_4 and T_5 have no successors, so these two tasks are the candidates for being placed immediately before T_3. The algorithm chooses T_5 because at time 8 this task incures lower cost to the schedule. Continuing this way Algorithm 4.4.2 will terminate with the schedule $(T_2, T_1, T_4, T_5, T_3)$. □

Problem $1|pmtn,prec,r_j|G_{max}$

In case $1|pmtn, prec, r_j| G_{max}$, i.e. if preemptions are permitted, the problem is much easier. Baker et al. [BLLRK83] presented an algorithm which is an extension of Algorithm 4.4.1. First, release dates are modified so that $r_j + p_j \le r_k$ whenever T_j precedes T_k. This is being done by replacing r_k by $\max\{r_k, \max\{r_j + p_j \mid T_j \prec T_k\}\}$ for $k = 2, \cdots, n$. The block structures are obtained as in Algorithm 4.4.1. As the block structures are determined by scheduling tasks in order of nondecreasing values of r_j, this implies that we can ignore precedence constraints at that level. Then, for each block $\mathcal{B}$, the subset $L \subseteq \mathcal{B}$ of tasks that have no successor in $\mathcal{B}$ is determined. The selection of task $T_l \in \mathcal{B}$ subject to equation (4.4.1) is replaced by the selection of task $T_l \in \mathcal{B}$ such that $G_l(C(\mathcal{B})) = \max_{T_j \in L} \{G_j(C(\mathcal{B}))\}$. This ensures that the selected task has no successors within block $\mathcal{B}$.

We mention that this algorithm can still be implemented to run in $O(n^2)$ time.

Example 4.4.4 [BLLRK83] To illustrate the last algorithm consider five tasks $\{T_1, \cdots, T_5\}$ whose processing times and release times are given by the vectors $p = [4\,2, 4, 2, 4]$ and $r = [0, 2, 0, 8, 14]$, respectively. The precedence constraints and cost functions are specified in Figure 4.4.2(a), (b). From the precedence constraints we obtain the modified release dates $r' = [0, 2, 4, 8, 14]$. Taking modified release dates instead of r, Algorithm 4.4.1 determines two blocks, $\mathcal{B}_1 = \{T_1, T_2, T_3, T_4\}$ from time 0 to 12, and $\mathcal{B}_2 = \{T_2\}$ from 14 until 18 (Figure 4.4.2(a). Block $\mathcal{B}_2$ consists of a single task and therefore represents an optimal part of the schedule. For block $\mathcal{B}_1$, we find the subset of tasks without successors $L_1 = \{T_3, T_4\}$ and select task T_3 since $G_3(12) < G_4(12)$. By re-scheduling the tasks in $\mathcal{B}_1$ while processing task T_3 (only if no other task is available), we obtain two subblocks: $\mathcal{B}_{11} = \{T_1, T_2\}$ from time 0 to 6 and $\mathcal{B}_{12} = \{T_4\}$ from 8 until 12 (Figure 4.4.2(b)). Block $\mathcal{B}_{12}$ needs no further attention. For block $\mathcal{B}_{11}$ we find $L_{11} - \{T_1, T_2\}$ and select task T_1 since $G_1(6) < G_2(6)$. By rescheduling the tasks in $\mathcal{B}_{11}$ again we finally obtain an optimal schedule (Figure 4.4.2(c)). □

4.4.2 Minimizing Mean Cost

From [LRKB77] we know that the general problem $1||\Sigma G_j$ of scheduling tasks, such that the sum of values $G_j(C_j)$ is minimal, is NP-hard. If tasks have unit processing times, i.e. for $1 \mid p_j = 1 \mid \Sigma G_j$, the problem is equivalent to finding a permutation $(\alpha_1, \cdots, \alpha_n)$ of the task indices $1, \cdots, n$ that minimizes $\Sigma G_j(C_{\alpha_j})$. This is a weighted bipartite matching problem, which can be solved in $O(n^3)$ time [LLRKS89]. For the case of arbitrary processing times, Rinnoy Kan et al. [RKLL75] presented a branch an bound algorithm. The computation of lower bounds on the costs of an optimal schedule follows an idea similar to that used in the $p_j = 1$ case. Suppose that $p_1 \leq \cdots \leq p_n$, and define $t_k = p_1 + \cdots + p_k$ for $k = 1, \cdots, n$. Then $G_j(t_k)$ is a lower bound on the cost of scheduling T_j in position k, and an overall lower bound is obtained by solving the weighted bipartite matching problem with coefficients $G_j(t_k)$. In addition to lower bounds, elimination criteria are used to discard partial schedules in the search tree. These criteria are generally of the form: if the cost functions and processing times of T_i and T_j satisfy a certain relationship, then there is an optimal schedule in which T_i precedes T_j.

A number of results are available for special kinds of cost functions. If all cost functions depend linearly on the task completion times, Smith [Smi56] proved that an optimal schedule is obtained by scheduling the tasks in order of nondecreasing values of $G_j(p)/p_j$ where $p = \Sigma p_j$.

For the case that cost of each task T_j is a quadratic function of its completion time, i.e. $G_j(C_j) = c_j C_j^2$ for some constant c_j, branch and bound algorithms were developed by Townsend [Tow78] and by Bagga et al. [BK81]. Both make use of task interchange relations similar to those discussed in Section 4.2 (see equ. (4.2.1)) to obtain sufficient conditions for the preference of a task T_i over another task T_j. For instance, following [BK81], if $c_i \geq c_j$ and $p_i \leq p_j$ for tasks T_i, T_j, then there will always be a schedule where T_i is performed prior to T_j, and whose total cost will not be greater than the cost of any other schedule where T_i is started later than T_j. Such a rule can be obviously used to reduce the number of created nodes in the tree of a branch and bound procedure.

A similar problem was discussed by Gupta and Sen [GS83] where each task has a given due date, and the objective is to minimize the sum of squares of lateness values, $\sum_{j=1}^{n} L_j^2$. If the tasks can be arranged in a schedule such that every pair of adjacent tasks T_i, T_j (i.e. T_i is executed immediately before T_j) satisfies the conditions

$$p_i \leq p_j \text{ and } \frac{d_i}{p_i} \leq \frac{d_j}{p_j},$$

then the schedule can be proved to be optimal. For general processing times and due dates, a branch and bound algorithm was presented in [GS83].

The problems of minimizing mean cost are equivalent to maximization problems where each task is assigned a *profit* that urges tasks to finish as early as possible. The profit of a task is described by a nonincreasing and concave function G_j on the finishing time of the task. Fisher and Krieger [FK84] discussed a class of heuristics for scheduling n tasks on a single processor to maximize the sum of profits $\Sigma G_j(C_j - p_j)$.

(a)

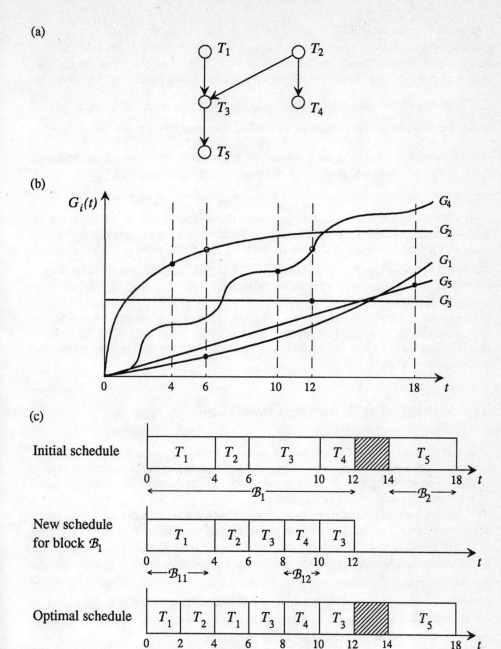

(b)

(c)

Figure 4.4.2 *An example problem* $1 \mid pmtn, prec, r_j \mid G_{max}$
   (a) *task set with precedence constraints,*
   (b) *cost functions specifying penalties associated with task completion times,*
   (c) *block schedules and an optimal preemptive schedule.*

The heuristic used in [FK84] is based on linear approximations of the functions G_j. Suppose several tasks have already been scheduled for processing in the interval $[0, t)$, and we must choose one of the remaining tasks to start at time t. Then the approximation of G_j is the linear funciton through the points $(t, C_j(t))$ and $(p, C_j(p))$ where $p = \sum_{j=1}^{n} p_j$. The task chosen maximizes $(C_j(t) - C_j(p))/t$. The main result presented in [FK84] is that the heuristic always obtains at least 2/3 of the optimal profit.

Finally we mention that there are a few results available for the case that, in addition to the previous assumptions, precedence constraints restrict the order of task execution. For the total weighted exponential cost function criterion $\sum_{j=1}^{n} w_j \exp(-cC_j)$, where c is some given "discount rate", Monma and Sidney [MS87] were able to prove that the job module property (see end of Section 4.2) is satisfied. As a consequence, for certain classes of precedence constraints that are built up iteratively from prime modules, the problem $1 \mid prec \mid \sum w_j \exp(-cC_j)$ can be solved in polynomial time. As an example, series-parallel precedence constraints are of that property. For more details we wefer the reader to [MS87].

Dynamic programming algorithms for general precedence constraints and for the special case of series-parallel precedence graphs can be found in [BS78a, BS78b, and BS81], where each task is assigned an arbitrary cost function that is nonnegative and nondecreasing in time.

4.5 Minimizing Change-Over Cost

This section deals with the scheduling of tasks on a single processor where under certain circumstances a cost is inferred when the processor switches from one task to another. The reason for such "change-over" cost might be machine setups required before tasks of special types can be processed.

First we present a more theoretical approach where a set of tasks subject to precedence constraints is given. The purpose of the precedence relation $\prec$ is twofold: on one hand it defines the usual precedence constraints of the form $T_i \prec T_j$ where task T_j cannot be started before task T_i has been completed. On the other hand, if $T_i \prec T_j$, then we say that processing T_j immediately after T_i does not require any additional setup on the processor, so processing T_j does not incur any change-over cost. But if $T_i \nprec T_j$, i.e. T_j is not an immediate successor of T_i, then processing T_j immediately after T_i will require processor setup and hence will cause change-over cost.

The types of problems we are considering in Section 4.5.1 assume unit change-over cost for the setups. The problem then is to find schedules that minimize the number of setups.

In Section 4.5.2 we discuss a more practically oriented model where jobs of different types are considered, and each job consists of a number of tasks. Processor setup is required, and consequently change-over cost is incurred, if the processor changes from one job type to another. Hence the tasks of each job should be scheduled in sequences or *lots* of certain sizes on the processor. The objective is then to determine sizes of task lots, where each lot is processed nonpreemptively, such that certain inventory and deadline conditions are observed, and change-over cost is minimized. The problem can also be regarded as a special instance of the so-called multi-product lot scheduling problem with capacity constraints. For a detailed analysis of this problem and its various special modifications we refer e.g. to [BY82, LRK80] and [Sch82]. All these models consider setup cost.

Generally speaking, *setups* are events that may occur every time processing of a task or job is initiated again after a pause in processing. In many real processing systems such setups are connected with change-over costs.

4.5.1 Setup Scheduling

Consider a finite partially ordered set $G = (\mathcal{T}, \leq)$, where $\leq$ is the reflexive, antisymmetric and transitive binary relation obtained from a given precedence relation $\prec$ as described in Section 2.3.2. Then, a *linear extension* of G is a linear order $(\mathcal{T}, \leq_L)$ that extends $(\mathcal{T}, \leq)$, i.e. for all $T', T'' \in \mathcal{T}, T' \leq T''$ implies $T' \leq_L T''$. For $\mathcal{T} = \{T_1, T_2, \cdots, T_n\}$, if the sequence $(T_{\alpha_1}, T_{\alpha_2}, \cdots, T_{\alpha_n})$ from left to right defines the linear order $\leq_L$, i.e. $T_{\alpha_1} \leq_L T_{\alpha_2} \leq_L \cdots \leq_L T_{\alpha_n}$, then $(T_{\alpha_1}, T_{\alpha_2}, \cdots, T_{\alpha_n})$ is obviously a schedule for $(\mathcal{T}, \prec)$.

Let $L = (T_{\alpha_1}, T_{\alpha_2}, \cdots, T_{\alpha_n})$ be a linear extension of $G = (\mathcal{T}, \leq)$ where $\leq$ is determined from precedence relation $\prec$. Two consecutive elements $T_{\alpha_i}, T_{\alpha_{i+1}}$ of L are separated by a *jump* (or *setup*) if and only if $T_{\alpha_i} \not\prec T_{\alpha_{i+1}}$. The total number of jumps of L is denoted by $s(L, G)$. The *jump number* $s(G)$ of G is the minimum number of jumps in some linear extension, i.e.

$$s(G) = \min\{s(L, G) \mid L \text{ is a linear extension of } G\}.$$

A linear extension L of G with $s(L, G) = s(G)$ is called *jump-* (or *setup-*) *optimal*. The problem of finding a schedule with minimum number of setups is often called *jump number problem*.

If we assume that a jump causes change-over cost in the schedule, a jump-optimal schedule for $(\mathcal{T}, \prec)$ would obviously be one in which the total change-over cost is at minimum.

The notion of jump number has been introduced by Chein and Martin [CM72]. The problem of determining the setup number $s(G)$ and producing an optimal linear extension for any given ordered set G has been considered by numerous authors. While good algorithms have been found for certain restricted classes of ordered sets, it has been shown by W. R. Pulleyblank [Pul75] that finding the setup number even for partial orders of height one [2] is an *NP*-hard problem.

For a general poset $G = (\mathcal{T}, \leq)$, let $K_1, K_2, \cdots, K_r$ be any minimum family of disjoint chains (for definition of a chain we refer to Chapter 2.3.2) whose set union of tasks is $\mathcal{T}$. The concatenation $K_1 \oplus K_2 \oplus \cdots \oplus K_r$ of these chains obviously is not necessarily a linear extension of G. On the other hand, any linear extension L of a finite poset G can be expressed as a linear sum $K_1 \oplus K_2 \oplus \cdots \oplus K_r$ of chains, chosen so that

---

[2] A partial order G is of height one if each directed path in G has at most two vertices.

in each chain neighboring tasks T_h and T_k are in relation $T_h < T_k$, and, for chains K_i, K_{i+1} ($i = 1, \cdots, r-1$), the last task of K_i does not precede the first task of K_{i+1}, $i = 1, \cdots, r-1$. Notice that a linear extension represents a schedule for $(T, <)$ in an obvious way. Setups occur exactly between two neighboring chains, i.e. between K_i and K_{i+1} for $i = 1, \cdots, r-1$.

The problem of scheduling precedence constrained tasks so that the number of setups is minimum is now formalized to the question of finding a linear extension that consists of a minimum number of chains.

One way of solving this problem heuristically is to determine so-called *greedy linear extensions*.

Algorithm 4.5.1 *Greedy linear extension of a partially ordered set* $(T, \leq)$.
```
begin
i := 0;
while  T ≠ ∅  do
    begin i := i+1;
    Let Tᵢ ∈ T be a task such that Tᵢ := {T ∈ T | T ≤ Tᵢ} forms a maximal chain, i.e.
        there is no successor task T' of Tᵢ for which {T ∈ T | T ≤ T'} is a chain;
    Let Kᵢ be the chain of tasks of Tᵢ;
    T := T - Tᵢ;
    end;
r := i;        -- r is the number of chains obtained
L := K₁ ⊕ K₂ ⊕ ⋯ ⊕ Kᵣ;
end;
```

From the way the chains are constructed in this algorithm it is clear that $L = K_1 \oplus K_2 \oplus \cdots \oplus K_r$ is a linear extension of $G = (T, \leq)$, and hence is a schedule for $(T, <)$. Greedy linear extensions can be characterized in the following way.

A linear extension L of G is *greedy* if and only if, for some r, L can be represented as $L = K_1 \oplus K_2 \oplus \cdots \oplus K_r$, where each K_i is a chain in G, the last task of K_i does not precede the first task of K_{i+1} (for $i = 1, \cdots, r-1$), and for each K_i and for any $T \in T$ which succeedes immediately the last task of $K_i < T$ in G, there is a $T' \in K_{i+1} \cup \cdots \cup K_r$ such that $T' < T$.

Example 4.5.2 To demonstrate how Algorithm 4.5.1 works, consider the precedence graph shown in Figure 4.5.1(a). The algorithm first chooses task T_3, thus getting the first chain $K_1 = (T_3)$. If the tasks chosen next are T_2 and then T_1, then we get the chains K_2 and K_3 shown encircled in Figure 4.5.1(a). The corresponding schedule is presented in Figure 4.5.1(b). □

It can be shown that for any finite poset G there is a greedy linear extension L of G satisfying $s(G) = s(G, L)$. On the other hand, optimal linear extensions need not be greedy. Also, greedy linear extensions may be far from optimum. So, for example, the setup number for the direct product of a two-element chain with an n-element chain is 1, yet there is a greedy linear extension with $n-1$ setups.

For some special classes of precedence graphs greedy linear extensions are known to be always optimal with respect to number of setups. Series-parallel graphs and N-free graphs are examples of such classes. For other examples and results we refer the interested reader to [ER85] and [RZ86].

Another important class of precedence graphs are interval orders (see Sections 2.1 and 2.3.2). Since interval orders model the sequential and overlapping structure of a set of intervals on the real line, they have many applications in several fields such as scheduling, VLSI routing in computer science, seriation in archeology, and in difference relations in measurement theory [Fis85, Gol80, Moh89]. Faigle and Schrader [FS85a and FS85b] presented a heuristic algorithm for the jump number problem for an interval order. But Ali and Deogun [AD90] were able to develop an optimization algorithm of time complexity $O(n^2)$ for n elements. They also presented a simple formula that allows to determine the minimal number of setups directly from the given interval order.

(a)

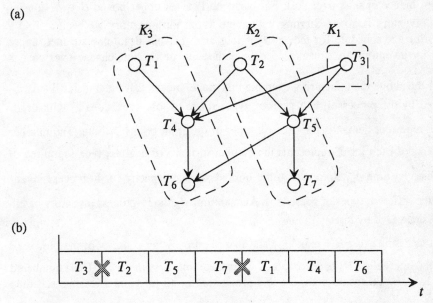

(b)

Figure 4.5.1 *An example for Algorithm 4.5.1*
    (a) precedence graph and a chain decomposition,
    (b) corresponding schedule. Crosses (×) mark setups.

4.5.2 Lot Size Scheduling

The problem investigated in this subsection arizes if tasks are scheduled in lots due to time and cost considerations. Let us consider for example the production of gearboxes of different types on a *transfer line*. The time required to manufacture one gearbox is assumed to be the same for all types. Changing from production of one gearbox type to another requires a change of machine installment to another state. As these change-overs are costly and time consuming the objective is to minimize the number of change-overs or the sum of their cost. The whole situation may be complicated by additional productional or environmental constraints. For example, there are varying demands of gearbox types over time. Storage capacity for *in-process inventory* of the produced items is limited. In-process inventory always increases if the production of a gearbox is finished; it is always decreased if produced items are delivered at given points in time where demand has to be fulfilled. A feasible schedule will assign gearbox productions to the processor in such a way that lots of gearboxes of the same type are manufactured without change-overs.

Now, the lot size scheduling problem can be formulated as follows. Consider n different types of jobs where set $\mathcal{J}_j$ contains all jobs of the jth type, $j = 1, \cdots, n$, and let $\mathcal{J} = \bigcup_{j=1}^{n} \mathcal{J}_j$ be the set of all jobs. Set $\mathcal{J}_j$ includes the jobs $J_j^1, \cdots, J_j^K$ with deadlines $\tilde{d}_{j1}, \cdots, \tilde{d}_{jK}$, respectively. Each job J_j^k itself consists of a number n_{jk} of unit processing time tasks. Whereas task preemption is not allowed, the processor may switch between jobs, even of different types. Only changing from a job of one type to that of another type is assumed to induce change-over cost. For each job type an upper bound $B_j \in I\!N^0$ on in-process inventory is given. Starting with some initial job inventory we want to find a feasible *lot size* schedule for the set $\mathcal{J}$ of jobs such that all deadlines are met, upper bounds on inventory are not exceeded, and the sum of all unit change-over cost is minimized.

For the above manufacturing example this model means that the transfer line is represented by the processor, and gearbox types relate to job types. Jobs J_j^k with deadlines $\tilde{d}_{jk}$ represent demands for gearbox types at different points in time. The number n_{jk} of tasks of each job J_j^k represents the number of items of gearbox type j required to be finished by time $\tilde{d}_{jk}$. B_j relates to the limited storage capacity for in-process inventory of the different types of gearboxes. At each time $\tilde{d}_{jk}$ the in-process inventory of job type j is decreased by n_{jk}.

Let us assume that $H = \max_{jk} \{\tilde{d}_{jk}\}$ and that the processing capacity of the processor during the interval $[0, H]$ is decomposed in discrete *unit time intervals* (UTI) numbered by $h = 1, \cdots, H$. To ensure both, feasible production of all jobs and a feasible schedule without idle time we assume that $H = \sum_{j=1}^{n} n_j$ where $n_j = \sum_{k=1}^{K} n_{jk}$ represents the total number of tasks of $\mathcal{J}_j$. The lot size scheduling problem can now be formulated by the following *mathematical programming problem*. Let x_{jh} be a variable which represents the assignment of a job of type j to some UTI h such that $x_{jh} = 1$ if a job of this type is produced during interval h and $x_{jh} = 0$ otherwise. Let y_{jh} be a variable which represents unit change-over cost such that $y_{jh} = 1$ if jobs of different types are processed in UTI $h-1$ and UTI h, and $y_{jh} = 0$ otherwise. Obviously, y_{jh} represents unit change-over cost. I_{jh} represents in-process inventory of job type j at the end of UTI h, and n_{jh} is the corresponding processing requirement (we set $n_{jh} = 0$ if there is no job with deadline $\tilde{d}_{jk} = h$). Let B_j denote the upper bound on inventory of job type j.

$$Minimize \quad \sum_{j=1}^{n} \sum_{h=1}^{H} y_{jh} \tag{4.5.1}$$

$$subject \ to \quad I_{jh-1} + x_{jh} - I_{jh} = n_{jh}, \qquad j = 1, \cdots, n, \ h = 1, \cdots, H, \tag{4.5.2}$$

$$\sum_{j=1}^{n} x_{jh} \le 1, \qquad h = 1, \cdots, H, \tag{4.5.3}$$

$$0 \le I_{jh} \le B_j, \qquad j = 1, \cdots, n, \ h = 1, \cdots, H, \tag{4.5.4}$$

$$x_{jh} \in \{0, 1\}, \qquad j = 1, \cdots, n, \ h = 1, \cdots, H, \tag{4.5.5}$$

$$y_{jh} = \begin{cases} 1 & \text{if } x_{jh} - x_{jh-1} > 0 \\ 0 & \text{otherwise}, \end{cases} \qquad j = 1, \cdots, n, \ h = 1, \cdots, H. \tag{4.5.6}$$

The above constraints can be interpreted as follows. Equations (4.5.2) assure that the deadlines of all jobs are observed, (4.5.3) assure that at no time more than one job type is being processed, (4.5.4) restrict the in-process inventory to the given upper bounds. Equations (4.5.5) and (4.5.6) constrain all variables to binary numbers. The objective function (4.5.1) minimizes the total number of change-overs, respectively the sum of their unit cost. Note that for (4.5.1)-(4.5.6) a feasible solution only exists if the cumulative processing capacity up to each deadline is not less than the total number of tasks to be finished by this time.

The problem of minimizing the number of change-overs under the assumption that different jobs of different types have also different deadlines was first investigated in [Gla68] by applying some *enumerative method*. There exist also *dynamic programming algorithms* for both, the problem with sequence-independent change-over cost [GL88, Mit72] and for the problem with sequence-dependent change-over cost [DE77]. For other enumerative methods see [MV90] and the references given therein. A closely related question to the problem discussed here has been investigated in [BD78], where each task has a fixed completion deadline and an integer processing time. The question studied is whether there exists a nonpreemptive schedule that meets all deadlines and has minimum sum of change-over cost. For arbitrary integer processing times the problem is already *NP*-hard for unit change-over cost, three tasks per job type and two distinct deadlines, i.e. $K = 2$. Another similar problem was investigated in [HKR87] where the existence of unit change-over cost depends on some given order of tasks, i.e. tasks are indexed with $1, 2, \cdots$, and change-over cost occurs only if a task is followed by some other task with larger index. This problem is solvable in polynomial time.

Schmidt [Sch92] proved that the lot size scheduling problem formulated by (4.5.1)-(4.5.6) is *NP*-hard for $n = 3$ job types. Now we show that it can be solved in polynomial time if $n = 2$ job types have to be considered only. The algorithm uses an idea which can be described by the rule "schedule all jobs such that no unforced change-overs occur". This rule always generates an optimal schedule if the earliest deadline has to be observed only by jobs of the same type. In case the earliest deadline has to be observed by jobs of either type the rule by itself is not necessarily optimal.

To find a feasible schedule with minimum sum of change-over cost we must assign all jobs to a number $Z \le H$ of nonoverlapping production intervals $z = 1, \cdots, Z$ such that all deadlines are met, upper bounds on inventory are not exceeded, and the number of all change-overs is minimum. Each production interval z represents the number of consecutive UTIs assigned only to jobs of the same type, i.e. there exists only one setup for each z.

For simplicity reasons we now denote the two job types by q and r. Considering any production interval z, we may assume that a job of type q (r) is processed in UTIs $h, h+1, \cdots, h^*$, and UTIs $h-1$ and h^*+1 are either assigned to the job of type r (q) or $h = 1$ or $h^* = H$. Now consider an assignment of jobs of type q to the first h^* UTIs only; if $h^* < H$ it has to be decided whether to continue processing of jobs of type q at h^*+1 or start a job of type r in this UTI. Let

$$U_{rh^*} = \min\{(i-h^*) - (\sum_{h=h^*+1}^{i} n_{rh} - I_{rh^*}) \mid i = h^*+1, \cdots, H\} \qquad (4.5.7)$$

be the remaining available processing capacity minus the processing capacity required to meet all future deadlines of $\mathcal{J}_r$,

$$V_{qh^*} = \sum_{h=1}^{H} n_{qh} - \sum_{h=1}^{h^*} x_{qh} \qquad (4.5.8)$$

be the number of not yet processed tasks of $\mathcal{J}_q$, and

$$W_{qh^*} = B_q - I_{qh^*} \qquad (4.5.9)$$

be the the the remaining storage capacity available for job type q at the end of UTI h^*. In-process inventory is calculated according to

$$I_{qh^*} = \sum_{h=1}^{h^*} (x_{jh} - n_{jh}). \qquad (4.5.10)$$

To generate a feasible schedule for job types q and r it is sufficient to change the assignment from type q (r) to type r (q) at the beginning of UTI h^*+1, $1 \le h^* < H$, if $U_{rh^*} \cdot V_{qh^*} \cdot W_{qh^*} = 0$ for the corresponding job types in UTI h^*. Applying this *UVW*-rule is equivalent to scheduling according to the above mentioned "no unforced change-overs" strategy. The following algorithm makes appropriate use of the *UVW*-rule.

Algorithm 4.5.3 *Lot size scheduling of two job types on a single processor* [Sch92].
```
begin
j := 1;
while j < 3 do
    begin
    for h := 1 to H do
        begin
        Calculate Ujh, Vjh, Wjh according to (4.5.7)-(4.5.9);
        if  Ujh·Vjh·Wjh = 0
        then
            begin
            Calculate the number of change-overs;
            Assign a job of the other type;
            end
        else  Assign a job of the type under consideration;
        end;
    j := j+1;
```

Choose the schedule with minimum number of change-overs;
    end;
end;

Using Algorithm 4.5.3 we generate for each job type $\jmath_j$ a number Z_j of production intervals $z_j = 1, \cdots, Z_j$ which are called q-intervals in case jobs of type q are processed, and r-intervals else, where $Z_q + Z_r = Z$. We first show that there is no schedule having less change-overs than the one generated by the UVW-rule, if the assignment of the first UTI ($h = 1$) and the length of the first production interval ($z = 1$; either a q- or an r-interval) are fixed. For $n = 2$ there are only two possibilities to assign a job type to $h = 1$. It can be shown by a simple exchange argument that there does not exist a schedule with less change-overs and the first production interval ($z = 1$) does not have UVW-length, if we fix the job type to be processed in the first UTI. Note that fixing the job type for $h = 1$ corresponds to an application of the UVW-rule considering an assignment of $h = 0$ to a job of types q or r. From this we conclude that if there is no such assignment of $h = 0$ then for finding the optimal schedule it is necessary to apply the UVW-rule twice and either assign job types q or r to $h = 1$. Let us first assume that $z = 1$ is fixed by length and job type assignment.

Lemma 4.5.4 *Changing the length of any production interval $z > 1$, as generated by the UVW-rule, cannot decrease the total number of change-overs.*

Proof. Increasing the length of any production interval z without decreasing the length of any other production interval is not possible because this would cause infeasibility.

The length of $z = 1$ is fixed and changing it will not be considered. Since $\sum_{j=1}^{n} n_j = H$, all UTIs of $[0, H]$ are assigned for processing. Each individual production interval $z_j > 1$ starts with some UTI h in which processing of a job of type j must begin to avoid infeasibility. Let us assume we could decrease some production interval $z_j > 1$ then $z_j + 1$ could not be eliminated, it only must begin earlier. Since z_j cannot be eliminated totally, z_j and $z_j + 1$ would still exist, but now with different production interval lengths. Induction over the number of production intervals will show that decreasing the length of any production interval $z > 1$ of the concerned job type cannot eliminate another production interval of the same job type. It remains to show that decreasing the length of any q-interval $z_q > 1$ cannot eliminate any r-interval and vice versa. The production intervals constructed according to the UVW-rule result in a tight schedule and for any two consecutive q-intervals z_q and $z_q + 1$ there will be in between an r-interval. Decreasing the length of z_q by one UTI would result in the consequence that $z_q + 1$ had to start one UTI earlier and so the length of the r-interval which is bounded by z_q and $z_q + 1$ cannot be changed. The same argument applies for decreasing the length of any r-interval $z_r > 1$ and its consequence for q-intervals. $\square$

Lemma 4.5.5 *Having generated an UVW-schedule it might be possible to reduce the total number of production intervals by changing assignment and length of the first production interval $z = 1$.*

Proof. From the result of Lemma 4.5.4 we know that it is sufficient to investigate all possible job type assignments and lengths of $z = 1$ to find an optimal schedule. Let us assume that a feasible schedule was constructed by assigning UTI $h = 1$ to a job of type q. From the application of the UVW-rule we know that if $U_{qh-1}V_{rh-1}W_{rh-1} = 0$, then some job of type q must begin to be processed in UTI h. Now consider the case $h = 1$; there was no processing yet at all, and let us assume $V_{r0} > 0$, $U_{q0} > 0$, and $W_{r0} > 0$. In this case there would be no need to start processing of a job of type q in UTI $h = 1$. Since $H = \sum_{h=1}^{H} n_{qh} + n_{rh}$ we have to assign $h = 1$ for processing nevertheless. Using the UVW-rule two assignment patterns of production intervals are possible: (i) In case W gets binding for q, or V gets binding for r we can have at most two change-overs of kind $q - r$ and then $r - q$. If we interchange the first q-interval with the first r-interval we get a new feasible schedule and the number of change-overs is reduced by one. Decreasing the length of the first r-interval might again increase the number of change-overs by one. With the result of Lemma 4.5.4 we know that no further improvement is possible and the optimal schedule is found. (ii) In case U gets binding for r, or V or W get binding for q we have at most one change-over of kind $q - r$ followed possibly by a second pair of $q - r$ intervals. Now we might again reduce the number of change-overs by one. To do this we have appropriately to divide the UTIs of the first r-interval into two sets U_1 and U_2. Then we move all UTIs of U_1 to the beginning of the schedule and the remaining UTIs of U_2 (if there are any) we combine with the second r-interval if both changes are feasible. After this rearrangement the pattern of the first three production intervals is $r - q - r$. There are possibly different positive lengths feasible for $z = 1$. For each of them the resulting schedule is optimal due to Lemma 4.5.4. $\square$

We are now ready to see that for $n = 2$ job types with unit change-over costs and upper bounds on inventory there exists an $O(H)$ time algorithm. This can be proved by a simple task exchange argument based on the observation that a schedule whose first production interval was constructed by the UVW-rule can never be better than a schedule with a corresponding interval having no UVW-lengths. Using the results of Lemmas 4.5.4 and 4.5.5 we simply apply the UVW-rule twice, if necessary, starting with either job types. To get the optimal schedule we take that with less change-overs. This is exactly what Algorithm 4.5.3 does. As the resulting number of production intervals is minimum the schedule is optimal under the unit change-over cost criterion. For generating each schedule we have to calculate U, V, and W at most H times. The calculations of each V and W require constant time. Hence it follows that the time complexity of calculating all U is not more than $O(H)$ if appropriate data structures are used. The following example problem demonstrates the approach of Algorithm 4.5.3.

h:	1	2	3	4	5	6	7	8	9	10
Schedule S_1:	$\mathcal{J}_1$	$\mathcal{J}_1$	$\mathcal{J}_2$	$\mathcal{J}_2$	$\mathcal{J}_2$	$\mathcal{J}_2$	$\mathcal{J}_1$	$\mathcal{J}_1$	$\mathcal{J}_2$	$\mathcal{J}_2$
Schedule S_2:	$\mathcal{J}_2$	$\mathcal{J}_2$	$\mathcal{J}_1$	$\mathcal{J}_1$	$\mathcal{J}_1$	$\mathcal{J}_1$	$\mathcal{J}_2$	$\mathcal{J}_2$	$\mathcal{J}_2$	$\mathcal{J}_2$

Table 4.5.1   *Schedules for Example* 4.5.6.

Example 4.5.6 $\mathcal{J} = \{\mathcal{J}_1, \mathcal{J}_2\}$, $\tilde{d}_{11} = 3$, $\tilde{d}_{12} = 7$, $\tilde{d}_{13} = 10$, $\tilde{d}_{21} = 3$, $\tilde{d}_{22} = 7$, $\tilde{d}_{23} = 10$, $B_1 = B_2 = 10$, $n_{11} = 1$, $n_{12} = 2$, $n_{13} = 1$, $n_{21} = 1$, $n_{22} = 1$, $n_{23} = 4$, and zero initial inventory.

Table 4.5.1 shows the two schedules obtained when starting with either job type. Schedule S_2 has minimum number of change-overs and thus is optimal. $\square$

References

AD90   H. H. Ali, and J. S. Deogun, A polynomial algorithm to find the jump number of interval orders, Preprint, Univ. of Nebraska Lincoln, 1990.

AH73   D. Adolphson, and T. C. Hu, Optimal linear ordering, *SIAM J. Appl. Math.* 25, 1973, 403-423.

BA87   U. Bagchi, and R. H. Ahmadi, An improved lower bound for minimizing weighted completion times with deadlines, *Oper. Res.* 35, 1987, 311-313.

Ban80   S. P. Bansal, Single machine scheduling to minimize weighted sum of completion times with secondary criterion - a branch-and-bound approach, *European J. Oper. Res.* 5, 1980, 177-181.

BD78   J. Bruno, P. Downey, Complexity of Task Sequencing with Deadlines, Set-Up Times and Changeover Costs. *SIAM J.Comput.* 7, 1978, 393-404.

BFR71   P. Bratley, M. Florian, P. Robillard, Scheduling with earliest start and due date constraints, *Naval Res. Logist. Quart.* 18, 1971, 511-517.

BFR73   P. Bratley, M. Florian, P. Robillard, On sequencing with earliest starts and due dates with application to computing bounds for the (n/m/G/Fmax) problem, *Naval Res. Logist. Quart.* 20, 1973, 57-67.

BH89   V. Bouchitte, M. Habib, The calculation of invariants of ordered sets, in: I. Rival (ed.), *Algorithms and Order*, Kluwer Academic Publishers 1989, 231-279.

BK81   P. C. Bagga, K. R. Kalra, Single machine scheduling problem with quadratic functions of completion time - a modified approach, *J. Inform. Optim. Sci.* 2, 1981, 103-108.

Bla76   J. Błażewicz, Scheduling dependent tasks with different arrival times to meet deadlines, in: E. Gelenbe,H. Beilner (eds.), *Modelling and Performance Evaluation of Computer Systems*, North Holland, Amsterdam, 1976, 57-65.

BLLRK83   K. R. Baker, E. L. Lawler, J. K. Lenstra, A. H. G. Rinnooy Kan, Preemptive scheduling of a single machine to minimize maximum cost subject to release dates and precedence constraints, *Oper. Res.* 31, 1983, 381-386.

BM83   H. Buer, R. H. Möhring, A fast algorithm for the decomposition of graphs and posets, *Math. Oper. Res.*8, 1983, 170-184.

BR82   L. Bianco, and S. Ricciardelli, Scheduling of a single machine to minimize total weighted completion time subject to release dates, *Naval Res. Logist. Quart.* 29, 1982, 151-167.

BS74   K. R. Baker, and Z.-S. Su, Sequencing with due dates and early start times to minimize maximum tardiness, *Naval Res. Logist. Quart.* 21, 1974, 171-176.

BS78a   K. R. Baker, and L. Schrage, Dynamic programming solution for sequencing problems with precedence constraints, *Oper. Res.* 26, 1978, 444-449.

BS78b   K. R. Baker, and L. Schrage, Finding an optimal sequence by dynamic programming: An extension to precedence related tasks, *Oper. Res.* 26, 1978, 111-120.

BS81   R. N. Burns, and G. Steiner, Single machine scheduling with series-parallel precedence constraints, *Oper. Res.* 29, 1981, 1195-1207.

Bur76   R. N. Burns, Scheduling to minimize the weighted sum of completion times with secondary criteria, *Naval Res. Logist. Quart.* 23, 1976, 25-129.

BY82   G .R. Bitran, H. H. Yanasse, Computational Complexity of the Capacitated Lot Size Problem. *Management Sci.* 28, 1982, 1174-1186.

Car82   J. Carlier, The one-machine sequencing problem, *European J. Oper. Res.* 11, 1982, 42-47.

CM72   M. Chein, P. Martin, Sur le nombre de sauts d'une foret, *C. R. Acad. Sc. Paris* 275, serie A, 1972, 159-161.

CMM67   R. W. Conway, W. L. Maxwell, L. W. Miller, *Theory of Scheduling.* Addison-Wesley, Reading, Mass., 1967.

Cof76   E. G. Coffman, Jr. (ed.), *Scheduling in Computer and Job Shop Systems*, J. Wiley, New York, 1976.

CS86   S. Chand, H. Schneeberger, A note on the single-machine scheduling problem with minimum weighted completion time and maximum allowable tardiness, *Naval Res. Logist. Quart.* 33, 1986, 551-557.

DD81   M. I. Dessouky, and J. S. Deogun, Sequencing jobs with unequal ready times to minimize mean flow time, *SIAM J.Comput.* 10, 1981, 192-202.

DE77   W. C. Driscoll, H. Emmons, Scheduling Production on One Machine with Changeover Costs. *AIIE Trans.* 9, 1977, 388-395.

DL90   J. Du, and J. Y.-T. Leung, Minimizing total tardiness on one machine is NP-hard, *Math. Oper. Res.* 15, 1990, 483-495.

EFMR83   J. Erschler, G. Fontan, C. Merce, and F. Roubellat, A new dominace concept in scheduling n jobs on a single machine with ready times and due dates, *Oper. Res.* 31, 1983, 114-127.

Emm75   H. Emmons, One machine sequencing to minimize mean flow time with minimum number tardy, *Naval Res. Logist. Quart.* 22, 1975, 585-592.

ER85   M. H. El-Zahar, and I. Rival, Greedy linear extensions to minimize jumps, *Discrete Appl. Math.* 11, 1985, 143-156.

Fis85   P. C. Fishburn, *Interval orders and interval graphs*, John Wiley & Sons, New York, 1985.

FK84   M. L. Fisher, A. M. Krieger, Analysis of a linearization heuristic for single machine scheduling to maximize profit, *Math. Programming* 28, 1984, 218-225.

FS85a   U. Faigle, and R. Schrader, A setup heuristic for interval orders, *Oper. Res. Lett.* 4, 1985, 185-188.

FS85b   U. Faigle, and R. Schrader, Interval orders without odd crowns are defect optimal, Report 85382-OR, University of Bonn, 1985.

FTM71   M. Florian, P. Trepant, and G. McMahon, An implicit enumeration algorithm for the machine sequencing problem, *Management Sci.* 17, 1971, B782-B792.

GJ76   M. R. Garey, and D. S. Johnson, Scheduling tasks with non-uniform deadlines on two processors, *J. Assoc. Comput. Mach.* 23, 1976, 461-467.

GJ79   M. R. Garey, D. S. Johnson, *Computers and Intractability: A Guide to the Theory of NP-Completeness*. W. H. Freeman, San Francisco, 1979.

GJST81 M. R. Garey, D. S. Johnson, B. B. Simons, and R. E. Tarjan, Scheduling unit-time tasks with arbitrary release times and deadlines, *SIAM J.Comput*. 10, 1981, 256-269.

GK87   S. K. Gupta, and J. Kyparisis, Single machine scheduling research, *OMEGA Internat. J. Management Sci*. 15, 1987, 207-227.

GL78   G. V. Gens, and E. V. Levner, Approximation algorithm for some scheduling problems, *Engrg. Cybernetics* 6, 1978, 38-46.

GL81   G. V. Gens, and E. V. Levner, Fast approximation algorithm for job sequencing with deadlines, *Discrete Appl. Math*. 3, 1981, 313-318.

GL88   A. Gascon, R. C. Leachman, A Dynamic Programming Solution to the Dynamic, Multi-Item, Single-Machine, Scheduling Problem. *Oper. Res*. 36, 1988, 50-56.

Gla68   C. R. Glassey, Minimum Changeover Scheduling of Several Products on One Machine. *Oper. Res*. 16, 1968, 342-352.

GLLRK79 R. L. Graham, E. L. Lawler, J. K. Lenstra, A. H. G. Rinnoy Kan, Optimization and approximation in deterministic sequencing and scheduling: a survey, *Ann. Discrete Math*. 5, 1979, 287-326.

Gol80   M. C. Golumbic, *Algorithmic graph theory and perfect graphs*, Academic Press, New York, 1980.

GS83   S. K. Gupta, T. Sen, Minimizing the range of lateness on a single machine, *Engrg Costs Production Economics* 7, 1983, 187-194.

GS84   S. K. Gupta, T. Sen, Minimizing the range of lateness on a single machine, *J. Oper Res. Soc*. 35, 1984, 853-857.

HKR87   T. C. Hu, Y. S. Kuo, F. Ruskey, Some optimum algorithms for scheduling problems with changeover costs. *Oper. Res*. 35, 1987, 94-99.

Hor72   W. A. Horn, Single-machine job sequencing with tree-like precedence ordering and linear delay penalties, *SIAM J. Appl. Math*. 23, 1972, 189-202.

Hor74   W. A. Horn, Some simple scheduling algorithms, *Naval Res. Logist. Quart*. 21, 1974, 177-185.

HS88   L. A. Hall, and D. B. Shmoys, Jackson's rule for one-machine scheduling: Making a good heuristic better, Department of Mathematics, Massachusetts Institute of Technology, Cambridge, 1988.

IIN81   T. Ichimori, H. Ishii, T. Nishida, Algorithm for one machine job sequencing with precedence constraints, *J. Oper. Res. Soc. Japan* 24, 1981, 159-169.

IK78   O. H. Ibarra, and C. E. Kim, Approximation algorithms for certain scheduling problems, *Math. Oper. Res*. 3, 1978, 197-204.

Jac55   J. R. Jackson, Scheduling a production line to minimize maximum tardiness, Research Report 43, Management Sci. Res. Project, UCLA, 1955.

Kan81   J. J. Kanet, Minimizing the average deviation of job completion times about a common due date, *Naval Res. Logist. Quart*. 28, 1981, 643-651.

Kar72   R. M. Karp, Reducibility among combinatorial problems, in: R. E. Miller, J. W. Thatcher (eds.), *Complexity of Computer Computations*, Plenum Press, New York, 1972, 85-103.

KIM78   H. Kise, T. Ibaraki, and H. Mine, A solvable case of a one-machine scheduling problem with ready and due times, *Oper. Res.* 26, 1978, 121-126.

KIM79   H. Kise, T. Ibaraki, and H. Mine, Performance analysis of six approximation algorithms for the one-machine maximum lateness scheduling problem with ready times, *J. Oper. Res. Soc. Japan* 22, 1979, 205-224.

KK83   K. R. Kalra, K. Khurana, Single machine scheduling to minimize waiting cost with secondary criterion, *J. Math. Sci.* 16-18, 1981-1983, 9-15.

Law64   E. L. Lawler, On scheduling problems with deferral costs, *Management Sci.* 11, 1964, 280-288.

Law73   E. L. Lawler, Optimal sequencing of a single machine subject to precedence constraints, *Management Sci.* 19, 1973, 544-546.

Law76   E. L. Lawler, Sequencing to minimize the weighted number of tardy jobs, *RAIRO Rech. Opér.* 10, 1976, Suppl. 27-33.

Law77   E. L. Lawler, A 'pseudopolynomial' algorithm for sequencing jobs to minimize total tardiness, *Ann. Discrete Math.* 1, 1977, 331-342.

Law78   E. L. Lawler, Sequencing jobs to minimize total weighted completion time subject to precedence constraints, *Ann. Discrete Math.* 2, 1978, 75-90.

Law82   E. L. Lawler, Sequencing a single machine to minimize the number of late jobs, Preprint, Computer Science Division, University of California, Berkeley, 1982.

Law83   E. L. Lawler, Recent results in the theory of machine scheduling, in: A. Bachem, M. Grötschel, B. Korte (eds.), *Mathematical Programming: The State of the Art*, Bonn 1982, Springer, Berlin, 1983, 202-234.

LD78   R. E. Larson, M. I. Dessouky, Heuristic procedures for the single machine problem to minimize maximum lateness, *AIIE Trans.* 10, 1978, 176-183.

LDD85   R. E. Larson, M. I. Dessouky, and R. E. Devor, A forward-backward procedure for the single machine problem to minimize maximum lateness, *IIE Trans.* 17, 1985, 252-260.

Len77   J. K. Lenstra, *Sequencing by Enumerative Methods*, Mathematical Centre Tracts 69, Mathematisch Centrum, Amsterdam, 1977.

LLLRK84   J. Labetoulle, E. L. Lawler, J. K. Lenstra, and A. H. G. Rinnoy Kan, Preemptive scheduling of uniform machines subject to release dates, in: W. R. Pulleyblank (ed.), *Progress in Combinatorial Optimization*, Academic Press, New York, 1984, 245-261.

LLRK76   B. J. Lageweg, J. K. Lenstra, A. H. G. Rinnooy Kan, Minimizing maximum lateness on one machine: Computational experience and some applications, *Statist. Neerlandica* 30, 1976, 25-41.

LLRK82   E. L. Lawler, J. K. Lenstra, and A. H. G. Rinnooy Kan, Recent development in deterministic sequencing and scheduling: a survey, in: M. A. H. Dempster, J. K. Lenstra, A. H. G Rinnooy Kan (eds.), *Deterministic and Stochastic Scheduling*, D. Reidel Publishing Company, Dortrecht. 1982, 35-73.

LLRKS89   E. L. Lawler, J. K. Lenstra, A. H. G. Rinnoy Kan, D. B. Shmoys, Sequencing and Scheduling: Algorithms and Complexity, Report BS-R8909, Dept. Operations Research, Statisitcs, and System Theory, Centre for Mathematics and Computer Science, Amsterdam, 1989.

LM69   E. L. Lawler, J. M. Moore, A functional equation and its application to resource allocation and sequencing problems, *Management Sci.* 16, 1969, 77-84.

LRK73   J. K. Lenstra, and A. H. G. Rinnooy Kan, Towards a better algorithm for the job-shop scheduling problem - I. Report BN 22, 1973, Mathematisch Centrum, Amsterdam.

LRK78   J. K. Lenstra, and A. H. G. Rinnooy Kan, Complexity of scheduling under precedence constraints, *Oper. Res.* 26, 1978, 22-35.

LRK80   J. K. Lenstra, and A. H. G. Rinnoy Kan, Complexity results for scheduling chains on a single machine, *European J. Oper. Res.* 4, 1980, 270-275.

LRKB77   J. K. Lenstra, A. H. G. Rinnoy Kan, and P. Brucker, Complexity of Machine Scheduling Problems, *Ann. Discrete Math.* 1, 1977, 343-362.

LY90   J. Y-T. Leung, and G. H. Young, Minimizing total tardiness on a single machine with precedence constraints, *ORSA J. Comput*, to appear.

McN59   R. NcNaughton, Scheduling with deadlines and loss functions, *Management Sci.* 6, 1959, 1-12.

MF75   G. B. McMahon, and M. Florian, On scheduling with ready times and due dates to minimize maximum lateness, *Oper. Res.* 23, 1975, 475-482.

Mit72   S. Mitsumori, Optimal Production Scheduling of Multicommodity in Flow Line. *IEEE Trans. Systems Man Cybernet.* CMC-2, 1972, 486- 493.

Miy81   S. Miyazaki, One machine scheduling problem with dual criteria, *J. Oper. Res. Soc. Japan* 24, 1981, 37-51.

Moe89   R. H. Möhring, Computationally tractable classes of ordered sets, in: I. Rival (ed.), *Algorithms and Order*, NATO Advanced Study Institute Series, 1989, 105-193.

Mon82   C. L. Monma, Linear-time algorithms for scheduling on parallel processors, *Oper. Res.* 30, 1982, 116-124.

Moo68   J. M. Moore, An n job, one machine sequencing algorithm for minimizing the number of late jobs, *Management Sci.* 15, 1968, 102-109.

MR85   R. H. Möhrig, F. J. Radermacher, Generalized results on the polynomiality of certain weighted sum scheduling problems, *Methods of Oper. Res.* 49, 1985, 405-417.

MS87   C. L. Monma, J. B. Sidney, Optimal sequencing via modular decomposition: characterization of sequencing functions, *Math. Oper. Res.* 12, 1987, 22-31.

MS89   J. H. Muller, J. Spinrad, Incremental modular decomposition, *J. Assoc. Comput. Mach.* 36, 1989, 1-19.

MV90   T. L. Magnanti, R. Vachani, A strong cutting plane algorithm for production scheduling with changeover costs, *Oper. Res.* 38, 1990, 456-473.

Pos85   M. E. Posner, Minimizing weighted completion times with deadlines, *Oper. Res.* 33, 1985, 562-574.

Pot80a   C. N. Potts, An algorithm for the single machine sequencing problem with precedene constraints, *Math. Programming Study* 13, 1980, 78-87.

Pot80b   C. N. Potts, Analysis of a heuristic for one machine sequencing with release dates and delivery times, *Oper. Res.* 28, 1980, 1436-1441.

Pot85   C. N. Potts, A Lagrangian based branch and bound algorithm for a single machine sequencing with precedence constraints to minimize total weighted completion time, *Management Sci.* 31, 1985, 1300-1311.

Pul75   W. R. Pulleyblank, On minimizing setups in precedence constrained scheduling, Report 81105-OR, University of Bonn, 1981.

PW83   C. N. Potts, and L. N. van Wassenhove, An algorithm for single machine sequencing
          with deadlines to minimize total weighted completion time, *European J. Oper. Res.*
          12, 1983, 379-387.

Rag86   M. Raghavachari, A V-shape property of optimal schedule of jobs about a common
          due date, *European J. Oper. Res.* 23, 1986, 401-402.

RDS87   F. M. E. Raiszadeh, A single machine bicriterion scheduling problem and an
          optimizing branch-and-bound procedure, *J. Inform. Optim. Sci.* 8, 1987, 311-321.

RKLL75   A. H. G. Rinnooy Kan, B. J. Lageweg, J. K. Lenstra, Minimizing total costs in one-
          machine scheduling, *Oper. Res.* 23, 1975, 908-927.

RZ86   I. Rival, and N. Zaguiga, Constructing greedy linear extensions by interchanging
          chains, *Order* 3, 1986, 107-121.

Sah76   S. Sahni, Algorithms for scheduling independent tasks, *J. Assoc. Comput. Mach.* 23,
          1976, 116-127.

Sch71   L. E. Schrage, Obtaining optimal solutions to resource constrained network
          scheduling problems, *AIIE Systems Engineering Conference,* Phoenix, Arizona, 1971.

Sch82   L. E. Schrage, The Multiproduct Lot Scheduling Problem. in: M. A. H. Dempster, J.
          K. Lenstra, A. H. G Rinnooy Kan (eds.), *Deterministic and Stochastic Scheduling,*
          Reidel, 1982.

Sch92   G. Schmidt, Minimizing changeover costs on a single machine, in: W. Bühler, F.
          Feichtinger, F.-J. Radermacher, P. Feichtinger (eds.), *DSOR Proceedings* 90, Vol 1,
          Springer, 1992. 425-432.

Sid73   J. B. Sidney, An extension of Moore's due date algorithm, in: S. E. Elmaghraby (ed.),
          Symposium on the Theory of Scheduling and Its Applications, Springer, Berlin, 1973,
          393-398.

Sid75   J. B. Sidney, Decomposition algorithms for single-machine sequencing with preced-
          ence relations and deferral costs, *Oper. Res.* 23, 1975, 283-298.

Sim78   B. Simons, A fast algorithm for single processor scheduling, *Proc. 19th Annual IEEE
          Symp. Foundations of Computer Science,* 1978, 50-53.

Smi56   W. E. Smith, Various optimizers for single-stage production, *Naval Res. Logist.
          Quart.* 3, 1956, 59-66.

SS86   J. B. Sidney, G. Steiner, Optimal sequencing by modular decomposition: polynomial
          algorithms, *Oper. Res.* 34, 1986, 606-612.

Tow78   W. Townsend, The single machine problem with quadratic penalty function of
          completion times: A branch and bound solution. *Management Sci.* 24, 1978, 530-534.

VB83   F. J. Villarreal, R. L. Bulfin, Scheduling a single machine to minimize the weighted
          number of tardy jobs, *AIIE Trans.* 15, 1983, 337-343.

5 Parallel Processor Scheduling

This chapter is devoted to the analysis of scheduling problems in parallel processor environment. As before the three main criteria to be analyzed are schedule length, mean flow time and lateness. Then, some more developed models of multiprocessor systems are described, including semi-identical processors and uniform k-processor systems. Corresponding results are presented in the four following sections.

5.1 Minimizing Schedule Length

In this section we will analyze the schedule length criterion. Complexity analysis will be complemented, wherever applicable, by a description of the most important approximation as well as enumerative algorithms. The presentation of the results will be divided into subcases depending on the type of processors used, the type of precedence constraints, and to a lesser extent task processing times and the possibility of task preemption.

5.1.1 Identical Processors

Problem $P \mid \mid C_{max}$

The first problem considered is $P \mid \mid C_{max}$ where a set of independent tasks is to be scheduled on identical processors in order to minimize schedule length. We start with complexity analysis of this problem which leads to the conclusion that the problem is not easy to solve since even simple cases such as scheduling on two processors can be proved to be *NP*-hard [Kar72].

Theorem 5.1.1 *Problem $P2 \mid \mid C_{max}$ is NP-hard.*

Proof. As a known *NP*-complete problem we take PARTITION [Kar72] which is formulated as follows.

> *Instance:*   Finite set $\mathcal{A}$ and a size $s(a_i) \in I\!N$ for each $a_i \in \mathcal{A}$.
>
> *Answer:*   "Yes" if there exists a subset $\mathcal{A}' \subseteq \mathcal{A}$ such that
>
> $$\sum_{a_i \in \mathcal{A}'} s(a_i) = \sum_{a_i \in \mathcal{A} - \mathcal{A}'} s(a_i) .$$
>
> Otherwise "No".

Given any instance of PARTITION defined by the positive integers $s(a_i)$, $a_i \in \mathcal{A}$, we define a corresponding instance of the decision counterpart of $P2 \mid \mid C_{max}$ by assuming $n = |\mathcal{A}|$, $p_j = s(a_j)$, $j = 1, 2, \cdots, n$, and a threshold value for the schedule length, $y =$

$(1/2) \sum\limits_{a_i \in \mathcal{A}} s(a_i)$. It is obvious that there exists a subset $\mathcal{A}'$ with the desired property for the instance of PARTITION if ond only if, for the corresponding instance of $P2 \parallel C_{\max}$, there exists a schedule with $C_{\max} \leq y$ (cf. Figure 5.1.1). This proves the theorem. $\square$

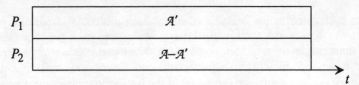

Figure 5.1.1 *A schedule for Theorem* 5.1.1.

Since there is no hope of finding an optimization polynomial time algorithm for $P \parallel C_{\max}$, one may try to solve the problem along the lines presented in Section 3.2. Firstly, we may relax some constraints imposed on problem $P \parallel C_{\max}$ and allow preemptions of tasks. It appears that problem $P \mid pmtn \mid C_{\max}$ can be solved very efficiently. It is easy to see that the length of a preemptive schedule cannot be smaller than the maximum of two values: the maximum processing time of a task and the mean processing requirement on a processor [McN59], i.e.:

$$C_{\max}^* = \max\{\max_j\{p_j\}, \frac{1}{m} \sum_{j=1}^{n} p_j\} . \tag{5.1.1}$$

The following algorithm given by McNaughton [McN59] constructs a schedule whose length is equal to $C_{\max}^*$.

Algorithm 5.1.2 *McNaughton's rule for* $P \mid pmtn \mid C_{\max}$ [McN59].
```
begin
```
$C_{\max}^* := \max\{\sum\limits_{j=1}^{n} p_j/m, \max\limits_j\{p_j\}\};$ -- minimum schedule length

$t := 0;\ i := 1;\ j := 1;$
```
repeat
    if  t + p_j < C*_max
    then
        begin
```
        Assign task T_j to processor P_i, starting at time t;

        $t := t + p_j;\ \ j := j + 1;$

          -- task T_j can be fully assigned to processor P_i,

          -- assignment of the next task will continue at time $t + p_j$
```
        end
    else
        begin
```
        Starting at time t, assign task T_j for $C_{\max}^* - t$ units to processor P_i;

          -- task T_j is preempted at time $C_{\max}^*$,

          -- processor P_i is now busy until $C_{\max}^*$,

          -- assignment of T_j will continue on the next processor at time 0

$$p_j := p_j - (C^*_{max} - t); \quad t := 0; \quad i := i+1;$$
    end;
until $j = n;$ -- all tasks have been scheduled
end;

Note that the above algorithm is an optimization procedure since it always finds a schedule whose length is equal to C^*_{max}. Its time complexity is $O(n)$.

We see that by allowing preemptions we made the problem easy to solve. However, there still remains the question of practical applicability of the solution obtained this way. It appears that in particular in multiprocessor systems with a common primary memory the assumption of task preemptions can be justified. In cases where task preemption is not allowed, as for instance in most manufacturing systems, one may try to find an approximation algorithm for the original problem and evaluate its worst case as well as its mean behavior. We will present such an analysis below.

One of the most often used general approximation strategies for solving scheduling problems is *list scheduling*, whereby a priority list of the tasks is given, and at each step the first available processor is selected to process the first available task on the list [Gra66] (cf. Section 3.2). The accuracy of a given list scheduling algorithm depends on the order in which tasks appear on the list. Unfortunately, this strategy may result in an unexpected behavior of constructed schedules, since the schedule length for problem $P \mid prec \mid C_{max}$ (with arbitrary precedence constraints) may increase if:

– the number of processors increases,

– task processing times decrease,

– precedence constraints are weakened, or

– the priority list changes.

(a)

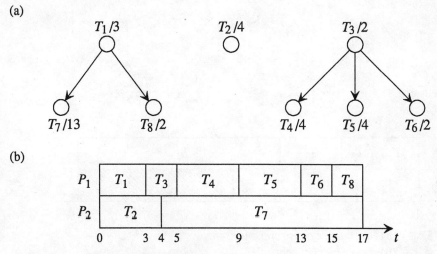

(b)

Figure 5.1.2   (a) *A task set, $m = 2$, $L = (T_1, T_2, T_3, T_4, T_5, T_6, T_7, T_8)$,*
        (b) *an optimal schedule.*

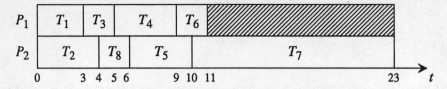

Figure 5.1.3 *Priority list changed: A new list $L' = (T_1, T_2, T_3, T_4, T_5, T_6, T_8, T_7)$.*

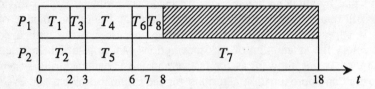

Figure 5.1.4 *Processing times decreased; $p'_j = p_j - 1, j = 1, 2, \cdots, n$.*

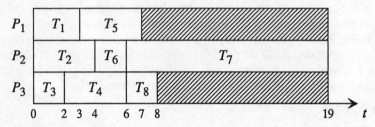

Figure 5.1.5 *Number of processors increased, $m = 3$*

(a)

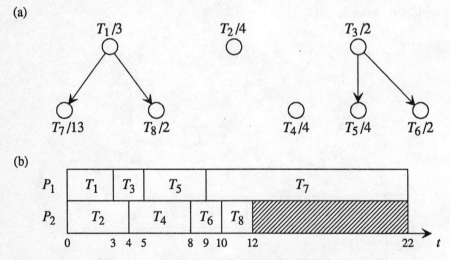

(b)

Figure 5.1.6 (a) *Precedence constraints weakened,*
(b) *a resulting list schedule.*

Figures 5.1.2 through 5.1.6 indicate the effects of changes of the above mentioned parameters. These list scheduling anomalies have been discovered by Graham [Gra66], who has also evaluated the maximum change in schedule length that may be induced by varying one or more problem parameters. We will quote this theorem since its proof is one of the shortest in that area and illustrates well the technique used in other proofs of that type. Let there be defined a task set $\mathcal{T}$ together with precedence constraints $\prec$. Let the processing times of the tasks be given as a vector p, let $\mathcal{T}$ be scheduled on m processors using list L, and let the obtained value of schedule length be equal to C_{max}. On the other hand, let the above parameters be changed: a vector of processing times $p' \leq p$ (for all the components), relaxed precedence constraints $\prec' \subseteq \prec$, priority list L' and the number of processors m'. Let the new value of schedule length be C'_{max}. Then the following theorem is valid.

Theorem 5.1.3 [Gra66] *Under the above assumptions,*

$$\frac{C'_{max}}{C_{max}} \leq 1 + \frac{m-1}{m'}. \tag{5.1.2}$$

Proof. Let us consider schedule S' obtained by processing task set $\mathcal{T}$ with primed parameters. Let the interval $[0, C'_{max})$ be divided into two subsets, $\mathcal{A}$ and $\mathcal{B}$, defined in the following way: $\mathcal{A} = \{t \in [0, C'_{max}) \mid$ all processors are busy at time t$\}$, $\mathcal{B} = [0, C'_{max}) - \mathcal{A}$.

Notice that both $\mathcal{A}$ and $\mathcal{B}$ are unions of disjoint half-open intervals. Let T_{j_1} denote a task completed in S' at time C'_{max}, i.e. $C_{j_1} = C'_{max}$. Two cases may occur.

1. The starting time s_{j_1} of T_{j_1} is an interior point of $\mathcal{B}$. Then by the definition of $\mathcal{B}$ there is some processor P_i which for some $\varepsilon > 0$ is idle during interval $[s_{j_1} - \varepsilon, s_{j_1})$. Such a situation may only occur if we have $T_{j_2} \prec T_{j_1}$ and $C_{j_2} = s_{j_1}$ for some task T_{j_2}.

2. The starting time of T_{j_1} is not an interior point of $\mathcal{B}$. Let us also suppose that $s_{j_1} \neq 0$. Define $x_1 = \sup\{x \mid x < s_{j_1}, \text{ and } x \in \mathcal{B}\}$ or $x_1 = 0$ if set $\mathcal{B}$ is empty. By the construction of $\mathcal{A}$ and $\mathcal{B}$, we see that $x \in \mathcal{A}$, and processor P_i is idle in time interval $[x_1 - \varepsilon, x_1)$ for some $\varepsilon > 0$. But again, such a situation may only occur if some task $T_{j_2} \prec' T_{j_1}$ is processed during this time interval.

It follows that either there exists a task $T_{j_2} \prec' T_{j_1}$ such that $y \in [C_{j_2}, s_{j_1})$ implies $y \in \mathcal{A}$ or we have : $x < s_{j_1}$ implies either $x \in \mathcal{A}$ or $x < 0$.

The above procedure can be inductively repeated, forming a chain $T_{j_3}, T_{j_4}, \cdots$, until we reach task T_{j_r} for which $x < s_{j_r}$ implies either $x \in \mathcal{A}$ or $x < 0$. Hence there must exist a chain of tasks

$$T_{j_r} \prec' T_{j_{r-1}} \prec' \cdots \prec' T_{j_2} \prec' T_{j_1} \tag{5.1.3}$$

such that at each moment $t \in \mathcal{B}$, some task T_{j_k} is being processed in S'. This implies that

$$\sum_{\phi \in S'} p'_{\phi} \leq (m'-1) \sum_{k=1}^{r} p'_{j_k} \tag{5.1.4}$$

where the sum on the left-hand side is made over all idle-time tasks ϕ' in S'. But by (5.1.3) and the hypothesis $\prec' \subseteq \prec$ we have

$$T_{j_r} \prec T_{j_{r-1}} \prec \cdots \prec T_{j_2} \prec T_{j_1}. \tag{5.1.5}$$

Hence,

$$C_{\max} \geq \sum_{k=1}^{r} p_{j_k} \geq \sum_{k=1}^{r} p'_{j_k}. \tag{5.1.6}$$

Furthermore, by (5.1.4) and (5.1.6) we have

$$C'_{\max} = \frac{1}{m'}(\sum_{k=1}^{n} p'_k + \sum_{\phi' \in S'} p'_{\phi'}) \leq \frac{1}{m'}(m\,C_{\max} + (m'-1)\,C_{\max}). \tag{5.1.7}$$

It follows that

$$\frac{C'_{\max}}{C_{\max}} \leq 1 + \frac{m-1}{m'}$$

and the theorem is proved. $\square$

From the above theorem, the *absolute performance ratio* for an arbitrary list scheduling algorithm solving problem $P \| C_{\max}$ can be derived.

Corollary 5.1.4 [Gra66] *For an arbitrary list scheduling algorithm LS for $P \| C_{\max}$ we have*

$$R_{LS} = 2 - \frac{1}{m}. \tag{5.1.8}$$

Proof: The upper bound of (5.1.8) follows immediately from (5.1.2) by taking $m' = m$ and by considering the list leading to an optimal schedule. To show that this bound is achievable let us consider the following example: $n = (m-1)m + 1$, $p = [1, 1, \cdots, 1, 1, m]$, $\prec$ is empty, $L = (T_n, T_1, T_2, \cdots, T_{n-1})$ and $L' = (T_1, T_2, \cdots, T_n)$. The corresponding schedules for $m = 4$ are shown in Figure 5.1.7. $\square$

It follows from the above considerations that an arbitrary list scheduling algorithm can produce schedules almost twice as long as optimal ones. An improvement could be gained if tasks are ordered properly. One of the simplest algorithms is the *LPT algorithm* in which the tasks are arranged in order of nonincreasing p_j.

Algorithm 5.1.5 *LPT Algorithm for $P \| C_{\max}$.*
begin
Order tasks on a list in nonincreasing order of their processing times;   -- i.e. $p_1 \geq \cdots \geq p_n$
for $i = 1$ **step** 1 **until** m **do** $s_i := 0$;
    -- processors P_i are assumed to be idle from time $s_i = 0$ on, $i = 1, \cdots, m$
$j := 1$;
repeat
    $s_k := \min\{s_i\}$;
    Assign task T_j to processor P_k at time s_k;

-- the first nonassigned task from the list is scheduled on the first processor

-- that becomes free

$s_k := s_k + p_j;\ j := j+1;$

until $j = n;$ -- all tasks have been scheduled

end;

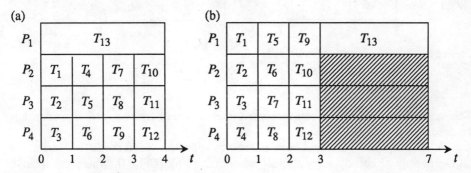

Figure 5.1.7 *Schedules for Corollary 5.1.4*
(a) an optimal schedule,
(b) an approximate schedule.

It is easy to see that the time complexity of this algorithm is $O(n \log n)$ since its most complex activity is to sort the set of tasks. The worst case behavior of the *LPT* rule is analyzed in Theorem 5.1.6.

Theorem 5.1.6 [Gra66] *If the LPT algorithm is used to solve problem $P \| C_{\max}$, then*

$$R_{LPT} = \frac{4}{3} - \frac{1}{3m}. \quad \Box \tag{5.1.9}$$

Space limitations prevent us from including here the proof of the upper bound in the above theorem. However, we will give an example showing that this bound can be achieved. Let $n = 2m + 1$, $p = [2m-1, 2m-1, 2m-2, 2m-2, \cdots, m+1, m+1, m, m, m]$. For $m = 3$, Figure 5.1.8 shows two schedules, an optimal one and an *LPT* schedule.

We see that in the worst case an *LPT* schedule can be up to 33% longer than an optimal schedule. However, one is led to expect better performance from the *LPT* algorithm than is indicated by (5.1.9), especially when the number of tasks becomes large. In [CS76] another absolute performance ratio for the *LPT* rule was proved, taking into account the number k of tasks assigned to a processor whose last task terminates the schedule.

Theorem 5.1.7 *For the assumptions stated above, we have*

$$R_{LPT}(k) = 1 + \frac{1}{k} - \frac{1}{km}. \quad \Box \tag{5.1.10}$$

(a)   (b)

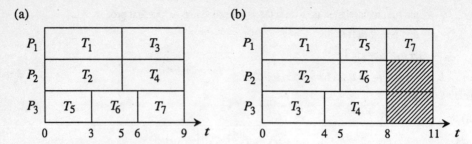

Figure 5.1.8 *Schedules for Theorem* 5.1.6
          (a) *an optimal schedule,*
          (b) *LPT schedule.*

This result shows that the worst-case performance bound for the *LPT* algorithm approaches one as fast as $1 + 1/k$.

On the other hand, it would be of interest to know how good the *LPT* algorithm is on the average. Recently such a result was obtained by [CFL84], where the relative error was found for two processors on the assumption that task processing times are independent samples from the uniform distribution on $[0, 1]$.

Theorem 5.1.8 *Under the assumptions already stated, we have the following bounds for the mean value of schedule length for the LPT algorithm, $E(C_{\max}^{LPT})$, for problem $P2||$ $C_{\max}$.*

$$\frac{n}{4}+\frac{1}{4(n+1)} \le E(C_{\max}^{LPT}) \le \frac{n}{4}+\frac{e}{2(n+1)},\qquad(5.1.11)$$

where $e = 2.7\cdots$ is the base of natural logarithm. $\square$

Taking into account that $n/4$ is a lower bound on $E(C_{\max}^*)$ we get $E(C_{\max}^{LPT})/E(C_{\max}^*) < 1 + O(1/n^2)$. Therefore, as n increases, $E(C_{\max}^{LPT})$ approaches the optimum no more slowly than $1 + O(1/n^2)$ approaches 1. The above bound can be generalized to cover also the case of m processors for which we have [CFL83]:

$$E(C_{\max}^{LPT}) \le \frac{n}{2m} + O(\frac{m}{n}).$$

Moreover, it is also possible to prove [FRK86, FRK87] that $C_{\max}^{LPT} - C_{\max}^*$ almost surely converges to 0 as $n \to \infty$ if the task processing time distribution has a finite mean and a density function f satisfying $f(0) > 0$. It is also shown that if the distribution is uniform or exponential, the rate of convergence is $O(\log(\log n)/n)$. This result, obtained by a complicated analysis, can also be guessed from simulation studies. Such an experiment was reported by Kedia [Ked70] and we present the summary of the results in Table 5.1.1. The last column presents the ratio of schedule lengths obtained by the *LPT* algorithm and the optimal preemptive one. Task processing times are drawn from the uniform distribution of the given parameters.

To conclude the above analysis we may say that the *LPT* algorithm behaves quite well and may be useful in practice. However, if one wants to have better performance guarantees, other approximation algorithms should be used, as for example *MULTIFIT* introduced by Coffman et al. [CGJ78] or the algorithm proposed by Hochbaum and Shmoys [HS87]. A comprehensive treatment of approximation algorithms for this and related problems is given by Coffman et al. [CGJ84].

n, m		Intervals of task processing time distribution	C_{max}	$C_{max}^{LPT} / C_{max}^*$
6	3	1, 20	20	1.00
9	3	1, 20	32	1.00
15	3	1, 20	65	1.00
6	3	20, 50	59	1.05
9	3	20, 50	101	1.03
15	3	20, 50	166	1.00
8	4	1, 20	23	1.09
12	4	1, 20	30	1.00
20	4	1, 20	60	1.00
8	4	20, 50	74	1.04
12	4	20, 50	108	1.02
20	4	20, 50	185	1.01
10	5	1, 20	25	1.04
15	5	1, 20	38	1.03
20	5	1, 20	49	1.00
10	5	20, 50	65	1.06
15	5	20, 50	117	1.03
25	5	20, 50	198	1.01

Table 5.1.1 *Mean performance of the LPT algorithm.*

We now pass to the third way of analyzing problem $P \| C_{max}$. Theorem 5.1.1. gave a negative answer to the question about the existence of an optimization polynomial time algorithm for solving $P2 \| C_{max}$. However, we have not proved that our problem is *NP*-hard in the strong sense and we may try to find a pseudopolynomial optimization algorithm. It appears that, based on a dynamic programming approach, such an algorithm can be constructed using ideas presented by Rothkopf [Rot66]. Below the algorithm is presented for $P \| C_{max}$; it uses Boolean variables $x_j(t_1, t_2, \cdots, t_m)$, $j = 1, 2, \cdots, n$, $t_i = 0, 1, \cdots, C$, $i = 1, 2, \cdots, m$, where C denotes an upper bound on the optimal schedule length C_{max}^*. The meaning of these variables is the following

$$x_j(t_1, t_2, \cdots, t_m) = \begin{cases} \textbf{true} & \text{if tasks } T_1, T_2, \cdots, T_j \text{ can be scheduled on processors } P_1, P_2, \cdots, P_m \text{ in such a way that } P_i \text{ is busy in time interval } [0, t_i], i = 1, 2, \cdots, m. \\ \textbf{false} & \text{otherwise.} \end{cases}$$

Now, we are able to present the algorithm.

Algorithm 5.1.9 *Dynamic programming for* $P \| C_{max}$ [Rot66].

begin

for all $(t_1, t_2, \cdots, t_m) \in \{0, 1, \cdots, C\}^m$ **do** $x_0(t_1, t_2, \cdots, t_m) := $ **false;**

$x_0(0, 0, \cdots, 0) := $ **true;**

    -- initial values for Boolean variables are now assigned

for $j = 1$ **step** 1 **until** n **do**

    for all $(t_1, t_2, \cdots, t_m) \in \{0, 1, \cdots, C\}^m$ **do**

$$x_j(t_1, t_2, \cdots, t_m) = \bigvee_{i=1}^{m} x_{j-1}(t_1, t_2, \cdots, t_{i-1}, t_i - p_j, t_{i+1}, \cdots, t_m); \qquad (5.1.12)$$

$$C_{max}^* := \min\{\max\{t_1, t_2, \cdots, t_m\} \mid x_n(t_1, t_2, \cdots, t_m) = true\}; \qquad (5.1.13)$$

    -- optimal schedule length has been calculated

Starting from the value C_{max}^*, assign tasks $T_n, T_{n-1}, \cdots, T_1$ to appropriate processors
    using formula (5.1.12) backwards;

end;

The above procedure solves problem $P \| C_{max}$ in $O(nC^m)$ time; thus for fixed m it is a pseudopolynomial time algorithm. As a consequence, for small values of m and C the algorithm can be used even in computer applications. To illustrate the use of the above algorithm let us consider the following example.

Example 5.1.10 Let $n = 3$, $m = 2$ and $p = [2, 1, 2]$. Assuming bound $C = 5$ we get the cube given in Figure 5.1.9(a) where particular values of variables $x_j(t_1, t_2, \cdots, t_m)$ are stored. In Figures 5.1.9(b) through 5.1.9(e) these values are shown, respectively, for $j = $ 0, 1, 2, 3 (only true values are depicted). Following Figure 5.1.9(e) and equation (5.1.13), an optimal schedule is constructed as shown in Figure 5.1.9(f). □

The interested reader may find a survey of some other enumerative approaches for the problem in question in [LLRKS89].

Problem $P \mid prec \mid C_{max}$

Let us now pass to the case of dependent tasks. At first tasks are assumed to be scheduled nonpreemptively. It is obvious that there is no hope of finding a polynomial time optimization algorithm for scheduling tasks of arbitrary length since $P \| C_{max}$ is already *NP*-hard. However, one can try to find such an algorithm for unit processing times of all the tasks. The first algorithm has been given for scheduling *forests*, consisting either of *in-trees* or of *out-trees* [Hu61]. We will first present Hu's algorithm for the case of an in-tree, i.e. for the problem $P \mid in\text{-}tree, p_j = 1 \mid C_{max}$. The algorithm is based on the notion of a *task level* in an in-tree which is defined as the number of tasks in the path to the root of the graph. The algorithm by Hu, which is also called *level algorithm* or *critical path algorithm* is as follows.

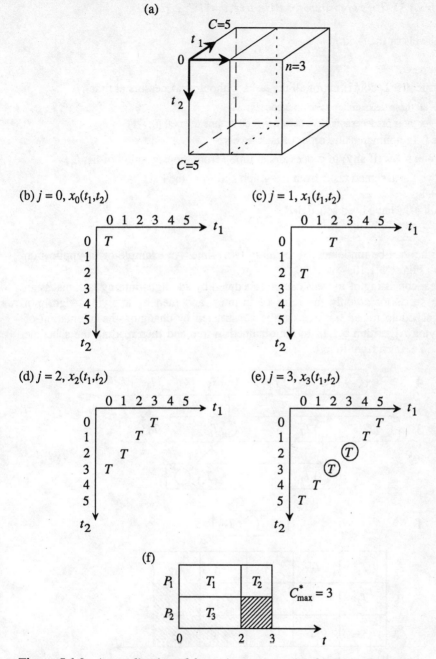

Figure 5.1.9 *An application of dynamic programming for Example 5.1.10*
(a) *a cube of Boolean variables,*
(b)-(e) *values of $x_j(t_1,t_2)$ for j = 0, 1, 2, 3, respectively (here T stands for true),*
(f) *an optimal schedule.*

Algorithm 5.1.11 *Hu's algorithm for P | in-tree, $p_j=1$ | C_{max}* [Hu61].
begin
Calculate levels of the tasks;
$t := 0$;
repeat
    Construct list L_t consisting of all the tasks without predecessors at time t;
        -- all these tasks either have no predecessors
        -- or their predecessors have been assigned in time interval $[0, t-1]$
    Order L_t in nonincreasing order of task levels;
    Assign m tasks (if any) to processors at time t from the beginning of list L_t;
    Remove the assigned tasks from the graph and from the list;
    $t := t+1$;
until all tasks have been scheduled;
end;

The algorithm can be implemented to run in O(n) time. An example of its application is shown in Figure 5.1.10.

A forest consisting of in-trees can be scheduled by adding a dummy task that is an immediate successor of only the roots of in-trees, and then by applying Algorithm 5.1.11. A schedule for an out-tree can be constructed by changing the orientation of arcs, applying Algorithm 5.1.11 to the obtained in-tree and then reading the schedule backwards, i.e. from right to left.

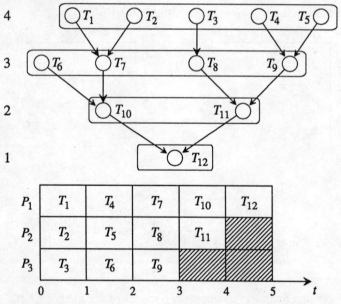

Figure 5.1.10 *An example of the application of Algorithm 5.1.11 for three processors.*

It is interesting to note that the problem of scheduling opposing forests (that is, combinations of in-trees and out-trees) on an arbitrary number of processors is *NP*-hard [GJTY83]. However, if the number of processors is limited to 2, the problem is easily solvable even for arbitrary precedence graphs [CG72, FKN69, Gab82]. We present the algorithm given by Coffman and Graham [CG72] since it can be further extended to cover the preemptive case. The algorithm uses *labels* assigned to tasks, which take into account the levels of the tasks and the numbers of their immediate successors. The following algorithm assigns labels to the tasks, and then uses them to find the shortest schedule for problem $P2 \mid prec, p_j = 1 \mid C_{max}$.

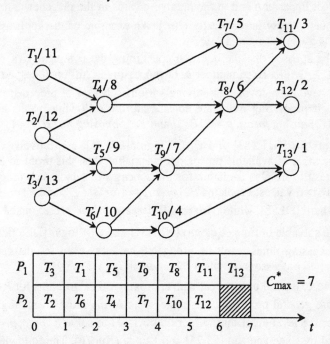

Figure 5.1.11 *An example of the application of Algorithm 5.1.12 (tasks are denoted by T_j/label).*

Algorithm 5.1.12 *Algorithm by Coffman and Graham for $P2 \mid prec, p_j = 1 \mid C_{max}$* [CG72].
begin
Assign label 1 to any task T_0 for which $isucc(T_0) = \varnothing$;
-- recall that $isucc(T)$ denotes the set of all immediate successors of T
$j := 1$;
repeat
    Construct set S consisting of all unlabeled tasks whose successors are labeled;
    for all $T \in S$ **do**
        begin
        Construct list $L(T)$ consisting of labels of tasks belonging to $isucc(T)$;
        Order $L(T)$ in decreasing order of the labels;
        end;
    Order these lists in increasing lexicographic order $L(T_{[1]}) \prec \cdots \prec L(T_{[|S|]})$;
    Assign label $j + 1$ to task $T_{[1]}$;
    $j := j + 1$;

```
until j = n;          -- all tasks have been assigned labels
call Algorithm 5.1.11;
     -- here the above algorithm uses labels instead of levels when scheduling tasks
end;
```

A careful analysis shows that the above algorithm can be implemented to run in time which is almost linear in n and in the number of arcs in the precedence graph [Set76]; thus its time complexity is practically $O(n^2)$. An example of the application of Algorithm 5.1.12 is given in Figure 5.1.11.

It must be stressed that the question concerning the complexity of problem $Pm \mid prec, p_j = 1 \mid C_{max}$ with a fixed number m of processors is still open despite the fact that many papers have been devoted to solving various subcases of precedence constraints. If tasks of unit processing times are considered, the following results are available. Problems $P3 \mid opposing\ forest, p_j = 1 \mid C_{max}$ and $Pk \mid opposing\ forest, p_j = 1 \mid C_{max}$ are solvable in time $O(n)$ [GJTY83] and $O(n^{2k-2}\log n)$ [DW85], respectively. On the other hand, if the number of available processors is variable, then this problem becomes NP-hard. Some results are also available for the subcases in which task processing times may take only two values. Problems $P2 \mid prec, p_j = 1\ or\ 2 \mid C_{max}$ and $P \mid prec, p_j = 1\ or\ k \mid C_{max}$ are NP-hard [DL88], while problems $P2 \mid tree, p_j = 1\ or\ 2 \mid C_{max}$ and $P2 \mid tree, p_j = 1\ or\ 3 \mid C_{max}$ are solvable in time $O(n\log n)$ [NLH81] and $O(n^2\log n)$ [DL89], respectively. Arbitrary processing times result in strong NP-hardness even for the case of chains scheduled on two processors (problem $P2 \mid chains \mid C_{max}$) [DLY91].

Furthermore, several papers deal with approximation algorithms for $P \mid prec, p_j = 1 \mid C_{max}$ and more general problems. We quote some of the most interesting results. The application of the level algorithm (Algorithm 5.1.11) to solve $P \mid prec, p_j = 1 \mid C_{max}$ has been analyzed by Chen and Liu [CL75] and Kunde [Kun76]. The following bound has been proved.

$$R_{level} = \begin{cases} \dfrac{4}{3} & \text{for } m = 2 \\[2ex] 2 - \dfrac{1}{m-1} & \text{for } m \geq 3. \end{cases}$$

Algorithm 5.1.12 is slightly better, its bound is $R = 2 - \dfrac{2}{m}$ for $m \geq 2$ [LS77].

In this context one should not forget the results presented in Theorems 5.1.3 through 5.1.6, where list scheduling anomalies have been analyzed.

Problem $P \mid pmtn, prec \mid C_{max}$

The analysis also showed that preemptions can be profitable from the viewpoint of two factors. First, they can make problems easier to solve, and second, they can shorten the schedule. Recently Coffman and Garey [CG91] proved that for problem $P2 \mid prec \mid C_{max}$ the least schedule length achievable by a nonpreemptive schedule is no more than 4/3 the least schedule length achievable when preemptions are allowed. While the proof of this fact seems to be tedious, a very simple example showing that this bound is met can easily be given for a set of three independent tasks of equal length (cf. Figure 5.1.12).

(a)

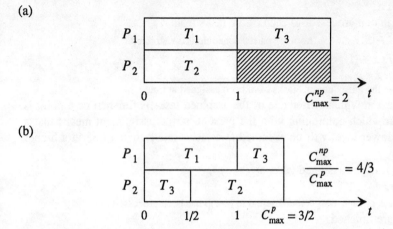

(b)

Figure 5.1.12   *An example of 4/3 conjecture*
(a) *nonpreemptive scheduling,*
(b) *preemptive scheduling.*

In the general case of dependent tasks scheduled on processors in order to minimize schedule length, one can construct optimal preemptive schedules for tasks of arbitrary length and with other parameters the same as in Algorithm 5.1.11 or 5.1.12. The approach again uses the notion of the *level* of task T_j in a precedence graph, by which is now understood the sum of processing times (including p_j) of tasks along the longest path between T_j and a terminal task (a task with no successors). Let us note that the level of a task being executed is decreasing. We have the following algorithm [MC69, MC70] for the problems $P2 \mid pmtn, prec \mid C_{max}$ and $P \mid pmtn, forest \mid C_{max}$. The algorithm uses a notion of a *processor shared schedule*, in which a task receives some fraction β (≤ 1) of the processing capacity of a processor.

Algorithm 5.1.13 *Algorithm by Muntz and Coffman for* $P2 \mid pmtn, prec \mid C_{max}$ *and* $P \mid pmtn, forest \mid C_{max}$ [MC69, MC70].
begin
for all $T \in \mathcal{T}$ **do** Compute the level of task T;
$t := 0; h := m;$
repeat
    Construct set Z of tasks without predecessors at time t;
    while $h > 0$ **and** $|Z| > 0$ **do**
        begin
        Construct subset S of Z consisting of tasks at the highest level;
        if $|S| > h$
        then
            begin
            Assign $\beta := h/|S|$ of a processing capacity to each of the tasks from S;

```
            h := 0;         -- a processor shared partial schedule is constructed
            end
        else
            begin
            Assign one processor to each of the tasks from S;
            h := h - |S|;   -- a "normal" partial schedule is constructed
            end;
        Z := Z - S;
        end;    -- the most "urgent" tasks have been assigned at time t
```

Calculate time τ at which **either** one of the assigned tasks is finished **or** a point is reached at which continuing with the present partial assignment means that a task at a lower level will be executed at a faster rate β than a task at a higher level;

Decrease levels of the assigned tasks by $(\tau - t)\beta$;

$t := \tau$; h := m;

```
            -- a portion of each assigned task equal to (τ-t)β has been processed
```

until all tasks are finished;

call Algorithm 5.1.2 to re-schedule portions of the processor shared schedule to get a normal one;

end;

The above algorithm can be implemented to run in $O(n^2)$ time. An example of its application to an instance of problem $P2 \mid pmtn, prec \mid C_{max}$ is shown in Figure 5.1.13.

At this point let us also consider another class of the precedence graphs for which the scheduling problem can be solved in polynomial time. To do this we have to present precedence constraints in the form of an activity network (task-on-arc precedence graph, viz. Section 3.1) whose nodes (events) are ordered in such a way that the occurrence of node i is not later than the occurrence of node j, if $i < j$. Now, let S_I denote the set of all the tasks which may be performed between the occurrence of event (node) I and $I + 1$. Such sets will be called *main sets*. Let us consider *processor feasible sets*, i.e. those main sets and those subsets of the main sets whose cardinalities are not greater than m, and number these sets from 1 to some K. Now, let Q_j denote the set of indices of processor feasible sets in which task T_j may be performed , and let x_i denote the duration of set i. Then, a linear programming problem can be formulated in the following way [WBCS77, BCSW76a] (another *LP* formulation for unrelated processors is presented in Section 5.1.2):

$$\textit{Minimize} \qquad C_{max} = \sum_{i=1}^{K} x_i \qquad\qquad (5.1.14)$$

$$\textit{subject to} \qquad \sum_{i \in Q_j} x_i = p_j, \ j = 1, 2, \cdots, n,$$

$$\qquad\qquad\qquad\qquad\qquad\qquad\qquad\qquad\qquad (5.1.15)$$

$$x_i \geq 0, \ i = 1, 2, \cdots, K.$$

It is clear that the solution of the *LP* problem depends on the order of nodes in the activity network, hence an optimal solution is found when this topological order is unique. Such a situation takes place for a *uniconnected activity network* (*uan*), i.e. one in which any two nodes are connected by a directed path in only one direction. An example of a uniconnected activity network together with the corresponding precedence graph is shown in Figure 5.1.14. On the other hand, the number of variables in the above *LP* problem depends polynomially on the input length, when the number of processors m is fixed. We may then use a non-simplex algorithm (e.g. from [Kha79] or [Kar84]) which solves any *LP* problem in time polynomial in the number of variables and constraints. Hence, we may conclude that the above procedure solves problem $Pm \mid pmtn, uan \mid C_{max}$ in polynomial time.

(a)

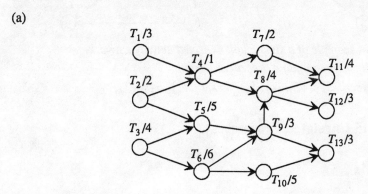

(b)

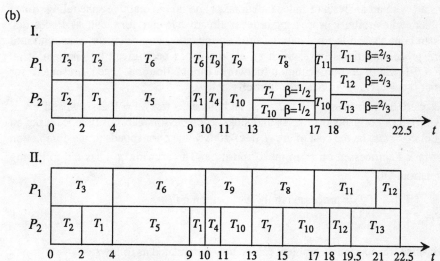

Figure 5.1.13 *An example of the application of Algorithm 5.1.13*
        (a) *a task set (nodes are denoted by T_j / p_j),*
        (b) *I: a processor-shared schedule, II: an optimal schedule.*

For general precedence graphs, however, we know from Ullman [Ull76] that the problem is *NP*-hard. In that case a heuristic algorithm such as Algorithm 5.1.13 my be chosen. The worst-case behavior of Algorithm 5.1.13 applied in the case of $P \mid pmtn$, $prec \mid C_{max}$ has been analyzed by Lam and Sethi [LS77]

$$R_{Alg.5.1.13} = 2 - \frac{2}{m}, \qquad m \geq 2.$$

(a)   (b)

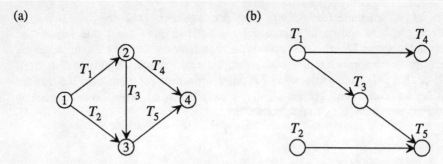

Figure 5.1.14   (a) *An example of a simple uniconnected activity network,*
(b) *The corresponding precedence graph.*
Main sets $S_1 = \{T_1, T_2\}$, $S_2 = \{T_2, T_3, T_4\}$, $S_3 = \{T_4, T_5\}$.

5.1.2 Uniform and Unrelated Processors

Problem $Q \mid p_j = 1 \mid C_{max}$

Let us start with an analysis of independent tasks and nonpreemptive scheduling. Since
the problem with arbitrary processing times is already *NP*-hard for identical processors,
all we can hope to find is a polynomial time optimization algorithm for tasks with unit
standard processing times only. Such an approach has been given by Graham et al.
[GLLRK79] where a transportation network formulation has been presented for
problem $Q \mid p_j = 1 \mid C_{max}$. We describe it briefly below.

Let there be n sources j, $j = 1, 2, \cdots, n$ and mn sinks (i, k), $i = 1, 2, \cdots, m$ and $k = 1$,
$2, \cdots, n$. Sources correspond to tasks and sinks to processors and positions of tasks on
them. Let $c_{ijk} = k/b_i$ be the cost of arc $(j, (i, k))$; this value corresponds to the completion
time of task T_j processed on P_i in the kth position. The arc flow x_{ijk} has the following
interpretation:

$$x_{ijk} = \begin{cases} 1 & \text{if } T_j \text{ is processed in the } k^{th} \text{ position on } P_i \\ 0 & \text{otherwise.} \end{cases}$$

The min-max transportation problem can be now formulated as follows:

Minimize	$\displaystyle \max_{i,j,k} \{c_{ijk} x_{ijk}\}$	(5.1.16)
subject to	$\displaystyle \sum_{i=1}^{m} \sum_{k=1}^{n} x_{ijk} = 1 \text{ for all } j,$	(5.1.17)
	$\displaystyle \sum_{j=1}^{n} x_{ijk} \leq 1 \quad \text{ for all } i, k,$	(5.1.18)
	$x_{ijk} \geq 0 \quad \text{ for all } i, j, k.$	(5.1.19)

This problem can be solved by a standard transportation procedure (cf. Section 2.3)
which results in $O(n^3)$ time complexity, or by a procedure due to Sevastjanov [Sev91].

Below we sketch this last approach. It is clear that the minimum schedule length is given as

$$C^*_{max} = \sup \{t \mid \sum_{i=1}^{m} \lfloor tb_i \rfloor < n \}. \tag{5.1.20}$$

On the other hand, a lower bound on the schedule length for the above problem is

$$C' = n / \sum_{i=1}^{m} b_i \leq C^*_{max}. \tag{5.1.21}$$

Bound C' can be achieved e.g. by a preemptive schedule. If we assign $k_i = \lfloor C'b_i \rfloor$ tasks to processor P_i, $i = 1, 2, \cdots, m$, respectively, then these tasks may be processed in time interval $[0, C']$. However, $l = n - \sum_{i=1}^{m} k_i$ tasks remain unassigned. Clearly $l \leq m-1$, since $C'b_i - \lfloor C'b_i \rfloor < 1$ for each i. The remaining l tasks are then assigned one by one to those processors P_i for which $\min_i \{(k_i + 1) / b_i\}$ is attained at a given stage, where, of course, k_i is increased by one after the assignment of a task to a particular processor P_i. This procedure is repeated until all tasks are assigned. We see that this approach results in an $O(m^2)$-algorithm for solving problem $Q \mid p_j = 1 \mid C_{max}$.

Example 5.1.14 To illustrate the above algorithm let us assume that $n = 9$ tasks are to be processed on $m = 3$ uniform processors whose processing speeds are given by the vector $b = [3, 2, 1]$. We get $C' = 9/6 = 1.5$. The numbers of tasks assigned to processors at the first stage are, respectively, 4, 3, and 1. A corresponding schedule is given in Figure 5.1.15(a), where task T_9 has not yet been assigned. An optimal schedule is obtained if this task is assigned to processor P_1, cf. Figure 5.1.15(b). □

Since other problems of nonpreemptive scheduling of independent tasks are *NP*-hard, one may be interested in applying certain heuristics. One heuristic algorithm which is a list scheduling algorithm, has been presented by Liu and Liu [LL74a]. Tasks are ordered on the list in nonincreasing order of their processing times and processors are ordered in nonincreasing order of their processing speeds. Now, whenever a machine becomes free it gets the first nonassigned task of the list; if there are two or more free processors, the fastest is chosen. The worst-case behavior of the algorithm has been evaluated for the case of an $m+1$ processor system, m of which have processing speed factor equal to 1 and the remaining processor has processing speed factor b. The bound is as follows.

$$R = \begin{cases} \dfrac{2(m+b)}{b+2} & \text{for } b \leq 2 \\[3mm] \dfrac{m+b}{2} & \text{for } b > 2. \end{cases}$$

It is clear that the algorithm does better if, in the first case ($b \leq 2$), m decreases faster than b, and if b and m decrease in case of $b > 2$. Other algorithms have been analyzed by Liu and Liu [LL74b, LL74c] and by Gonzalez et al. [GIS77].

(a)

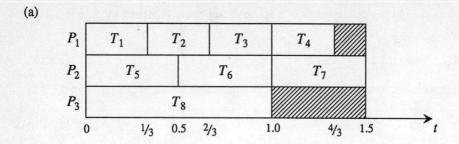

(b)

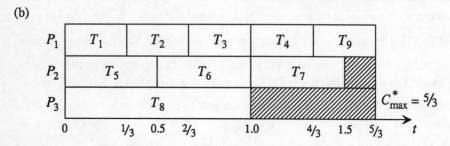

Figure 5.1.15 *Schedules for Example* 5.1.14

             (a) a *partial schedule,*

             (b) *an optimal schedule.*

Problem $Q \,|\, pmtn \,|\, C_{max}$

By allowing preemptions, i.e. for the problem $Q\,|\,pmtn\,|\,C_{max}$, one can find optimal schedules in polynomial time. We will present an algorithm given by Horvath et al. [HLS77] despite the fact that there is a more efficient one by Gonzalez and Sahni [GS78]. We do this because the first algorithm covers more general precedence constraints than the second, and it generalizes the ideas presented in Algorithm 5.1.13. The algorithm is based on two concepts: the *task level*, defined as previously as processing requirement of the unexecuted portion of a task, but now expressed in terms of a standard processing time, and *processor sharing*, i.e. the possibility of assigning only a fraction β $(0 \le \beta \le \max\{b_i\})$ of processing capacity to some task. Let us assume that tasks are indexed in order of nonincreasing p_j's and processors are in order of nonincreasing values of b_i. It is quite clear that the minimum schedule length can be estimated by

$$C^*_{max} \ge C = \max\Big\{ \max_{1 \le k \le m} \{\frac{X_k}{B_k}\}, \{\frac{X_n}{B_m}\}\Big\} \tag{5.1.22}$$

where X_k is the sum of processing requirements (i.e. standard processing times p_j) of the first k tasks, and B_k is the collective processing capacity (i.e. the sum of processing speed factors b_i) of the first k processors. The algorithm presented below constructs a schedule of length equal to C for the problem $Q\,|\,pmtn\,|\,C_{max}$.

Algorithm 5.1.15 *Algorithm by Horvath, Lam and Sethi for $Q|pmtn|C_{max}$* [HLS77]
begin
for all $T \in \mathcal{T}$ **do** Compute level of task T;
$t := 0$; $h := m$;
repeat
    while $h > 0$ **do**
        begin
        Construct subset S of $\mathcal{T}$ consisting of tasks at the highest level;
           -- the most "urgent" tasks are chosen
        if $|S| > h$
        then
           begin
           Assign the tasks of set S to the h remaining processors to be processed at

$$\text{the same rate } \beta = \sum_{i=m-h+1}^{m} b_i / |S|;$$

           $h := 0$;   -- tasks from set S share the h slowest processors
           end
        else
           begin
           Assign tasks from set S to be processed at the same rate β on the fastest
              $|S|$ processors;
           $h := h - |S|$;   -- tasks from set S share the fastest $|S|$ processors
           end;
        end;   -- the most urgent tasks have been assigned at time t
    Calculate time moment τ at which either one of the assigned tasks is finished or a
    point is reached at which continuing with the present partial assignment causes
    that a task at a lower level will be executed at a faster rate β than a higher
    level task;
        -- note, that the levels of the assigned tasks decrease during task execution
    Decrease levels of the assigned tasks by $(\tau - t)\beta$;
    $t := \tau$; $h := m$;   -- a portion of each assigned task equal to $(\tau - t)\beta$ has been processed
until all tasks are finished;
    -- the schedule constructed so far consists of a sequence of intervals during each
    -- of which certain tasks are assigned to the processors in a shared mode.
    -- In the next loop task assignment in each of these intervals is determined
for each interval of the processor shared schedule **do**
    begin
    Let y be the length of the interval;
    if g tasks share g processors
    then Assign each task to each processor for y/g time units
    else
        begin
        Let p be the processing requirement of each of the g tasks in the interval;
        Let b be the processing speed factor of the slowest processor;
        if $p/b < y$
        then call Algorithm 5.1.2
        -- tasks can be assigned as in McNaughton's rule, ignoring different processor speeds
        else

```
      begin
      Divide the interval into g subintervals of equal lengths;
      Assign the g tasks so that each task occurs in exactly h intervals, each
          time on a different processor;
        end;
      end;
    end;
 -- a normal preemptive schedule has now been constructed
 end;
```

The time complexity of Algorithm 5.1.15 is $O(mn^2)$. An example of its application is shown in Figure 5.1.16.

(a)

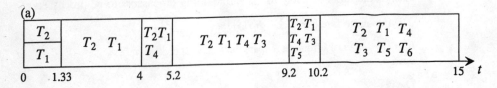

0   1.33   4   5.2   9.2   10.2   15 t

(b)

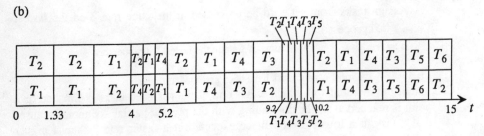

0   1.33   4   5.2   9.2   10.2   15 t

Figure 5.1.16 *An Example of the application of Algorithm 5.1.15: $n = 6$, $m = 2$, $p =$*
[20, 24, 10, 12, 5, 4], $b = [4, 1]$
(a) a processor shared schedule,
(b) an optimal schedule.

Problem $Q \,|\,pmtn, prec\,|\,C_{max}$

When considering dependent tasks, only preemptive polynomial time optimization algorithms are known. Algorithm 5.1.15 also solves problem $Q2\,|\,pmtn, prec\,|\,C_{max}$, if the level of a task is understood as in Algorithm 5.1.13 where standard processing times for all the tasks were assumed. When considering this problem one should also take into account the possibility of solving it for unconnected activity networks via the slightly modified linear programming approach (5.1.14)-(5.1.15). It is also possible to solve the problem by using another *LP* formulation which is described below.

It is also possible to solve problem $Q\,|\,pmtn, prec\,|\,C_{max}$ approximately by the two machine aggregation approach, developed in the framework of flow shop scheduling [RS83] (cf. Section 7.1). In this case the two fastest processors are used only, and the worst case bound is

$$\frac{C_{\max}}{C_{\max}^*} \leq \begin{cases} \sum_{i=1}^{m/2} \max\{b_{2i-1}/b_1, b_{2i}/b_2\} & \text{if } m \text{ is even,} \\ \sum_{i=1}^{\lfloor m/2 \rfloor} \max\{b_{2i-1}/b_1, b_{2i}/b_2\} + b_m/b_1 & \text{if } m \text{ is odd.} \end{cases}$$

Problem $R \mid pmtn \mid C_{\max}$

Let us pass now to the case of unrelated processors. This case is the most difficult. We will not speak about unit-length tasks, because unrelated processors with unit length tasks would reduce to the case of indentical or uniform processors. Hence, no polynomial time optimization algorithms are known for problems other than preemptive ones. Also, very little is known about approximation algorithms for this case. Some results have been obtained by Ibarra and Kim [IK77], but the obtained bounds are not very encouraging. Thus, we will pass to the preemptive scheduling model.

Problem $R \mid pmtn \mid C_{\max}$ can be solved by a *two-phase method*. The first phase consists in solving a linear programming problem formulated independently by Błażewicz et al. [BCSW76a, BCW77] and by Lawler and Labetoulle [LL78]. The second phase uses the solution of this *LP* problem and produces an optimal preemptive schedule.

Let $x_{ij} \in [0, 1]$ denote a part of T_j processed on P_i. The *LP* formulation is as follows:

$$\text{Minimize} \quad C_{\max} \tag{5.1.23}$$

$$\text{subject to} \quad C_{\max} - \sum_{j=1}^{n} p_{ij} x_{ij} \geq 0, \quad i = 1, 2, \cdots, m \tag{5.1.24}$$

$$C_{\max} - \sum_{i=1}^{m} p_{ij} x_{ij} \geq 0, \quad j = 1, 2, \cdots, n \tag{5.1.25}$$

$$\sum_{i=1}^{m} x_{ij} = 1, \quad j = 1, 2, \cdots, n. \tag{5.1.26}$$

Solving the above problem, we get $C_{\max} = C_{\max}^*$ and optimal values x_{ij}^*. However, we do not know how to schedule the task parts, i.e. how to assign these parts to processors in time. A schedule may be constructed in the following way. Let $T = [t_{ij}^*]$ be the $m \times n$ matrix defined by $t_{ij}^* = p_{ij} x_{ij}^*$, $i = 1, 2, \cdots, m$, $j = 1, 2, \cdots, n$. Notice that the elements of T reflect optimal values of processing times of particular tasks on the processors. The jth column of T corresponding to task T_j will be called *critical* if $\sum_{i=1}^{m} t_{ij}^* = C_{\max}^*$. By Y we denote an $m \times m$ diagonal matrix whose element y_{kk} is the total idle time on processor P_k, i.e. $y_{kk} = C_{\max}^* - \sum_{j=1}^{n} t_{kj}^*$. Columns of Y correspond to dummy tasks. Let $V = [T,Y]$ be an $m \times (n+m)$ matrix. Now set $\mathcal{U}$ containing m positive elements of matrix V can be defined as having exactly one element from each critical column and at most one element from other columns, and having exactly one element from each row. We see that $\mathcal{U}$ corresponds to a task set which may be processed in parallel in an optimal schedule. Thus, it may be used to construct a partial schedule of length $\delta > 0$. An optimal schedule is then produced as the union of the partial schedules. This procedure is summarized in Algorithm 5.1.16 [LL78].

Algorithm 5.1.16 *Construction of an optimal schedule corresponding to LP solution for $R \mid pmtn \mid C_{\max}$.*
begin
$C := C_{\max}^*;$
while $C > 0$ **do**
   begin
   Construct set $\mathcal{U};$
      -- thus a subset of tasks to be processed in a partial schedule has been chosen
   $v_{\min} := \min_{v_{ij} \in \mathcal{U}} \{v_{ij}\};$

   $v_{\max} := \max_{j \in \{j' \mid v_{ij'} \notin \mathcal{U} \text{ for } i = 1, \cdots, m\}} \{\sum_i v_{ij}\};$

   if $C - v_{\min} \geq v_{\max}$
   then $\delta := v_{\min}$
   else $\delta := C - v_{\max};$
      -- the length of the partial schedule is equal to δ
   $C := C - \delta;$
   for each $v_{ij} \in \mathcal{U}$ **do** $v_{ij} := v_{ij} - \delta;$
      -- matrix V is changed;
      -- note that due to the way δ is defined, the elements of V can never become negative
   end;
end;

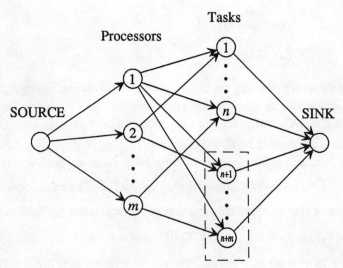

Figure 5.1.17 *Finding set $\mathcal{U}$ by the network flow approach.*

The proof of correctness of the algorithm can be found in [LL78].

Now we only need an algorithm that finds set $\mathcal{U}$ for a given matrix V. One of the possible algorithms is based on the network flow approach. In this case the network has m nodes corresponding to machines (rows of V) and $n+m$ nodes corresponding to tasks (columns of V), cf. Figure 5.1.17. A node i from the first group is connected by an arc to a node j of the second group if and only if $v_{ij} > 0$. Arc flows are constrained by b from below and by $c = 1$ from above, where the value of b is 1 for arcs joining the source with processor-nodes and critical task nodes with the sink, and $b = 0$ for the other arcs. Obviously, finding a feasible flow in this network is equivalent to finding set $\mathcal{U}$. The following example illustrates the second phase of the described method.

(a)

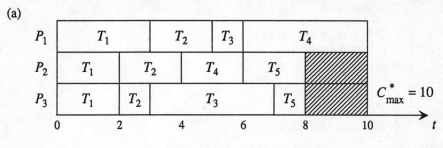

(b)

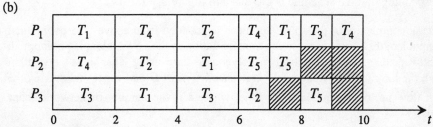

Figure 5.1.18 (a) *A linear programming solution for an instance of* $R \mid pmtn \mid C_{max}$, (b) *an optimal schedule.*

Example 5.1.17 Suppose that for a certain scheduling problem a linear programming solution of the two phase method has the form given in Figure 5.1.18(a). An optimal schedule is then constructed in the following way. First, matrix V is calculated.

$$
V^* = \begin{array}{c} \\ P_1 \\ P_2 \\ P_3 \\ \\ \end{array}
\begin{array}{ccccc} T_1\, T_2\, T_3\, T_4\, T_5 & & T_6\, T_7\, T_8 \\
\left[\begin{array}{ccccc} \underline{3} & 2 & 1 & 4 & 0 \\ 2 & 2 & 0 & \underline{2} & 2 \\ 2 & 1 & \underline{4} & 0 & 1 \end{array}\right] & \left[\begin{array}{ccc} 0 & 0 & 0 \\ 0 & 2 & 0 \\ 0 & 0 & 2 \end{array}\right] \\
7\ 5\ 5\ 6\ 3 & 0\ 2\ 2 \end{array}
$$

Then elements constituting set $\mathcal{U}$ are chosen according to Algorithm 5.1.16, as depicted above. The value of a partial schedule length is $\delta = 2$. Next, the while-loop of Algorithm 5.1.16 is repeated yielding the following sequence of matrices V_i.

$$
V_1 = \left[\begin{array}{ccccc} 1 & 2 & 1 & \underline{4} & 0 \\ 2 & \underline{2} & 0 & 0 & 2 \\ \underline{2} & 1 & 2 & 0 & 1 \end{array}\right] \left[\begin{array}{ccc} 0 & 0 & 0 \\ 0 & 2 & 0 \\ 0 & 0 & 2 \end{array}\right]
$$

$$V_2 = \begin{bmatrix} 1 & 2 & 1 & 2 & 0 \\ 2 & 0 & 0 & 0 & 2 \\ 0 & 1 & 2 & 0 & 1 \end{bmatrix} \begin{bmatrix} 0 & 0 & 0 \\ 0 & 2 & 0 \\ 0 & 0 & 2 \end{bmatrix}$$

$$V_3 = \begin{bmatrix} 1 & 0 & 1 & 2 & 0 \\ 0 & 0 & 0 & 0 & 2 \\ 0 & 1 & 0 & 0 & 1 \end{bmatrix} \begin{bmatrix} 0 & 0 & 0 \\ 0 & 2 & 0 \\ 0 & 0 & 2 \end{bmatrix}$$

$$V_4 = \begin{bmatrix} 1 & 0 & 1 & 1 & 0 \\ 0 & 0 & 0 & 0 & 1 \\ 0 & 0 & 0 & 0 & 1 \end{bmatrix} \begin{bmatrix} 0 & 0 & 0 \\ 0 & 2 & 0 \\ 0 & 0 & 2 \end{bmatrix}$$

$$V_5 = \begin{bmatrix} 0 & 0 & 1 & 1 & 0 \\ 0 & 0 & 0 & 0 & 0 \\ 0 & 0 & 0 & 0 & 1 \end{bmatrix} \begin{bmatrix} 0 & 0 & 0 \\ 0 & 2 & 0 \\ 0 & 0 & 1 \end{bmatrix}$$

$$V_6 = \begin{bmatrix} 0 & 0 & 0 & 1 & 0 \\ 0 & 0 & 0 & 0 & 0 \\ 0 & 0 & 0 & 0 & 0 \end{bmatrix} \begin{bmatrix} 0 & 0 & 0 \\ 0 & 1 & 0 \\ 0 & 0 & 1 \end{bmatrix}$$

A corresponding optimal schedule is presented in Figure 5.1.18(b). □

The overall complexity of the above approach is bounded from above by a polynomial in the input length. This is because the transformation to the LP problem is polynomial, and the LP problem may be solved in polynomial time using Khachiyan's algorithm [Kha79]; the loop in Algorithm 5.1.16 is repeated at most $O(mn)$ times and solving the network flow problem requires $O(z^3)$ time, where z is the number of network nodes [Kar74].

Problem $R \mid pmtn, prec \mid C_{\max}$

If dependent tasks are considered, i.e. in the case $R \mid pmtn, prec \mid C_{\max}$, linear programming problems similar to those discussed in (5.1.14)-(5.1.15) or (5.1.23)-(5.1.26) and based on the activity network presentation, can be formulated. For example, in the latter formulation one defines x_{ijk} as a part of task T_j processed on processor P_i in the main set S_k. Solving the LP problem for x_{ijk}, one then applies Algorithm 5.1.16 for each main set. If the activity network is uniconnected, an optimal schedule is constructed in this way, otherwise only an approximate schedule is obtained.

We complete this chapter by remarking that introduction of ready times into the model considered so far is equivalent to the problem of minimizing maximum lateness. We will consider this type of problems in Section 5.3.

5.2 Minimizing Mean Flow Time

5.2.1 Identical Processors

Problem $P \mid\mid \Sigma C_j$

In the case of identical processors and equal ready times preemptions are not profitable from the viewpoint of the value of the mean flow time [McN59]. Thus, we can limit ourselves to considering nonpreemptive schedules only.

When analyzing the nature of criterion ΣC_j, one might expect that, as in the case of one processor (cf. Section 4.2), by assigning tasks in nondecreasing order of their processing times the mean flow time will be minimized. In fact, a proper generalization of this simple rule leads to an optimization algorithm for $P \mid\mid \Sigma C_j$ (Conway et al. [CMM67]). It is as follows.

Algorithm 5.2.1 *SPT rule for problem* $P \mid\mid \Sigma C_j$ [CMM67].
begin
Order tasks on list L in nondecreasing order of their processing times;
while $L \neq \varnothing$ **do**
  begin
  Take the m first tasks from the list (if any) and assign these tasks arbitrarily to the
    m different processors;
  Remove the assigned tasks from list L;
  end;
Process tasks assigned to each processor in *SPT* order;
end;

The complexity of the algorithm is obviously $O(n\log n)$.

In this context let us also mention that introducing different ready times makes the problem strongly *NP*-hard even for the case of one processor (see Section 4.2 and [LRKB77]). Also, if we introduce different weights, then the 2-processor problem without release times, $P2 \mid\mid \Sigma w_j C_j$, is already *NP*-hard [BCS74].

Problem $P \mid prec \mid \Sigma C_j$

Let us now pass to the case of dependent tasks. Here, $P \mid out\text{-}tree, p_j = 1 \mid \Sigma C_j$ is solved by an adaptation of Algorithm 5.1.11 (Hu's algorithm) to the out-tree case [Ros–], and $P2 \mid prec, p_j = 1 \mid \Sigma C_j$ is strongly *NP*-hard [LRK78]. In the case of arbitrary processing times recent results by Du et al. [DLY91] indicate that even simplest precedence constraints result in computational hardness of the problem. That is problem $P2 \mid chains \mid \Sigma C_j$ is already *NP*-hard in the strong sense. On the other hand, it was also proved in [DLY91] that preemption cannot reduce the mean weighted flow time for a set of chains. Together with the last result this implies that problem $P2 \mid chains, pmtn \mid \Sigma C_j$ is also NP-hard in the strong sense. Unfortunately, no approximation algorithms for these problems are evaluated from their worst-case behavior point of view.

5.2.2 Uniform and Unrelated Processors

The results of Section 5.2.1 also indicate that scheduling dependent tasks on uniform or unrelated processors is an NP-hard problem in general. No approximation algorithms have been investigated either. Thus, we will not consider this subject.

On the other hand, in the case of independent tasks, preemptions may be worthwhile, thus we have to treat nonpreemptive and preemptive scheduling separately.

Problem $Q \mid \mid \Sigma C_j$

Let us start with uniform processors and nonpreemptive schedules. In this case the flow time has to take into account processor speed; so the flow time of task $T_{i[k]}$ processed in the kth position on processor P_i is defined as $F_{i[k]} = (1/b_i)\sum_{j=1}^{k} p_{i[j]}$. Let us denote by n_i the number of tasks processed on processor P_i. Thus, $n = \sum_{i=1}^{m} n_i$. The mean flow time is then given by

$$\overline{F} = \frac{\sum_{i=1}^{m} \frac{1}{b_i} \sum_{k=1}^{n_i} (n_i - k + 1)p_{i[k]}}{n}. \tag{5.2.1}$$

It is easy to see that the numerator in the above formula is the sum of n terms each of which is the product of a processing time and one of the following coefficients:

$$\frac{1}{b_1}n_1, \frac{1}{b_1}(n_1-1), \cdots, \frac{1}{b_1}, \frac{1}{b_2}n_2, \frac{1}{b_2}(n_2-1), \cdots, \frac{1}{b_2}, \cdots, \frac{1}{b_m}n_m, \frac{1}{b_m}(n_m-1), \cdots, \frac{1}{b_m}.$$

It is known from [CMM67] that such a sum is minimized by matching n smallest coefficients in nondecreasing order with processing times in nonincreasing order. An $O(n\log n)$ implementation of this rule has been given by Horowitz and Sahni [HS76].

Problem $Q \mid pmtn \mid \Sigma C_j$

In the case of preemptive scheduling, it is possible to show that there exists an optimal schedule for $Q \mid pmtn \mid \Sigma C_j$ in which $C_j \leq C_k$ if $p_j < p_k$. On the basis of this observation, the following algorithm has been proposed by Gonzalez [Gon77].

Algorithm 5.2.2 *Algorithm by Gonzalez for $Q \mid pmtn \mid \Sigma C_j$ [Gon77].*
begin
Order processors in nonincreasing order of their processing speed factors;
Order tasks in nondecreasing order of their standard processing times;
for $j = 1$ **to** n **do**

```
begin
    Schedule task T_j to be completed as early as possible, preempting when necessary;
        -- tasks will create a staircase pattern "jumping" to a faster processor
        -- whenever a shorter task has been finished
    end;
end;
```

The complexity of this algorithm is $O(n \log n + mn)$. An example of its application is given in Figure 5.2.1.

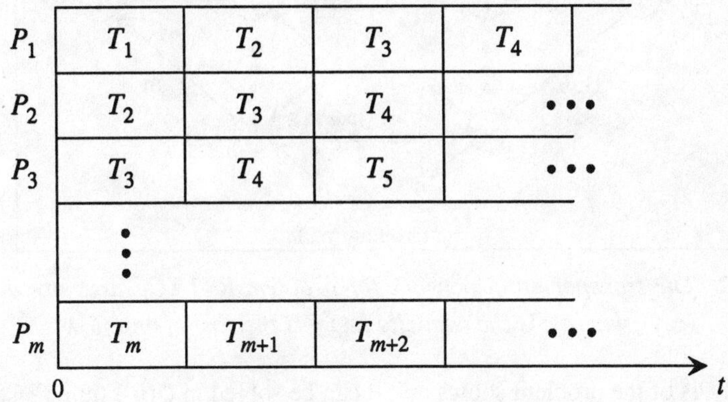

Figure 5.2.1 *An example of the application of Algorithm 5.2.2.*

Problem $R \| \Sigma C_j$

Let us now turn to the case of unrelated processors and consider problem $R \| \Sigma C_j$. An approach to its solution is based on the observation that task $T_j \in \{T_1, \cdots, T_n\}$ processed on processor $P_i \in \{P_1, \cdots, P_m\}$ as the last task contributes its processing time p_{ij} to $\bar{F}$. The same task processed in the last but one position contributes $2p_{ij}$, and so on [BCS74]. This reasoning allows one to construct an $(mn) \times n$ matrix Q presenting contributions of particular tasks processed in different positions on different processors to the value of $\bar{F}$:

$$Q = \begin{bmatrix} [p_{ij}] \\ 2[p_{ij}] \\ \cdot \\ \cdot \\ \cdot \\ n[p_{ij}] \end{bmatrix}$$

The problem is now to choose n elements from matrix Q such that
- exactly one element is taken from each column,
- at most one element is taken from each row,
- the sum of selected elements is minimum.

We see that the above problem is a variant of the assignment problem (cf. [Law76]), which may be solved in a natural way via the transportation problem. The corresponding transportation network is shown in Figure 5.2.2.

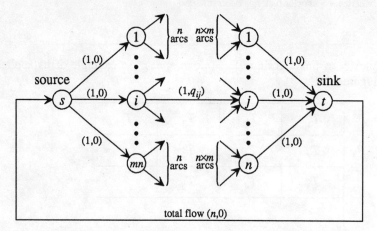

Figure 5.2.2 *The transportation network for problem R || ΣC$_j$: arcs are denoted by (c, y), where c is the capacity and y is the cost of unit flow*

Careful analysis of the problem shows that it can be solved in $O(n^3)$ time [BCS74]. The following example illustrates this technique.

Example 5.2.3 Let us consider the following instance of problem $R || \Sigma C_j$: $n = 5$, $m = 3$, and matrix p of processing times

$$p = \begin{bmatrix} 3 & 2 & 4 & 3 & 1 \\ 4 & 3 & 1 & 2 & 1 \\ 2 & 4 & 5 & 3 & 4 \end{bmatrix}.$$

Using this data matrix Q is constructed as follows:

$$Q = \begin{bmatrix}
3 & 2 & 4 & 3 & 1 \\
4 & 3 & 1 & 2 & 1 \\
2 & 4 & 5 & 3 & 4 \\
6 & 4 & 8 & 6 & 2 \\
8 & 6 & 2 & 4 & 2 \\
4 & 8 & 10 & 6 & 8 \\
9 & 6 & 12 & 9 & 3 \\
12 & 9 & 3 & 6 & 3 \\
6 & 12 & 15 & 9 & 12 \\
12 & 8 & 16 & 12 & 4 \\
16 & 12 & 4 & 8 & 4 \\
8 & 16 & 20 & 12 & 16 \\
15 & 10 & 20 & 15 & 5 \\
20 & 15 & 5 & 10 & 5 \\
10 & 20 & 25 & 15 & 20
\end{bmatrix}.$$

On the basis of this matrix a network as shown in Figure 5.2.2 is constructed. Solving the transportation problem results in the selection of the underlined elements of matrix Q. They correspond to the schedule shown in Figure 5.2.3. $\square$

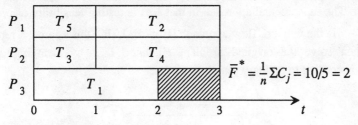

Figure 5.2.3 *An optimal schedule for Example 5.2.3.*

To end this section, we mention that the complexity of problem $R \mid pmtn \mid \Sigma C_j$ is still an open question.

5.3 Minimizing Due Date Involving Criteria

5.3.1 Identical Processors

In Section 4.3 we have seen that single processor problems with due date optimization criteria are *NP*-hard in most cases. In the following we will concentrate on minimization of L_{max} criterion. It seems to be quite natural that in this case the general rule should be to schedule tasks according to their earliest due dates (*EDD*-rule, cf. Section 4.3.1). However, this simple rule of Jackson [Jac55] produces optimal schedules under very restricted assumptions only. In other cases more sophisticated algorithms are necessary, or the problems are *NP*-hard.

Problem $P \mid\mid L_{max}$

Let us start with nonpreemptive scheduling of independent tasks. Taking into account simple transformations between scheduling problems (cf. Section 3.4) and the relationship between the C_{max} and L_{max} criteria, we see that all the problems that are *NP*-hard under the C_{max} criterion remain *NP*-hard under the L_{max} criterion. Hence, for example, $P2 \mid\mid L_{max}$ is *NP*-hard. On the other hand, unit processing times of tasks make the problem easy, and $P \mid p_j=1, r_j \mid L_{max}$ can be solved by an obvious application of the *EDD* rule [Bla77]. Moreover, problem $P \mid p_j=p, r_j \mid L_{max}$ can be solved in polynomial time by an extension of the single processor algorithm (see Section 4.3.1; see also [GJST81]). Unfortunately very little is known about the worst-case behavior of approximation algorithms for the *NP*-hard problems in question.

Problem $P \mid pmtn \mid L_{\max}$

The preemptive mode of processing makes the solution of the scheduling problem much easier. The fundamental approach in that area is testing feasibility of problem $P \mid pmtn, r_j, \tilde{d}_j \mid -$ via the network flow approach [Hor74]. Using this approach repetitively, one can then solve the original problem $P \mid pmtn \mid L_{\max}$ by changing due dates (deadlines) according to a binary search procedure.

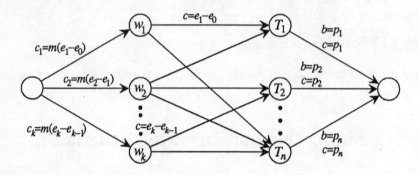

Figure 5.3.1 *Network corresponding to problem $P \mid pmtn, r_j, \tilde{d}_j \mid -$.*

Let us now describe Horn's approach for testing feasibility of problem $P \mid pmtn, r_j, \tilde{d}_j \mid -$, i.e. deciding whether or not for a given set of ready times and deadlines there exists a schedule with no late task. Let the values of ready times and deadlines of an instance of $P \mid pmtn, r_j, \tilde{d}_j \mid -$ be ordered on a list in such a way that $e_0 < e_1 < \cdots < e_k$, $k \le 2n$, where e_i stands for some r_j or $\tilde{d}_j$. We construct a network that has two sets of nodes, besides source and sink (cf. Figure 5.3.1). The first set corresponds to time intervals in a schedule, i.e. node w_i corresponds to interval $[e_{i-1}, e_i]$, $i = 1, 2, \cdots, k$. The second set corresponds to the task set. The capacity of an arc joining the source of the network to node w_i is equal to $m(e_i - e_{i-1})$ and thus corresponds to the total processing capacity of m processors in this interval. If task T_j could be processed in interval $[e_{i-1}, e_i]$ (because of its ready time and deadline) then w_i is joined to T_j by an arc of capacity $e_i - e_{i-1}$. Node T_j is joined to the sink of the network by an arc with capacity equal to p_j and with a lower bound on arc flow which is also equal to p_j. We see that finding a feasible flow pattern corresponds to constructing a feasible schedule and this test can be made in $O(n^3)$ time (cf. Section 2.3.3). A schedule is constructed on the basis of flow values on arcs between interval and task nodes. Let us consider the following example.

Example 5.3.1 Let $n = 5$, $p = [5, 2, 3, 3, 1]$, $r = [2, 0, 1, 0, 2]$, and $d = [8, 2, 4, 5, 8]$. The corresponding network is shown in Figure 5.3.2(a), and a feasible flow pattern is depicted in Figure 5.3.2(b). On the basis of this flow the feasible schedule shown in Figure 5.3.2(c) is constructed. □

(a)

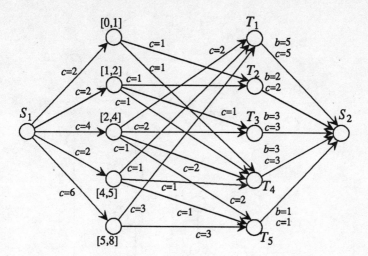

(b)

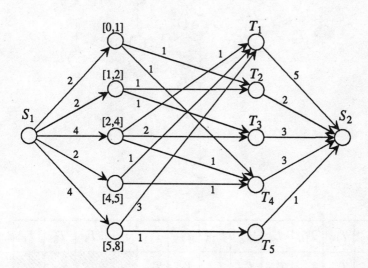

(c)

| P_1 | T_2 | T_2 | T_3 | | T_1 | T_1 | |
| P_2 | T_4 | T_3 | T_4 | T_1 | T_4 | T_5 | |

0   1   2   4   5   8 t

Figure 5.3.2 *Finding a feasible schedule via network flow approach (Example 5.3.1)*

    (a) *a corresponding network,*

    (b) *a feasible flow pattern,*

    (c) *a schedule.*

(a)

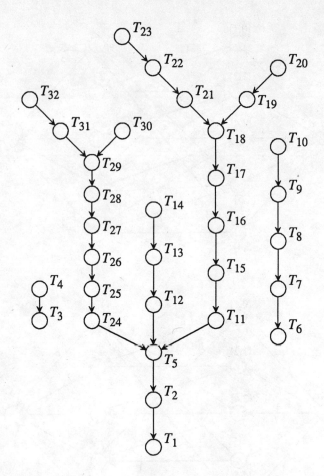

(b)

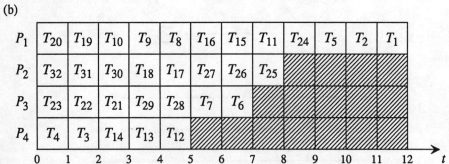

Figure 5.3.3 *An example of the application of Algorithm 5.3.2; n = 32, m = 4, d = [16, 20, 4, 3, 15, 14, 17, 6, 6, 4, 10, 8, 9, 7, 10, 9, 10, 8, 2, 3, 6, 5, 4, 11, 12, 9, 10, 8, 7, 5, 3, 5]*

(a) *the task set,*

(b) *an optimal schedule.*

In the next step a binary search can be conducted on the optimal value of L_{max}, with each trial value of L_{max} inducing deadlines which are checked for feasibility by means of the above network flow computation. This procedure can be implemented to solve problem $P \mid pmtn, r_j \mid L_{max}$ in $O(n^3 \min\{n^2, \log n + \log \max\{p_j\}\})$ time [LLLRK84].

Problem $P \mid prec, p_j = 1 \mid L_{max}$

Let us now pass to dependent tasks. A general approach in this case consists in assigning modified due dates to tasks, depending on the number and due dates of their successors. Of course, the way in which modified due dates are calculated depends on the parameters of the problem in question. When scheduling nonpreemptable tasks on a multiple processor system only unit processing times can result in polynomial time scheduling algorithms. Let us start with in-tree precedence constraints and assume that if $T_i < T_j$ then $i > j$. The following algorithm minimizes L_{max} (isucc(j) denotes the immediate successor of T_j) [Bru76b].

Algorithm 5.3.2 *Algorithm by Brucker for $P \mid in\text{-}tree, p_j = 1 \mid L_{max}$* [Bru76b].
```
begin
```
$d_1^* := 1 - d_1;$
```
for k = 2 step 1 until n do
    begin
```
Calculate modified due date of T_k according to the formula

$$d_k^* := \max\{1 + d_{isucc(k)}^*, 1 - d_k\};$$
```
    end;
```
Schedule tasks in nonincreasing order of their modified due dates subject to precedence
    constraints;
```
end;
```

This algorithm can be implemented to run in $O(n \log n)$ time. An example of its application is given in Figure 5.3.3. Surprisingly out-tree precedence constraints result in the *NP*-hardness of the problem [BGJ77].

However, when we limit ourselves to two processors, a different way of computing modified due dates can be proposed which allows one to solve the problem in $O(n^2)$ time [GJ76]. In the algorithm below $g(k, d_i^*)$ is the number of successors of T_k having modified due dates not greater than d_i^*.

Algorithm 5.3.3 *Algorithm by Garey and Johnson for problem $P2 \mid prec, p_j = 1 \mid L_{max}$* [GJ76].
```
begin
```
$Z := T;$
```
while Z ≠ ∅ do
    begin
```
Choose $T_k \in Z$ which is not yet assigned a modified due date and all of whose
    successors have been assigned modified due dates;
Calculate a modified due date of T_k as:

$$d_k^* := \min\{d_k, \min\{(d_i^* - \lceil \tfrac{1}{2}g(k, d_i^*) \rceil) \mid T_i \in \text{succ}(T_k)\}\};$$

$$\mathcal{Z} := \mathcal{Z} - \{T_k\};$$

end;

Schedule tasks in nondecreasing order of their modified due dates subject to precedence constraints;

end;

For $m > 2$ this algorithm may not lead to optimal schedules, as demonstrated in the example in Figure 5.3.4. However, the algorithm can be generalized to cover the case of different ready times too, but the running time is then $O(n^3)$ [GJ77] and this is as much as we can get in nonpreemptive scheduling.

Problem $P \mid pmtn, prec \mid L_{\max}$

Preemptions allow one to solve problems with arbitrary processing times. In [Law82b] algorithms have been presented that are preemptive counterparts of Algorithms 5.3.2 and 5.3.3 and the one presented by Garey and Johnson [GJ77] for nonpreemptive scheduling and unit-length tasks. Hence problems $P \mid pmtn, in\text{-}tree \mid L_{\max}$, $P2 \mid pmtn$, $prec \mid L_{\max}$ and $P2 \mid pmtn, prec, r_j \mid L_{\max}$ are solvable in polynomial time. Algorithms for these problems employ essentially the same techniques for dealing with precedence constraints as the corresponding algorithms for unit-length tasks. However, the algorithms are more complex and will not be presented here.

5.3.2 Uniform and Unrelated Processors

Problem $Q \mid\mid L_{\max}$

From the considerations of Section 5.3.1 we see that nonpreemptive scheduling to minimize $L_{\max}$ is in general a hard problem. Only for the problem $Q \mid p_j = 1 \mid L_{\max}$ a polynomial time optimization algorithm is known. This problem can be solved via a transportation problem formulation as in (5.1.16)-(5.1.19), where now $c_{ijk} = k/b_i - d_j$. Thus, from now on we will concentrate on preemptive scheduling.

Problem $Q \mid pmtn \mid L_{\max}$

We will consider uniform processors first. One of the most interesting algorithms in that area has been presented for problem $Q \mid pmtn, r_j \mid L_{\max}$ by Federgruen and Groenevelt [FG86]. It is a generalization of the network flow approach to the feasibility testing of problem $P \mid pmtn, r_j, \tilde{d}_j \mid -$ described above. The feasibility testing procedure for problem $Q \mid pmtn, r_j, \tilde{d}_j \mid -$ uses tripartite network formulation of the scheduling problem, where the first set of nodes corresponds to tasks, the second corresponds to processor-interval (period) combination and the third corresponds to interval nodes.

The source is connected to each task node, the arc to the jth node having capacity p_j, $j =$ 1, 2,$\cdots$,n. A task node is connected to all processor-interval nodes for all intervals during which the task is available. All arcs leading to a processor-interval node that corresponds to a processor of type r (processors of the same speed may be represented by one node only) and an interval of length τ, have capacity $(b_r - b_{r+1})\tau$, with the con-

(a)

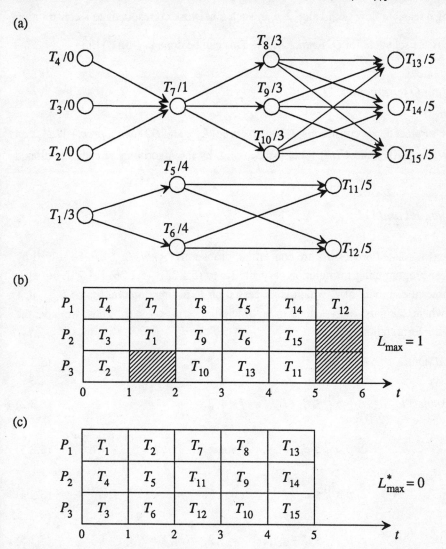

(b)

(c)

Figure 5.3.4 *Unoptimal schedules generated by Algorithm 5.3.3 for m=3, n–15, and all due dates $d_j = 5$*

(a) *a task set (all tasks are denoted by T_j^*/d_j),*

(b) *a schedule constructed by Algorithm 5.3.3,*

(c) *an optimal schedule.*

vention $b_{m+1} = 0$. Every node (w_i, r) corresponding to processor type r and interval w_i of length τ_i, $i = 1, 2, \cdots, k$, is connected to interval node w_i and has capacity $\sum_{j=1}^{r} m_j(b_r - b_{r+1})\tau_i$, where m_j denotes the number of processors of the jth type (cf. Figure 5.3.5). Finally, all interval nodes are connected to the sink with uncapacitated arcs. Finding a feasible flow with value $\sum_{j=1}^{n} p_j$ in such a network corresponds to a construction of a feasible schedule for $Q \mid pmtn, r_j, \tilde{d}_j \mid -$. This can be done in $O(mn^3)$ time.

Problem $Q \mid pmtn, prec \mid L_{max}$

In case of precedence constraints, $Q2 \mid pmtn, prec \mid L_{max}$ and $Q2 \mid pmtn, prec, r_j \mid L_{max}$ can be solved in $O(n^2)$ and $O(n^6)$ time, respectively, by the algorithms already mentioned [Law82b].

Problem $R \mid pmtn \mid L_{max}$

As far as unrelated processors are concerned, problem $R \mid pmtn \mid L_{max}$ can be solved by an linear programming formulation very similar to (5.1.23) - (5.1.26) [LL78], but now x_{ij}^k denotes the amount of T_j which is processed on P_i in time interval $[d_{k-1} + L_{max}, d_k + L_{max}]$ where due dates are assumed to be ordered, $d_1 < d_2 < \cdots < d_n$. Thus, we have the following formulation:

$$\textit{Minimize} \quad L_{max} \tag{5.3.1}$$

$$\textit{subject to} \quad \sum_{i=1}^{m} p_{ij} x_{ij}^{(1)} \leq d_1 + L_{max}, \quad j = 1, 2, \cdots, n \tag{5.3.2}$$

$$\sum_{i=1}^{m} p_{ij} x_{ij}^{(k)} \leq d_k - d_{k-1}, \quad j = k, k+1, \cdots, n, \; k = 2, 3, \cdots, n \tag{5.3.3}$$

$$\sum_{j=1}^{n} p_{ij} x_{ij}^{(1)} \leq d_1 + L_{max}, \quad i = 1, 2, \cdots, m \tag{5.3.4}$$

$$\sum_{j=k}^{n} p_{ij} x_{ij}^{(k)} \leq d_k - d_{k-1}, \quad i = 1, 2, \cdots, m, \; k = 2, 3, \cdots, n \tag{5.3.5}$$

$$\sum_{i=1}^{m} \sum_{k=1}^{j} x_{ij}^{(k)} = 1 \qquad j = 1, 2, \cdots, n. \tag{5.3.6}$$

Solving the *LP* problem we obtain n matrices $T^{(k)} = [t_{ij}^{(k)*}]$, $k = 1, \cdots, n$; then an optimal solution is constructed by an application of Algorithm 5.1.16 to each matrix separately.

In this context let us also mention that the case when precedence constraints form a unconnected activity network, can also be solved via the same modification of the *LP* problem as described for the C_{max} criterion [Slo81].

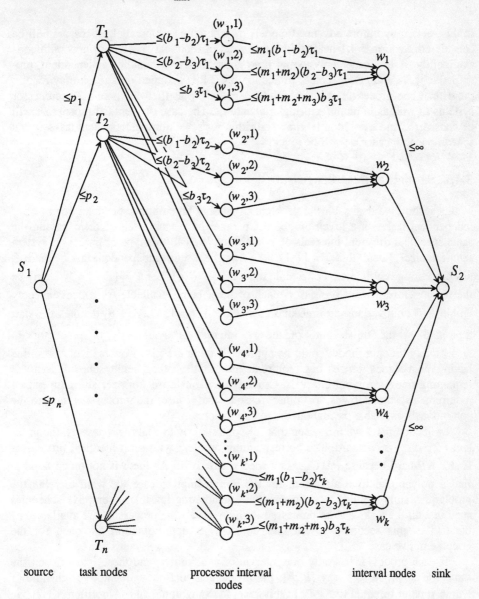

Figure 5.3.5 *A network corresponding to scheduling problem $Q \mid pmtn, r_j, d_j \mid -$ for three processor types.*

5.4 Other Models

In this section two more advanced models of scheduling on parallel processors will be considered. Section 5.4.1 deals with processors of identical speeds but noncontinuous availability. A low order polynomial time algorithm for scheduling independent, preemptable tasks will be presented. In Section 5.4.2 it is assumed that a task may require more than one processor at a time. Such a model is justified in some microprocessor systems as well as in manufacturing applications. The case of identical processors will be considered and a polynomial time algorithm for scheduling independent tasks with a schedule length criterion will be given.

5.4.1 Semi-Identical Processors

In this section we deal with the problem of finding preemptive schedules for a set of independent tasks on a given number of parallel processors each of them having the same speed but different intervals of availability. We call this type of processor system *semi-identical*. Recall that $\mathcal{T} = \{T_j \mid j = 1, \cdots, n\}$ be a set of independent tasks, where T_j has processing requirements of p_j time units $(j = 1, \cdots, n)$. Let $\mathcal{P} = \{P_i \mid i = 1, \cdots, m\}$ be the set of semi-identical processors each of them being available for processing only within $N(i)$ nonoverlapping time intervals $[B_i^r, F_i^r]$, $r = 1, \cdots, N(i)$. B_i^r denotes the start time and F_i^r the finish time of the rth interval of availability of processor P_i, respectively. Such a model could be applied, if there are given two sets of tasks, one having preassigned processing requirements and the other being scheduled in the remaining free processing intervals. Other applications arise from certain maintenance requirements, breakdowns, or other reasons that cause the processors not to be continuously available throughout the planning horizon.

In Section 5.1.1 we have seen that for continuously available processors, the problem $P2 \mid\mid C_{\max}$ is *NP*-hard. The corresponding problem with semi-identical processors is also *NP*-hard because $P \mid\mid C_{\max}$ is a special case of it. As there is not much hope to find a polynomial time algorithm for the nonpreemptive case we want to relax the problem. Mainly we will be concerned with generating feasible preemptive schedules such that all the tasks can be processed in the intervals the processors are available. At the end of this section we will also consider an approximation approach for the nonpreemptive case.

If each processor has only one interval of availability, and these intervals are the same for all processors, say $[B, F]$, the problem is to find a preemptive schedule of length smaller or equal to $F - B$. In this case, McNaughton's rule (Algorithm 5.1.2) can be applied which generates schedules with at most $m - 1$ preemptions.

If each of the processors is available during an interval $[B, F_i]$, i.e. availability starts at the same time but not necessarily finishes at the same time (or vice versa) the problem is closely related to the minimum makespan problem for uniform processor systems (see Section 5.1.2). Assume that the processors are ordered according to nonincreasing finish times F_i. For $i = 1, \cdots, m$, the quantity F_i/F_m may now be interpreted as the *speed* of processor P_i in a uniform processor model. In analogy to the results of Gonzalez and Sahni [GS78] one can show that a feasible preemptive schedule with schedule length smaller than or equal to F_m, can be constructed in $O(n+m\log m)$ time inducing at most $2(m-1)$ preemptions, provided a feasible schedule exists. This schedule has then to be transformed into a feasible schedule of the original problem which causes some additional effort.

Next, following Schmidt [Sch84], we will present an $O(n+m\log m)$ algorithm for the general problem with arbitrary start and finish times. This algorithm generates at most $Q-1$ preemptions if the distribution of the intervals of processor availability satisfies a so-called staircase pattern, or at most $O(mQ)$ preemptions for arbitrary intervals, where $Q = \sum_{i=1}^{m} N(i)$.

First we assume that the processing intervals of all processors form a staircase pattern as shown in Figure 5.4.1. We will say that the system of m semi-identical processors has the property of a *staircase pattern* if all the intervals of availability of processor P_{i-1} cover all the intervals of availability of processor P_i. If we define the processing capacity of processor P_i in the rth interval by $PC_i^r := F_i^r - B_i^r$ and its total processing capacity by $PC_i = \sum_{r=1}^{N(i)} PC_i^r$ then the property of the staircase pattern implies $PC_i^r \le PC_{i-1}^r$ and $PC_i \le PC_{i-1}$ for $1 < i \le m$.

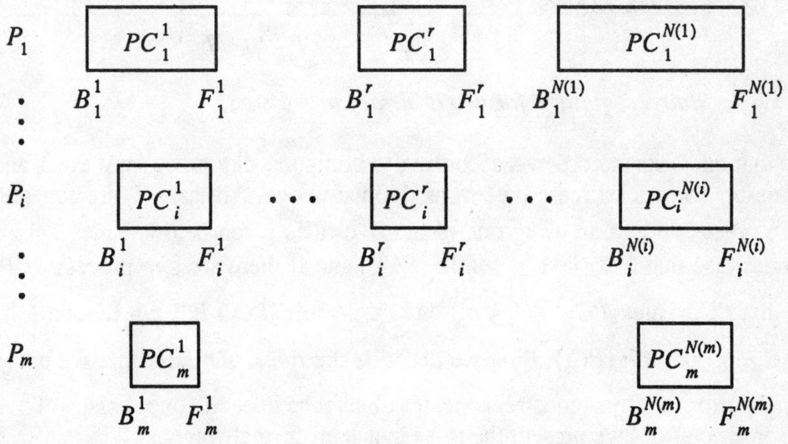

Figure 5.4.1 *Processor system satisfying a staircase pattern.*

Let us further assume that $n \ge m$; in case $n < m$ only the first n processors will be used to schedule the task set. Further discussions are based on the assumption that for the problem in question the following system of inequalities holds.

$$p_1 \le PC_1 \qquad (5.4.1-1)$$

$$p_1 + p_2 \le PC_1 + PC_2 \qquad (5.4.1-2)$$

$$\cdots$$

$$p_1 + p_2 + \cdots + p_{m-1} \le PC_1 + PC_2 + \cdots + PC_{m-1} \qquad (5.4.1\text{--m-1})$$

$$p_1 + p_2 + \cdots + p_n \le PC_1 + PC_2 + \cdots + PC_m \qquad (5.4.1\text{--m})$$

where

$$p_1 \ge p_2 \ge \cdots \ge p_n \ and \ PC_1 \ge PC_2 \ge \cdots \ge PC_m. \qquad (5.4.2)$$

Let us now regard two arbitrary processors P_k and P_l with $PC_k > PC_l$ as shown in Figure 5.4.2. Let Φ_k^a, Φ_k^b, and Φ_k^c denote the processing capacities of processor P_k in the intervals $[B_k^1, B_l^1]$, $[B_l^1, F_l^{N(l)}]$, and $[F_l^{N(l)}, F_k^{N(k)}]$, respectively. Then obviously, $PC_k = \Phi_k^a + \Phi_k^b + \Phi_k^c$.

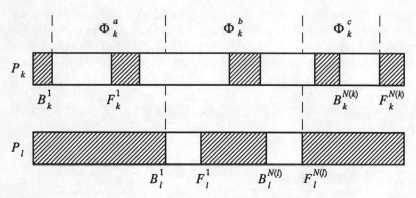

Figure 5.4.2 *Staircase pattern for two arbitrary processors.*

Assume that the tasks are ordered according to nonincreasing processing times and that the processors form a staircase pattern as defined above. All tasks T_j are scheduled in the given order one by one using one of the five rules given below. Rules 1-4 are applied in the case that $1 \le j < m$, $p_j > \min_i \{PC_i\}$, and if there are two processors P_k and P_l such that $PC_l = \max_i \{PC_i \mid PC_i < p_j\}$ and $PC_k = \min_i \{PC_i \mid PC_i \ge p_j\}$. Rule 5 is used if $m \le j \le n$ or $p_j \le \min_i \{PC_i\}$. First we describe the rules, and after that we prove that their application always constructs a feasible schedule, if one exists. To avoid cumbersome notations we present the rules in a semi-formal way.

Rule 1. *Condition*: $p_j = PC_k$.

Schedule task T_j on processor P_k such that all the intervals $[B_k^r, F_k^r]$, $r = 1, \cdots, N(k)$, are completely filled; combine processors P_k and P_l to form a *composite processor*, denoted again by P_k, which is available in all free processing intervals of the original processor P_l, i.e. define $PC_k = PC_l$ and $PC_l = 0$.

Rule 2. *Condition*: $p_j - PC_l > \max\{\Phi_k^a, \Phi_k^c\}$ and $p_j - \Phi_k^b \ge \min\{\Phi_k^a, \Phi_k^c\}$.

Schedule task T_j on processor P_k in its free processing intervals within $[B_l^1, F_l^{N(l)}]$. If Φ_k^a (Φ_k^c) is minimum use all the free processing intervals of P_k in $[B_k^1, B_l^1]$ ($[F_l^{N(l)}, F_k^{N(k)}]$) to schedule T_j, and schedule the remaining processing requirements of that task (if there is any) in the free processing intervals of P_k within $[F_l^{N(l)}, F_k^{N(k)}]$ ($[B_k^1, B_l^1]$) from left to right (right to left) such that the rth processing interval is completely filled with T_j before the interval $r+1^{st}$ ($r-1^{st}$) is used, respectively. Combine processors P_k and P_l to a composite processor P_k which is available in the remaining free processing intervals of the original processors P_k and P_l, i.e. define $PC_k = PC_k + PC_l - p_j$ and $PC_l = 0$.

Rule 3. *Condition*: $p_j - PC_l > \max\{\Phi_k^a, \Phi_k^c\}$ and $p_j - \Phi_k^b < \min\{\Phi_k^a, \Phi_k^c\}$.

If Φ_k^a (Φ_k^c) is minimum, schedule task T_j on processor P_k such that its free processing intervals in $[B_k^1, B_l^1]$ ($[F_l^{N(l)}, F_k^{N(k)}]$) are completely filled with T_j; further fill processor P_k in the intervals $[B_l^r, F_l^r]$, $r = 1, \cdots, N(l)$, completely with T_j and use the remaining processing capacity of P_k in the interval $[B_l^1, F_l^{N(l)}]$ to schedule task T_j with its remaining processing requirement such that T_j is scheduled from left to right (right to left) where the $r+1^{st}$ ($r-1^{st}$) interval is not used before the rth interval has been completely filled with T_j, respectively. After doing this there will be some time t in the interval $[B_l^1, F_l^{N(l)}]$ up to (after) this time task T_j is continuously scheduled on processor P_k. Time t always exists because $p_j - \min\{\Phi_k^a, \Phi_k^c\} < \Phi_k^b$. Now schedule T_j with its processing requirement which is scheduled after (before) t on processor P_l in the corresponding time intervals. Combine processors P_k and P_l to a composite processor P_k which is available in the remaining free processing intervals of the original processors P_k and P_l, i.e. define $PC_k = PC_k + PC_l - p_j$ and $PC_l = 0$.

Rule 4. *Condition*: $p_j - PC_l \leq \max\{\Phi_k^a, \Phi_k^c\}$.

Schedule task T_j on processor P_l such that all its intervals $[B_l^r, F_l^r]$, $r = 1, \cdots, N(l)$ are completely filled with T_j. If Φ_k^a (Φ_k^c) is maximum, schedule task T_j with its remaining processing requirement on processor P_k in the free processing intervals of $[B_k^1, B_l^1]$ ($[F_l^{N(l)}, F_k^{N(k)}]$) from left to right (right to left) such that the rth processing interval is completely filled with T_j before the $r+1^{st}$ ($r-1^{st}$) interval is used, respectively. Combine processors P_k and P_l to a composite processor P_k which is available in the remaining free processing intervals of the original processor P_k, i.e. define $PC_k = PC_k + PC_l - p_j$ and $PC_l = 0$.

Rule 5. *Condition*: remaining cases.

Schedule task T_j and the remaining tasks in any order in the remaining free processing intervals successively from left to right starting with processor P_k; switch to a processor P_i, $i < k$ only if the $i+1^{st}$ processor is already completely filled.

To show the optimality of rules 1-5 we first prove the following lemma.

Lemma 5.4.1 *After having scheduled a task T_j, $j \in \{1,\cdots,m-1\}$, on some processor P_k according to rules 1 or 2, or on P_k and P_l according to rules 3 or 4, the following observations are true:*

(1) *The remaining free processing intervals of processor P_k and P_l are disjoint.*

(2) *Combining processors P_k and P_l to a composite processor P_k results in a new stair-case pattern.*

(3) *If all inequalities in (5.4.1) and (5.4.2) hold before scheduling task T_j, the remaining processing requirements and processing capacities after scheduling T_j still satisfy inequalities (5.4.1) and (5.4.2).*

(4) *The number of completely filled or completely empty intervals equals $\sum_{i=1}^{m} N(i) - K$ where K is the number of only partially filled intervals, and $(K \le j < m)$.*

Proof. After scheduling task T_j according to rules 1-4 the remaining free processing intervals of processors P_k and P_l are disjoint; this follows from the description of the rules, and thus observation (1) is true.

After application of any of the four scheduling rules the composite processor has free processing capacities in all the intervals $[B_l^r, F_l^r]$. From this and from the fact that before scheduling task T_j the processors $P_1,\cdots,P_k$ and $P_{l+1},\cdots,P_m$ formed a staircase pattern, observation (2) follows.

In order to prove (3), suppose that tasks $T_1,\cdots,T_{z-1}$ are already scheduled, and consider scheduling of the next task, T_z. Suppose inequalities of (5.4.1) and (5.4.2) are true before T_z is scheduled. Notice that inequalities (5.4.2) do not depend on the way how tasks are scheduled. We want to show that (5.4.1) remains true after task T_z has been scheduled. Let PC_i^z denote the processing capacity of processor P_i after task T_z has been scheduled, and let T_{z+1} be scheduled immediately after T_z. We distinguish two cases.

Case 1: Task T_z is scheduled on processor P_1 with rules 1 or 2, or on processors P_1 and P_2 with rules 3 or 4. After scheduling task T_z processors P_1 and P_2 are combined to *composite processor* P_1 with processing capacity $PC_1^z = PC_1^{z-1} + PC_2^{z-1} - p_z$. Since inequalities (5.4.1) were satisfied before scheduling T_z we have $p_z + p_{z+1} \le PC_1^{z-1} + PC_2^{z-1} \le PC_1^z + p_z$ i.e. $p_{z+1} \le PC_1^z$, and the first inequality of (5.4.1) holds. The processing capacities of processors P_i, $2 < i \le m$, remain unchanged and thus inequalities (3) to (m) of (5.4.1) hold, too. We now change inequality number (q) of (5.4.1) to (q-1), $2 < q \le m$, renumber processor P_i by P_{i-1} for $i = 3,\cdots,m$, and introduce a dummy processor P_m with $PC_m = 0$. Thus we get a system of m processors and the remaining $n-z$ tasks satisfying the inequalities of (5.4.1).

Case 2: Task T_z is scheduled on processor P_k, $1 < k < m$ with rules 1 or 2, or on processors P_k and P_{k+1} with rules 3 or 4. After scheduling task T_z, processors P_k and P_{k+1} are combined to a composite processor P_k with free capacity $PC_k^z = PC_k^{z-1} + PC_{k+1}^{z-1} - p_z$. Because inequalities (1) to (m) of (5.4.1) were satisfied before scheduling T_z we have $\sum_{j=z}^{k+z} p_j \leq \sum_{i=1}^{k+1} PC_i^{z-1} \leq \sum_{i=1}^{k-1} PC_i^z + PC_k^z + p_z$, and together with $\sum_{j=z+1}^{k+z} p_j \leq \sum_{i=1}^{k-1} PC_i^z + PC_k^z$ inequality (k) follows. The processing capacities of processors P_i, $i \in \{1, \cdots, k-1, k+2, \cdots, m\}$, remain unchanged and thus the remaining inequalities also hold. Again we change the numbers of inequalities (q) of (5.4.1) to (q-1), $k+1 < q \leq m$, and renumber processor P_i to P_{i-1} for $i = k+2, \cdots, m$, and introduce a dummy processor P_m with $PC_m = 0$. The resulting system of m processors and $n-z$ tasks again satisfies the inequalities of (5.4.1).

Induction on the number of tasks proves that repeated application of rules 1-4 keeps inequalities of (5.4.1) satisfied and thus observation (3) of the lemma is proved.

It remains to show that observation (4) holds. Application of rule 1 on a task T_j fills all assigned intervals completely and does not increase the number of existing partially filled intervals. The use of rules 2-4 adds at most one only partially filled interval. After scheduling some task T_z, at most z intervals are only partially filled, and with $z \leq K$ observation (4) is true. $\square$

We are now ready to prove the following theorem. The proof is constructive and leads to an algorithm that solves our problem.

Theorem 5.4.2 *For a system of m semi-identical processors with staircase patterns of availability and a given set $\mathcal{T}$ of n tasks there will always be a feasible preemptive schedule if and only if all inequalities of (5.4.1) and (5.4.2) hold.*

Proof. To prove the theorem we assume that $p_j > \min_i \{PC_i\}$ for $j = 1, \cdots, m-1$; otherwise the theorem is always true if and only if the mth inequality of (5.4.1) holds, as can easily be seen. There always exists a feasible preemptive schedule for T_1. Now assume that the first z tasks have been scheduled feasibly according to rules 1-4. We show that T_{z+1} also can be scheduled feasibly:

(1) $1 < z < m$: after scheduling task T_z all inequalities of (5.4.1) and (5.4.2) hold according to Lemma 5.4.1. Then $p_{z+1} \leq PC_1^z$, hence task T_{z+1} can be scheduled feasibly on processor P_1.

(2) $m \leq z \leq n$: after scheduling the first $m-1$ tasks using rules 1-4, $m-1$ processors are completely filled with tasks. Since $PC_2^{z-1} = PC_3^{z-1} = \cdots = PC_m^{z-1} = 0$ and $PC_1^{z-1} \geq \sum_{j=z}^n p_j$, task T_z can be scheduled on processor P_1, and the remaining tasks can also be scheduled on this processor by means of rule 5. $\square$

The following algorithm makes appropriate use of the five scheduling rules.

Algorithm 5.4.3 *Algorithm by Schmidt [Sch84] for semi-identical processors.*
begin
Order the m largest tasks T_j according to nonincreasing processing times and schedule
    them in the given order;

```
for all i ∈ {1,···,m}  do  PCᵢ := ∑_{r=1}^{N(i)} PCᵢʳ;
repeat
    if j < m and pⱼ > min{PCᵢ}
                       i
    then
        begin
        Find processor Pₗ with PCₗ = max{PCᵢ | PCᵢ < pⱼ} and processor Pₖ with PCₖ
                                    i

            = min{PCᵢ | PCᵢ ≥ pⱼ};
              i

        if PCₖ = pⱼ
        then call rule 1
        else
            begin
            Calculate Φₖᵃ, Φₖᵇ, and Φₖᶜ;
            if pⱼ − PCₗ > max{Φₖᵃ,Φₖᶜ}
            then
                    if pⱼ−Φₖᵇ ≥ min {Φₖᵃ,Φₖᶜ}
                    then call rule 2 else call rule 3;
                else call rule 4;
                end
            end
        else call rule 5;
until j = n;
end;
```

Theorem 5.4.4   *Given a system of m processors $P_1,\cdots,P_m$ of noncontinuous availability, where each processor P_i is available in $N(i)$ time intervals. Then, if the processor system forms a staircase pattern and the tasks satisfy the inequalities of (5.4.1) and (5.4.2), Algorithm 5.4.3 generates a feasible preemptive schedule with at most $(\sum_{i=1}^{m}N(i))-1$ preemptions.*

Proof. The feasibility of the schedule has already been proved in Theorem 5.4.2. What remains to prove is the upper bound of preemptions. Using scheduling rules 1-5, a task T_j will only be preempted between two intervals if one of them is completely filled with T_j and the other interval is at least partially filled with T_j. From observation (4) of Lemma 5.4.1 we can conclude that after having scheduled the first $m-1$ tasks with rules 1-4, at most $(\sum_{i=1}^{m-1}N(i)) - 1$ preemptions are induced. From the discussion in the proof of observation (3) we know that after scheduling the first $m-1$ tasks according to rules 1-4, the last $m-1$ processors have zero processing capacity, and thus the number of induced preemptions is in fact $\sum_{i=1}^{m-1}N(i)$. There is an original or a composite processor P_1 with $PC_1 \geq \sum_{j=m}^{n} p_j$. As this processor is available during $N(m)$ intervals, scheduling the last $n - m + 1$ tasks according to rule 5 induces at most $N(m)-1$ additional preemptions; thus the total number of preemptions will be $(\sum_{i=1}^{m} N(i)) - 1$. It is easy to show that the same argument applies if there are less than $m - 1$ tasks scheduled according to rules 1-4. Thus Algorithm 5.4.3 generates at most $(\sum_{i=1}^{m} N(i)) - 1$ preemptions. The tightness of this bound can be easily verified. $\square$

Theorem 5.4.5 *The time complexity of Algorithm 5.4.3 is $O(n + m\log m)$.*

Proof. Ordering the tasks by their processing times requires $O(n + m\log m)$ time, because the m largest tasks can be found in $O(n)$ time, and sorting them requires $O(m\log m)$ time. The "if-part" of the "repeat-loop" of Algorithm 5.4.3 can be implemented to run in $O(\log m)$ time using balanced search trees for the PC_i values. Insertions, deletions and searches can be carried out in $O(\log m)$ time. Since this part of the "repeat-loop" is called at most $O(m)$ times the time complexity of this part is $O(m\log m)$. The "else-part" of the "repeat-loop" can be implemented in $O(n)$ time and thus the overall time complexity of the algorithm is $O(n + m\log m)$. $\square$

Notice that if all processors are only available in a single processing interval and all these intervals have the staircase property the algorithm generates feasible schedules with at most $m - 1$ preemptions. If we further assume that $B_i = B$ and $F_i = F$ for all $i = 1, \cdots, m$ Algorithm 5.4.3 reduces to McNaughton's rule [McN59] with time complexity $O(n)$ and at most $m - 1$ preemptions.

There is a number of more general problems that can be solved by similar approaches.

(1) Consider the general problem where the intervals of m semi-identical processors are arbitrarily distributed as shown in Figure 5.4.3(a) for an example problem with $m = 3$ processors. Reordering the original intervals leads to a staircase pattern which is illustrated in Figure 5.4.3(b). Now each processor P'_i, with $PC'_i > 0$ is a *composite processor* combining processors $P_i, P_{i+1}, \cdots, P_m$, and each interval $[B''_i, F''_i]$ is a *composite interval* combining intervals of availability of processors $P_i, P_{i+1}, \cdots, P_m$. The numbers in the different intervals of Figure 5.4.3(b) correspond to the number of original processors where that interval of availability is related to. After reordering the original intervals this way the problem consists of at most $Q' \le Q = \sum_{i=1}^{m} N(i)$ intervals of availability. Using Algorithm 5.4.3, $O(m)$ preemptions are possible in each interval and thus $O(mQ)$ is an upper bound on the number of preemptions which will be generated for the original problem.

(2) If there is no feasible preemptive schedule for the problem at least one of the inequalities of (5.4.1) is violated; this means that the processing capacity of at least one processor is insufficient. We now increase the processing capacity in such a way that all the tasks can be feasibly processed. An *overtime cost function* is introduced that measures the required increase of processing capacity. Assume that an increase of one time unit of processing capacity results in an increase of one unit of cost. If inequality (5.4.1-q) is violated we have to increase the total capacity of the first q processors by

$\sum\limits_{j=1}^{q}(p_j - PC_j)$ in case of $1 \leq q < m$; hence the processing capacity of each of the pro-

cessors $P_1, \cdots, P_q$ is increased by $\dfrac{1}{q}\sum\limits_{j=1}^{q}(p_j - PC_j)$. If inequality (5.4.1-m) is violated, the

cost minimum increase of all processing capacities is achieved if the processing

capacity of each processor is increased by $\dfrac{1}{m}(\sum\limits_{j=1}^{n}p_j - \sum\limits_{j=1}^{m}PC_j)$. Now Algorithm 5.4.3 can

be used to construct a feasible preemptive schedule of minimum total overtime cost.
Checking and adjusting the m inequalities can be done in $O(m)$ time, and then
Algorithm 5.4.3 can be applied. Hence a feasible schedule of minimal overtime cost
can be constructed in $O(n + m\log m)$ time.

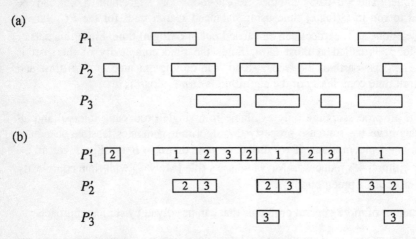

Figure 5.4.3 *Example for arbitrary processing intervals*
        (a) general intervals of availability,
        (b) corresponding staircase pattern.

(3) If each task T_j also has a deadline $\tilde{d}_j$ the problem is not only to meet start and finish
times of all intervals but also all deadlines. The problem can be solved by using a
similar approach where the staircase patterns and the given deadlines are considered.
Since all the tasks may have different deadlines, the resulting time complexity is
$O(nm\log n)$. A detailed description of this procedure can be found in [Sch88]. There it
is also proved there the algorithm generates at most $Q + m(s-1) - 1$ preemptions if the
semi-identical processor system forms a staircase pattern, and $m(Q + s - 1) - 1$ preemptions in the general case, where s is the number of different deadlines. We mention that
this approach is not only dedicated to the deadline problem. It can also be applied to a
problem where all the tasks have different ready times and the same deadline, as these
two situations are of the same structure.

At the end of this section we want turn to the problem of scheduling tasks nonpreemptively on semi-identical processors. If the processors P_i have arbitrary start times B_i but
are continuously available from then on, minimizing C_{max} is a possible criterion. Lee
[Lee91] showed for this problem that the application of the *LPT* rule results in a worst

case bound of $(\frac{3}{2} - \frac{1}{2m})C^*_{\max}$. If the *LPT* rule is modified appropriately the bound can be improved to $\frac{4}{3}C^*_{\max}$. This modification uses dummy tasks to simulate start times $B_i > 0$. For each such processor a task T_j with processing time $p_j = B_i$ is inserted. These tasks are merged into the original task set and then all tasks are scheduled according to *LPT* under the additional restriction that only one dummy task may be assigned to each processor. After finishing the schedule all dummy tasks are moved to the head of the processors followed by the remaining tasks assigned to each P_i.

This approach can also be used to give an exact answer to the single interval $[B, F_i]$ or $[B_i, F]$ nonpreemptive problem. First we apply an approximation algorithm and if a solution exists we are done. If we do not succeed in finding a feasible solution we can use the worst case ratio as an upper bound and the solution of the preemptive case as a lower bound in some enumerative approach.

5.4.2 Scheduling Multiprocessor Tasks

One of the assumptions imposed in Chapter 3 was that each task is processed on at most one processor at a time. However, in recent years with the rapid development of manufacturing as well as microprocessor and especially multi-microprocessor systems, the above assumption has ceased to be justified in some important applications. There are, for example, self-testing multi-microprocessor systems in which one processor is used to test others or diagnostic systems in which testing signals stimulate the tested elements and their corresponding outputs are simultaneously analyzed [Avi78, DD81]. When formulating scheduling problems in such systems, one must take into account the fact that some tasks have to be processed on more than one processor at a time. These problems create a new direction in processor scheduling theory.

Following Błażewicz et al. [BDW84, BDW86] we will set up the subject more precisely. Tasks are to be processed on a set of identical processors. The set of tasks is divided into k subsets $\mathcal{T}^1 = \{T^1_1, T^1_2, \cdots, T^1_{n_1}\}$, $\mathcal{T}^2 = \{T^2_1, T^2_2, \cdots, T^2_{n_2}\}$, $\cdots$, $\mathcal{T}^k = \{T^k_1, T^k_2,$ $\cdots, T^k_{n_k}\}$, where $n = n_1 + n_2 + \cdots + n_k$. Each task T^1_i, $i = 1, 2, \cdots, n$, requires exactly one of the processors for its processing and its processing time is equal to p^1_i. Similarly, each task T^l_i, where $1 < l \le k$, requires l arbitrary processors simultaneously for its processing during a period of time whose length is equal to p^l_i. We will call tasks from $\mathcal{T}^l$ *width-l* tasks or $\mathcal{T}^l$-tasks. All the tasks considered here are assumed to be *independent*, i.e. there are no precedence constraints among them. A schedule will be called *feasible* if, besides the usual conditions, each $\mathcal{T}^l$-task is processed by l processors at a time, $l = 1, \cdots, k$. The schedule length is taken as optimality criterion.

Let us start with nonpreemptive scheduling. It is clear that the general problem is *NP*-hard (cf. Section 5.1), thus, we may concentrate on unit-length tasks. Let us start with the problem of scheduling tasks which belong to two sets only: $\mathcal{T}^1$ and $\mathcal{T}^k$, for arbitrary k. This problem can be solved optimally by the following algorithm.

Algorithm 5.4.6 *Scheduling unit tasks from sets* $\mathcal{T}^1$ *and* $\mathcal{T}^k$ *to minimize* $C_{\max}$
[BDW86].
begin
Calculate the length of an optimal schedule according to the formula

$$C_{\max}^* = \max\{\lceil \frac{n_1 + kn_k}{m} \rceil, \lceil n_k / \lfloor \frac{m}{k} \rfloor \rceil\}; \tag{5.4.3}$$

Schedule $\mathcal{T}^k$-tasks in time interval $[0, C_{\max}^*]$ using first-fit algorithm;
  -- see Section 7.1 for the description of the first-fit algorithm
Assign $\mathcal{T}^1$-tasks to the remaining free processors;
end;

It should be clear that (5.4.3) gives a lower bound on the schedule length of an optimal schedule and this bound is always met by a schedule constructed by Algorithm 5.4.6.

If tasks belong to sets $\mathcal{T}^1, \mathcal{T}^2, \cdots, \mathcal{T}^k$, where k is a fixed integer, the problem can be solved by an approach similar to that for the problem of nonpreemptive scheduling of unit processing time tasks under fixed resource constraints [BE83]. We will describe that approach in Section 7.1.

Now, we will pass to preemptive scheduling. First, let us consider the problem of scheduling tasks from sets $\mathcal{T}^1$ and $\mathcal{T}^k$ in order to minimize schedule length. In [BDW84, BDW86] it has been proved that among minimum-length schedules for the problem there always exists a feasible *normalized schedule*, i.e. one in which first all $\mathcal{T}^k$-tasks are assigned in time interval $[0, C_{\max}^*]$ using McNaughton's rule (Algorithm 5.1.2), and then all $\mathcal{T}^1$-tasks are assigned, using the same rule, in the remaining part of the schedule (cf. Fig. 5.4.4).

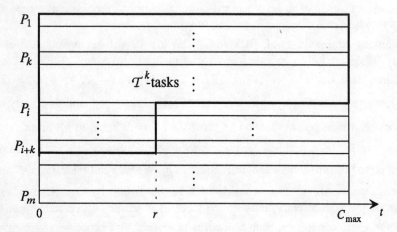

Figure 5.4.4 *An example normalized schedule.*

Following the above result, we will concentrate on finding an optimal schedule among normalized ones. A lower bound on the schedule length $C_{\max}$ can be obtained as follows. Define

$$X = \sum_{i=1}^{n_1} p_i^1, \quad Y = \sum_{i=1}^{n_k} p_i^k, \quad Z = X + kY,$$

$$p_{max}^1 = \max_{T_i^1 \in \mathcal{T}^1} \{p_i^1\}, \quad p_{max}^k = \max_{T_i^k \in \mathcal{T}^k} \{p_i^k\}.$$

Then,

$$C_{max} \geq C = \max\{Z/m, \, Y/\lfloor m/k \rfloor, \, p_{max}^1, \, p_{max}^k\}. \tag{5.4.4}$$

It is clear that no feasible schedule can be shorter than the maximum of the above values, i.e. mean processing requirement on one processor, mean processing requirement of $\mathcal{T}^k$-tasks on k processors, the maximum processing time among $\mathcal{T}^1$-tasks, and the maximum processing time among $\mathcal{T}^k$-tasks. If $mC > Z$, then in any schedule there will be an idle time of minimum length $IT = mC - Z$. On the basis of bound (5.4.4) and the reasoning preceding it one can try to construct a preemptive schedule of minimum length equal to C. However, this will not always be possible, and one has to lengthen the schedule. Below we present the reasoning that allows to find the optimal schedule length. Let $l = \lfloor Y/C \rfloor$. It is quite clear that the optimal schedule length C_{max}^* must obey the inequality

$$C \leq C_{max}^* \leq Y/l.$$

We know that there exists an optimal normalized schedule where tasks are arranged in such a way that kl processors are devoted entirely to $\mathcal{T}^k$-tasks, k processors are devoted to $\mathcal{T}^k$-tasks in time interval $[0, r]$, and $\mathcal{T}^1$-tasks are scheduled in the remaining time (cf. Fig. 5.4.4). Let m_1 be the number of processors that can process $\mathcal{T}^1$-tasks during time interval $[0, r]$, i.e. $m_1 = m - (l+1)k$. In a normalized schedule which completes all tasks by some time B, where $C \leq B \leq Y/l$, we will have $r = Y - Bl$. Thus, the optimum value C_{max}^* will be the smallest value of B ($B \geq C$) such that the $\mathcal{T}^1$-tasks can be scheduled on m_1 processors available during the interval $[0, B]$ and on $m_1 + k$ processors available in the interval $[r, B]$. Below we give necessary and sufficient conditions for the unit width tasks to be scheduled. To do this, let us assume that these tasks are ordered in such a way that $p_1^1 \geq p_2^1 \geq \cdots \geq p_{n_1}^1$. For a given pair B, r with $r = Y - Bl$, let $p_1^1, p_2^1, \cdots, p_j^1$ be the only processing times greater than $B - r$. Consider now two cases.

Case 1: $j \leq m_1 + k$. Then $\mathcal{T}^1$-tasks can be scheduled if and only if

$$\sum_{i=1}^{j} [p_i^1 - (B - r)] \leq m_1 r. \tag{5.4.5}$$

To prove that this condition is indeed necessary and sufficient, let us first observe that if (5.4.5) is violated the $\mathcal{T}^1$-tasks cannot be scheduled. Suppose now that (5.4.5) holds. Then one should schedule the excesses (exceeding $B - r$) of "long" tasks T_1^1, $\cdots, T_j^1$, and (if (5.4.5) holds without equality) some other tasks on m_1 processors in time interval $[0, r]$ using McNaughton's rule. After this operation the interval is completely filled with unit width tasks on m_1 processors.

Case 2: $j > m_1 + k$. In that case $\mathcal{T}^1$-tasks can be scheduled if and only if

$$\sum_{i=1}^{m_1+k} [p_i^1 - (B-r)] \leq m_1 r. \qquad (5.4.6)$$

Other long tasks will have enough space on the left hand side of the schedule because condition (5.4.4) is obeyed.

Next we describe how the optimum value of schedule length (C_{max}^*) can be found.

Let $W_j = \sum_{i=1}^{j} p_i^1$. Inequality (5.4.5) may then be rewritten as

$$W_j - j(B-r) \leq m_1(Y-Bp).$$

Solving it for B we get

$$B \geq \frac{(j-m_1)Y + W_j}{(j-m_1)p+j}.$$

Define

$$H_j = \frac{(j-m_1)Y + W_j}{(j-m_1)p+j}.$$

Thus, we may write

$$C_{max}^* = \max\{C, H_1, H_2, \cdots, H_{n_1}\}.$$

Finding the above maximum can clearly be done in $O(n_1 \log n_1)$ time by sorting the unit-width tasks by p_i^1. But one can do better by taking into account the following facts.

1. $H_i \leq C$ for $i \leq m_1$ or $i \geq m_1 + k$.

2. H_i has no local maxima for $i = m_1 + 1, \cdots, m_1 + k - 1$.

Thus, to find a maximum over $H_{m_1+1}, \cdots, H_{m_1+k-1}$ and C we only need to apply a linear time median finding algorithm [AHU74] and a binary search. This will result in an $O(n_1)$ algorithm that calculates C_{max}^*. (Finding the medians takes $O(n_1)$ the first time, $O(n_1/2)$ the second time, $O(n_1/4)$ the third time, etc.) Thus the total time to find the medians is $O(n_1)$.

Now we are in the position to present an optimization algorithm for scheduling width-1 and width-k tasks.

Algorithm 5.4.7 *Scheduling preemptable tasks from sets $\mathcal{T}^1$ and $\mathcal{T}^k$ to minimize C_{max}* [BDW86]
begin
Calculate the minimum schedule length C_{max}^*;
call Algorithm 5.1.2 to schedule $\mathcal{T}^k$-tasks in interval $[0, C_{max}^*]$ using McNaughton's
    rule;
$l := \lfloor Y/C_{max}^* \rfloor$; $m_1 := m-(l+1)k$; $r := Y - C_{max}^* l$;

Calculate the number j of long $\mathcal{T}^1$-tasks that exceed $C^*_{max} - r$;

```
if j≤m₁+k then
   begin
```
Call Algorithm 5.1.2 to schedule the excesses of the long tasks and possibly some other tasks on m_1 processors in interval $[0, r]$;

Call Algorithm 5.1.2 to schedule the remaining processing requirement in interval $[r, C^*_{max}]$ on $m_1 + k$ processors;

```
   end
else
   begin
```
Call Algorithm 5.1.2 to schedule part $\left((m_1 + k)(C^*_{max} - r)/\sum_{i=1}^{j} p_i^1\right) p_h^1$ of each long task

T_h^1 in interval $[r, C^*_{max}]$ on $m_1 + k$ processors;

     -- if among smaller tasks not exceeding $(C^*_{max} - r)$ there are some tasks longer than r,

     -- then this excess must be taken into account in denominator of the above rate

Call Algorithm 5.1.2 to schedule the rest of the task set in interval $[0, r]$ on m_1 processors;

```
   end;
end;
```

The optimality of the above algorithm follows from the preceding discussion. Its time complexity is $O(n_1 + n_k)$, thus we get $O(n)$.

Considering the general case of preemptively scheduling tasks from sets $\mathcal{T}^1$, $\mathcal{T}^2, \ldots, \mathcal{T}^k$, we can use the very useful linear programming approach presented in equations (5.1.14)-(5.1.15) to solve this problem in polynomial time.

Finally we will briefly comment on the possible extensions and refinements that are of practical interest, too. First, one may consider additional resources besides central processors; this model will be considered in Section 7.2. Then, a set of uniform (instead of identical) processors may be assumed; this subject is partially covered by [BDCW90]. Also, one could consider a model, where some kind of dedicated tests are given, where each test (each task) is to be carried out by a priori specified set of processors. Preliminary results in that area have been obtained in [BDOS92, KK85, JM84 and Kub87]. A recent survey including also some results taking into account timing constraints caused by a network connecting parallel processors is given in [VLL90].

References

AH73   D. Adolphson, and T. C. Hu, Optimal linear ordering, *SIAM J. Appl. Math.* 25, 1973, 403-423.

AIIU74   A. V. Aho, J. E. Hopcroft, J. D. Ullman, *The Design and Analysis of Computer Algorithms*, Addison-Wesley, Reading, Mass., 1974.

Ash72   S. Ashour, *Sequencing Theory*, Springer Verlag Berlin, 1972.

Avi78   A. Avizienis, Fault tolerance: the survival attribute of digital systems, *Proc. IEEE* 66, 1978, 1109-1125.

Bak74   K. Baker, *Introduction to Sequencing and Scheduling*, J. Wiley, New York, 1974.

BCS74   J. Bruno, E. G. Coffman, Jr., R. Sethi, Scheduling independent tasks to reduce mean finishing time, *Comm. ACM* 17, 1974, 382-387.

BCSW76a   J. Błażewicz, W. Cellary, R. Słowiński, and J. Węglarz, Deterministyczne problemy szeregowania zadań na równoległych procesorach. Cz. I. *Zbiory zadań niezależnych, Podstawy Sterowania* 6, 1976, 155-178.

BCSW76b   J. Błażewicz, W. Cellary, R. Słowiński, and J. Węglarz, Deterministyczne problemy szeregowania zadań na równoległych procesorach, Cz. II. *Zbiory zadań niezależnych, Podstawy Sterowania* 6, 1976, 297-320.

BCW77   J. Błażewicz, W. Cellary, and J. Węglarz, A strategy for scheduling splittable tasks to reduce schedule length, *Acta Cybernet.* 3, 1977, 99-106.

BDOS92   J. Błażewicz, M. Drozdowski, P. dell'Olmo, M. G. Speranza, Scheduling multiprocessor tasks on three dedicated processors, *Inform. Process. Lett.* 1992, to appear.

BDSW90   J. Błażewicz, M. Drozdowski, G. Schmidt, D. de Werra, Scheduling independent two processor tasks on a uniform duo-processor system, *Discrete Appl. Math.* 28, 1990, 11-20.

BDW84   J. Błażewicz, M. Drabowski, J. Węglarz, Scheduling independent 2-processor tasks to minimize schedule length, *Inform. Process. Lett.* 18, 1984, 267-273.

BDW86   J. Błażewicz, M. Drabowski, J. Węglarz, Scheduling multiprocessor tasks to minimize schedule length, *IEEE Trans. Comput.* C-35, 1986, 389-393.

BE83   J. Błażewicz, K. Ecker, A linear time algorithm for restricted bin packing and scheduling problems, *Oper. Res. Lett.* 2, 1983, 80-83.

BGJ77   P. Brucker, M. R. Garey, and D. S. Johnson, Scheduling equal-length tasks under treelike precedence constraints to minimize maximum lateness, *Math. Oper. Res.* 2, 1977, 275-284.

Bla77   J. Błażewicz, Simple algorithms for multiprocessor scheduling to meet deadlines, *Inform. Process. Lett.* 6, 1977, 162-164.

Bru76a   J. Bruno, Scheduling algorithms for minimizing the mean weighted flow-time, E. G. Coffman, Jr. (ed.), *Computer and Job-Shop Scheduling Theory*, John Wiley & Sons, New York, 1976.

Bru76b   P. J. Brucker, Sequencing unit-time jobs with treelike precedence on m machines to minimize maximum lateness, *Proceedings IX International Symposium on Mathematical Programming, Budapest,* 1976.

CD73   E. G. Coffman, Jr., P. J. Denning, *Operating Systems Theory*, Prentice-Hall, Englewood Cliffs, N. J., 1973.

CFL83   E. G. Coffman, Jr., G. N. Frederickson, G. S. Luecker, Probabilistic analysis of the LPT processor scheduling heuristic, (unpublished paper), 1983.

CFL84   E. G. Coffman, Jr., G. N. Frederickson, G. S. Luecker, A note on expected makespans for largest-first sequences of independent task on two processors, *Math. Oper. Res.* 9, 1984, 260-266.

CG72   E. G. Coffman, Jr., R. L. Graham, Optimal scheduling for two-processor systems, *Acta Inform.* 1, 1972, 200-213.

CG91   E. G. Coffman, Jr., M. R. Garey, Proof of the 4/3 conjecture for preemptive versus nonpreemptive two-processor scheduling, Report Bell Laboratories, Murray Hill, 1991.

CGJ78   E. G. Coffman, Jr., M. R. Garey, D. S. Johnson, An application of bin-packing to multiprocessor scheduling, *SIAM J.Comput.* 7, 1978, 1-17.

CGJ84   E. G. Coffman, Jr., M. R. Garey, D. S. Johnson, Appoximation algorithms for bin packing - an updated survey, in: G. Ausiello, M. Lucertini, P. Serafini (eds.), *Algorithm Design for Computer System Design*, Springer Verlag, Vienna, 1984, 49-106.

CL75   N.-F. Chen, C. L. Liu, On a class of scheduling algorithms for multiprocessors computing systems, in: T.-Y. Feng (ed.), *Parallel Processing*, Lecture Notes in Computer Science 24, Springer Verlag, Berlin, 1975, 1-16.

CMM67   R. W. Conway, W. L. Maxwell, and L. W. Miller, *Theory of Scheduling*, Addison-Wesley, Reading, Mass., 1967.

Cof73   E. G. Coffman, Jr., A survey of mathematical results in flow-time scheduling for computer systems, *GI - 3. Jahrestagung, Hamburg*, Springer Verlag Berlin, 1973, 25-46.

Cof76   E. G. Coffman, Jr. (ed.), *Scheduling in Computer and Job Shop Systems*, J. Wiley, New York, 1976.

CS76   E. G. Coffman, Jr., and R. Sethi, A generalized bound on LPT sequencing, *RAIRO-Informatique* 10, 1976, 17-25.

DD81   M. Dal Cin, E. Dilger, On the diagnostability of self-testing multimicroprocessor systems, *Microprocessing and Microprogramming* 7, 1981, 177-184.

DL88   J. Du, J. Y-T. Leung, Scheduling tree-structured tasks with restricted execution times, *Inform. Process. Lett.* 28, 1988, 183-188.

DL89   J. Du, J. Y-T. Leung, Scheduling tree-structured tasks on two processors to minimize schedule length, *SIAM J. Discrete Math.* 2, 1989, 176-196.

DLY91   J. Du, J. Y-T. Leung, G. H. Young, Scheduling chain structured tasks to minimize makespan and mean flow time, *Inform. and Comput.* 92, 1991, 219-236.

DW85   D. Dolev, M. K. Warmuth, Scheduling flat graphs, *SIAM J.Comput.* 14, 1985, 638-657.

FB73   E. B. Fernandez, B. Bussel, Bounds on the number of processors and time for multiprocessor optimal schedules, *IEEE Trans. Comput.* C22, 1973, 745-751.

FG86   A. Federgruen, H. Groenevelt, Preemptive scheduling of niform machines by ordinary network flow techniques, *Management Sci.* 32, 1986, 341-349.

FKN69   M. Fujii, T. Kasami, K. Ninomiya, Optimal sequencing of two equivalent processors, *SIAM J. Appl. Math.* 17, 1969, 784-789, Err: *SIAM J. Appl. Math.* 20, 1971, 141.

Fre82   S. French, *Sequencing and Scheduling: An Introduction to the Mathematics of the Job-Shop*, Horwood, Chichester, 1982.

FRK86   J. B. G. Frenk, A. H. G. Rinnooy Kan, The rate of convergence to optimality of the LPT rule, *Discrete Appl. Math.* 14, 1986, 187-197.

FRK87   J. B. G. Frenk, A. H. G. Rinnooy Kan, The asymptotic optimality of the LPT rule, *Math. Oper. Res.* 12, 1987, 241-254.

Gab82   H. N. Gabow, An almost linear algorithm for two-processor scheduling, *J. Assoc. Comput. Mach.* 29, 1982, 766-780.

Gar -   M. R. Garey, Unpublished result.

Gar73   M. R. Garey, Optimal task sequencing with precedence constraints, *Discrete Math.* 4, 1973, 37-56.

GG73   M. R. Garey, R. L. Graham, Bounds for multiprocessor scheduling with limited resources, *4th Symposium on Operating System Principles,* 1966, 104-111.

GG75   M. R. Garey, R. L. Graham, Bounds for multiprocessor scheduling with resource constraints, *SIAM J.Comput.* 4, 1975, 187-200.

GIS77   T. Gonzalez, O. H. Ibarra, S. Sahni, Bounds for LPT schedules on uniform processors, *SIAM J.Comput.* 6, 1977, 155-166.

GJ76   M. R. Garey, D. S. Johnson, Scheduling tasks with nonuniform deadlines on two processors, *J. Assoc. Comput. Mach.* 23, 1976, 461-467.

GJ77   M. R. Garey, D. S. Johnson, Two-processor scheduling with start-times and deadlines, *SIAM J.Comput.* 6, 1977, 416-426.

GJ79   M. R. Garey, D. S. Johnson, *Computers and Intractability: A Guide to the Theory of NP-Completeness.* W. H. Freeman, San Francisco, 1979.

GJST81   M. R. Garey, D. S. Johnson, B. B. Simons, R. E. Tarjan, Scheduling unit time tasks with arbitrary release times and deadlines, *SIAM J.Comput.* 10, 1981, 256-269.

GJTY83   M. R. Garey, D. S. Johnson, R. E. Tarjan, M. Yannakakis, Scheduling opposing forests, SIAM J. *Algebraic and Discrete Meth.* 4, 1983, 72-93.

GLLRK79   R. L. Graham, E. L. Lawler, J. K. Lenstra, A. H. G. Rinnoy Kan, Optimization and approximation in deterministic sequencing and scheduling theory: a survey, *Ann. Discrete Math.* 5, 1979, 287-326.

Gon77   T. Gonzalez, Optimal mean finish time preemptive schedules, Technical Report 220, Computer Science Depatment, Pennsylvania Stat Univ. 1977.

Gra66   R. L. Graham, Bounds for certain multiprocessing anomalies, *Bell System Tech. J.* 45, 1966, 1563-1581.

Gra69   R. L. Graham, Bounds on multiprocessing timing anomalies, *SIAM J. Appl. Math.* 17, 1969, 263-269.

Gra76   R. L. Graham, Bounds on performance of scheduling algorithms, Chapter 5 in [Cof76].

GS78   T. Gonzalez, S. Sahni, Preemptive scheduling of uniform processor systems, *J. Assoc. Comput. Mach.* 25, 1978, 92-101.

GS78   T. Gonzalez, S. Sahni, Preemptive scheduling for uniform processor systems, *J. Assoc. Comput. Mach.* 25, 1978, 81-101.

HLS77   E. G. Horvath, S. Lam, R. Sethi, A level algorithm for preemptive scheduling, *J. Assoc. Comput. Mach.* 24, 1977, 32-43.

Hor73   W. A. Horn, Minimizing average flow time with parallel machines, *Oper. Res.* 21, 1973, 846-847.

Hor74   W. A. Horn, Some simple scheduling algorithms, *Naval Res. Logist. Quart.* 21, 1974, 177-185.

HS76   E. Horowitz, S. Sahni, Exact and aproximate algorithms for scheduling non-identical processors, *J. Assoc. Comput. Mach.* 23, 1976, 317-327.

HS87   D. S. Hochbaum, D. B. Shmoys, Using dual approximation algorithms for scheduling problems: theoretical and practical results, *J. Assoc. Comput. Mach.* 34, 1987, 144-162.

Hu61   T. C. Hu, Parallel sequencing and assembly line problems, *Oper. Res.* 9, 1961, 841-848.

IK77   O. H. Ibarra, C. E. Kim, Heuristic algorithms for scheduling independent tasks on nonidentical processors, *J. Assoc. Comput. Mach.* 24, 1977, 280-289.

Jac55   J. R. Jackson, Scheduling a production line to minimize maximum tardiness, Res. Report 43, Management Research Project, University of California, Los Angeles, 1955.

JM84   D. S. Johnson, C. L. Monma, A scheduling problem with simultaneous machine requirement, TIMS XXVI, Copenhagen, 1984.

Joh83   D. S. Johnson, The NP-completeness column: an ongoing guide, *J. Algorithms* 4, 1983, 189-203.

Kar72   R. M. Karp, Reducibility among combinatorial problems, in: R. E. Miller, J. W. Thatcher (eds.), *Complexity of Computer Computations*, Plenum Press, New York, 1972, 85-104.

Kar74   A. W. Karzanov, Determining the maximal flow in a network by the method of preflows, *Soviet Math. Dokl.* 15, 1974, 434-437.

Kar84   N. Karmarkar, A new polynomial-time algorithm for linear programming, *Combinatorica* 4, 1984, 373-395.

KE75   O. Kariv, S. Even. An $O(n^{2.5})$ algorithm for maximum matching in general graphs, *16th Annual Symposium on Foundations of Computer Science IEEE*, 1975, 100-112.

Ked70   S. K. Kedia, A job scheduling problem with parallel machines, Unpublished Report, Dept. of Ind. Eng. University of Michigan, Ann Arbor, 1970.

Kha79   L. G. Khachiyan, A polynomial algorithm for linear programming (in Russian), *Dokl. Akad. Nauk SSSR*, 244, 1979, 1093-1096.

KK82   N. Karmarkar, R. M. Karp, The differing method of set partitioning, Report UCB/CSD 82/113, Computer Science Division, University of California, Berkeley, 1982.

KK85   H. Krawczyk, M. Kubale, An approximation algorithm for diagnostic test scheduling in multicomputer systems, *IEEE Trans. Comput.* C-34, 1985, 869-872.

Kub87   M. Kubale, The complexity of scheduling independent two-processor tasks on dedicated processors, *Inform. Proc. Lett.* 24, 1987, 141-147.

Kun76   M. Kunde, Beste Schranke beim LP-Scheduling, Bericht 7603, Institut für Informatik und Praktische Mathematik, University Kiel, 1976.

Law73   E. L. Lawler, Optimal sequencing of a single machine subject to precedence constraints, *Management Sci.* 19, 1973, 544-546.

Law76   E. L. Lawler, *Combinatorial optimization: Networks and Matroids*, Holt, Rinehart and Winston, New York, 1976.

Law82a   E. L. Lawler, Recent results in the theory of machine scheduling, in: A. Bachem, M. Grötschel, B. Korte (eds.) *Mathematical Programing: The State of Art*, Bonn 1982, Springer Verlag, Berlin, 1982, 202-234.

Law82b   E. L. Lawler, Preemptive scheduling in precedence-constrained jobs on parallel machines, in: M. A. H. Dempster, J. K. Lenstra, A. H. G. Rinnooy Kan (eds.), *Deterministic and Stochastic Scheduling*, Reidel, Dordrecht, 1982, 101-123.

Lee91   C.-Y. Lee, Parallel machine scheduling with nonsimultaneous machine available time, *Discrete Appl. Math.* 30, 1991, 53-61.

Len81b   J. K. Lenstra, Sequencing by enumerative methods, Mathematical Centre Tracte 69, Mathematisch Centrum, Amsterdam, 1981.

LL74a   J. W. S. Liu, C. L. Liu, Performance analysis of heterogeneous multiprocessor computing systems, in E. Gelenbe, R. Mahl (eds.), *Computer Architecture and Networks*, North Holland, Amsterdam, 1974, 331-343.

LL74b   J. W. S. Liu, C. L. Liu, Performance analysis of heterogeneous multiprocessor computing systems, in: E.Gelenbe, R. Mahl (eds), *Computer Architecture and Networks*, North Holland, Amsterdam, 1974, 331-343.

LL74c   J.W.S. Liu, C.L. Liu, Bounds on scheduling algorithms for heterogeneous computing systems, Technical Report UIUCDCS-R-74-632, Dept. of Computer Science, University of Illinois at Urbana-Champaign, 1974.

LL78   E. L. Lawler, J. Labetoulle, Preemptive scheduling of unrelated parallel processors by linear programing, *J. Assoc. Comput. Mach.* 25, 1978, 612-619.

LLLRK82   J. Lageweg, J. K. Lenstra, E. L. Lawler, A. H. G. Rinnooy Kan, Computer Aided complexity classification of combinatorial problems, *Comm. ACM* 25, 1982, 817-822.

LLLRK84   J. Labetoulle, E. L. Lawler, J. K. Lenstra, A. H. G. Rinnooy Kan, Preemptive scheduling of uniform processors subject to release dates, in: W. R. Pulleyblank (ed.), *Progress in Combinatorial Optimization*, Academic Press, New York, 1984, 245-261.

LLRK82   E. L. Lawler, J. K. Lenstra, A. H. G. Rinnooy Kan, Recent developments in deterministic sequencing and scheduling: a survey, in M. A. H. Dempster, J. K. Lenstra, A. H. G. Rinnooy Kan (eds.), *Deterministic and Stochastic Scheduling*, Reidel, Dordrecht, 1982, 35-73.

LLRKS89   E. L. Lawler, J. K. Lenstra, A. H. G. Rinnooy Kan, D. B. Shmoys, Sequencing and scheduling: algorithms and complexity, Report Centre Mathematics and Computer Science, Amsterdam, 1989.

LRK78   J. K. Lenstra, A. H. G. Rinnooy Kan, Complexity of scheduling under precedence constraints, *Oper. Res.* 26, 1978, 22-35.

LRK84   J. K. Lenstra, A. H. G. Rinnooy Kan, Scheduling theory since 1981: an annotated bibliography, in M. O'h Eigearthaigh, J. K. Lenstra, A. H. G. Rinnooy Kan (eds.), *Combinatorial Optimization: Annotated Bibliographies,* J. Wiley, Chichester, 1984.

LRKB77   J. K. Lenstra, A. H. G. Rinnooy Kan, P. Brucker, Complexity of machine scheduling problems, *Ann. Discrete Math.* 1, 1977, 343-362.

LS77   S. Lam, R. Sethi, Worst case analysis of two scheduling algorithms, *SIAM J.Comput.* 6, 1977, 518-536.

MC69   R. Muntz, E. G. Coffman, Jr., Optimal preemptive scheduling on two-processor systems, *IEEE Trans. Comput.* C-18, 1969, 1014-1029.

MC70   R. Muntz, E. G. Coffman, Jr., Preemptive scheduling of real time tasks on multipro-
            cessor systems, *J. Assoc. Comput. Mach.* 17, 1970, 324-338.

McN59   R. McNaughton, Scheduling with deadlines and loss functions, *Management Sci.* 6,
            1959, 1-12.

NLH81   K. Nakajima, J. Y-T. Leung, S. L. Hakimi, Optimal two processor scheduling of tree
            precedence constrained tasks with two execution times, *Performance Evaluation* 1,
            1981, 320-330.

Rin78   A. H. G. Rinnooy Kan, *Machine Scheduling Problems: Classification, Complexity
            and Computations*, Nijhoff, The Hague, 1978.

RG69   C. V. Ramamoorthy, M. J. Gonzalez, A survey of techniques for recognizing parallel
            processable streams in computer programs, AFIPS Conference Proceedings, Fall Joint
            Computer Conference, 1969, 1-15.

Ros–   unpublished result.

Rot66   M. H. Rothkopf, Scheduling independent tasks on parallel processors, *Management
            Sci.* 12, 1966, 347-447.

RS83   H. Röck, G. Schmidt, Machine aggregation heuristics in shop scheduling, *Methods
            Oper. Res.* 45, 1983, 303-314.

Sah79   S. Sahni, Preemptive scheduling with due dates, *Oper. Res.* 5, 1979, 925-934.

SC80   S. Sahni, Y. Cho, Scheduling independent tasks with due times on a uniform
            processor system, *J. Assoc. Comput. Mach.* 27, 1980, 550-563.

Sch84   G. Schmidt, Scheduling on semi-identical processors, *Z. Oper Res.* A28, 1984, 153-
            162.

Sch88   G. Schmidt, Scheduling independent tasks with deadlines on semi-identical
            processors, *J. Opl. Res. Soc.* 39, 1988, 271-277.

Set76   R. Sethi, Algorithms for minimal-length schedules, Chapter 2 in [Cof76].

Set77   R. Sethi, On the complexity of mean flow time scheduling, *Math. Oper. Res.* 2, 1977,
            320-330.

Sev91   S. V. Sevastjanov, Private communication, 1991.

Slo78   R. Słowiński, Scheduling preemptible tasks on unrelated processors with additional
            resources to mionimize schedule length, in G. Bracci, R. C. Lockemann (eds.),
            Lecture Notes in Computer Science, vol 65, Springer Verlag, Berlin, 1978, 536-547.

SW77   R. Słowiński, J. Węglarz, Minimalno-czasowy modelsieciowy z roznymi sposobami
            wykonywania czynnosci, *Przeglad Statystyczny* 24, 1977, 409-416.

Ull76   J. D. Ullman, Complexity of sequencing problems, Chapter 4 in [Cof76].

VLL90   B. Veltman, B. J. Lageweg, J. K. Lenstra, Multiprocessor scheduling with
            communication delays, Centre for Mathematics and Computer Science, Report BS -
            R9018, 1990.

WBCS77   J. Węglarz, J. Błażewicz, W. Cellary, and R.Słowiński, An automatic revised simplex
            method for constrained resource network scheduling, *ACM Trans. Math. Software* 3,
            1977, 295-300.

Wer84   D. de Werra, Preemptive scheduling linear programming and network flows, *SIAM J.
            Algebra and Discrete Math.* 5, 1984, 11-20.

6 Static Shop Scheduling

In this chapter we will consider scheduling tasks on dedicated processors (machines). As we said in Section 3.1 we assume that tasks form n subsets (or jobs), belonging to set $\mathcal{J}$, and two adjacent tasks of a job are to be performed on different machines. Unfortunately, most scheduling problems of this kind are *NP*-hard, which is especially true for optimality criteria other than C_{max}. In the first two sections we will concentrate first on polynomial time algorithms, where special cases of flow shop and open shop scheduling problems will be considered. Then the job shop scheduling problem will be discussed and two approaches, a heuristic based on simulated annealing and an exact based on branch and bound will be presented.

6.1 Flow Shop Scheduling

Recall that in flow shop scheduling problems jobs visit machines in a fixed order, $P_1, \cdots, P_m$. At each machine, a specified task of a job is being performed. Let T_{1j}, $T_{2j}, \cdots, T_{mj}$ denote the tasks forming job $\mathcal{J}_j \in \mathcal{J}$, and p_{ij} be the time required to process task T_{ij} on machine P_i.

Problems $F2 \mid\mid C_{max}$ and $F2 \mid\mid \Sigma C_j$

One of the most classical algorithms in this area is that for problem $F2 \mid\mid C_{max}$ due to S. Johnson [Joh54]. It is as follows.

Algorithm 6.1.1 *Johnson's algorithm for $F2 \mid\mid C_{max}$* [Joh54].
begin
Construct a set of jobs $\mathcal{J}_1 := \{ J_j \in \mathcal{J} \mid p_{1j} \le p_{2j} \}$;
Schedule jobs from set $\mathcal{J}_1$ in nondecreasing order of their p_{1j}'s on both machines;
Schedule jobs from set $\mathcal{J} - \mathcal{J}_1$ in nonincreasing order of their p_{2j}'s on both machines;
end;

It is clear that this algorithm requires $O(n \log n)$ time. An example of its application for $n=5$, $m=2$ and the following matrix of processing times

$$p = \begin{pmatrix} 4 & 4 & 30 & 6 & 2 \\ 5 & 1 & 4 & 30 & 3 \end{pmatrix}$$

is given in Figure 6.1.1.

The algorithm can be extended to cover also the special case of three machine scheduling in which $\min_j \{p_{1j}\} \ge \max_j \{p_{2j}\}$ or $\min_j \{p_{3j}\} \ge \max_j \{p_{2j}\}$. In this case the job processing times on the second machine are of no relevance for the optimality of the schedule, and an optimal schedule can be obtained by applying Algorithm 6.1.1 to processing times $(p_{1j}+p_{2j}, p_{2j}+p_{3j})$.

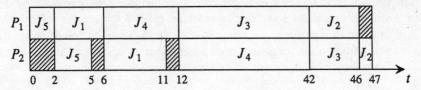

Figure 6.1.1 *An optimal schedule for a flow shop scheduling example.*

There exist also polynomial time algorithms for the case of unit processing times and tree precedence graphs. Problems $F2 \mid tree, p_j = 1 \mid C_{max}$ and $F2 \mid tree, p_j = 1 \mid \Sigma C_j$ are solvable in polynomial time [Lag–]. However, more complicated assumptions concerning problem parameters (e.g. general precedence constraints, more machines involved or other criteria) make the problem strongly *NP*-hard.

As far as the preemptive scheduling is concerned, the situation is the same as described above, i.e. $F2 \mid pmtn \mid C_{max}$ is solved by Algorithm 6.1.1, but other problems are strongly *NP*-hard. The only exception is $F2 \mid pmtn \mid \Sigma C_j$, which is still open.

Problem $Fm \mid\mid C_{max}$

$Fm \mid\mid C_{max}$ including its *permutation schedule* variant where identical job sequences on each machine are required, and $Fm \mid pmtn \mid C_{max}$ as well, are unary *NP*-hard for a fixed number of $m \geq 3$ machines [GJS76, GS78]. But we know from before that these problems are polynomially solvable for $m = 2$, and there is no advantage to preemption. It follows that these polynomial time algorithms could be used to generate *approximation schedules* for more complicated cases. Some results of that kind can be found in [GS78, Bar81, Pot85] and [RS83]. In the first paper, an approximation algorithm H_1 based on Algorithm 6.1.1 has been proposed for problem $F \mid\mid C_{max}$. Its worst case behavior is proved to be

$$R_{H_1} = \lceil m/2 \rceil.$$

We will refer to this result later again.

In the second paper, a quite complicated approximation algorithm A has been proposed whose absolute error does not depend on n and is proved to be

$$C_{max}^A - C_{max}^* = (m-1)(3m-1)p_{max}/2.$$

Potts [Pot85] analyzed several approximation algorithms for the problem $F2 \mid r_j \mid C_{max}$. The best algorithm, RJ', consists in the repeated application of a certain variant of Johnson's Algorithm 6.1.1; its absolute performance ratio can be estimated as

$$R_{RJ'} = 5/3.$$

An extensive survey of some other approximation algorithms using mainly geometric methods may be found in [Sev92].

In the following we concentrate on the basic ideas of *machine aggregation heuristics* using pairs of machines as introduced by Gonzalez and Sahni [GS78] and Röck and Schmidt [RS83]. These concepts can be applied to a variety of other *NP*-hard problems with polynomially solvable two-machine cases (cf. Sections 5.1 and 7.1). They lead to worst case performance ratios of $\lceil m/2 \rceil$, and the derivation of most of the results may be based on the following more general lemma which can also be applied in cases of open shop problems modeled by unrelated parallel machines.

Lemma 6.1.2 [RS83] *Let S be a nonpreemptive schedule of a set $\mathcal{T}$ of n tasks on $m \geq 3$ unrelated machines P_i, $i = 1,\cdots,m$. Consider the complete graph $(\mathcal{P}, \mathcal{E})$ of all pairs of machines, where $\mathcal{E} = \{\{P_i, P_j\} \mid i, j = 1,\cdots,m, \text{ and } i \neq j\}$. Let $\mathcal{M}$ be a maximum matching for $(\mathcal{P}, \mathcal{E})$. Then there exists a schedule S' where*

(1) *each task is processed on the same machine as in S, and S' has at most n preemptions,*

(2) *all ready times, precedence and resource constraints under which S was feasible remain satisfied,*

(3) *no pair $\{P_i, P_j\}$ of machines is active in parallel at any time unless $\{P_i, P_j\} \in \mathcal{M}$, and*

(4) *the finish time of each task increases by a factor of at most $\lceil m/2 \rceil$.*

Proof. In case of odd m add an idle dummy machine P_{m+1} and match it with the remaining unmatched machine, so that an even number of machines can be assumed. Decompose S into subschedules $S(q,f)$, $q \in \mathcal{M}$, $f \in \{f_q^1, f_q^2, \cdots, f_q^{K_q}\}$ where $f_q^1 < f_q^2 < \cdots < f_q^{K_q}$ is the sequence of distinct finish times of the tasks which are processed on the machine pair q. Without loss of generality we assume that $K_q \geq 1$. Let $f_q^0 = 0$ be the start time of the schedule and let $S(q, f_q^k)$ denote the subschedule of the machine pair q during interval $[f_q^{k-1}, f_q^k]$. The schedule S' which is obtained by arranging all these subschedules of S one after the other in the order of nondecreasing endpoints f, has the desired properties because (1) each task can preempt at most one other task, and this is the only source of preemption. (2) and (3): each subschedule $S(q,f)$ is feasible in itself, and its position in S' is according to nondecreasing endpoints of f. (4): the finish time C_j' of task $T_j \in \mathcal{T}$ in S' is located at the endpoint of the corresponding subschedule $S(q(j), C_j)$ where $q(j)$ is the machine pair on which T_j was processed in S, and C_j is the finish time of T_j in S. Due to the nondecreasing endpoint order of the subschedules it follows that $C_j' \leq \lceil m/2 \rceil C_j$. $\square$

For certain special problem structures Lemma 6.1.2 can be specialized so that preemption is kept out. Then, the aggregation approach can be applied to problems $F \mid\mid C_{\max}$ and $O \mid\mid C_{\max}$, and to some of their variants as well which remain solvable in case of $m = 2$ machines. We assume that for flow shops the machines are numbered in such a way that it reflects the order each job is assigned to the machines.

We present two aggregation heuristics that are based on special conditions restricting the use of machines.

Condition C1: No pair P_i, P_j of machines is allowed to be active in parallel at any time unless $\{P_i, P_j\} \in \mathcal{M}_1 = \{\{P_{2l-1}, P_{2l}\} \mid l = 1, \cdots, \lfloor m/2 \rfloor\}$.

Condition C2: Let $(\mathcal{P}, \mathcal{E})$ be a bipartite graph where $\mathcal{E} = \{\{P_a, P_b\} \mid a \in \{1, \cdots, \lceil m/2 \rceil\}$, $b \in \{\lceil m/2 \rceil + 1, \cdots, m\}$, and let $\mathcal{M}_2$ be a maximal matching for $(\mathcal{P}, \mathcal{E})$. Then no pair $\{P_i, P_j\}$ of machines is allowed to be active in parallel at any time unless $\{P_i, P_j\} \in \mathcal{M}_2$.

The following Algorithms 6.1.3 and 6.1.4 are based on conditions C1 and C2, respectively.

Algorithm 6.1.3 *Aggregation heuristic H_1 for $F \| C_{max}$* [GS78].
begin
for each pair $q_i = \{P_{2i-1}, P_{2i}\} \in \mathcal{M}_1$
    begin
    Find an optimal subschedule S_i^* for the two machines P_{2i-1} and P_{2i};
    if m is odd **then**
        $S_{\lceil m/2 \rceil}^* :=$ an arbitrary schedule of the tasks on the remaining unmatched machine P_m;
    $S := S_1^* \oplus S_2^* \oplus \cdots \oplus S_{\lceil m/2 \rceil}^*$;
    end;
end;

As already mentioned, for $F \| C_{max}$ this heuristic was shown in [GS78] to have the worst case performance ratio of $C_{max}(H_1)/C_{max}^* \leq \lceil m/2 \rceil$. The given argument can be extended to $F \mid pmtn \mid C_{max}$ and $O \| C_{max}$, and also to some resource constrained models. Tightness examples which reach $\lceil m/2 \rceil$ can also be constructed, but heuristic H_1 is not applicable if permutation flow shop schedules are required.

In order to be able to handle this restriction consider the following Algorithm 6.1.4 which is based on conditon C2. Assume for the moment that all machines with index less that or equal $\lceil m/2 \rceil$ are represented as a virtual machine P_1', and those with an index larger than $\lceil m/2 \rceil$ as a virtual machine P_2'. We again consider the given scheduling problem as a two machine problem.

Algorithm 6.1.4 *Aggregation heuristic H_2 for $F \| C_{max}$ and its permutation variant* [RS83].
begin
Solve the flow shop problem for two machines P_1', P_2' where each job J_j has processing time $a_j = \sum_{i=1}^{\lceil m/2 \rceil} p_{ij}$ on P_1' and procssing time $b_j = \sum_{i=\lceil m/2 \rceil + 1}^{m} p_{ij}$ on P_2', respectively;
Let S be the two-machine schedule thus obtained;
Schedule the jobs on the given m machines according to the two machine schedule S;
end;

The worst case performance ratio of Algorithm 6.1.4 can be derived with the following Lemma 6.1.5.

Lemma 6.1.5 For each problem $F \| C_{max}$ (permutation flow shops included) and $O \| C_{max}$, the application of H_2 guarantees $C_{max}(H_2)/C_{max}^* \leq \lceil m/2 \rceil$.

Proof. Let S be an optimal schedule of length C_{max}^* for an instance of the problem under consideration. As $\mathcal{M}_2$ from condition C2 is less restrictive than $\mathcal{M}_1$, it follows from Lemma 6.1.2 that there exists a preemptive schedule S' which remains feasible under C2, and whose length is $C_{max}'/C_{max}^* \leq \lceil m/2 \rceil$. By construction of $\mathcal{M}_2$, S' can be interpreted as a preemptive schedule of the job set on the two virtual machines P_1', P_2', where P_1' does all processing which is required on the machines $P_1, \cdots, P_{\lceil m/2 \rceil}$, and P_2' does all processing which is required on the machines $P_{\lceil m/2 \rceil+1}, \cdots, P_m$. Since on two machines there is no advantage to preemption tasks, the schedule S generated by algorithm H_2 has length $C_{max}(H_2) \leq C_{max}' \leq \lceil m/2 \rceil C_{max}^*$. $\square$

H_2 can be implemented to run in $O(n(m + \log n))$ for $F \| C_{max}$ and also for its permutation variant using Algorithm 6.1.1. It is easy to adapt Lemma 6.1.2 to a given preemptive schedule S so that the $\lceil m/2 \rceil$ bound for H_2 extends to $F \| pmtn \| C_{max}$ as well.

The following example shows that the $\lceil m/2 \rceil$ bound of H_2 is tight for $F \| C_{max}$. Take m jobs J_j, $j = 1, \cdots, m$, with processing times $p_{ij} = p > 0$ for $i = j$, whereas $p_{ij} = \varepsilon \to 0$ for $i \neq j$. H_2 uses the processing times $a_j = p + (\lceil m/2 \rceil - 1)\varepsilon$, $b_j = \lfloor m/2 \rfloor \varepsilon$ for $j \leq \lceil m/2 \rceil$, and $a_j = \lceil m/2 \rceil \varepsilon$, $b_j = p + (\lceil m/2 \rceil - 1)\varepsilon$ for $j > \lceil m/2 \rceil$. Consider job sets $\mathcal{J}^k$ which consist of k copies of each of these m jobs. For an optimal flow shop schedule for $\mathcal{J}^k$ we get $C_{max}^* = kp + (m-1)(k+1)\varepsilon$. The optimal two machine flow shop schedule for $\mathcal{J}^k$ produced by H_2 may start with all k copies of $J_{\lceil m/2 \rceil+1}, J_{\lceil m/2 \rceil+2}, \cdots, J_m$ and then continue with all k copies $J_1, J_2, \cdots, J_{\lceil m/2 \rceil}$. On m machines this results in a length of $C_{max}(H_2) = (m-1+k\lfloor m/2 \rfloor)\varepsilon + \lceil m/2 \rceil pk$. It follows that $C_{max}(H_2)/C_{max}^*$ approaches $\lceil m/2 \rceil$ as $\varepsilon \to 0$.

Problem $F2 \| no\text{-}wait \| C_{max}$

An interesting subcase of flow shop scheduling is that with *no-wait constraints* where no intermediate storage is considered and a job once finished on one machine must immediately be started on the next one.

The two-machine case, i.e. problem $F2 \| no\text{-}wait \| C_{max}$, may be formulated as a special case of scheduling jobs on one machine whose *state* is described by a single real valued variable x (the so-called *one state-variable machine problem*) [GG64, RR72]. Job J_i requires a starting state $x = A_i$ and leaves with $x = B_i$. There is a cost for changing the machine state x in order to enable the next job to start. The cost c_{ij} of J_j following J_i is given by

$$c_{ij} = \begin{cases} \int\limits_{B_i}^{A_j} f(x)dx & \text{if } A_j \geq B_i, \\[2em] \int\limits_{A_j}^{B_i} g(x)dx & \text{if } B_i > A_j, \end{cases}$$

where $f(x)$ and $g(x)$ are integrable functions satisfying $f(x) + g(x) \geq 0$. The objective is to find a minimal cost sequence for the n jobs. Let us observe that problem $F2 \mid no\text{-}wait \mid C_{\max}$ may be modeled in the above way if $A_j = p_{1j}$, $B_j = p_{2j}$, $f(x) = 1$ and $g(x) = 0$. Cost c_{ij} then corresponds to the idle time on the second machine when J_j follows J_i, and hence a minimal cost sequence for the one state-variable machine problem also minimizes the completion time of the schedule for problem $F2 \mid no\text{-}wait \mid C_{\max}$. On the other hand, the first problem corresponds also to a special case of the traveling salesman problem which can be solved in $O(n^2)$ time [GG64]. Unfortunately, more complicated assumptions concerning the structure of the flow shop problem result in its NP-hardness. So, for example, $Fm \mid no\text{-}wait \mid C_{\max}$ is unary NP-hard for fixed $m \geq 3$ [Roc84].

As far as approximation algorithms are concerned H_1 is not applicable here, but H_2 turns out to work.

Lemma 6.1.6 *For $F \mid no\text{-}wait \mid C_{\max}$, the application of H_2 guarantees $C_{\max}(H_2)/C_{\max}^* \leq \lceil m/2 \rceil$.*

Proof. It is easy to see that solving the two machine instance by H_2 is equivalent to solving the given instance of the m machine problem under the additional condition C2. It remains to show that for each no-wait schedule S of length $C_{\max}$ there is a corresponding schedule S' which is feasible under C2 and has length $C_{\max}' \leq \lceil m/2 \rceil C_{\max}$. Let $J_1, J_2, \cdots, J_n$ be the sequence in which the jobs are processed in S and let s_{ij} be the start time of job J_j, $j = 1, \cdots, n$, on machine P_i, $i = 1, \cdots, m$. As a consequence of the no-wait requirement, the successor J_{j+1} of J_j cannot start to be processed on machine P_{i-1} before J_j starts to be processed on machine P_i. Thus for $q = \lceil m/2 \rceil$ we have $s_{q+1,j} \leq s_{q,j+1} \leq \cdots \leq s_{1,j+q}$ and for the finish time C_j of job J_j we get $C_j \leq s_{m,j+1} \leq s_{m-1,j+2} \leq \cdots \leq s_{q+1,j+m-q} \leq s_{q+1,j+q}$. This shows that if we would remove the jobs between J_j and J_{j+q} from S, then S would satisfy C2 in the interval $[s_{q+1,j}, s_{q+1,j+q}]$. Hence, for each $k = 1, \cdots, q$ the sub-schedule S_k of S which covers only the jobs of the subsequence $J_k, J_{k+q}, J_{k+2q}, \cdots, J_{k+\lfloor(n-k)/q\rfloor q}$ of $J_1, \cdots, J_n$ satisfies C2. Arrange these subschedules in sequence. None is longer than $C_{\max}$, and each job appears in one of them. The resulting schedule S' is feasible and has length $C_{\max}' \leq qC_{\max}$. $\square$

Using the algorithm of Gilmore and Gomory [GG64], H_2 runs in $O(n(m + \log n))$ time. The tightness example given above applies to the no-wait flow shop as well, since the optimal schedule is in fact a no-wait schedule, and on two machines it is optimal to have any alternating sequence of jobs $J_b, J_a, J_b, J_a \cdots$ with $a \in \{1, \cdots, \lceil m/2 \rceil\}$ and $b \in$

$\{\lceil m/2 \rceil + 1, \cdots, m\}$, and in case of odd m this may be followed by all copies of J_1. When ε tends to zero, the length of such a schedule on m machines approaches $\lceil m/2 \rceil kp$, thus $C_{max}(H_2)/C^*_{max}$ approaches $\lceil m/2 \rceil$.

An interesting fact about the lengths of no-wait and normal flow shop schedules, respectively, has been proved in [Len–]. It appears that the no-wait constraint may lengthen the optimal flow shop schedule considerably, since $C^*_{max}(no\text{-}wait)/C^*_{max} < m$ for $m \geq 2$.

6.2 Open Shop Scheduling

We recall that the formulation of an open shop scheduling problem is the same as for the flow shop problem except that the order of processing tasks comprising one job may be arbitrary.

Problem $O2 \mid\mid C_{max}$

Let us consider nonpreemptive scheduling first. Problem $O2 \mid\mid C_{max}$ can be solved in $O(n)$ time [GS76]. We give here a simplified description of the algorithm presented in [LLRK82]. For convenience let us denote $a_j = p_{1j}$, $b_j = p_{2j}$, $\mathcal{A} = \{J_j \mid a_j \geq b_j\}$, $\mathcal{B} = \{J_j \mid a_j < b_j\}$, $K_1 = \Sigma a_j$ and $K_2 = \Sigma b_j$.

Algorithm 6.2.1 *Gonzalez-Sahni algorithm for $O2 \mid\mid C_{max}$* [GS76].
begin
Choose any two jobs J_k and J_l for which $a_k \geq \max_{J_j \in \mathcal{A}} \{b_j\}$ and $b_l \geq \max_{J_j \in \mathcal{B}} \{a_j\}$;

Set $\mathcal{A}' := \mathcal{A} - \{J_k, J_l\}$;
Set $\mathcal{B}' := \mathcal{B} - \{J_k, J_l\}$;
Construct separate schedules for $\mathcal{B}' \cup \{J_l\}$ and $\mathcal{A}' \cup \{J_k\}$ using patterns shown in Figure 6.2.1;   -- other tasks from $\mathcal{A}'$ and $\mathcal{B}'$ are scheduled arbitrarily
Join both schedules in the way shown in Figure 6.2.2;
Move tasks from $\mathcal{B}' \cup \{J_l\}$ processed on P_2 to the right;
        -- it has been assumed that $K_1 - a_l \geq K_2 - b_k$; the opposite case is symmetric
Change the order of processing on P_2 in such a way that T_{2k} is processed first on this machine;
end;

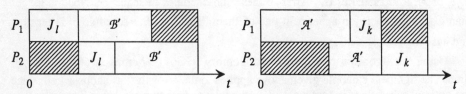

Figure 6.2.1 *A schedule for Algorithm 6.2.1*

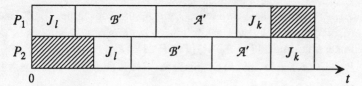

Figure 6.2.2 *A schedule for Algorithm 6.2.1*

The above problem becomes *NP*-hard as the number of machines increases to 3. As far as heuristics are concerned we refer to the machine aggregation algorithms introduced in Section 6.1 which in the case of open shop use Algorithm 6.2.1.

Problem $O \mid pmtn \mid C_{max}$

Again preemptions result in a polynomial time algorithm. That is, problem $O \mid pmtn \mid C_{max}$ can be optimally solved by taking

$$C_{max}^* = \max \{\max_j \{\sum_{i=1}^m p_{ij}\}, \max_i \{\sum_{j=1}^n p_{ij}\}\}$$

and then applying Algorithm 5.1.16 [GS76].

Problems $O2 \mid\mid \Sigma C_j$ and $O2 \mid\mid L_{max}$

Let us mention here that problems $O2 \mid\mid \Sigma C_j$ and $O2 \mid\mid L_{max}$ are *NP*-hard, as proved in [AC82] and [LLRK81], respectively, and problem $O \mid pmtn, r_j \mid L_{max}$ is solvable via the linear programming approach [CS81].

As far as heuristics are concerned, arbitrary list scheduling and the *SPT* algorithm have been evaluated for $O \mid\mid \Sigma C_j$ [AC82]. Their asymptotic performance ratios are $R_L^\infty = n$ and $R_{SPT}^\infty = m$, respectively. Since the number of tasks is usually much larger than the number of machines, the bounds indicate the advantage of *SPT* schedules over arbitrary ones.

6.3 Job Shop Scheduling

In case of job shop scheduling a number of tasks per job, their assignment to machines and an order of processing is arbitrary but known a priori. In this section one polynomially solvable case of the job shop scheduling problem will be presented. Then a branch and bound, and heuristic algorithms, respectively, will be given.

6.3.1 Basic Ideas

Let us consider the following example.

Example 6.3.1 Assume we have two jobs J_1 and J_2, three machines P_1, P_2 and P_3, and each job consists of three tasks, with the following vectors of assignments of tasks, machines and processing times: $[T_{11}, P_1, 3]$, $[T_{21}, P_2, 1]$, $[T_{31}, P_3, 3]$ and $[T_{12}, P_1, 2]$, $[T_{22}, P_3, 2]$, $[T_{32}, P_2, 1]$. A feasible but not optimal schedule is shown in Figure 6.3.1. □

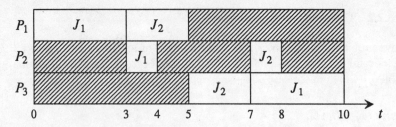

Figure 6.3.1 *Feasible schedule for Example* 6.3.1.

It is well known that job shop scheduling is not only a model with a broad application area but also one of the computationally hardest problems investigated so far in this book; the job shop scheduling problem is already *NP*-hard for only two machines. No heuristic with performance guarantee has been developed until now. There are, however, some special cases for which polynomial time algorithms exist:

- two machine job shops and all tasks have unit processing time; solvable in time linear in the total number of tasks [HA82, Bru81];

- two jobs job shops; solvable in $O(n_1 n_2 \log n_1 n_2)$ time [Ake56, HN63, Bru88] where n_1 and n_2 are the number of tasks of the first and the second job, respectively;

- two machine job shops where jobs do not have more than two tasks; solvable in $O(n \log n)$ time [Jac56].

Below we present an algorithm by Jackson for solving problem $J2 | n_j \leq 2 | C_{max}$. The algorithm divides jobs into four *classes* $\mathcal{J}_1$, $\mathcal{J}_2$, $\mathcal{J}_{12}$ and $\mathcal{J}_{21}$, where $\mathcal{J}_i$, $i = 1, 2$, denotes a subset of jobs consisting of only one task which is to be performed on machine P_i and $\mathcal{J}_{hi}$, $hi = 12, 21$, denotes a subset of jobs consisting of two tasks which are to be performed on machine P_h and P_i, respectively. The algorithm is as follows.

Algorithm 6.3.2 *Jackson's algorithm for $J2 | n_j \leq 2 | C_{max}$* [Jac56].
begin
Call Algorithm 6.1.1 for the job set $\mathcal{J}_{12}$;
Call Algorithm 6.1.1 for the job set $\mathcal{J}_{21}$;
Assign jobs to machine P_1 in order $\mathcal{J}_{12}, \mathcal{J}_1, \mathcal{J}_{21}$;
Assign jobs to machine P_2 in order $\mathcal{J}_{21}, \mathcal{J}_2, \mathcal{J}_{12}$;
    -- jobs in sets $\mathcal{J}_{12}$ and $\mathcal{J}_{21}$ are ordered by Algorithm 6.1.1
    -- jobs in sets $\mathcal{J}_1$ and $\mathcal{J}_2$ appear in any order
end;

The complexity of this algorithm is $O(n\log n)$, since its most complex function is ordering the jobs. Unfortunately, this is as far as we can use polynomial time, optimization algorithms, since other problems of scheduling in job shops are strongly *NP-hard*.

On the other hand there exist many enumerative algorithms for solving the general job shop scheduling problem. The notorious 10-machine, 10-job problem introduced by [FT63] still serves as a benchmark for these approaches. No optimal solution was found until 1987, when Carlier and Pinson [CP89] developed an algorithm which had to compute roughly 22.000 nodes consuming five hours of computing time on a minicomputer PRIME 2655. One of the most efficient optimization algorithms developed in the meantime is described in [BJS92]; using this algorithm the above mentioned 10x10 - problem was solved on a SUN workstation within 16 minutes calculating roughly 4.000 nodes. The solution is generated by a branch and bound algorithm using the disjunctive graph representation due to [RS64].

For a job shop scheduling problem a *disjunctive graph* $G = (\mathcal{V}, C \cup \mathcal{D})$ consists of a set of nodes $\mathcal{V} = \mathcal{T} \cup \{s, t\}$, a set of conjunctive arcs C and a set of so-called *disjunctive arcs* $\mathcal{D}$. $\mathcal{V}$ represents the tasks of all jobs and contains additionally two nodes s and t which are respectively source and sink nodes of G. Each node T_{ij} has a weight equal to the corresponding task processing time; the weight of s and t is zero. C represents the processing order of the tasks and $\mathcal{D}$ represents their machine requirements, i.e. for every pair of tasks requiring the same machine two directed arcs with opposite directions are introduced. A *schedule* (may be partial) corresponds to an acyclic subgraph of G containing only directed conjunctive and disjunctive arcs. The (chosen) set of disjunctive arcs of this subgraph is called *selection* and will be denoted by S. If S contains all nodes and exactly one disjunctive arc from each pair we call S a *complete selection*. Figure 6.3.2 shows the disjunctive graph and the complete selection (lines marked with dots) corresponding to the solution given in Figure 6.3.1. The length of the corresponding schedule is given by the length of the *longest path* in G, i.e. the critical path. For the problem in Example 6.3.1, the longest path is given by the arcs (s, T_{11}), (T_{11}, T_{12}), (T_{12}, T_{22}), (T_{22}, T_{31}) and (T_{31}, t).

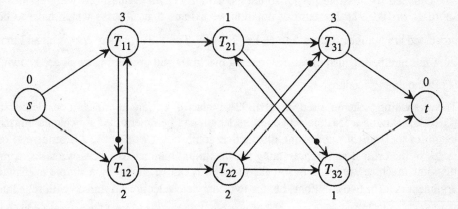

Figure 6.3.2 *Graph representation of Example 6.3.1.*

Some heuristics are also based on the disjunctive graph model. For example, in [ABZ88] a so-called *shifting bottleneck procedure* is presented where in each iteration single machine scheduling problems are solved. This method can also be combined with partial enumeration. In [LAL88] and [MSS88] simulated annealing heuristics are applied which we started to discuss already in Section 2.5. The approaches are appealing for great problem sizes or under conditions where short computing times are required. For the 10x20 problem of [ABZ88] the branch and bound algorithm of [BJS92] stopped with some suboptimal solution requiring three days of computing time; with simulated annealing a solution 5% better than the subotimal one was found in roughly five minutes on a slower computer [MSS88].

Below we review the branch and bound approach and then we investigate the approaches using simulated annealing with a short comment on the bottleneck heuristic. At the end of this section we discuss empirical results of the four solution approaches concerning solution quality and computing times.

6.3.2 Branch and Bound Algorithm

For Example 6.3.1 (as for other instances of $J \mid \mid C_{\max}$) a complete selection with minimum longest path length from s to t, i.e. an optimal solution, can be found by means of a branch and bound algorithm. Apart from the root node each node r of the search tree represents some selection S_r; for the root node no selection is given. The successors of each node are generated by choosing additional disjunctive arcs such that the selection of the predecessor node is a partial set of the selection of the successor nodes. The generation of successor nodes stops if a feasible solution (complete selection) has been found or if it can be shown that the node under investigation does not contain an optimal solution. For each node of the search tree a lower bound (*LB*) and an upper bound (*UB*) can be calculated. For cyclic, i.e. infeasible solutions the lower bound is set to infinity; upper bounds are determined by $C_{\max}$ values of actually best feasible schedules. Two major questions which have great influence on the efficiency of the algorithm have still to be answered: (1) what branching procedure should be used and (2) how should be the branching procedure chosen, i.e. how should the lower bounds be calculated for feasible partial solutions. To answer these questions we present the approach of [BJS92]. For ease of notation we assume that all tasks which have to be processed are numbered from 1 to N, i.e. $T = \{T_1, T_2, \cdots, T_N\}$, where $N = \sum_{j=1}^{n} n_j$, and that from this numbering also the corresponding machines and processing times are known.

(1) Branching Procedure

The branching scheme used in [BJS92] is based on an approach considered in [GNZ86]. Having a feasible schedule, its length can be determined by calculating the length of the *critical path* of the disjunctive graph $G = (\mathcal{V}, C \cup S)$. All sequences of nodes of the critical path representing the maximum number of successive tasks using the same machine are forming so-called *blocks*. It can be shown by a simple exchange argument that for two solutions, i.e. for two complete selections S and S' with schedule lengths $C_{\max}^{S'} < C_{\max}^{S}$ at least one task of one block in the schedule S' is processed before the first or after the last task of the corresponding block in a schedule S.

Let y be some feasible solution generated from all possible solutions $\mathcal{Y}_r$ of a particular node r of the search tree and let S be the corresponding schedule. Let us further assume that y is generated by means of some heuristic. Now according to the above observation y can only be improved if in at least one block of S the first or the last task is exchanged with some other task of the same block. Considering these conditions the following branching scheme to generate successors from node r is used.

Let $\mathcal{B}_1, \cdots, \mathcal{B}_k$ be the blocks in S. For a block $\mathcal{B}_i$ with tasks $T_1^i, \cdots, T_{m_i}^i$ there exists a set of "before-candidates" $\mathcal{E}_i^B := \mathcal{B}_i - \{T_1^i\}$ and a set of "after-candidates" $\mathcal{E}_i^A := \mathcal{B}_i - \{T_{m_i}^i\}$. Both arc sets represent interchange possibilities. Furthermore, let us assume that there exists a permutation of length $2K$ of arc sets O_i and Q_i with $O_i := \{(T_1^i, T) \mid T \in \mathcal{E}_i^B\}$ and $Q_i := \{(T, T_{m_i}^i) \mid T \in \mathcal{E}_i^A\}$. Now using this permutation a set S_T^B of fixed disjunctive arcs concerning "before-candidates" and a set S_T^A of fixed disjunctive arcs concerning "after-candidates" is determined. Sets which contain cycles in itself or form cycles in conjunction with S_r are eliminated because of infeasibility. The sets S_T^B and S_T^A are added to the already fixed disjunctions S_r. These solutions represent successor nodes of node r in the search tree.

For the branching scheme the order of the successors of a search tree node r has also to be determined. To decide this, and moreover to answer the questions of fixing additional disjunctive arcs and of calculating lower bounds, the variables *head* and *tail* have to be introduced. Calculations of heads and tails are based on all conjunctive and fixed disjunctive arcs represented by a special search tree node r: the head h_j of task T_j is an earliest possible starting time of that task and the tail q_j of task T_j is the lower bound of the time period between the finish time of T_j and C_{max}^*. A simple way to determine heads and tails is to calculate the longest path from s to T_j and from T_j to t, respectively.

For computational purposes one objective of the branching scheme is to add large numbers of fixed disjunctions to the set S_r in each branching step. The approach to reach this goal relies on a method given by [CP88], uses heads and tails and is based on the following inequalities.

$$h_k + p_k + \sum_{T_j \in \mathcal{T}_k} p_j + \min_{T_j \in \mathcal{T}_k} \{p_j\} \geq UB, \tag{6.3.1}$$

$$\min_{T_j \in \mathcal{T}_k} \{h_j\} + \sum_{T_j \in \mathcal{T}_k} p_j + p_k + q_k \geq UB, \tag{6.3.2}$$

$$\min_{T_j \in \mathcal{T}_k} \{h_j\} + \sum_{T_j \in \mathcal{T}_k} p_j + p_k + \min_{T_j \in \mathcal{T}_k} \{q_j\} \geq UB. \tag{6.3.3}$$

$\mathcal{T}_i$ is the set of tasks which have to be processed on a given machine P_i, T_k some task of $\mathcal{T}_i$, and $\mathcal{T}_k \subseteq \mathcal{T}_i - \{T_k\}$. For $|\mathcal{T}_k| \geq 2$ it can be shown that

(1) if inequalities (6.3.1) and (6.3.3) hold then in all solutions task T_k has to be processed *after* all tasks of $\mathcal{T}_k$ and that

(2) if inequalities (6.3.2) and (6.3.3) hold then in all solutions task T_k has to be processed *before* all tasks of $\mathcal{T}_k$.

In case of (1) the pair $(\mathcal{T}_k, T_k)$ is called a *primal pair*; now all disjunctive arcs $\{(T_j, T_k) \mid T_j \in \mathcal{T}_k\}$ (primal arcs) can be fixed. (2) leads to the *dual pair* $(T_k, \mathcal{T}_k)$ and now disjunctive arcs $\{(T_k, T_j) \mid T_j \in \mathcal{T}_k\}$ (dual arcs) can be fixed. For calculating all primal and dual pairs an efficient method has been suggested in [BJS92]. If $|\mathcal{T}_k| = 1$ then T_j has to be processed before T_k in every solution if

$$h_k + p_k + p_j + q_j \geq UB \qquad\qquad (6.3.4)$$

holds; then the arc (T_j, T_k) (direct arc) will be fixed.

The branching scheme now fixes as many arcs as possible according to that approach; after each iteration of arc-fixing new heads and tails have to be calculated. The tree is traversed using a depth-first search strategy.

(2) Calculation of lower bounds

For each node r of the search tree with a set $\mathcal{S}_r$ of fixed disjunctive arcs a lower bound is calculated for each successor node s of r. If its value exceeds the value of the current upper bound the node under investigation can be discarded from the solution process.

The first idea for calculating lower bounds is to determine the longest path in the disjunctive graph considering only already fixed disjunctive arcs and all given conjunctive arcs. The calculation can be improved depending on different steps of the solution process. The corresponding cases to distinguish are:

(a) during the computation of sets $\mathcal{E}_i^B$ and $\mathcal{E}_i^A$, task T_j is moved before or after block $\mathcal{B}$,

(b) during the computation of heads and tails and

(c) after the computation of heads and tails.

For details we refer to [BJS92]. The calculation of all these lower bounds is advantageous because every time a lower bound exceeds the upper bound all further considerations for the node under investigation can be stopped. With these ideas the following algorithm describes the solution procedure.

Algorithm 6.3.3 *Branch and bound algorithm for* $J \| C_{\max}$ *for node* r [BJS92].
begin
Calculate a schedule $S \in \mathcal{Y}_r$ using some heuristic;
    -- $\mathcal{Y}_r$ contains all possible schedules which can be generated from search tree node r
Calculate the critical path CP;
if $C_{\max}^S < UB$
then
    begin
    $UB := C_{\max}^S$;
    Calculate the blocks of CP;
    Calculate the sets $\mathcal{E}_i^B$ and $\mathcal{E}_i^A$;
    while there exists a task $T_j \in \mathcal{E}_i^v$ with $i = 1, \cdots, k$, and $v = A$ or B **do**

```
    begin
      Delete T_j from E_i^v;
      Choose selections for the corresponding successor s of node r;
      Calculate a lower bound LB(s) for node s;
      if LB(s) < UB then call Branch and Bound (s) recursively;
      end
    end
end;
```

For finding a first feasible schedule a priority rule is used which is based on the calculation of special lower bounds. That task is scheduled next which induces the smallest lower bound and all of its predecessors are already scheduled [BJS92].

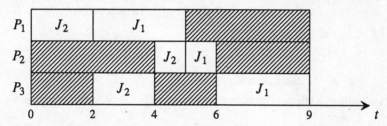

Figure 6.3.3 *Optimal schedule for Example* 6.3.1.

Applying the branch and bound algorithm to Example 6.3.1 gives a lower bound of 8, the initial solution with an upper bound of 10 shown in Figure 6.3.1 and the optimal solution with $C_{max} = 9$ is shown in Figure 6.3.3.

6.3.3 Simulated Annealing

As an alternative to optimization algorithms heuristic approaches could be used to find suboptimal schedules for job shop problems. For practical applications mainly priority rules are suggested; unfortunately none of the rules seems to outperform any other for practical problem settings. Recently *simulated annealing* (*SA*) was also applied to job shop scheduling problems.

For the success of *SA* techniques (cf. Section 2.5) the definition of *neighborhoods* of seed solutions is critical. Recall that a neighborhood $\mathcal{N}_i$ of some solution i is defined as the set of solutions that can be reached from i by exactly one transition. For job shop scheduling problems the neighborhoods can be defined using transitions of the critical path of the disjunctive graph. To find a schedule S_j with a makespan smaller than this of the seed schedule S_i, the critical path has to be shortened. This is only possible - as we saw in the last section - if we interchange the sequence of tasks belonging to the critical path. Unfortunately, in the case of job shop problems very few interchanges lead to schedules that are better than some good seed solution.

Moreover the movements of the seed are also controlled by some prespecified *acceptance probability* for inferior solutions. $AP_{ij}(k)$ represents the probability to accept an inferior schedule S_j to seed schedule S_i as the current seed schedule. Its value is calculated by min $\{1, \exp(-(C_{max}^j - C_{max}^i)/c_k)\}$ where C_{max}^j and C_{max}^i are the lengths of schedules S_j, S_i, and c_k is a positive control parameter of annealing at stage k.

In [LAL88] and [MSS88] two simulated annealing approaches to job shop scheduling have been suggested. The approach given in [MSS88] is called a *controlled search SA* and is a specialization of Algorithm 2.5.1 introduced in Section 2.5.

Algorithm 6.3.4 *simulated annealing algorithm for* $J \| C_{max}$ [MSS88].
begin
Generate S_i; -- initial seed schedule generated by a heuristic
for $k = 1, \cdots, K$ **do** -- number of stages in SA
    for $m = 1, \cdots, M_k$ **do** -- number of searches in each stage
        begin
        Generate S_j from $\mathcal{N}_i$; -- $\mathcal{N}_i$ is the neighborhood of schedule S_i
        if $C_{max}^j - C_{max}^i < 0$
        then $i := j$
        else
            if $AP_{ij}(k) > $ random $[0, 1)$
    -- $AP_{ij}(k)$ is the acceptance probability of new schedule S_j from schedule S_i at stage k
            then $i := j$
            else perform a local search from S_j and find schedule S_{i_0};
        if $C_{max}^{i_0} - C_{max}^i < 0$ **then** $i := i_0$;
        Keep the best solution found so far;
        end
end;

In [MSS88] a constant acceptance probability for each stage, i.e. $AP_{ij}(k) = AP(k)$ is assumed. The search is restricted to neighborhoods defined with respect to *semi-active schedules*, i.e. those feasible schedules that cannot be improved in terms of makespan by shifting a task to the left without changing the task sequence on at least one machine. A *critical path* of a semi-active schedule is defined again by a set of tasks that forms a longest path in the disjunctive graph. With $\mathcal{N}_i^1$ a set of semi-active schedules is used which can be obtained by interchanging single pairs of adjacent tasks belonging to a critical path of the semi-active schedule S_i. Due to feasibility conditions such a pair of tasks must come from the same machine and must belong to different jobs. Taking into account the observation that neighborhood $\mathcal{N}_i^1$ includes only a few adjacent pairs that improve the makespan by exactly one interchange, an extended search neighborhood $\mathcal{N}_i^2$ is defined where multi adjacent pairwise interchanges are possible.

To generate the initial seed schedule the shifting bottleneck method without partial enumeration (*SB1*) proposed by [ABZ88] is used. *SB1* schedules one machine at a time. The *length of the longest path* in a disjunctive graph from the source node to a node T_j determines the earliest start time r_j of task T_j. The length of a longest path from node T_j to the sink node of the graph determines the latest finish time q_j of task T_j. This corresponds to the delivery time model for a single machine discussed in Section 4.1.2

where each task T_j has ready time r_j, processing time p_j and amount of time q_j in the system after its completion. This problem can be solved optimally using a branch and bound procedure due to [Car82]. Each unscheduled machine gets a *priority index* determined by the value of the objective function of the single machine problem. The machine with largest priority index is the *bottleneck machine* and is scheduled next. Once a bottleneck machine has been scheduled, the machines previously scheduled are reoptimized one by one solving the corresponding single machine problems again. The cycle of the reoptimization for the scheduled machines continues until no further improvement is possible or it was already reoptimized three times. Whenever a cycle of reoptimization is completed the machines are reordered according to nonincreasing priority indices.

If a solution in the neighborhood is not accepted, *deterministic local search* within *SA* can be applied to the rejected schedule. The search terminates when a local optimum has been found or an upper limit on the number of iterations has been reached. If the solution obtained by deterministic local search is superior to seed solution S_i it replaces the seed solution; otherwise S_i is retained. We will denote this approach by *SA1*. On the other hand, another simulated annealing algorithm has been proposed in [LAL88] where a neighborhood $\mathcal{N}_i$ of some schedule S_i is defined by exchanging the sequence of pairs of tasks being processed on the same machine, belonging to the critical path, and being connected by an arc. With this the size of the neighborhood is bounded by $m(n-1)$ where n is the number of jobs and m is the number of machines. The cost of each schedule is determined by the length of a critical path. The cooling schedule which is used in [LAL88] is described in [AL85]. We will denote this algorithm by *SA2*.

6.3.4 Computational Results

The branch and bound algorithm, the two *SA* algorithms and the shifting bottleneck algorithm without (*SB1*) and with partial enumeration (*SB2*) are now evaluated. The tests have taken into account *accuracy* (solution quality) and time to compute the solutions. Test problems from Fisher and Thompson [FT63] and from Adams et al. [ABZ88] have been used, where the sequence of machines has been randomly generated for each job. For all instances the number of tasks of each job equals the number of machines, and each job has precisely one task on each machine. For the problems presented in [FT63] the processing times of the tasks are randomly chosen integers from the intervals (1, 10) for the 6-machine, 6-job problem, and from (1, 99) for the two other ones. For the instances of [ABZ88] the processing times are chosen from the discrete uniform distribution on the interval (5, 99). The results are shown in Table 6.3.1 where the first number in each entry denotes the best solution found and the second number gives the elapsed CPU time in seconds.

Now we comment briefly on the way how particular results presented in the table were obtained. As far as the shifting bottleneck method is concerned, the best result obtained either by this method or by its combination with partial enumeration, are presented. On the other hand, testing *SA2* algorithm [LAL88], more than one solution was generated for each problem instance and with this the numbers in the entries are average values.

ALGORITHM ────────────── PROBLEM	Branch and bound [BJS92]	Shifting bottleneck SB [ABZ88]	Simulated annealing $SA1$ [MSS88]	Simulated annealing $SA2$ [LAL88]
6x6 [FT63]	55/0	55/1	---	56^*/8
10x10 [FT63]	930/1138	930/426	946/494	933.4^*/57772
5x20 [FT63]	1179 1)	1178/40	---	1173.8^*/62756
5x10 [ABZ88]	666/0	666/1	2)	707^*/6
	655/3	669/6	655/2	671^*/24
	597/1	605/16	597/17	617.6(606)/129
	590/4	593/23	590/17	593.8^*/121
	593/0	593/0	2)	594.4^*/5
5x15 [ABZ88]	926/0	926/1	2)	937.2^*/16
	890/0	890/1	2)	900.6^*/66
	863/0	863/2	863/1	905.8^*/16
	951/0	951/0	2)	965.2^*/13
	958/0	959/0	2)	958^*/14
5x20 [ABZ88]	1222/0	1222/1	2)	1229.6^*/32
	1039/1	1039/0	2)	1042.8^*/34
	1150/0	1150/1	2)	1154.6^*/32
	1292/0	1292/0	2)	1292^*/27
	1207/4	1207/2	2)	1299.8^*/34
10x10 [ABZ88]	945/58	978/120	959/80	981(956)/110
	784/15	787/96	784/48	792.4^*/112
	848/64	859/113	848/54	872.2(861)/112
	842/340	860/120	842/59	853.4(848)/830
	902/343	914/145	907/51	908.4^*/667
10x15 [ABZ88]	1059 1)	1084/181	1071/105	1067.6(1063)/1991
	927/6700	944/210	927/94	944.2(938)/2163
	1032/3451	1032/113	1032/12	1051^*/275
	935/89062	976/217	973/102	966.6(952)/2098
	977/273162	1017/215	991/92	1004.4(992)/2133
10x20 [ABZ88]	1218/43800	1224/372	1218/31	1219^*/4342
	1270 1)	1291/419	1274/146	$1273.6^{(*)}$/4535
	1276 1)	1250/451	1216/156	1244.8(1224)/4354
	1202 1)	1239/446	1196/138	1260.4(1203)/581
	1355/239	1355/276	1355/8	1355^*/3956
10x30 [ABZ88]	1784/7	1784/19	2)	1784^*/1517
	1850/1	1850/15	2)	1850^*/1752
	1719/75	1719/13	2)	1726.6^*/1880
	1721/12	1721/14	2)	1775.6^*/1886
	1888/23	1888/11	2)	2011.2^*/434
15x15 [ABZ88]	1268/113419	1305/368	1292/320	1300(1293)/5346
	1424 1)	1423/419	1435/295	1442.4(1433)/5287

1 Optimality could not be proved within a time of 72 hours.
2 No SA was necessary since the starting solution using SB1 was already optimal.

1232 [1]	1255/540	1231/345	1227.2$^{(*)}$/5480
1233/94739	1273/335	1251/337	1258.2(1248)/5766
1238 [1]	1269/450	1235/309	1247.4$^{(*)}$/5373

Table 6.3.1 *The results of an experimental comparison of four algorithms for* $J \| C_{max}$.

As far as computing time is concerned, the computer used for testing *SA2* method, i.e. VAX-785, here is considered to be a standard one. Hence, the computing times appearing in column 4 are the same as given in [LAL88]. The computing times given in [ABZ88] and [MSS88] are halved in columns 2 and 3 repetively, following the suggestion of [LAL88] since they were obtained on a slower machine VAX-780. On the other hand, computing times given in [BJS92] should be multiplied by a factor of 6 to 9 because of the fast computer, i.e. Sun 4/20.

The branch and bound algorithm was implemented in C on a Sun 4/20 [BJS92] with an iterative not recursive implementation using a stack of search tree nodes which resulted in a much faster code. Also some special data structures concerning local data like blocks on a critical path, before- and after-candidates, lower bounds and global data like conjunctive arcs and upper bounds were used. In 83.7 percent of all cases the algorithm found the optimal solution or best solution known so far and in 67 percent of these cases it was either the only algorithm which found this result or the fastest solution method (taking into account original computing times).

In [MSS88] *SA1* algorithm has been tested on a VAX 780. Firstly, the authors generated an initial seed schedule using the shifting bottleneck method *SB1* of [ABZ88]. In case the optimal solution was already given by the start solution no *SA* had to be applied; this happened in 39% of all investigated cases (compare columns 2 and 3). For the remaining 25 cases *SA1* was started with an initial acceptance probability of 0.5 and then lineary and discretely decreased to 0.2. Limiting the number M_k of searches at each stage, the number K of stages and the number of iterations in the deterministic local search it turned out that in 52 percent of all cases where *SA1* was applied it found the optimal solution or best solution known so far and in 69.2 percent of these cases it was either the only algorithm which found this result or the fastest solution method. Solution times are calculated here using the time for generating the initial solution and the time for *SA1*.

In [LAL88] simulated annealing algorithm *SA2* has been tested on VAX-785. The authors applied the algorithm five times to each problem instance and *decrement* combination. For the decrement rule they used distance parameters of 0.1, 0.01, 0.001 and 0.0001 for the problems in [FT63], 1.0 and 0.1 for the 10x30 problem and 1.0, 0.1, 0.01 for the remaining problems. Initial and final value of the control parameter c was set to 0.95 and 10-6 respectively. Large (small) values of the distance parameter correspond to a fast (slow) decrement of c. The smaller the distance parameter, the better the solution and the longer the computing time were. When *SA2* was compared to pure iterative improvement methods, the authors report that the latter is easily outperformed by *SA2*. The authors recorded the best and the average schedule length and also average computing times for all runs on each distance parameter and problem instance combination. In column 4 of Table 6.3.1 the modified best average schedule length for each problem instance and the corresponding average computing time is shown, i.e. the average values of these schedule lengths where the first time the best schedule was generated. When an optimal solution was found during the recorded runs, the corresponding average schedule length is marked with an asterisk. If no optimal solution was found, the best found schedule length is put in brackets; if the generated schedule represents the best known solution so far but it is not proved to be the optimal solution then the asterisk is put in brackets. In 69.8 percent of all cases *SA2* found the optimal solution or best solution known so far and in 13.3 percent of these cases it was either the only algorithm which found this result or the fastest solution method.

Comparing the optimization algorithm with the different heuristics it can be observed that branch and bound did not find the optimal or best solution known so far in seven cases or 16.3 percent of all problem instances; in these cases the heuristics were more successful. Further it can be observed that using a theoretical combination of *SA* and *SB1* in 36 cases or with 83.7 percent the best solution could have been found. This points out that *SA* combined with some good heuristic can increase performance significantly. For the problems investigated here such a combination finds optimal or best known solutions as often as the optimization algorithm does.

From the results another observation can be made. If the relative ratio between jobs and machines is not smaller than 2, all heuristics find the optimal or best solution known so far; if the ratio is 1.5 in 3 of 5 cases branch and bound algorithm finds better solutions and if the ratio is 1, in 3 of 10 cases branch and bound algorithm finds better solutions. From this we might also conclude that it should be favourable to use *SA* or its combination with *SB1* as a start solution for branch and bound method.

References

AC82   J. O. Achugbue, F.Y.Chin, Scheduling the open shop to minimize mean flow time, *SIAM J.Comput.* 11, 1982, 709-720.

ABZ88   J. Adams, E. Balas, D. Zawack, The shifting bottleneck procedure for job shop scheduling, *Management Sci.* 34, 1988, 391-401.

Ake56   S. H. Akers, A graphical approach to production scheduling problems, *Oper. Res.* 4, 1956, 244-245.

AL85   E. H. L. Aarts, P. J. M. van Laarhoven, Statistical cooling: a general approach to combinatorial optimization problems, *Philips J. of Research* 40, 1985, 193-226.

Bar81   I. Barany, A vector-sum theorem and its application to improving flow shop guarantees, *Math. Oper. Res.* 6, 1981, 445-452.

BJS92   P. Brucker, B. Jurisch, B. Sievers, A branch & bound algorithm for the job-shop scheduling problem, Osnabrücker Schriften zur Mathematik, Universität Osnabrück, 1992.

Bru81   P. Brucker, Minimizing maximum lateness in a two-machine unit-time job shop, *Computing* 27, 1981, 367-370.

Bru88   P. Brucker, An efficient algorithm for the job-shop problem with two jobs, *Computing* 40, 1988, 353-359.

Car82   J. Carlier, The one machine sequencing problem, *European J. Oper. Res.* 11, 1982, 42-47.

CP88   J. Carlier, E. Pinson, A polynomial time algorithm for determining efficient immediate selections for the job-shop problem, Technical Report, Angers/Compiegne, 1989.

CP89   J. Carlier, E. Pinson, An algorithm for solving the job-shop problem, *Management Sci.* 35, 1989, 164-176.

CS81   Y. Cho, S. Sahni, Preemptive scheduling of independent jobs with release and due times on open, flow and job shops, *Oper. Res.* 29, 1981, 511-522.

FT63   H. Fisher, G. L. Thompson, Probabilistic learning combinations of local job-shop scheduling rules, in: J.F. Muth, G.L. Thompson (eds.), *Industrial Scheduling*, Englewood Cliffs, N.J., Prentice Hall, 1963, 225-251.

GG64   P. C. Gilmore, R. E. Gomory, Sequencing a one-state variable machine: a solvable case of the traveling salesman problem, *Oper. Res.* 12, 1964, 655-679.

GJS76   M. R. Garey, D. S. Johnson, R. Sethi, The complexity of flowshop and jobshop scheduling. *Math. Oper. Res.* 1, 1976, 117-129.

GNZ86   J. Grabowski, E. Nowicki, S. Zdrzalka, A block approach for single machine scheduling with release dates and due dates, *European J. Oper. Res.* 26, 1986, 278-285.

GS76   T. Gonzalez, S. Sahni, Open shop scheduling to minimize finish time, *J. Assoc. Comput. Mach.* 23, 1976, 665-679.

GS78   T. Gonzalez, S. Sahni, Flowshop and jobshop schedules: complexity and approximation. *Oper. Res.* 26, 1978, 36-52.

HA82   H. Hefetz, I. Adiri, An efficient optimal algorithm for the two machine unit-time jobshop schedule-length problem, *Math. Oper. Res.* 7, 1982, 354-360.

HN63   W. H. Hardgrave, G. L. Nemhauser, A geometric model and a graphical algorithm for a sequencing problem, *Oper. Res.* 11, 1963, 889-900.

Jac56   J. R. Jackson, An extension of Johnson's results on job lot scheduling, *Naval Res. Logist. Quart.* 3, 1956, 201-203.

Joh54   S. M. Johnson, Optimal two-and-three-stage production schedules, *Naval Res. Logist. Quart.* 1, 1954, 61-68.

Lag–   B. J. Lageweg, unpublished.

LAL88   P. J. M. van Laarhoven, E. H. L. Aarts, J. K. Lenstra, Job shop scheduling by simulated annealing, Report OS-R8809, CWI, 1988.

LLRK81 E. L. Lawler, J. K. Lenstra, A. H. G. Rinnooy Kan, Minimizing maximum lateness in two machine open shop, *Math. Oper. Res.* 6, 1981, 153-158. Erratum: *Math. Oper. Res.* 7, 1982, 635.

LLRK82 E. L. Lawler, J. K. Lenstra, A. H. G.Rinnooy Kan, Recent developments in deterministic sequencing and scheduling: a survey, in: M. A. H. Dempster, J. K. Lenstra, A. H. G. Rinnooy Kan (eds.) *Deterministic and Stochastic Scheduling*, Reidel, Dordrecht, 1982, 35-73.

Len–   J. K. Lenstra, unpublished result.

MSS88   H. Matsuo, C. J. Suh, R. S. Sullivan, A controlled search simulated annealing method for the general job shop scheduling problem, WP #03-04-88, Department of Management, Graduate School of Business, University of Texas, Austin 1988.

Pot85   C. N. Potts, Analysis of heuristics for two-machine flow- shop sequencing subject to release dates, *Math. Oper. Res.* 10, 1985, 576-584

Roc84   H. Röck, The three machine no-wait flow shop problem is NP- complete, *J. Assoc. Comput. Mach.* 31, 1984, 336-345.

RR72   S. S. Reddi, C. V. Ramamoorthy, On the flow-shop sequencing problem with no wait in process, *Oper.Res.Quart.* 23, 1972, 323-331.

RS64   B. Roy, B. Sussmann, Les problémes d'ordonnancement avec contraintes disjontives, Note DS #9 bis, SEMA, Paris, 1964.

RS83   H. Röck, G. Schmidt, Machine aggregation heuristics in shop scheduling, *Methods of Oper. Res.* 45, 1983, 303-314.

Sev92   S. V. Sevastjanov, On some geometric methods in scheduling theory: A survey, *Discrete Appl. Math.* 1992, to appear.

7 Resource Constrained Scheduling

The scheduling model we consider now is more complicated than the previous ones, because any task, besides processors, may require for its processing some additional scarce resources. Resources, depending on their nature, may be classified into types and categories. The classification into *types* takes into account only the functions resources fulfill: resources of the same type are assumed to fulfill the same functions. The classification into *categories* will concern two points of view. First, we differentiate three categories of resources from the viewpoint of resource constraints. We will call a resource *renewable*, if only its total usage i.e. temporary availability at every moment is constrained (in other words this resource can be used once more when returned by a task currently using it). A resource is called *nonrenewable*, if only its total consumption, i.e. integral availability up to any given moment is constrained (in other words this resource once used by some task cannot be assigned to any other task). A resource is called *doubly constrained*, if both total usage and total consumption are constrained. Secondly, we distinguish two resource categories from the viewpoint of resource divisibility: *discrete* (i.e. discretely-divisible) and *continuous* (i.e. continuously-divisible) resources. In other words, by a discrete resource we will understand a resource which can be allocated to tasks in discrete amounts from a finite set of possible allocations, which in particular may consist of only one unit per task. Continuous resources, on the other hand, can be allocated in arbitrary a priori unknown amounts less than or equal to some given maximum value.

In the next three sections we will consider several basic subcases of the resource constrained scheduling problem. In Sections 7.1 and 7.2 problems with renewable, discrete resources will be considered. In Section 7.1 it will in particular be assumed that any task requires one arbitrary processor and some units of additional resources, while in Section 7.2 tasks may require more than one processor at a time (cf. also Section 5.4.2). Section 7.3 is devoted to an analysis of scheduling with continuous resources.

7.1 Classical Model

The resources to be considered in this section are assumed to be discrete and renewable. Thus, we may assume that s types of additional resources $R_1, R_2, \cdots, R_s$ are available in $m_1, m_2, \cdots, m_s$ units, respectively. Each task T_j requires for its processing one processor and certain fixed amounts of additional resources specified by the resource requirement vector $R(T_j) = [R_1(T_j), R_2(T_j), \cdots, R_s(T_j)]$, where $R_l(T_j)$ $(0 \le R_l(T_j) \le m_l)$, $l = 1, 2, \cdots, s$, denotes the number of units of resource R_l required for the processing of T_j. We will assume here that all required resources are granted to a task before its processing begins or resumes (in the case of preemptive scheduling), and they are returned by the task after its completion or in the case of its preemption. These assumptions define a very simple rule to prevent system deadlocks (see e.g. [CD73]) which is often used in practice, despite the fact that it may lead to a not very efficient use of additional resources.

We see that such a model is of special value in manufacturing systems where tasks, besides processors, may require additional limited resources for their processing, such as manpower, tools, space, etc. One should also not forget about computer applications where additional resources can stand for primary memory, mass storage, channels and I/O devices. Before discussing basic results in that area we would like to introduce a missing part of the notation scheme introduced in Section 3.4 that describes additional resources. In fact, they are denoted by parameter $\beta_2 \in \{\varnothing, res\ \lambda\delta\rho\}$, where

$\beta_2 = \varnothing$: no resource constraints,

$\beta_2 = res\ \lambda\delta\rho$: there are specified resource constraints;

$\lambda, \delta, \rho \in \{\cdot, k\}$ denote respectively the number of resource types, resource limits and resource requirements. If

$\lambda, \delta, \rho = \cdot$ then the number of resource types, resource limits and resource requirements are respectively arbitrary, and if

$\lambda, \delta, \rho = k$, then, respectively, the number of resource types is equal to k, each resource is available in the system in the amount of k units and the resource requirements of each task are at most equal to k units.

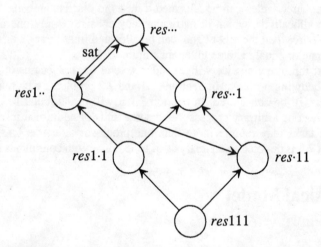

Figure 7.1.1 *Polynomial transformations among resource constrained scheduling problems.*

At this point we would also like to present possible transformations among scheduling problems Π that differ only by their resource requirements (see Figure 7.1.1). In this figure six basic resource requirements are presented. All but two of these transformations are quite obvious. Transformation $\Pi(res\cdots) \propto \Pi(res1\cdots)$ has been proved for the case of saturation of machines and additional resources and will not be presented here. The second, $\Pi(res1\cdots) \propto \Pi(res\cdot11)$, has been proved in [BBKR86]; to sketch its proof, for a given instance of the first problem we construct a corresponding instance of the second problem by assuming the parameters all the same, except resource constraints. Then for each pair T_i, T_j such that $R_1(T_i) + R_1(T_j) > m_1$ (in the first problem), resource R_{ij} available in the amount of one unit is defined in the second problem. Tasks T_i, T_j require a unit of R_{ij}, while other tasks do not require this resource. It follows that $R_1(T_i) + R_1(T_j) \leq m_1$ in the first problem if and only if for each resource R_k, $R_k(T_i) + R_k(T_j) \leq 1$ in the second problem.

We will now pass to the presentation of some important results obtained for the above model of resource constrained scheduling. Space limitations prohibit us even from only quoting all such results, however, an extensive survey may be found in [BCSW86]. As an example we chose the problem of scheduling tasks on parallel identical processors to minimize schedule length. Basic algorithms in this area will be presented.

Let us first consider the case of independent tasks and nonpreemptive scheduling.

Problem $P2 \mid res \cdots, p_j = 1 \mid C_{\max}$

The problem of scheduling unit-length tasks on two processors with arbitrary resource constraints and requirements can be solved optimally by the following algorithm.

Algorithm 7.1.1 *Algorithm by Garey and Johnson for* $P2 \mid res \cdots, p_j = 1 \mid C_{\max}$ [GJ75].
begin
Construct an n-node (undirected) graph G with each node labelled as a distinct task and
    with an edge joining T_i to T_j if and only if $R_l(T_i) + R_l(T_j) \leq m_l$, $l = 1, 2, \cdots, s$;
Find a maximum matching $\mathcal{F}$ of graph G;
Put the minimal value of schedule length $C_{\max}^* = n - |\mathcal{F}|$;
Process in parallel the pairs of tasks joined by the edges comprising set $\mathcal{F}$; process
    other tasks individually;
end;

Notice that the key idea here is the correspondence between maximum matching in a graph displaying resource constraints and the minimum-length schedule. The complexity of the above algorithm clearly depends on the complexity of the algorithm determining the maximum matching. There are several algorithms for finding it, the complexity of the most efficient by Kariv and Even [KE75] being $O(n^{2.5})$. An example of the application of this algorithm is given in Figure 7.1.2 where it is assumed that $n = 6$, $m = 2$, $s = 2$, $m_1 = 3$, $m_2 = 2$, $R(T_1) = [1, 2]$, $R(T_2) = [0, 2]$, $R(T_3) = [2, 0]$, $R(T_4) = [1, 1]$, $R(T_5) = [2, 1]$, and $R(T_6) = [1, 0]$.

An even faster algorithm can be found if we restrict ourselves to the one-resource case. It is not hard to see that in this case an optimal schedule will be produced by ordering tasks in nonincreasing order of their resource requirements and assigning tasks in that order to the first free processor on which a given task can be processed because of resource constraints. Thus, problem $P2 \mid res1 \cdots, p_j = 1 \mid C_{\max}$ can be solved in $O(n \log n)$ time.

If in the last problem tasks are allowed only for 0-1 resource requirements, the problem can be solved in $O(n)$ time even for arbitrary ready times and an arbitrary number of machines, by first assigning tasks with unit resource requirements up to m_1 in each slot, and then filling these slots with tasks having zero resource requirements [Bła78].

(a)   (b) $\mathcal{F} = \{(T_1, T_6), (T_2, T_3), (T_4, T_5)\}$

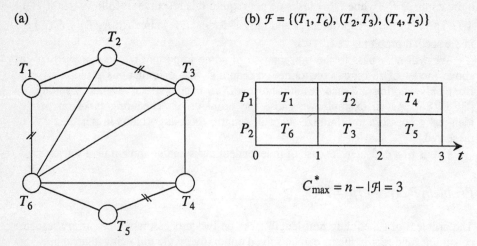

$$C^*_{max} = n - |\mathcal{F}| = 3$$

Figure 7.1.2 *An application of Algorithm 7.1.1*
   (a) *graph G corresponding to the scheduling problem,*
   (b) *an optimal schedule.*

Problem $P \mid res\ sor, p_j = 1 \mid C_{max}$

When the number of resource types, resource limits and resource requirements are fixed (i.e. constrained by positive integers s, o, r, respectively), problem $P \mid res\ sor, p_j = 1 \mid C_{max}$ is still solvable in linear time, even for an arbitrary number of processors [BE83]. We describe this approach below, since it has more general application. Depending on the resource requirements $(R_1(T_i), R_2(T_i), \cdots, R_s(T_i)) \in \{0, 1, \cdots, r\}^s$, the tasks can be distributed among a sufficiently large (and fixed) number of classes. For each possible resource requirements we define one such class. The correspondence between the resource requirements and the classes will be described by a 1-1 function $f: \{0, 1, \cdots, r\}^s \rightarrow \{1, 2, \cdots, k\}$, where k is the number of different possible resource requirements, i.e. $k = (r+1)^s$. For a given instance, let n_i denote the number of tasks belonging to the ith class, $i = 1, 2, \cdots, k$. Thus all the tasks of class i have the same resource requirement $f^{-1}(i)$. Observe that most of the input information describing an instance of problem $P \mid res\ sor, p_j = 1 \mid C_{max}$ is given by the resource requirements of n given tasks (we bypass for the moment the number m of processors, the number s of additional resources and resource limits o). This input may now be replaced by the vector $v = (v_1, v_2, \cdots, v_k) \in I\!N_0^k$, where v_i is the number of tasks having resource requirements equal to $f^{-1}(i)$, $i = 1, 2, \cdots, k$. Of course, the sum of the components of this vector is equal to the number of tasks, i.e. $\sum_{i=1}^{k} v_i = n$.

We now introduce some definitions useful in the following discussion. An *elementary instance* of $P \mid res\, sor, p_j = 1 \mid C_{max}$ is defined as a sequence $R(T_1), R(T_2), \cdots, R(T_u)$, where each $R(T_i) \in \{1, 2, \cdots, r\}^s - \{(0, 0, \cdots, 0)\}$, with properties $u \le m$ and $\sum_{i=1}^{u} R(T_i) \le (o, o, \cdots, o)$. Note that the minimal schedule length of an elementary instance is always equal to 1. An *elementary vector* is a vector $v \in I\!N_0^k$ which corresponds to an elementary instance. If we calculate the number L of different elementary instances, we see that L cannot be greater than $(o+1)^{(r+1)^s-1}$; however, in practice L will be much smaller than this upper bound. Denote the elementary vectors (in any order) by $b_1, b_2, \cdots, b_L$.

We observe two facts. First, any input $R(T_1), R(T_2), \cdots, R(T_n)$ can be considered as a union of elementary instances. This is because any input consisting of one task is elementary. Second, each schedule is also constructed from elementary instances, since all the tasks which are executed at the same time form an elementary instance.

Now, taking into account the fact that the minimal length of a schedule for any elementary instance is equal to one, we may formulate the original problem as that of finding a decomposition of a given instance into the minimal number of elementary instances. One may easily see that this is equivalent to finding a decomposition of the vector $v = (v_1, v_2, \cdots, v_k) \in I\!N_0^k$ into a linear combination of elementary vectors $b_1, b_2, \cdots, b_L$, for which the sum of coefficients is minimal: Find $e_1, e_2, \cdots, e_L \in I\!N_0^k$ such that $\sum_{i=1}^{L} e_i b_i = v$ and $\sum_{i=1}^{L} e_i$ is minimal.

Thus, we have obtained a linear integer programming problem, which in the general case, would be *NP*-hard. Fortunately, in our case the number of variables L is fixed. It follows that we can apply a result due to Lenstra [Len83] which states that the linear programming problem with fixed number of variables can be solved in polynomial time depending on both, the number of constraints of the integer linear programming problem and $\log a$, but not on the number of variables, where a is the maximum of all the coefficients in the linear integer programming problem. Thus, the complexity of the problem is $O(2^{L^2}(k \log a)^{cL})$, for some constant c. In our case the complexity of that algorithm is $O(2^{L^2}(k \log n)^{cL}) < O(n)$. Since the time needed to construct the data for this integer programming problem is $O(2^s(L + \log n)) = O(\log n)$, we conclude that the problem $P \mid res\, sor, p_j = 1 \mid C_{max}$ can be solved in linear time.

Problem $Pm \mid res\, sor \mid C_{max}$

Now we generalize the above considerations for the case of non-unit processing times and tasks belonging to a fixed number k of classes only. That is, the set of tasks may be divided into k classes and all the tasks belonging to the same class have the same processing and resource requirements. If the number of processors m is fixed, then the following algorithm, based on dynamic programming, has been proposed by Błażewicz et al. [BKS89]. A schedule will be built step by step. In every step one task is assigned to a processor at a time. All these assignments obey the following rule: if task T_i is assigned after task T_j, then the starting time of T_i is not earlier than the starting time of

T_j. At every moment an assignment of processors and resources to tasks is described by a *state of the assignment process*. For any state a *set of decisions* is given each of which transforms this state into another state. A *value of each decision* will reflect the length of a partial schedule defined by a given state to which this decision led. Below, this method will be described in a more detail.

The state of the assignment process is described by an $m \times k$ matrix X, and vectors Y and Z. Matrix X reflects numbers of tasks from particular classes already assigned to particular processors. Thus, the maximum number of each entry may be equal to n. Vector Y has k entries, each of which represents the number of tasks from a given class not yet assigned. Finally, vector Z has m entries and they represent classes which recently assigned tasks (to particular processors) belong to.

The initial state is that for which matrices X and Z have all entries equal to 0 and Y has entries equal to the numbers of tasks in the particular classes in a given instance.

Let S be a state defined by X, Y and Z. Then, there is a decision leading to state S' consisting of X', Y' and Z' if and only if

$$\exists\, t \in \{1, \cdots, k\} \text{ such that } Y_t > 0, \tag{7.1.1}$$

$$|\mathcal{M}| = 1, \tag{7.1.2}$$

where $\mathcal{M}$ is any subset of

$$\mathcal{F} = \{ i \mid \sum_{1 \le j \le k} X_{ij} p_j = \min_{1 \le g \le m} \{ \sum_{1 \le j \le k} X_{gj} p_j \} \},$$

and finally

$$R_l(T_t) \le m_l - \sum_{1 \le j \le k} R_l(T_j) \,|\{g \mid Z_g = j\}|, \qquad l = 1, 2, \cdots, s; \tag{7.1.3}$$

where this new state is defined by the following matrices

$$X'_{ij} = \begin{cases} X_{ij} + 1 & \text{if } i \in \mathcal{M} \text{ and } j = t, \\ X_{ij} & \text{otherwise,} \end{cases}$$

$$Y'_j = \begin{cases} Y_j - 1 & \text{if } j = t, \\ Y_j & \text{otherwise,} \end{cases} \tag{7.1.4}$$

$$Z'_i = \begin{cases} t & \text{if } i \in \mathcal{M}, \\ Z_i & \text{otherwise.} \end{cases}$$

In other words, a task from class t may be assigned to processor P_i, if this class is non-empty (inequality (7.1.1) is fulfilled), there is at least one free processor (equation (7.1.2)), and resource requirements of this task are satisfied (equation (7.1.3)).

If one (or more) conditions (7.1.1) through (7.1.3) are not satisfied, then no task can be assigned at this moment. Thus, one must simulate an assignment of an idle-time task. This is done by assuming the following new state S'':

$$X''_{ij} = \begin{cases} X_{ij} & \text{if } i \notin \mathcal{F}, \\ X_{hj} & \text{otherwise,} \end{cases}$$

$$Y'' = Y, \tag{7.1.5}$$

$$Z_i'' = \begin{cases} Z_i & \text{if } i \notin \mathcal{F}, \\ 0 & \text{otherwise.} \end{cases}$$

where h is one of these g, $1 \le g \le m$, for which

$$\sum_{1 \le j \le k} X_{gj} p_j = \min_{\substack{1 \le i \le m \\ i \notin \mathcal{F}}} \left\{ \sum_{1 \le j \le k} X_{ij} p_j \right\}.$$

This means that the above decision leads to state S'' which repeats a pattern of assignment for processor P_h, i.e. one which will be free as the first from among those which are busy now.

A decision leading from state S to S' has its value equal to

$$\max_{1 \le i \le m} \left\{ \sum_{1 \le j \le k} X_{ij} p_j \right\}. \tag{7.1.6}$$

This value, of course, is equal to a temporary schedule length.

The final state is that for which the matrices Y and Z have all entries equal to 0. An optimal schedule is then constructed by starting from the final state and moving back, state by state, to the initial state. If there is a number of decisions leading to a given state, then we choose the one having the least value to move back along it. More clearly, if state S follows immediately S', and S (S' respectively) consists of matrices X, Y, Z (X', Y', Z' respectively), then this decision corresponds to assigning a task from $Y - Y'$ at the time $\min_{1 \le i \le m} \left\{ \sum_{1 \le j \le k} X_{ij} p_j \right\}$.

The time complexity of this algorithm clearly depends on the product of the number of states and the maximum number of decisions which can be taken at the states of the algorithm. A careful analysis shows that this complexity can be bounded by $O(n^{k(m+1)})$, thus, for fixed numbers of task classes k and of processors m, it is polynomial in the number of tasks.

Let us note that another dynamic programming approach has been described in [BKS89] in which the number of processors is not restricted, but a fixed upper bound on task processing times p is specified. In this case the time complexity of the algorithm is $O(n^{k(p+1)})$.

Problem $P \mid res \cdots, p_j = 1 \mid C_{\max}$

It follows that when we consider the nonpreemptive case of scheduling of unit length tasks we have five polynomial time algorithms and this is probably as much as we can get in this area, since other problems of nonpreemptive scheduling under resource constraints have been proved to be NP-hard. Let us mention the parameters that have an influence on the hardness of the problem. First, different ready times cause the strong NP-hardness of the problem even for two processors and very simple resource requirements, i.e. problem $P2 \mid res1\cdots, r_j, p_j = 1 \mid C_{\max}$ is already strongly NP-hard [BBKR86] (From Figure 7.1.1 we see that problem $P2 \mid res\cdot11, r_j, p_j = 1 \mid C_{\max}$ is strongly NP-hard as well). Second, an increase in the number of processors from 2 to 3 results in the strong NP-hardness of the problem. That is, problem $P3 \mid res1\cdots, r_j, p_j = 1 \mid C_{\max}$ is strongly NP-hard as proved by Garey and Johnson [GJ75]. (Note that this is the famous 3-PARTITION problem, the first strongly NP-hard problem). Again from Figure 7.1.1 we conclude that problem $P3 \mid res \cdot 11, r_j, p_j = 1 \mid C_{max}$ is NP-hard in the strong sense. Finally, even the simplest precedence constraints result in the NP-hardness of the scheduling problem, that is, the $P2 \mid res111, chains, p_j = 1 \mid C_{max}$ is NP-hard in the strong sense [BLRK83]. Because all these problems are NP-hard, there is a need to work out approximation algorithms. We quote some of the results. Most of the algorithms considered here are list scheduling algorithms which differ from each other by the ordering of tasks on the list. We mention three approximation algorithms analyzed for the problem [1].

1. *First fit (FF).* Each task is assigned to the earliest time slot in such a way that no resource and processor limits are violated.

2. *First fit decreasing (FFD).* A variant of the first algorithm applied to a list ordered in nonincreasing order of $R_{max}(T_j)$, where $R_{max}(T_j) = \max\{R_l(T_j)/m_l \mid 1 \le l \le s\}$.

3. *Iterated lowest fit decreasing (ILFD* - applies for $s = 1$ and $p_j = 1$ only). Order tasks as in the *FFD* algorithm. Put C as a lower bound on C_{max}^*. Place T_1 in the first time slot and proceed through the list of tasks, placing T_j in a time slot for which the total resource requirement of tasks already assigned is minimum. If we ever reach a point where T_j cannot be assigned to any of C slots, we halt the iteration, increase C by 1, and start over.

Below we will present the main known bounds for the case $m < n$. In [KSS75] several bounds have been established. Let us start with the problem $P \mid res1 \cdot \cdot, p_j = 1 \mid C_{max}$ for which the three above mentioned algorithms have the following bounds:

$$\frac{27}{10} - \left\lceil \frac{37}{10m} \right\rceil < R_{FF}^{\infty} < \frac{27}{10} - \frac{24}{10m},$$

$$R_{FFD}^{\infty} = 2 - \frac{2}{m},$$

$$R_{ILFD} \le 2.$$

We see that the use of an ordered list improves the bound by about 30%. Let us also mention here that problem $P \mid res \cdot \cdot \cdot, p_j = 1 \mid C_{max}$ can be solved by the approximation algorithm based on the two machine aggregation approach by Röck and Schmidt [RS83], described in Section 6.1 in the context of flow shop scheduling. The worst case behavior of this algorithm is $R = \left\lceil \frac{m}{2} \right\rceil$.

---

[1] Let us note that the resource constrained scheduling for unit task processing times is equivalent to a variant of the bin packing problem in which the number of items per bin is restricted to m. On the other hand, several other approximation algorithms have been analyzed for the general bin packing problem and the interested reader is referred to [CGJ84] for an excellent survey of the results obtained in this area.

Problem $P \mid res \cdots \mid C_{max}$

For arbitrary processing times some other bounds have been established. For problem $P \mid res \cdots \mid C_{max}$ the first fit algorithm has been analyzed by Garey and Graham [GG75]:

$$R_{FF}^{\infty} = \min\{\frac{m+1}{2}, s+2-\frac{2s+1}{m}\} \,.$$

Finally, when dependent tasks are considered, the first fit algorithm has been evaluated for problem $P \mid res \cdots, prec \mid C_{max}$ by the same authors:

$$R_{FF}^{\infty} = m \,.$$

Unfortunately, no results are reported on the probabilistic analysis of approximation algorithms for resource constrained scheduling.

Problem $P \mid pmtn, res1 \cdot 1 \mid C_{max}$

Now let us pass to preemptive scheduling. Problem $P \mid pmtn, res1 \cdot 1 \mid C_{max}$ can be solved via a modification of McNaughton's rule (Algorithm 5.1.2) by taking

$$C_{max}^{*} = \max\{\max_j\{p_j\}, \sum_{j=1}^{n} p_j/m, \sum_{T_j \in Z_R} p_j/m_1\}$$

as the minimum schedule length, where Z_R is the set of tasks for which $R_1(T_j) = 1$. The tasks are scheduled as in Algorithm 5.1.2, the tasks from Z_R being scheduled first. The complexity of the algorithm is obviously $O(n)$.

Problem $P2 \mid pmtn, res \cdots \mid C_{max}$

Let us consider now the problem $P2 \mid pmtn, res \cdots \mid C_{max}$. This can be solved via a transformation into the transportation problem [BLRK83].

Without loss of generality we may assume that task T_j, $j = 1, 2, \cdots, n$, spends exactly $p_j/2$ time units on each of the two processors. Let (T_j, T_i), $j \neq i$, denote a resource feasible task pair, i.e. a pair for which $R_l(T_j) + R_l(T_i) \leq m_l$, $l = 1, 2, \cdots, s$. Let Z be the set of all resource feasible pairs of tasks. Z also includes all pairs of the type (T_j, T_{n+1}), $j = 1, 2, \cdots, n$, where T_{n+1} is an idle time (dummy) task. Now we may construct a transportation network. Let $n+1$ sender nodes correspond to the $n+1$ tasks (including the idle time task) which are processed on processor P_1 and let $n+1$ receiver nodes correspond to the $n+1$ tasks processed on processor P_2. Stocks and requirements of nodes corresponding to T_j, $j = 1, 2, \cdots, n$, are equal to $p_j/2$, since the amount of time each task spends on each processor is equal to $p_j/2$. The stock and the requirement of two nodes corresponding to T_{n+1} are equal to $\sum_{j=1}^{n} p_j/2$, since these are the maximum amounts of time each processor may be idle. Then, we draw directed arcs (T_j, T_i) and

(T_i, T_j) if and only if $(T_j, T_i) \in Z$, to express the possibility of processing tasks T_j and T_i in parallel on processors P_1 and P_2. In addition we draw an arc (T_{n+1}, T_{n+1}). Then, we assign for each pair $(T_j, T_i) \in Z$ a cost associated with arcs (T_j, T_i) and (T_i, T_j) equal to 1, and a cost associated with the arc (T_{n+1}, T_{n+1}) equal to 0. (This is because an interval with idle times on both processors does not lengthen the schedule). Now, it is quite clear that the solution of the corresponding transportation problem, i.e. the set of arc flows $\{x_{ji}^*\}$, is simply the set of the numbers of time units during which corresponding pairs of tasks are processed (T_j being processed on P_1 and T_i on P_2).

The complexity of the above algorithm is $O(n^4 \log \Sigma p_j)$ since this is the complexity of finding a minimum cost flow in a network, and the number of vertices in the transportation network is $O(n)$.

Problem $Pm \mid pmtn, res \cdots \mid C_{max}$

Now let us pass to the problem $Pm \mid pmtn, res \cdots \mid C_{max}$. This problem can still be solved in polynomial time via the linear programming approach (5.1.15) - (5.1.16) but now, instead of the processor feasible set, the notion of a *resource feasible set* is used. By the latter we mean the set of tasks which can be simultaneously processed because of resource limits (including processor limit). At this point let us also mention that problem $P \mid pmtn, res \cdots 1 \mid C_{max}$ can be solved by the generalization of the other linear programming approach presented in (5.1.24) - (5.1.27). Let us also add that the latter approach can handle different ready times and the L_{max} criterion. On the other hand, both approaches can be adapted to cover the case of the uniconnected activity network in the same way as that described in Section 5.1.1.

Finally, we mention that for the problem $P \mid pmtn, res1 \cdots \mid C_{max}$, the approximation algorithms FF and FFD had been analyzed by Krause et al. [KSS75]:

$$R_{FF}^{\infty} = 3 - \frac{3}{m},$$

$$R_{FFD}^{\infty} = 3 - \frac{3}{m}.$$

Surprisingly, the use of an ordered list does not improve the bound.

7.2 Scheduling Multiprocessor Tasks

In this section we combine the model presented in Section 5.4.2 with the resource constrained scheduling. That is, each task is assumed to require one or more processors at a time, and possibly a number of additional resources during its execution. The tasks are scheduled preemptively on m identical processors so that schedule length is minimized.

We are given a set $\mathcal{T}$ of tasks of arbitrary processing times which are to be processed on a set of $\mathcal{P} = \{P_1, \cdots, P_m\}$ of m identical processors. There are also s additional types of resources, $R_1, \cdots, R_s$, in the system, available in the amounts of $m_1, \cdots, m_s \in \mathbb{N}^0$ units. The task set $\mathcal{T}$ is partitioned into subsets,

$$\mathcal{T}^j = \{T_1^j, \cdots, T_{n_j}^j\},$$

$j = 1, 2, \cdots, k$, k being a fixed integer $\leq m$, denoting a set of tasks each requiring j processors and no additional resources, and

$$\mathcal{T}^{jr} = \{T_1^{jr}, \cdots, T_{n_j^r}^{jr}\},$$

$j = 1, 2, \cdots, k$, k being a fixed integer $\leq m$, denoting a set of tasks each requiring j processors simultaneously and at most m_l units of resource type R_l, $l = 1, \cdots, s$ (for simplicity we write superscript r to denote "resource tasks", i.e. tasks or sets of tasks requiring resources). The resource requirements of any task T_i^{jr}, $i = 1, 2, \cdots, n_j^r$, $j = 1, 2, \cdots, k$, are given by the vector $R(T_i^{jr}) \leq (m_1, m_2, \cdots, m_s)$.

We will be concerned with preemptive scheduling, i.e. each task may be preempted at any time in a schedule, and restarted later at no cost (in that case, of course, resources are also preempted). All tasks are assumed to be independent, i.e. there are no precedence constraints or mutual exclusion constraints among them. A schedule will be called feasible if, besides the usual conditions each task from $\mathcal{T}^j \cup \mathcal{T}^{jr}$ for $j = 1, 2, \cdots, k$ is processed by j processors at a time, and at each moment the number of processed $\mathcal{T}^{jr}$-tasks is such that the numbers of resources used do not exceed the resource limits. Our objective is to find a feasible schedule of minimum length. Such a schedule will be called *optimal*.

First we present a detailed discussion of the case of one resource type ($s = 1$) available in r units, unit resource requirements, i.e. resource requirement of each task is 0 or 1, and $j \in \{1, k\}$ processors per task for some $k \leq m$. So the task set is assumed to be $\mathcal{T} = \mathcal{T}^1 \cup \mathcal{T}^{1r} \cup \mathcal{T}^k \cup \mathcal{T}^{kr}$. A scheduling algorithm of complexity $O(nm)$ where n is the number of tasks in set $\mathcal{T}$, and a proof of its correctness are presented for $k = 2$. Finally, a linear programming formulation of the scheduling problem is presented for arbitrary values of s, k, and resource requirements. The complexity of the approach is bounded from above by a polynomial in the input length as long as the number of processors is fixed.

Process of Normalization

First we prove that among minimum length schedules there exists always a schedule in a special normalized form: A feasible schedule of length C for the set $\mathcal{T}^1 \cup \mathcal{T}^{1r} \cup \mathcal{T}^k \cup \mathcal{T}^{kr}$ is called *normalized* if and only if $\exists w \in \mathbb{N}^0$, $\exists L \in [0, C)$ such that the number of $\mathcal{T}^k$-, $\mathcal{T}^{kr}$-tasks executed at time $t \in [0, L)$ is $w + 1$, and the number of $\mathcal{T}^k$-, $\mathcal{T}^{kr}$-tasks executed at time $t \in [L, C)$ is w (see Figure 7.2.1). We have the following theorem [BE91].

Theorem 7.2.1 *Every feasible schedule for the set of tasks* $\mathcal{T}^1 \cup \mathcal{T}^{1r} \cup \mathcal{T}^k \cup \mathcal{T}^{kr}$ *can be transformed into a normalized schedule.*

Proof. Divide a given schedule into columns such that within each column there is no change in task assignment. Note that since the set of tasks and the number of processors are finite, we may assume that the schedule consists only of a finite number of different columns. Given two columns A and B of the schedule, suppose for the moment that they are of the same length. Let n_A^j, n_A^{jr}, n_B^j, n_B^{jr} denote the number of T^j-, T^{jr}-tasks in columns A and B, respectively, $j \in \{1, k\}$. Let n_A^0 and n_B^0 be the numbers of unused processors in A and B, respectively. The proof is based on the following claim.

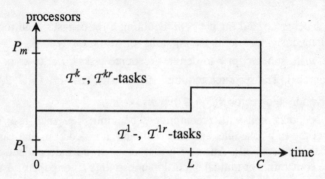

Figure 7.2.1 *A normalized form of a schedule*

Claim 7.2.2 *Let A and B be columns as above of the same length, and $n_B^k + n_B^{kr} \geq n_A^k + n_A^{kr} + 2$. Then it is always possible to shift tasks between A and B in such a way that afterwards B contains one task of type T^k or T^{kr} less than before.* (The claim is valid for any $k \geq 2$.)

Proof. We consider two different types of task shifts, Σ_1 and Σ_2. They are presented below in an algorithmic way. Algorithm 7.2.3 tries to perform a shift of one T^k-task from B to A, and, conversely, of some T^1- and T^{1r}-tasks from A to B. Algorithm 7.2.4 tries to perform a shift of some, say $j + 1$ T^{kr}-tasks from B to A, and, conversely, of j T^k-tasks and some T^1-, T^{1r}-tasks from A to B.

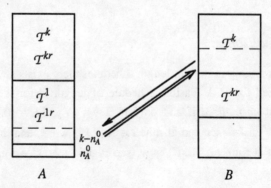

Figure 7.2.2 *Shift of tasks in Algorithm 7.2.3.*

Algorithm 7.2.3 *Shift* Σ_1.
```
begin
if n_B^k > 0 -- i.e. B has at least one task of type T^k
then
    begin
    Shift one task of type T^k from column B to column A;
            -- i.e. remove one of the T^k-tasks from B and assign it to A
    if n_A^0 < k
    then
        begin
        if n_A^1 + n_A^0 ≥ k
        then  Shift k - n_A^0 T^1-tasks from A to B
        else
            if There are at least k - n_A^0 - n_A^1 unused resources in B
            then
                begin
                Shift n_A^1 T^1-tasks from A to B;
                Shift k - n_A^0 - n_A^1 T^{1r}-tasks from A to B;
                end
            else  write('Σ_1 cannot be applied: resource conflict');
        end;
    end
else  write('Σ_1 cannot be applied: B has no T^k-task');
end;
```

Algorithm 7.2.4 *Shift* Σ_2.
```
begin
if n_B^{kr} > 0      -- i.e. B has at least one task of type T^{kr}
then
    begin
    if n_A^{1r} = 0
    then
        begin
        Shift one T^{kr}-task from B to A;
        if n_A^0 < k
            then
            if n_A^{kr} < r    -- i.e. no resource conflicts in A
                then  Shift k - n_A^0 T^1-tasks from A to B
                else  Write('Σ_2 cannot be applied: resource conflict');
        end
    else      -- i.e. in the case of n_A^{1r} > 0
        begin
        if there are numbers j, λ_1, and λ_2 such that
```

$$\lambda_1 + \lambda_2 = k - n_A^0 \text{ if } n_A^0 < k, \text{ and } 1 \text{ otherwise,}$$
$$0 \le j < \lambda_2,$$
$$j \le n_A^k, j < n_B^{kr},$$
$$\lambda_1 \le n_A^1, \lambda_2 \le n_A^{1r},$$
$$n_B^{kr} + \lambda_2 - j - 1 \le r,$$
$$n_A^{kr} + n_A^{1r} + j + 1 - \lambda_2 \le r$$

    then   -- perform the following shifts simultaneously
        begin
        Shift $j + 1$ T^{kr}-tasks from B to A;
        Shift j T^k-tasks from A to B;
        Shift λ_1 T^1-tasks from A to B;
        Shift λ_2 T^{1r}-tasks from A to B;
        end;
      else write('Σ_2 cannot be applied');
    end;
  end
else write('Σ_2 cannot be applied: B has no T^{kr}-task');
end;

Before we prove that it is always possible to change columns A and B in the proposed way by means of shifts Σ_1 and Σ_2 we formulate some assumptions and simplifications on the columns A and B (detailed proofs are left to the reader).

(a1) Without loss of generality we assume that all the tasks in A and B are pairwise independent, i.e. they are not parts of the same task.

(a2) $n_A^k + n_A^{kr} \le n_B^k + n_B^{kr} - 2$ (condition of Claim 7.2.2). From that we get

$$n_A^{1r} + n_A^1 + n_A^0 \ge n_B^{1r} + n_B^1 + n_B^0 + 2k.$$

(a3) We restrict our considerations to the case $n_A^{1r} \ge n_B^{1r} + k$ because otherwise shift Σ_1 or Σ_2 can be applied without causing resource problems.

(a4) Next we can simplify the considerations to the case $n_B^{1r} = 0$. Following (a3) and the fact that, whatever shift we apply, at most k tasks of type T^{1r} are shifted from A to B (and none from B to A) we conclude that we can continue our proof without considering n_B^{1r} tasks of type T^{1r} in both columns.

(a5) Now we assume $n_A^0 = 0$ or $n_B^0 = 0$ as we can remove all the processors not used in both columns.

(a6) Again we can simplify our considerations by assuming $n_B^0 = 0$ and $n_B^1 = 0$. For suppose $n_B^0 > 0$ or $n_B^1 > 0$, we can remove all the idle processors and T^1-tasks from column B and $n_B^0 + n_B^1$ idle processors or tasks of type T^1 or T^{1r} from column A. This can be done because there are enough tasks $\mathcal{T}^1$ and $\mathcal{T}^{1r}$ (or idle processors) left in column A.

The two columns are now of the form shown in Figure 7.2.3.

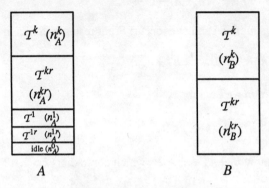

Figure 7.2.3 *Restructuring columns in Claim 7.2.2.*

Now we consider four cases (which exhaust all possible situations) and prove that in each of them either shift Σ_1 or Σ_2 can be applied. Let $\gamma = \min\{n_A^{1r}, \max\{k - n_A^0, 1\}\}$.

Case I: $n_B^{kr} + \gamma \le r$, $n_B^k > 0$. Here Σ_1 can be applied.

Case II: $n_B^{kr} + \gamma \le r$, $n_B^k = 0$. In this case Σ_2 can be applied.

Case III: $n_B^{kr} + \gamma > r$, $n_B^k > 0$.

If $0 \le n_A^{1r} \le k - n_A^0$

   or $n_A^{1r} > k - n_A^0$, $k - n_A^0 \le 0$,

   or $n_A^{1r} > k - n_A^0 > 0$, $n_A^0 + n_A^1 \ge k$,

   or $n_A^{1r} > k - n_A^0 > 0$, $n_A^0 + n_A^1 < k$, $n_B^{kr} + k - n_A^0 - n_A^1 \le r$,

we can always apply Σ_1. In the remaining subcase,

$$n_A^{1r} > k - n_A^0 > 0, \ n_A^0 + n_A^1 < k, \ n_B^{kr} + k - n_A^0 - n_A^1 > r,$$

Σ_1 cannot be applied and, because of resource limits in column B, a Σ_2-shift is possible only under the additional assumption

$$n_B^{kr} + k - n_A^0 - n_A^1 - n_A^k - 1 \le r.$$

What happens in the subcase $n_B^{kr} + k - n_A^0 - n_A^1 - n_A^k - 1 > r$ will be discussed in a moment.

Case IV: $n_B^{kr} + \gamma > r$, $n_B^k = 0$.

Now, Σ_2 can be applied, except when the following conditions hold simultaneously:

$$n_A^{1r} > k - n_A^0 > 0, \ n_A^0 + n_A^1 < k - 1, \text{ and}$$
$$n_B^{kr} + k - n_A^0 - n_A^1 - n_A^k - 1 > r.$$

We recognize that in cases III and IV under certain conditions neither of the shifts Σ_1, Σ_2 can be applied. These conditions can be put together as follows:

$$n_B^k \geq 0, \text{ and } n_B^{kr} + k - n_A^0 - n_A^1 - n_A^k - 1 > r.$$

We prove that this situation can never occur: From resource limits in column A we get

$$n_B^{kr} + k - n_A^0 - n_A^1 - n_A^k - 1 > r \geq n_A^{1r} + n_A^{kr}.$$

Together with $kn_B^{kr} \leq m$ we obtain

$$(k-1)(n_A^1 + n_A^{1r} + n_A^0) - k(k-1) < 0,$$

but from (a2) we know $n_A^1 + n_A^{1r} + n_A^0 \geq 2k$, which contradicts $k > 1$. $\square$

Having proved Claim 7.2.2, it is not hard to prove Theorem 7.2.1. Firstly, we observe that the number of different columns in each feasible schedule is finite. Then, applying shifts Σ_1 or Σ_2 a finite number of times we will get a normalized schedule (for pairs of columns of different lengths only a part of the the longer column remains unchanged but for one such column this happens only a finite number of times). $\square$

Before we describe an algorithm which determines a preemptive schedule of minimum length we prove some simple properties of optimal schedules [BE91].

Lemma 7.2.5 *In a normalized schedule it is always possible to process the tasks in such a way that the boundary between $\mathcal{T}^k$-tasks and $\mathcal{T}^{kr}$-tasks contains at most k steps.*

Proof. Suppose there are more than k steps, say $k + i$, $i \geq 1$, and the schedule is of the form given in Figure 7.2.4. Suppose the step at point L lies between the first and the last step of the $\mathcal{T}^k$-, $\mathcal{T}^{kr}$- boundary.

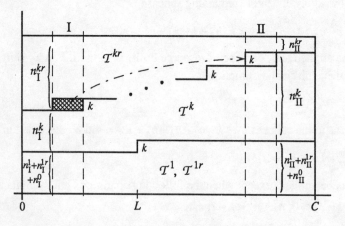

Figure 7.2.4 *k-step boundary between $\mathcal{T}^k$- and $\mathcal{T}^{kr}$-tasks*

We try to reduce the location of the first step (or even remove this step) by exchanging parts of T^{kr}-tasks from interval I with parts of T^k-tasks from interval II. From resource limits we know:

$$n_{II}^{1r} + n_{II}^{kr} \le r, \; n_I^{1r} + n_I^{kr} \le r.$$

As there are $k+i$ steps, we have $n_I^{kr} = n_{II}^{kr} + k + i$. Consider possible subcases:

(i) If $n_{II}^{1r} + n_{II}^{kr} < r$, then exchange the T^k- and T^{kr}-tasks in question. This exchange is possible because in I at least one T^{kr}-task can be found that is independent of all the tasks in II, and in II at least one T^k-task can be found that is independent of all the tasks in I.

(ii) If $n_{II}^{1r} + n_{II}^{kr} = r$, then the shift described in (i) cannot be performed directly. However, this shift can be performed simultaneously with replacement of a T^{1r}-task from II by a T^1-task (or idle time) from I, as can be easily seen.

If the step at point L in Figure 7.2.4 is the leftmost or rightmost step among all steps considered so far, then the step removal works in a similar way. $\square$

Corollary 7.2.6 *In case* $k = 2$ *we may assume that the schedule has one of the forms shown in Figure 7.2.5.* $\square$

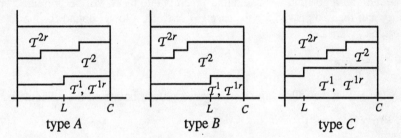

Figure 7.2.5 *Possible schedule types in Corollary 7.2.6.*

Lemma 7.2.7 *Let* $k = 2$. *In cases* (B) *and* (C) *of Figure 7.2.5 the schedule can be changed in such a way that one of the steps in the boundary between* T^k *and* T^{kr} *is located at point* L, *or it disappears.*

Proof. The same arguments as in the proof of Lemma 7.2.5 are used. $\square$

Corollary 7.2.8 *In case* $k = 2$, *every schedule can be transformed into one of the types given in Figure 7.2.6.* $\square$

Let us note that if in type $B1$ (Figure 7.2.6) not all resources are used during interval $[L, C)$, then the schedule can be transformed into type $B2$ or $C2$. If in type $C1$ not all resources are used during interval $[L, C)$, then the schedule can be transformed into type $B2$ or $C2$. A similar argument holds for schedules of type A.

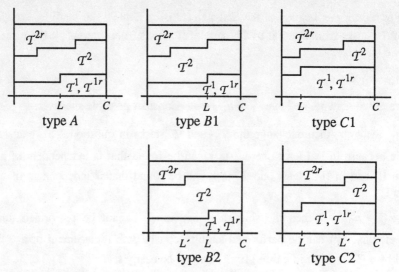

Figure 7.2.6 *Possible schedule types in Corollary 7.2.8.*

The Algorithm

In this section an algorithm of scheduling preemptable tasks will be presented and its optimality will then be proved for the case $k = 2$. Now, a lower bound for the schedule length can be given. Let

$$X^j = \sum_{T_i \in \mathcal{T}^j} p_i^j, \qquad\qquad X^{jr} = \sum_{T_i^{jr} \in \mathcal{T}^{jr}} p_i^{jr}, \qquad (j = 1, k).$$

It is easy to see that the following formula gives a lower bound on the schedule length,

$$C = \max\{C_{max}^r, C'\} \tag{7.2.1}$$

where

$$C_{max}^r = (X^{1r} + X^{kr})/r,$$

and C' is the optimum schedule length for all $\mathcal{T}^1$-, $\mathcal{T}^{1r}$-, $\mathcal{T}^k$-, $\mathcal{T}^{kr}$-tasks without considering resource limits (cf. Section 5.4.2).

In the algorithm presented below we are trying to construct a schedule of type **B2** or **C2**. However, this may not always be possible because of resource constraints causing "resource overlapping" in certain periods. In this situation we first try to correct the schedule by exchanging some critical tasks so that resource limits are not violated, thus obtaining a schedule of type **A**, **B1** or **C1**. If this is not possible, i.e. if no feasible schedule exists, we will have to re-compute bound C in order to remove all resource overlappings.

Let L and L' be the locations of steps as shown in the schedules of type **B2** or **C2** in Figure 7.2.6. Then

$$L = (X^2 + X^{2r}) \bmod C, \text{ and } L' = X^{2r} \bmod C. \tag{7.2.2}$$

In order to compute resource overlapping we proceed as follows. Assign $\mathcal{T}^2$- and $\mathcal{T}^{2r}$-tasks in such a way that only one step in the boundary between these two types of tasks occurs; this is always possible because bound C was chosen properly. The schedule thus obtained is of type **B2** or **C2**. Before the $\mathcal{T}^1$- and $\mathcal{T}^{1r}$-tasks are assigned we partition the free part of the schedule into two areas, LA (left area) and RA (right area) (cf. Figure 7.2.7). Note that a task from $\mathcal{T}^1 \cup \mathcal{T}^{1r}$ fits into LA or RA only if its length does not exceed L or $C-L$, respectively. Therefore, all "long" tasks have to be cut into two pieces, and one piece is assigned to LA, and the other one to RA. We do this by assigning a piece of length $C-L$ of each long task to RA, and the remaining piece to LA (see Section 5.4.2 for detailed reasoning). The *excess* $e(T_i)$ of each such task is defined as $e(T_i) = p_i - C + L$, if $p_i > C - L$, and 0 otherwise.

The task assignment is continued by assigning all excesses to LA, and, in addition, by putting as many as possible of the remaining $\mathcal{T}^{1r}$-tasks (so that no resource violations occur) and $\mathcal{T}^1$-tasks to LA. However, one should not forget that if there are more long tasks in $\mathcal{T}^1 \cup \mathcal{T}^{1r}$ than $z_1 + 2$ (cf. Figure 7.2.7), then each such task should be assigned according to the ratio of processing capacities of both sides LA and RA, respectively. All tasks not being assigned yet are assigned to RA. Hence only in RA resource limits may be violated. Take the sum OL of processing times of all $\mathcal{T}^{1r}$-tasks violating the resource limit. OL is calculated in the algorithm given below. Of course, OL is always less than or equal to $C-L$, and the $\mathcal{T}^{1r}$-tasks in RA can be arranged in such a way that at any time in $[L, C)$ no more than $r+1$ resources are required.

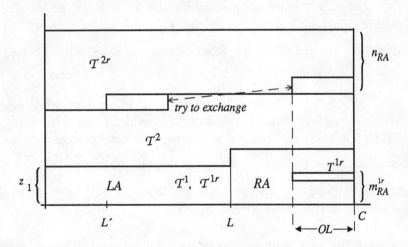

Figure 7.2.7 *Left and right areas in a normalized schedule*

Resource overlapping (OL) of $\mathcal{T}^{1r}$- and $\mathcal{T}^{2r}$-tasks cannot be removed by exchanging $\mathcal{T}^{1r}$-tasks in RA with $\mathcal{T}^1$-tasks in LA, because the latter are only the excesses of long tasks. So the only possibility to remove the resource overlapping is to exchange $\mathcal{T}^{2r}$-tasks in RA with $\mathcal{T}^2$-tasks in LA (cf. Figure 7.2.7). Suppose that $\tau (\leq OL)$ is the maximal amount of T^2-, T^{2r}-tasks that can be exchanged in that way. Thus resource overlapping in RA is reduced to the amount $OL - \tau$. If $OL - \tau = 0$, then all tasks are scheduled properly and we are done. If $OL - \tau > 0$, however, a schedule of length C does not exist. In order to remove the remaining resource overlapping (which is in fact $OL - \tau$) we have to increase the schedule length again.

Let n_{RA} be the number of T^2- or T^{2r}-tasks executed at the same time during $[L, C)$. Furthermore, let z_1 be the number of processors not used by T^2- or T^{2r}-tasks at time 0, let m_{RA}^{1r} be the number of processors executing T^{1r}-tasks in RA (cf. Figure 7.2.7), and let l_{RA}^1 be the number of T^1-tasks executed in RA and having excess in LA. The schedule length is then increased by some amount ΔC, i.e.

$$C = C + \Delta C, \text{ where } \Delta C = \min \{\Delta C_a, \Delta C_b, \Delta C_c\}, \tag{7.2.3}$$

and ΔC_a, ΔC_b, and ΔC_c are determined as follows.

(a) $$\Delta C_a = \frac{OL - \tau}{m_{RA}^{1r} + (m - z_1 - 2)/2 + l_{RA}^1}.$$

This formula considers the fact that the parts of T^{1r}-tasks violating resource limits have to be distributed among other processors. By lengthening the schedule the following processors will contribute processing capacity:

- m_{RA}^{1r} processors executing T^{1r}-tasks on the right hand side of the schedule,

- $(m - z_1 - 2)/2$ pairs of processors executing T^2- or T^{2r}-tasks and contributing to a decrease of L (and thus lengthening part RA),

- l_{RA}^1 processors executing T^1-tasks whose excesses are processed in LA (and thus decreasing their excesses, and hence allowing part of T^{1r} to be processed in LA).

(b) If the schedule length is increased by some Δ then L will be decreased by $n_{RA}\Delta$, or, as the schedule type may switch from **C2** to **B2** (provided L was small enough, cf. Figure 7.2.6), L would be replaced by $C + \Delta + L - n_{RA}\Delta$. In order to avoid the latter case we choose Δ in such a way that the new value of L will be 0, i.e. $\Delta C_b = \frac{L}{n_{RA}}$.

Notice that with the new schedule length $C + \Delta C$, $\Delta C \in \{\Delta C_a, \Delta C_b\}$, the length of the right area RA, will be increased by $\Delta C(n_{RA} + 1)$.

(c) Consider all tasks in T^1 with nonzero excesses. All tasks in T^1 whose excesses are less than $\Delta C(n_{RA} + 1)$ will have no excess in the new schedule. However, if there are tasks with larger excess, then the structure of a schedule of length $C + \Delta C$ will be completely different and we are not able to conclude that the new schedule will be optimal. Therefore we take the shortest task T_s of T^1 with nonzero excess and choose the new schedule length so that T_s will fit exactly into the new RA, i.e.

$$\Delta C_c = \frac{p_s - C + L}{1 + n_{RA}}.$$

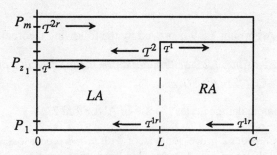

Figure 7.2.8 *Construction of an optimal schedule*

The above reasoning leads to the following algorithm [BE91].

Algorithm 7.2.9

Input: Number m of processors, number r of resource units, sets of tasks T^1, T^{1r}, T^2, T^{2r}.

Output: Schedule for $T^1 \cup T^{1r} \cup T^2 \cup T^{2r}$ of minimum length.

begin

Compute bound C according to formula (7.2.1);

repeat

Compute L, L' according to (7.2.2), and the excesses for the tasks of $T^1 \cup T^{1r}$;

Using bound C, find a normalized schedule for T^2- and T^{2r}-tasks by assigning T^{2r}-tasks from the top of the schedule (processors $P_m, P_{m-1}, \cdots,$) and from left to right, and by assigning T^2-tasks starting at time L, to the processors P_{z_1+1} and P_{z_1+2} from right to left (cf. Figure 7.2.8);

if the number of long T^1- and T^{1r}-tasks is $\leq z_1 + 2$

then

Take the excesses $e(T)$ of long T^1- and T^{1r}-tasks, and assign them to the left area LA of the schedule in the way depicted in Figure 7.2.8

else

Assign these tasks according to the processing capacities of both sides LA and RA of the schedule, respectively;

if LA is not completely filled

then Assign T^{1r}-tasks to LA as long as resource constraints are not violated;

if LA is not completely filled

then Assign T^1-tasks to LA;

Fill the right area RA with the remaining tasks in the way shown in Figure 7.2.8;

if resource constraints are violated in interval $[L, C]$

then

> Compute resource overlapping $OL - \tau$ and correct bound C according to (7.2.3);
>
>   **until** $OL - \tau = 0$;
>
> **end;**

The optimality of Algorithm 7.2.9 is proved by the following theorem [BE91].

Theorem 7.2.10 *Algorithm* 7.2.9 *determines a preemptive schedule of minimum length for* $T^1 \cup T^{1r} \cup T^2 \cup T^{2r}$ *in time* $O(nm)$. $\square$

The following example demonstrates the use of Algorithm 7.2.9.

Example 7.2.11 Consider a processor system with $m = 8$ processors, and $r = 3$ units of resource. Let the task set contain 9 tasks, and processing requirements as given in the following table:

	T_1	T_2	T_3	T_4	T_5	T_6	T_7	T_8	T_9
processing times	10	5	5	5	10	8	2	3	7
number of processors	2	2	2	2	1	1	1	1	1
number of resource units	1	0	0	0	1	1	1	0	0

Table 7.2.1

Then,

$$X^1 = 10, X^{1r} = 20, X^2 = 15, X^{2r} = 10,$$

$$C^r_{\max} = (X^{1r} + X^{2r})/r = 10, \ C' = (X^1 + X^{1r} + 2X^2 + 2X^{2r})/m = 10,$$

i.e. $C = 10$ and $L = 5$. The first loop of Algorithm 7.2.9 yields the schedule shown in Figure 7.2.9. In the schedule thus obtained a resource overlapping occurs in the interval [8,10). There is no way to exchange tasks, so $\tau = 0$, and an overlapping of amount 2 remains. From equation (7.2.3) we obtain $\Delta C_a = 1/3$, $\Delta C_b = 5/2$, and $\Delta C_c = 2/3$. Hence the new schedule length will be $C = 10 + \Delta C_a = 10.33$, and $L = 4.33$, $L' = 10.0$. In the second loop the algorithm determines the schedule shown in Figure 7.2.10, which is now optimal. $\square$

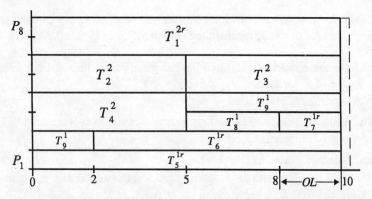

Figure 7.2.9 *Example schedule after the first loop of Algorithm 7.2.9.*

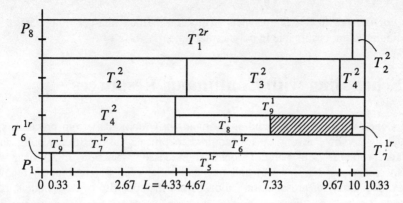

Figure 7.2.10 *Example schedule after the second loop of Algorithm 7.2.9.*

Linear Programming Approach to the General Case

In this section we will show that for a much larger class of scheduling problems one can find schedules of minimum length in polynomial time. We will consider tasks having arbitrary resource and processor requirements. That is, the task set $\mathcal{T}$ is now composed of the following subsets:

$\mathcal{T}^j, j = 1, \cdots, k$, tasks requiring j processors each and no resources, and

$\mathcal{T}^{jr}, j = 1, \cdots, k$, tasks requiring j processors each and some resources.

We present a linear programming formulation of the problem. Our approach is similar to the *LP* formulation of the project scheduling problem, cf. (5.1.15)-(5.1.16). We will need a few definitions. By a resource feasible set we mean here a subset of tasks that can be processed simultaneously because of their total resource and processor requirements. Let M be the number of different resource feasible sets. By variable x_i we denote the processing time of the ith resource feasible set, and by Q_j we denote the set of indices of those resource feasible sets that contain task $T_j \in \mathcal{T}$. Thus the following linear programming problem can be formulated:

$$\text{Minimize} \quad \sum_{i=1}^{M} x_i$$
$$\text{subject to} \quad \sum_{i \in Q_j} x_i = p_j \text{ for each } T_j \in \mathcal{T},$$
$$x_i \geq 0, i = 1, 2, \cdots, M.$$

As a solution of the above problem we get optimal values x_i^* of interval lengths in an optimal schedule. The tasks processed in the intervals are members of the corresponding resource feasible subsets. As before, the number of constraints of the linear programming problem is equal to n, and the number of variables is $O(n^m)$. Thus, for a fixed number of processors the complexity is bounded from above by a polynomial in the number of tasks. On the other hand, a linear programming problem may be solved (using e.g. Karmarkar's algorithm [Kar84]) in time bounded from above by a polynomial in the number of variables, the number of constraints, and the sum of logarithms of all the coefficients in the *LP* problem. Thus for a fixed number of processors, our scheduling problem is solvable in polynomial time.

7.3 Scheduling with Continuous Resources

In this section we consider scheduling problems in which, apart from processors, also continuously-divisible resources are required to process tasks. Basic results will be given for problems with parallel, identical processors (Section 7.3.2) or a single processor (Sections 7.3.3, 7.3.4) and one additional type of continuous, renewable resource. This order of presentation follows from the specifity of task models used in each case.

7.3.1 Introductory Remarks

Let us start with some comments concerning the concept of a continuous resource. As we remember, this is a resource which can be allotted to a task in an arbitrary, unknown in advance amount from a given interval. We will deal with renewable resources, i.e. such for which only usage, i.e. temporary availability is constrained at any time. This "temporary" character is important, since in practice it is often ignored for some doubly constrained resources which are then treated as nonrenewable. For example, this is the case of money for which usually only the consumption is considered, whereas they have also a "temporary" nature. Namely, money treated as a renewable resource mean in fact a "flow" of money, i.e. an amount available in a given period of a fixed length (week, month), also called rate of spending or rate of investment. The most typical example of a (renewable) continuous resource is power (electric, hydraulic, pneumatic) which, however, is in general doubly constrained since apart from the usage, also its consumption, i.e. energy, is constrained.

We should also stress that sometimes it is purposeful to treat a discrete (i.e. discretely-divisible) resource as a continuous one, since it can simplify scheduling algorithms. This approach is allowed when there are many alternative amounts of (discrete) resource available for processing each task. Such a situation occurs e.g. in multiprocessor systems where a common primary memory consists of hundreds of pages (see [Weg80]). Treating primary memory as a continuous resource we obtain a scheduling problem from the class we are interested in. Other examples we get when parallel "processors" are driven by a common power source. "Processors" mean here e.g. machines with proper drives, electrolitic tanks, or pumps for refuelling navy boats.

In the next two sections we will study scheduling problems with continuous resources for two models of task processing characteristic (time or speed) vs. (continuous) resource amount allotted. The first model is given in the form of a continuous function: task processing speed vs. resource amount allotted at a given time (Section 7.3.2), whereas the second one is given in the form of a continuous function: task processing time vs. resource amount allotted (Section 7.3.3). The first model is more natural in majority of practical situations, since it reflects directly the "temporary" nature of renewable resources. It is also more general and allows a deep a priori analysis of properties of optimal schedules due to the form of the function describing task processing speed in relation to the allotted amount of resource. This analysis leads even to analytical results in some cases, and in general to the simplest formulations of mathematical programming problems for finding optimal schedules. However, in situations when all tasks use constant resource amounts during their execution, both models are equivalent. Then rather the second model is used as the direct generalization of the traditional, discrete model.

In Section 7.3.4 we will consider another type of problems, where task processing times are constant, but their ready times are functions of a continuous resource. This is another generalization of the traditional scheduling model which is important in some practical situations.

7.3.2 Processing Speed vs. Resource Amount Model

Assume that we have m identical, parallel processors $P_1, P_2, \cdots, P_m$, and one additional, (continuous, renewable) resource available in amount $\hat{U}$. For its processing task $T_j \in \mathcal{T}$ requires one of the processors and an amount of a continuous resource $u_j(t)$ which is arbitrary and unknown in advance within interval $(0, \hat{U}]$.

The task processing model is given in the form:

$$\dot{x}_j(t) = dx_j(t)/dt = f_j[u_j(t)], x_j(0) = 0, x_j(C_j) = \tilde{x}_j \tag{7.3.1}$$

where $x_j(t)$ is the state of T_j at time t, f_j is a (positive) continuous, decreasing function, $f_j(0) = 0$, C_j is the (unknown in advance) completion time of T_j, and $\tilde{x}_j > 0$ is the known final state of T_j. Since a continuous resource is assumed to be renewable, we have

$$\sum_{j=1}^{n} u_j(t) \leq \hat{U} \text{ for each } t. \tag{7.3.2}$$

As we see, the above model relates task processing speed to the (continuous) resource amount allotted to this task at time t. Let us interprete the concept of a *task state*. By the state of task T_j at time t, $x_j(t)$, we mean a measure of the completion of T_j up to time t or a measure of work related to this completion. This can be, for example, the number of standard instructions of a computer program already processed, the volume of a fuel bunker already refueled, the amount of a product resulting from the performance of T_j up to time t, the number of man-hours or kilowatt-hours already spent in processing T_j, etc.

Let us point out that in practical situations it is often quite easy to construct this model, i.e. to define f_j, $j = 1, 2, \cdots, n$. For example, in computer systems analyzed in [Weg80], the f_j's are progress rate functions of programs, closely related to their lifetime curves, whereas in problems in which processors use electric motors, the f_j's are functions: rotational speed vs. current density.

Let us also notice that in the case of a continuous resource changes of the resource amount allotted to a task within interval $(0, \hat{U}]$ does not mean a task preemption.

To compare formally the model (7.3.1) with the model

$$p_j = \phi_j(u_j), u_j \in (0, \hat{U}] \tag{7.3.3}$$

where p_j is the processing time of T_j and ϕ_j is a (positive) continuous, increasing function, notice that the condition $x_j(C_j) = \tilde{x}_j$ is equivalent to

$$\int_0^{C_j} f_j[u_j(t)]dt = \tilde{x}_j. \qquad (7.3.4)$$

Thus, if $u_j(t) = u_j$, i.e. is constant for $t \in (0,C_j]$, we have

$$C_j = p_j = \tilde{x}_j/f_j(u_j), \text{ i.e. } \phi_j = \tilde{x}_j/f_j(u_j). \qquad (7.3.5)$$

In consequence, if T_j is processed using a constant resource amount u_j, (7.3.5) defines the relation between both models. It is worth to underline that, as we will see, on the basis of the model (7.3.1) one can easily and naturally find the conditions under which tasks are processed using constant resource amounts in an optimal schedule.

Assume now that the number n of tasks is less than or equal to the number m of machines, and that tasks are independent. The first assumption implies that in fact we deal only with the allocation of a continuous resource, since the assignment of tasks to machines is trivial. This is a "pure" (continuous) resource allocation problem, as opposed to a "mixed" (discrete-continuous) problem, when we deal simultaneously with scheduling on machines (considered as a discrete resource) and the allocation of a continuous resource.

Our goal is to find a piece-wise continuous vector function $u^*(t) = (u_1^*(t), u_2^*(t), \cdots, u_n^*(t))$, $u_j^*(t) \geq 0$, $j = 1, 2, \cdots, n$, such that (7.3.1) and (7.3.2) are satisfied, and $C_{max} = \max\{C_j\}$ reaches its minimum C_{max}^*. This problem was studied in a number of papers (see [Weg82] as a survey) under different assumptions concerning task and resource characteristics. Below we present few basic results useful in our future considerations. To this end we need some additional denotations.

Let us denote by $\mathcal{U}$ the set of *resource allocations*, i.e. all points $u = (u_1, u_2, \cdots, u_n) \in \mathbb{R}^n$, $u_j \geq 0$ for $j = 1, 2, \cdots, n$, satisfying the relation

$$\sum_{j=1}^n u_j \leq \hat{U}.$$

Further, we will denote by $\mathcal{V}$ the set defined as follows:

$$v = (v_1, v_2, \cdots, v_n) \in \mathcal{V} \text{ if and only if } u \in \mathcal{U}, \text{ and } v_j = f_j(u_j), j = 1, 2, \cdots, n. \quad (7.3.6)$$

As the functions f_j are monotonic for $j = 1, 2, \cdots, n$, it is obvious that (7.3.5) defines a univalent mapping between $\mathcal{U}$ and $\mathcal{V}$, and thus we can call the vectors v *transformed resource allocations*. It is easy to prove (see, e.g. [Weg82]) that C_{max}^* as a function of final states of tasks $\tilde{x} = (\tilde{x}_1, \tilde{x}_2, \cdots, \tilde{x}_n)$ can always be expressed as

$$C_{max}^*(\tilde{x}) = \min\{C_{max} > 0 \mid \tilde{x}/C_{max} \in \text{co}\mathcal{V}\} \qquad (7.3.7)$$

where co$\mathcal{V}$ is the *convex hull* of $\mathcal{V}$, i.e. the set of all convex combinations of the elements of $\mathcal{V}$. Notice that (7.3.7) gives a simple geometrical interpretation of an optimal solution of our problem. Namely, it says that C^*_{max} is always reached at the intersection point of the straight line given by the parametric equations

$$v_j = \tilde{x}_j/C_{max}, j = 1, 2, \cdots, n \qquad (7.3.8)$$

and the boundary of set $co\mathcal{V}$. Since, according to (7.3.6), the shape of $\mathcal{V}$, and thus $co\mathcal{V}$, depends on functions $f_j, j = 1, 2, \cdots, n$, we can study the form of optimal solutions in relation to these functions. Let us consider two special, but very important cases:

(i) f_j concave, $j = 1, 2, \cdots, n$, and

(ii) $f_j \le c_j u_j, c_j = f_j(\hat{U})/\hat{U}, j = 1, 2, \cdots, n$.

It is easy to check that in case (i) set $\mathcal{V}$ is already convex, i.e. $co\mathcal{V} = \mathcal{V}$. Thus, the intersection point defined above is always a transformed resource allocation (see Figure 7.3.1 for $n = 2$).

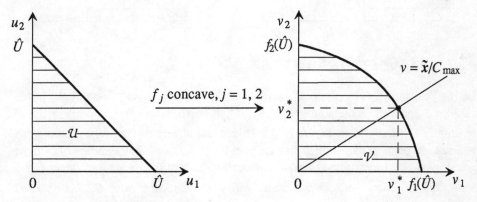

Figure 7.3.1 *The case of concave $f_j, j = 1, 2$.*

This means that in the optimal solution tasks are processed fully in parallel using constant resource amounts $u_j^*, j = 1, 2, \cdots, n$. To find these amounts let us notice that the equation of the boundary of $\mathcal{V}$ has the form $\sum_{j=1}^{n} f_j^{-1}(v_j) = \hat{U}$ (we substitute u_j from (7.3.6) for the equation of the boundary of $\mathcal{U}$, i.e. $\sum_{j=1}^{n} u_j = \hat{U}$), where f_j^{-1} is the function inverse to $f_j, j = 1, 2, \cdots, n$. Substituting v_j from (7.3.8), we get for the above equation

$$\sum_{j=1}^{n} f_j^{-1}(\tilde{x}_j/C_{max}) = \hat{U}. \qquad (7.3.9)$$

For given $\ddot{x}_j, j = 1, 2, \cdots, n$, the (unique) positive root of this equation is equal to the minimum value C^*_{max} of C_{max}. Of course

$$u_j^* = f_j^{-1}(\tilde{x}_j/C^*_{max}), j = 1, 2, \cdots, n. \qquad (7.3.10)$$

It is worth to note that equation (7.3.9) can be solved analytically for some important cases. In particular, this is the case of $f_j = c_j u_j^{1/\alpha_j}, c_j > 0, \alpha_j \in \{1, 2, 3, 4\}, j = 1, 2, \cdots, n$, when (7.3.9) reduces to an algebraic equation of an order ≤ 4. Furthermore, if $\alpha_j = \alpha \ge 1, j = 1, 2, \cdots, n$, we have

$$C^*_{max} = [\tfrac{1}{\hat{U}} \sum_{j=1}^{n} (\tilde{x}_j/c_j)^{\alpha}]^{1/\alpha} . \tag{7.3.11}$$

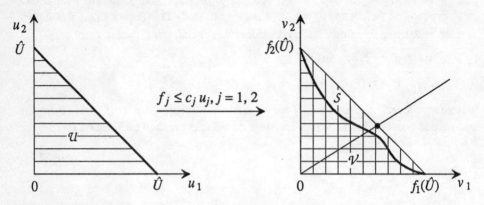

Figure 7.3.2 *The case of* $f_j \le c_j u_j$, $c_j = f_j(\hat{U})/\hat{U}, j = 1, 2.$

Let us pass to the case (ii). It is easy to check that now set $\mathcal{V}$ lies entirely inside simplex S spanned on the points $(0, \cdots, 0, f_j(\hat{U}), 0, \cdots, 0)$, where $f_j(\hat{U})$ appears on the jth position, $j = 1, 2, \cdots, n$ (see Figure 7.3.2). This means clearly that co$\mathcal{V} = S$, and that the intersection point of the straight line defined by (7.3.7) and the boundary of S most probably is not a transformed resource allocation (except for the case of linear f_j, $j = 1, \cdots, 2, \cdots, n$). However, one can easily verify that the same value C^*_{max} is obtained using transformed resource allocations whose convex combination yields the intersection point just discussed. These are, of course, the extreme points on which simplex S is spanned. This fact implies directly that in case (ii) there always exists the solution of the length $C^*_{max} = \sum_{j=1}^{n} \tilde{x}_j/f_j(\hat{U})$ in which single tasks are processed consecutively (on a single machine) using the maximum resource amount $\hat{U}$. Of course, this solution is not unique if we assume that there is no time loss concerned with a task preemption. However, there is no reason to preempt a task if it does not decrease C^*_{max}. Thus, in both cases (i) and (ii) there exist optimal solutions in which each task is processed using a constant resource amount. Consequently, in these cases the model (7.3.1) is mathematically equivalent to the model (7.3.3).

In the general case of arbitrary functions f_j, $j = 1, 2, \cdots, n$, one must search for transformed resource allocations whose convex combination fulfills (7.3.8) and gives the minimum value of C_{max} .

Assume now that tasks are dependent, i.e. that a nonempty relation $\prec$ is defined on $\mathcal{T}$. To represent $\prec$ we will use task-on-arc digraphs, also called activity networks (see Section 3.1). In this representation we can order nodes, i.e. events in such a way that the occurrence of node i is not later than the occurrence of node j if $i < j$. As is well known, such an ordering is always possible (although not always unique) and can be found in time $O(n^2)$ (see, e.g. [Law76]). Using this ordering one can utilize the results obtained for independent tasks to solve corresponding resource allocation problems for dependent tasks. To show how it works we will need some further denotations. Denote by $\mathcal{T}_k$ the subset of tasks which can be processed in the interval between the occurrence of nodes k and $k+1$, by $x_{jk} \geq 0$ a part of $T_j \in \mathcal{T}_k$ (i.e. a part of $\tilde{x}_j$) processed in the above interval, by $\Delta_k^*(\{x_{jk}\})_{T_j \in \mathcal{T}_k}$ the minimum length of this interval as a function of task parts $\{x_{jk}\}_{T_j \in \mathcal{T}_k}$, and by $\mathcal{K}_j$ the set of indices of $\mathcal{T}_k$'s such that $T_j \in \mathcal{T}_k$.

Of course, task parts $\{x_{jk}\}_{T_j \in \mathcal{T}_k}$ are independent for each $k = 1, 2, \cdots, K-1$, K being the total number of nodes in the network, and thus for calculating of Δ_k's as functions of these parts, we can utilize the results concerning independent tasks. To illustrate this approach let us start with the case (ii) discussed previously. Considering the optimal solution in which task parts are processed consecutively in each interval k we see that this is equivalent to the consecutive processing of entire tasks in an order defined by relation $\prec$. Moreover, this result is independent on the ordering of nodes in the network. Unfortunately, the last statement is not true in general for other cases of f_j's. Consider the case (i) of concave f_j, $j = 1, 2, \cdots, n$, and assume that nodes are ordered in the way defined above. Thus, for calculating $\Delta_k^*(\{x_{jk}\}_{T_j \in \mathcal{T}_k})$, $k = 1, 2, \cdots, K-1$, one must solve for each $\mathcal{T}_k$ an equation of type (7.3.9)

$$\sum_{T_j \in \mathcal{T}_k} f_j^{-1}(x_{jk}/\Delta_k) = \hat{U}. \tag{7.3.12}$$

of which Δ_k^* is the (unique) positive root for given $\{x_{jk}\}_{T_j \in \mathcal{T}_k}$. As mentioned before, this equation can be solved analytically for some important cases. The step which remains is to find a division of $\tilde{x}_j$'s into parts x_{jk}^*, $j = 1, 2, \cdots, n$; $k \in \mathcal{K}_j$ ensuring the minimum value of $C_{\max}$. This is equivalent to the solution of the following nonlinear programming problem:

$$\textit{Minimize} \quad C_{\max} = \sum_{k=1}^{K-1} \Delta_k^*(\{x_{jk}\}_{T_j \in \mathcal{T}_k}) \tag{7.3.13}$$

$$\textit{subject to} \quad \sum_{k \in \mathcal{K}_j} x_{jk} = \tilde{x}_j, j = 1, 2, \cdots, n, \tag{7.3.14}$$

$$x_{jk} \geq 0, j = 1, 2, \cdots, n, k \in \mathcal{K}_j. \tag{7.3.15}$$

It can be proved (see e.g. [Weg82]) that $C_{\max}$ is a convex function of x_{jk}'s for arbitrary f_j's, thus we have a convex programming problem with linear constraints. Its solution is the optimal solution of our problem for a given ordering of nodes. Using the Lagrange theorem one can verify that for $f_j = c_j u_j^{1/\alpha}$, $\alpha > 1$, when $C_{\max}^*$ is given by (7.3.11), the solution does not depend on the ordering of nodes. Of course, this is always true when the ordering of nodes is unique, i.e. for a uan (cf. Section 3.1). In general, however, in order to find a solution which is optimal over all possible orderings of nodes one must solve the corresponding convex programming problem for each of these orderings and choose a solution with the smallest value of $C_{\max}$. Notice that it may happen in the solution thus obtained that a task is preempted because the amount of continuous resource allotted to it is zero in some time interval. Thus, to solve the problem optimally for the nonpreemptive case, one must introduce nonpreemptibility conditions to the optimization problem (7.3.13)-(7.3.15). Since such conditions complicate the problem significantly, a more practical approach is to solve the preemptive version optimally, and then to allot some minimum resource amount to each preempted task, and at the same time reduce the resource allocations of the other tasks correspondingly.

To illustrate the way of formulating the optimization problem (7.3.13)-(7.3.15) let us consider a simple example.

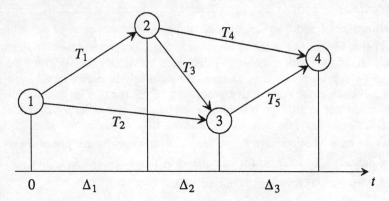

Figure 7.3.3 *Example uniconnected activity network*

Example 7.3.1 Consider the uan given in Figure 7.3.3. Let $\hat{U} = 1$, $f_j = u_j$ for $j = 1, 3, 5$, and $f_j = 2u_j^{1/2}$ for $j = 2, 4$. Subsets of tasks which can be processed between the occurrence of consecutive nodes are:

$$\mathcal{T}_1 = \{T_1, T_2\}, \ \mathcal{T}_2 = \{T_2, T_3, T_4\}, \ \mathcal{T}_3 = \{T_4, T_5\}$$

Sets of indices of $\mathcal{T}_k$'s such that $T_j \in \mathcal{T}_k$ are:

$$\mathcal{K}_1 = \{1\}, \ \mathcal{K}_2 = \{1, 2\}, \ \mathcal{K}_3 = \{2\}, \ \mathcal{K}_4 = \{2, 3\}, \ \mathcal{K}_5 = \{3\}.$$

Since all the functions f_j are concave, we use equation (7.3.12) to calculate $\Delta_k^*(\{x_{jk}\}_{T_j \in \mathcal{T}_k})$ for $k = 1, 2, 3$. For Δ_1^* we have

$$x_{11}/\Delta_1^* + x_{21}^2/4\Delta_1^{*2} = 1,$$

and thus $\Delta_1^*(x_{11}, x_{21}) = (x_{11} + \sqrt{x_{11}^2 + x_{21}^2})/2$. Similarly,

$$x_{22}^2/4\Delta_2^{*2} + x_{32}/\Delta_2^* + x_{42}^2/4\Delta_2^{*2} = 1,$$

$$\Delta_2^*(x_{22}, x_{32}, x_{42}) = (x_{32} + \sqrt{x_{22}^2 + x_{32}^2 + x_{22}^2})/2$$

and

$$x_{43}^2/4\Delta_3^{*2} + x_{53}/\Delta_3^* = 1,$$

$$\Delta_3^*(x_{43}, x_{53}) = (x_{53} + \sqrt{x_{43}^2 + x_{53}^2})/2.$$

The problem is to minimize the sum of the above functions subject to the constraints $x_{11} = \tilde{x}_1$, $x_{21} + x_{22} = \tilde{x}_2$, $x_{32} = \tilde{x}_3$, $x_{42} + x_{43} = \tilde{x}_4$, $x_{53} = \tilde{x}_5$, $x_{jk} \geq 0$ for all j, k. Eliminating five of the variables from the above constraints, a problem with two variables remains. □

Notice that the reasoning performed above for dependent tasks remains valid if we replace the assumption $n \leq m$ by $|T_k| \leq m$, $k = 1, 2, \cdots, K-1$.

Let us now consider the case that the number of machines is less than the number of tasks which can be processed simultaneously[2]. We start with independent tasks and $n > m$. To solve the problem optimally for the preemptive case we must, in general, consider all possible assignments of machines to tasks, i.e. all m-element combinations of tasks from T. Keeping for them denotion T_k, $k = 1, 2, \cdots, \binom{n}{m}$, we obtain a new optimization problem of type (7.3.13)-(7.3.15). For the nonpreemptive case we consider maximal sequences of m-tuples of tasks from T such that each task appears in at least one m-tuple and no task is preempted. For example, if $m = 3$ and $n = 5$, one such sequence would be $(\{T_1, T_2, T_3\}, \{T_2, T_3, T_4\}, \{T_3, T_4, T_5\})$. For each sequence we formulate and solve the problem of type (7.3.13)-(7.3.15) and choose the best solution.

It is easy to see that finding an optimal schedule is computationally very difficult in general, and thus it is purposeful to construct heuristics. For the nonpreemptive case the idea of a heuristic approach can be to choose one or several sequences of m-tuples of tasks described above and solve a problem of type (7.3.13)-(7.3.15) for each of them. Another idea, for an arbitrary problem type, consists of two steps:

(a) Schedule task from T on machines from P for task processing times $p_j = \tilde{x}_j/f_j(\hat{u}_j)$, $j = 1, 2, \cdots, n$, where the $\hat{u}_j$'s are fixed resource amounts.

(b) Allocate the continuous resource among parts of tasks processed in parallel in the schedule obtained in step (a).

Usually in both steps we take into account the same optimization criterion ($C_{\max}$ in our case), although heuristics with different criteria can also be considered. Of course, we tend to solve each step optimally. In majority of cases it can be done pretty easily for step (b) (numbers of task parts processed in parallel are less than or equal to m; see Figure 7.3.4 for $m = 2$, $n = 4$) when, as we remember, even analytic results can be obtained. However, the complexity of step (a) is radically different for preemptive and nonpreemptive scheduling. In the first case, the problem under consideration can be solved exactly in $O(n)$ time using McNaughton's algorithm, whereas in the second one it is NP-hard for any fixed value of m ([Kar72]; see also Section 5.1). In the latter case approximation algorithms as described in Section 5.1, or dynamic programming algorithms similar to that presented in Section 7.1 can be applied (here tasks are divided into classes with equal processing times).

---

[2] Recall that this assumption is not needed when in the optimal solution tasks are processed on a single machine, i.e. if $f_j \leq c_j u_j$, $c_j = f_j(\hat{U})/\hat{U}$, $j = 1, 2, ..., n$.

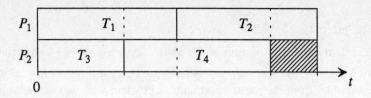

Figure 7.3.4 *Parts of tasks processed in parallel in an example schedule.*

The question remains how to define resource amounts $\hat{u}_j$, $j = 1, 2, \cdots, n$, in step 1°. There are many ways to do this; some of them were described in [BCSW86] and checked experimentally in the preemptive case. Computational experiments show that solutions produced by this heuristic differ from the optimum by several percent on average. However, further investigations in this area are still needed. Notice also that we can change the amounts $\hat{u}$ when performing steps (a) and (b) iteratively.

Let us stress once again that the above two-step approach is pretty general, since it combines (discrete) scheduling problems (step (a)) with problems of continuous resource allocation among independent tasks (step (b)). Thus, in step (a) we can utilize all the algorithms presented so far in this book, as well as many others, e.g. from constrained resource project scheduling (see, e.g. [SW89]). On the other hand, in step (b) we can utilize several generalizations of the results presented in this section. We will mention some of them below, but earlier we say few words about dependent tasks and $|\mathcal{T}_k| > m$ for at least one k. Of course, to solve the problem heuristically we can use the two-step approach. However, to solve it optimally in the preemptive case one must combine the reasoning presented for dependent tasks and $n \le m$, and that for independent tasks and $n > m$. It means that each problem of type (7.3.12)-(7.3.14) must be solved for all m-element subsets of sets $\mathcal{T}_k$, $k = 1, 2, \cdots, K-1$. In the nonpreemptive case nonpreemptability conditions of tasks processing must again be added to the optimization problem of type (7.3.13)-(7.3.15).

We end this section with few remarks concerning generalizations of the results presented for continuous resource allocation problems. First of all we can deal with a doubly constrained resource, when, apart from (7.3.2), also the constraint $\sum_{j=1}^{n} \int_0^{C_j} f_j[u_j(t)]dt \le \hat{V}$ is imposed, $\hat{V}$ being the consumption constraint [Weg81]. Secondly, each task may require many continuous resource types. The processing speed of task T_j is then given by $\dot{x}_j(t) = f_j[u_{j1}(t), u_{j2}(t), \cdots, u_{js}(t)]$, where $u_{jl}(t)$ is the amount of resource R_l allotted to T_j at time t, ans s is the number of different resource types. Thus in general we obtain multiobjective resource allocation problems of the type formulated in [Weg91]. Thirdly, other optimality criteria can be considered, such as $\int_0^{C_{\max}} g[u(t)]dt$ [NZ81], $\sum w_j C_j$ [NZ84a, NZ84b] or $L_{\max}$ [Weg89].

7.3.3 Processing Time vs. Resource Amount Model

In this section we consider problems of scheduling nonpreemptable tasks on a single machine, where task processing times are linear and continuous functions of a continuous resource. The task processing model is given in the form

$$p_j = b_j - a_j u_j, \underline{u}_j \le u_j \le \tilde{u}_j, j = 1, 2, \cdots, n \tag{7.3.16}$$

where $a_j > 0$, $b_j > 0$, and $\underline{u}_j$ and $\tilde{u}_j \in [0, b_j/a_j]$ are known constants. The continuous resource is available in maximal amount $\hat{U}$, i.e. $\sum_{j=1}^{n} u_j \le \hat{U}$. Although now the resource is not necessarily renewable (this is not a temporary model), we will keep denotations as introduced in Section 7.3.2. Scheduling problems using the above model were broadly studied by Janiak in a number of papers we will refer to in the sequel. Without loss of generality we can restrict our considerations to the case that lower bounds $\underline{u}_j$ of resource amounts alloted to the particular tasks are zero. This follows from the fact that in case of $\underline{u}_j > 0$ the model can be replaced by an equivalent one in the following way:

replace b_j by $b_j - a_j \underline{u}_j$ and $\tilde{u}_j$ by $\tilde{u}_j - \underline{u}_j$, $j = 1, 2, \cdots, n$, and $\hat{U}$ by $\hat{U} - \sum_{i=1}^{n} \underline{u}_i$; finally, set all $\underline{u}_j = 0$. Given a set of tasks $T = \{T_1, \cdots, T_n\}$, let $z = [z(1), \cdots, z(n)]$ denote a permutation of task indices that defines a feasible task order for the scheduling problem, and let Z be the set of all such permutations. A schedule for T can then be characterized by a pair $(z, u) \in Z \times U$. The value of a schedule (z, u) with respect to the optimality criterion γ will be denoted by $\gamma(z, u)$. A schedule with an optimal value of γ will briefly be denoted by (z^*, u^*).

Let us start with the problem of minimizing $C_{\max}$ for the case of equal ready times and arbitrary precedence constraints [Jan88a]. Using a slight modification of the notation introduced in Section 3.4, we denote this type of problems by $1 \,|\, prec, p_j = b_j - a_j u_j, \Sigma u_j \le \hat{U} \,|\, C_{\max}$. It is easy to verify that an optimal solution (z^*, u^*) of the problem is obtained if we chose an arbitrary permutation $z \in Z$ and allocate the continuous resource according to the following algorithm.

Algorithm 7.3.2 *for finding u^* for* $1 \,|\, prec, p_j = b_j - a_j u_j, \Sigma u_j \le \hat{U} \,|\, C_{\max}$ [Jan88a].
```
begin
for j := 1 to n do u_j^* := 0;
while T ≠ ∅ and Û > 0 do
    begin
    Find T_k ∈ T for which a_k = max{a_j};
             j
    u_j^* := min{ũ_k, Û};
    Û := Û - u_k^*;
    T := T - {T_k};
    end;
```

$u^* := [u_1^*, \cdots, u_n^*];$ -- u^* is an optimal resource allocation
end;

Obviously, the time complexity of this algorithm is $O(n\log n)$.

Consider now the problem with arbitrary ready times, i.e. $1 \mid prec, r_j, p_j = b_j - a_j u_j, \Sigma u_j \le \hat{U} \mid C_{max}$. One can easily prove that an optimal solution (z^*, u^*) of the problem is always found if we first schedule tasks according to an obvious modification of Algorithm 4.4.2 by Lawler - thus having determined z^* - and then allocate the resources according to Algorithm 7.3.3.

Algorithm 7.3.3 *for finding* u^* *for* $1 \mid prec, r_j, p_j = b_j - a_j u_j, \Sigma u_j \le \hat{U} \mid C_{max}$ [Jan88a].
begin
for $j := 1$ **to** n **do** $u_j^* := 0;$
$S_{z^*(1)} := r_{z^*(1)};$
$l := 1;$
for $j := 2$ **to** n **do** $S_{z^*(j)} := \max\{r_{z^*(j)}, S_{z^*(j-1)} + b_{z^*(j-1)}\};$
          -- starting times of tasks in permutation z^* for u^* have been calculated
$\mathcal{J} := z;$ -- Construct set $\mathcal{J}$
while $\mathcal{J} \ne \emptyset$ **or** $\hat{U} \ne 0$ **do**
     begin
     Find the biggest index k for which $r_{z^*(k)} = S_{z^*(k)};$
     $\mathcal{J} := \{z^*(j) \mid k < n, \text{ and } u_{z^*(j)}^* < u_{z^*(j)}\};$
     Find index t for which $a_{z^*(t)} = \max\{a_{z^*(j)} \mid z^*(j) \in \mathcal{J}\};$
     $d := \min\{S_{z^*(i)} - r_{z^*(i)} \mid t < i \le n\};$
     $y := \min\{u_{z^*(t)}, \hat{U}, d/a_{z^*(t)}\};$
     $u_{z^*(t)}^* := u_{z^*(t)}^* + y;$
     $\hat{U} := \hat{U} - y;$
     for $i := t$ **to** n **do** $S_{z^*(i)} := S_{z^*(i)} - y a_{z^*(t)};$
     $l := k;$
          -- new resource allocation and task starting times have been calculated
     end;
$u^* := [u_1^*, \cdots, u_n^*];$ -- u^* is an optimal resource allocation
end;

The complexity of this algorithm is $O(n^2)$, and this is the complexity of the whole approach for finding (z^*, u^*), since Algorithm 4.4.2 is also of complexity $O(n^2)$.

Let us now pass to the problems of minimizing maximum lateness L_{max}. Since problem $1 \mid prec, p_j = b_j - a_j u_j, \Sigma u_j \le \hat{U} \mid L_{max}$ is equivalent to problem $1 \mid prec, r_j, p_j = b_j - a_j u_j, \Sigma u_j \le \hat{U} \mid C_{max}$ (as in the case without additional resources), its optimal solution can always be obtained by finding z^* according to the Algorithm 4.4.2 and u^* according to a simple modification of Algorithm 7.3.3.

It is also easy to see that problem $1 \mid r_j, \, p_j = b_j - a_j u_j, \, \Sigma u_j \leq \hat{U} \mid L_{\max}$ is strongly NP-hard, since the restricted version $1 \mid r_j \mid L_{\max}$ is already strongly NP-hard (see Section 4.3). For the problem $1 \mid prec, \, r_j, \, p_j = b_j - a_j u_j, \, \Sigma u_j \leq \hat{U} \mid L_{\max}$ where in addition precedence constraints are given, an exact branch and bound algorithm was presented by Janiak [Jan86].

Finally, consider problems with the optimality criteria ΣC_j and $\Sigma w_j C_j$. Problem $1 \mid prec, \, p_j = b_j - a_j u_j, \, \Sigma u_j \leq \hat{U} \mid \Sigma C_j$ is NP-hard, and problem $1 \mid r_j, \, p_j = b_j - a_j u_j, \, \Sigma u_j \leq \hat{U} \mid \Sigma C_j$ is strongly NP-hard, since the corresponding restricted versions $1 \mid prec \mid \Sigma C_j$ and $1 \mid r_j \mid \Sigma C_j$ are NP-hard and strongly NP-hard, respectively (see Section 4.2). The complexity status of problem $1 \mid p_j = b_j - a_j u_j, \, \Sigma u_j \leq \hat{U} \mid \Sigma w_j C_j$ is still an open question. It is easy to verify for any given $z \in \mathcal{Z}$ the minimum value of $\Sigma w_j C_j$ in this problem is always obtained by allocating the resource according to the following algorithm of complexity $O(n \log n)$.

Algorithm 7.3.4 *for finding* u^* *for* $1 \mid p_j = b_j - a_j u_j, \, \Sigma u_j \leq \hat{U} \mid \Sigma w_j C_j$ [Jan88a].
```
begin
while T ≠ ∅ do
    begin
```
Find $z(k) \in z$ for which $a_{z(k)} \sum_{j=k}^{n} w_{z(j)} = \max_{z(i) \in z} \{a_{z(i)} \sum_{j=i}^{n} w_{z(j)}\}$;

$u^*_{z(k)} := \min\{\tilde{u}_{z(k)}, \, \max\{0, \, \hat{U}\}\}$;

$\hat{U} := \hat{U} - u^*_{z(k)}$;

$T := T - \{T_k\}$;
```
    end;
```
$u^* := [u^*_1, \cdots, u^*_n]$;   -- u^* is an optimal resource allocation
```
end;
```

An exact algorithm of the same complexity can also be given for this problem if for any two tasks $T_i, \, T_j$ either $T_i \prec T_j$ or $T_j \prec T_i$, where $T_i \prec T_j$ means that $b_i \leq b_j, \, a_i \geq a_j$, $\tilde{u}_i \geq \tilde{u}_j$, and $w_i \geq w_j$. Assume that the tasks are ordered in permutation z according to $\prec$. The algorithm allocates the resource among tasks in the following way: $u^*_{z^*(j)} = \min\{\tilde{u}_{z^*(j)}, \, \max\{0, \, \hat{U}_j\}\}$ for $j = 1, \, 2, \cdots, n$, where $\hat{U}_1 = \hat{U}$, $\hat{U}_{j+1} = \hat{U}_j - u^*_{z^*(j)}$, $j = 1, \, 2, \cdots, n-1$.

Now let us pass to the criterion which is specific to scheduling problems with additional continuous resources, namely to the criterion denoting the total resource utilization, i.e. $U = \sum_{j=1}^{n} u_j$. This criterion should be minimized subject to the constraint $\gamma < \hat{\gamma}$ where γ is a classical schedule performance measure and $\hat{\gamma}$ is a given value of γ. Of course, scheduling problems to minimize Σu_j are closely related to corresponding problems with criterion γ. Additionally, we use the fact that for the considered problems it is easy to calculate the maximum value $\tilde{\gamma}$ of γ.

We illustrate this idea for the criterion $\gamma = C_{max}$, i.e. for problem $1 \mid prec$, $p_j = b_j - a_j u_j$, $C_{max} < \hat{C} \mid \Sigma u_j$. It is obvious that the upper bound for C_{max}, $\tilde{C}^*_{max} = \min\limits_{z \in Z} C_{max}(z^*, 0) = C_{max}(z^*, 0)$. Thus, we have the following modification of Algorithm 7.3.2.

Algorithm 7.3.5 *for finding* u^* *for* $1 \mid prec$, $p_j = b_j - a_j u_j$, $C_{max} \le \hat{C} \mid \Sigma u_j$ [Jan91a].
begin
for $j := 1$ **to** n **do**
$u^*_j := 0;$
$U := 0;$

$C_{max} := \tilde{C}_{max};$
while $\mathcal{T} \neq \varnothing$ **and** $C_{max} > \hat{C}$ **do**
    begin
    Find $T_k \in \mathcal{T}$ for which $a_k = \max\limits_j \{a_j\};$

    $u^*_k := \min\{\tilde{u}_k, \max\{0, (C_{max} = \hat{C}/a_k)\};$
    $U := U + u^*_k;$
    $C_{max} := C_{max} - a_k u^*_k;$
    $\mathcal{T} := \mathcal{T} - \{T_k\};$
    end;
if $\mathcal{T} = \varnothing$ **and** $C_{max} > \hat{C}$ **then** no solution exists **else** $u^* := [u^*_1, \cdots, u^*_n];$
    -- u^* is an optimal resource allocation
end;

Knowing how to solve a problem for criteria γ and Σu_j, one can also find the set of all Pareto-optimal (i.e. efficient or nondominated) solutions (z^P, u^P) for *bi-criterion problems* ([Jan91a]). As an example, consider the problem $1 \mid r_j$, $p_j = b_j - a_j u_j \mid C_{max} \wedge \Sigma u_j$. Of course, $\underset{\sim}{C}_{max} = \min\limits_{z \in Z} C_{max}(z, \tilde{u}) = \sum\limits_{j=1}^{n} (b_j - a_j \tilde{u}_j)$ is a lower bound for C_{max}. In our problem, for each value $C_{max} \in [\underset{\sim}{C}_{max}, \tilde{C}_{max}]$, any feasible permutation $z \in Z$ can be taken as Pareto-optimal permutation z^P. In order to find the set $\mathcal{U}^P$ of all Pareto-optimal resource allocations u^P, we determine the Pareto curve (which is a convex, decreasing and piece-wise linear function) from the following algorithm of time complexity $O(n \log n)$.

Algorithm 7.3.6 *for finding the Pareto curve in* $1 \mid r_j$, $p_j = b_j - a_j u_j \mid C_{max} \wedge \Sigma u_j$ [Jan91a].
begin
for $j := 1$ **to** n **do** $u^*_{z(j)} := 0;$
$i := 0;$

$C^i_{max} := \tilde{C}_{max};$
$U^0 := 0;$

```
while  T ≠ ∅  do
    begin
    i := i+1;
    Find T_k ∈ T for which a_k = max{a_j};
                                   j
    u*_k := ũ_k;
    C^i_max := C^{i-1}_max − a_k ũ_k;
    U^i := U^{i-1} + ũ_k;
    a^i := 1/a_k;
    T := T − {T_k};
    for l := 1 to n do u^i_l := u*_l;
    end;
end;
```

Obtained pairs $(C^0_{max}, U^0), (C^1_{max}, U^1), \cdots, (C^n_{max}, U^n)$ are consecutive breakpoints of the Pareto curve; a^i is the slope of the ith segment of this curve, $i = 1, 2, \cdots, n$. The set $\mathcal{U}^P$ is the sum of n segments joining the points $a^i, u^{i+1}, i = 0, 1, 2, \cdots, n-1$.

To end this section let us mention some results obtained for the processing time vs. resource amount model in case of dedicated processors. Two-machine flow shop problems with linear task models were studied by Janiak [Jan88a, Jan89], where it was proved that the problem is *NP*-hard for the single criteria $\gamma = C_{max}$ and $\gamma = \Sigma u_j$, even for identical values of a_j on one of the machines and fixed processing times on the second machine. Approximation algorithms and an exact branch and bound algorithm were also presented in these papers. Flow shop and job shop problems with convex task models were considered in [Jan86, Jan88c, JG87] and [Jan88d].

7.3.4 Ready Time vs. Resource Amount Model

In this section we assume that task processing times are given constants but ready times are continuously dependent on the amount of allocated continuous resource, i.e.

$$r_j = f_j(u_j), \underline{u}_j \le u_j \le \tilde{u}_j, j = 1, 2, \cdots, n, \tag{7.3.17}$$

where all the lower and upper bounds of resource allocations, $\underline{u}_j$ and $\tilde{u}_j$, are known constants.

As in Section 7.3.3 tasks are assumed to be nonpreemptable. We only consider scheduling of tasks on a single machine. Problems of this type appear e.g. in the ingot preheating process in steel mills [Jan91b].

Problem $1 \mid r_j = f_j(u_j), \sum_{j=1}^{n} u_j \leq \hat{U} \mid C_{max}$

This problem is strongly *NP*-hard even in the special case of linear functions f_j (see (7.3.16)) and $\underline{u}_j = 0$, $j = 1, 2, \cdots, n$, and in the case of $a_j = a$, $j = 1, 2, \cdots, n$ [Jan91b].

However, for identical values of r_j, i.e. for $f_j = f$, $\underline{u}_j = \underline{u}$ and $\tilde{u}_j = \tilde{u}$ for all j, the problem can be solved in polynomial time. In this case we know from [Jan86b] that an optimal solution (z^*, u^*) is obtained by scheduling tasks according to nonincreasing processing times p_j (thus defining permutation z^*) and by allocating the continuous resource for z^* according to the following formulas: if

$$f(\tilde{u}_{z^*(1)}) + \sum_{j=1}^{n} p_{z^*(j)} \geq f(\underline{u}) + \sum_{j=2}^{n} p_{z^*(j)}$$

where

$$\tilde{u}_{z^*(1)} = \min\{(\hat{U} - (n-1)\underline{u}), \tilde{u}\},$$

then

$$u^*_{z^*(1)} = \tilde{u}_{z^*(1)}, u^*_{z(j)} = \underline{u}, j = 2, 3, \cdots, n.$$

Otherwise,

$$u^*_{z^*(j)} = f^{-1}(r - (\sum_{i=j}^{k-1} p_{z^*(i)} + d)), j = 1, 2, \cdots, k-1,$$

$$u_{z^*(k)} = f^{-1}(r - d), u^*_{z^*(j)} = \underline{u}, j = k+1, k+2, \cdots, n,$$

where $r = f(\underline{u})$, and $k-1$ is the maximal natural number such that

$$(\sum_{j=1}^{k-1} f^{-1}(r - \sum_{i=j}^{k-1} p_{z^*(i)}) + (n - (k-1))\underline{u} \leq \hat{U}) \text{ and } (f^{-1}(r - \sum_{j=1}^{k-1} p_{z^*(j)}) \leq \tilde{u}),$$

$$d = \min\{(r - \sum_{j=1}^{k-1} p_{z^*(i)} - f(\tilde{u})), d'\},$$

with d' following from the equation

$$\sum_{j=1}^{k-1} f^{-1}(r - \sum_{i=j}^{k-1} p_{z^*(i)} - d') + f^{-1}(r - d') + (n-k)\underline{u} = \hat{U}.$$

Thus, if we are able to calculate f, f^{-1} and d' in time $O(g(n))$, then (z^*, u^*) is calculated in $O(\max\{g(n), n\log n\})$ time, i.e. this time is polynomial if $g(n)$ is polynomial. For example, this is the case if f is linear. In special situations where f is linear and $b_j = b$ for $j = 1, 2, \cdots, n$, algorithms of time complexity $O(n\log n)$ exist. These situations are as follows:

(i) $\tilde{u}_j = \tilde{u}, p_j = p, j = 1, 2, \cdots, n,$

(ii) $a_j = a, p_j = p, j = 1, 2, \cdots, n.$

An optimal solution (z^*, u^*) is obtained by scheduling the tasks according to nonincreasing values of a_j in case (i), nonincreasing $\tilde{u}_j$ in case (ii), and by allocating the continuous resource using corresponding modifications of the above formulas [Jan86]. For arbitrary linear functions f_j, Janiak [Jan88a] was able to prove that for given $z \in Z$, an optimal resource allocation u_z^* can be calculated in $O(n^2)$ time using the following algorithm.

Algorithm 7.3.7 *for finding u^* for* $1 \mid r_j = b_j - a_j u_j, \ \Sigma u_j \le \hat{U} \mid C_{max}$ [Jan88a].
```
begin
for j := 1 to n do
    begin
```
$u_{z(j)}^* := 0;$

$C_{z(j)} := b_{z(j)} + \sum_{i=j}^{n} p_{z(i)};$

```
    end;
```
$\mathcal{J} := \{z(j) \mid j = 1, 2, \cdots, n\};$

$l := 0;$

$C_0 := 0;$

$\mathcal{J}_0 := 0;$

```
while 𝒥 ≠ ∅ do
    begin
```
$l := l + 1;$

Find set $\mathcal{J}_l = \{z(j) \mid z(j) \in \mathcal{J} \text{ and } C_{z(j)} = \min_{z(i) \in \mathcal{J}} \{C_{z(i)}\}\};$

$\mathcal{J} = \mathcal{J} - \mathcal{J}_l;$

```
    end;
```
$Q := \mathcal{J}_l;$

```
while not (Û = 0 or l = 0 or min {ũⱼ−uⱼ*} = 0) do
                                    j∈Q
    begin
```
$x := \min \{C_q - C_p, \ \hat{U} / \sum_{j \in Q} (1/a_j), \ \min_{j \in Q} \{a_j(\tilde{u}_j - u_j^*)\}\};$

       -- p and q are indices of tasks belonging to sets Q and $\mathcal{J}_{l-1}$, respectively

```
    for j ∈ Q do
```
$u_j^* := u_j^* + x/a_j;$

$\hat{U} := \hat{U} - \sum_{j \in Q} x/a_j;$

$l := l - 1;$

$Q := Q \cup \mathcal{J}_l;$

```
    end;
```
$u_z^* := [u_1^*, \cdots, u_n^*];$ -- u_z^* is an optimal resource allocation for permutation z
```
end;
```

In the same paper it has been shown that in the case of $a_j = a$, $\tilde{u}_j = \tilde{u}$, $p_j = p$ for $j = 1$, $2, \cdots, n$, an optimal solution (z^*, u^*) is obtained when tasks are scheduled in order of nondecreasing b_j and the resource is allocated according to Algorithm 7.3.7. The same is also true for problems in which the above permutation is in accordance with the nonincreasing orders of a_j, $\tilde{u}_j$ and p_j. Of course, Algorithm 7.3.7 can also be used for finding resource allocations for permutations $z \in Z$ defined heuristically. In [Jan89b] 25 such heuristics with the (best possible) worst case bound 2 were compared experimentally. The best results for "low" resource level ($\hat{U} = 0.2 \sum_{j=1}^{n} \tilde{u}_j$) were produced by ordering tasks according to nondecreasing b_j, whereas for "high" resource level ($\hat{U} = 0.9 \sum_{j=1}^{n} \tilde{u}_j$) sorting tasks according to nondecreasing values of $b_j - a_j \tilde{u}_j$ yields best results.

Problem $1 \mid r_j = f_j(u_j), C_{max} \le \hat{C} \mid \Sigma u_j$

Similarly as for $1 \mid r_j = f_j(u_j), \Sigma u_j \le \hat{U} \mid C_{max}$ it can be proved that the considered problem is already strongly NP-hard for $f_j = b_j - a_j u_j$, $j = 1, 2, \cdots, n$, and NP-hard for $a_j = a$, $j = 1, 2, \cdots, n$ (see [Jan91b]). Also similarly to the solution of the first problem, if $f_j = f$, $u_j = u$ for all j, the problem is solved optimally by scheduling tasks according to nonincreasing p_j (thus defining permutation z^*) and by allocating the resource according to the following condition. If

$$r + \sum_{j=1}^{n} p_j - \hat{C} \le p_{z^*(1)}, \text{ where } r = f(\underline{u}),$$

then

$$u_{z^*(1)}^* = f^{-1}(\hat{C} - \sum_{j=1}^{n} p_j), \ u_{z^*(j)}^* = \underline{u}, j = 2, 3, \cdots, n,$$

and otherwise

$$u_{z^*(j)}^* = f^{-1}(\hat{C} - \sum_{i=j}^{n} p_{z^*(i)}) = f^{-1}(C/r - \sum_{i=j}^{k-1} p_{z^*(i)} - d) \text{ for } j = 1, 2, \cdots, k-1,$$

$$u_{z^*(k)}^* = f^{-1}(\hat{C} - \sum_{i=k}^{n} p_{z^*(i)}) = f^{-1}(r - d),$$

$$u_{z^*(j)}^* = f^{-1}(r) = \underline{u}, j = k+1, k+2, \cdots, n,$$

where k is the maximal natural number such that

$$\sum_{i=1}^{k-1} p_{z^*(i)} \le r + \sum_{j=1}^{n} p_j - \hat{C},$$

$$d = r + \sum_{j=1}^{n} p_j - \hat{C} - \sum_{i=1}^{k-1} p_{z^*(i)} = r + \sum_{i=k}^{n} p_{z^*(i)} - \hat{C}.$$

Thus, if we are able to calculate f and f^{-1} in $O(g(n))$ time, then finding (z^*, u^*) needs $O(\max\{g(n), n\log n\})$ time.

Notice that for the considered problem it is generally sufficient to consider $\hat{C}$ for which $\underline{C}_{max} \le \hat{C} \le \tilde{C}_{max}$, where $\underline{C}_{max} = \min_{z \in Z} C_{max}(z, \tilde{u})$ and $\tilde{C}_{max} = \min_{z \in Z} C_{max}(z, \underline{u})$. In particular, for identical f_j, $\underline{u}_j$, $\tilde{u}_j$, $j = 1, 2, \cdots, n$, we have $C_{max}(z, \tilde{u} =) \underline{C}_{max} = f(\tilde{u}) + \sum_{j=1}^{n} p_j$ and

$C_{max}(z, \underline{u}) = \tilde{C}_{max} = f(\underline{u}) + \sum_{j=1}^{n} p_j$ for each $z \in Z$.

If functions f_j are not identical, then for given $z \in Z$ an optimal u_z^* is obtained in $O(n)$ time using the formula [Jan91b]

$$u_{z(j)}^* = \max\{0, (b_{z(j)} + \sum_{i=j}^{n} p_{z(i)} - \hat{C})/a_{z(j)}\}, j = 1, 2, \cdots, n. \tag{7.3.18}$$

This follows simply from the linear programming formulation of the problem. On the same basis it is easy to see that the cases:

(i) $b_j = b, \tilde{u}_j = \tilde{u}, p_j = p, j = 1, 2, \cdots, n,$

(ii) $b_j = b, a_j = a, p_j = p, j = 1, 2, \cdots, n,$

(iii) $a_j = a, \tilde{u}_j = \tilde{u}, p_j = p, j = 1, 2, \cdots, n$

are solvable in $O(n\log n)$ time by scheduling tasks according to nonincreasing a_j in case (i), nonincreasing $\tilde{u}_j$ in case (ii), and nonincreasing b_j in case (iii), and by allocating the resource according to (7.3.18). For each of these cases z^* does not depend on $\tilde{C}$, and $\underline{C}_{max} = C_{max}(z^*, \tilde{u})$, $\tilde{C}_{max} = C_{max}(z^*, 0)$.

Heuristics in which z is defined heuristically and u_z^* is calculated according to (7.3.18) were studied in [Jan91b]. The best results were obtained by scheduling tasks according to nondecreasing b_j. Unfortunately, the worst-case performance of these heuristics is not known.

On the basis of the presented results, the set of all Pareto-optimal solutions can be constructed for some bi-criterion problems of type $1 \mid r_j = f_j(u_j) \mid C_{max} \wedge \Sigma u_j$ using the ideas described in [Jan91a].

References

BBKR86   J. Błażewicz, J. Barcelo, W. Kubiak, H.Rock, Scheduling tasks on two processors with deadlines and additional resources, *European J. Oper. Res.* 26, 1986, 364-370.

BCSW86   J. Błażewicz, W. Cellary, R. Słowiński, J. Węglarz, *Scheduling under Resource Constraints: Deterministic Models*, J. C. Baltzer, Basel, 1986.

BE91   J. Błażewicz, K. Ecker, Scheduling multiprocessor tasks under unit resource constraints, *Int. Conf. on Optimization Techniques and Applications,* Singapore, April 1987, 161-169.

BKS89   J. Błażewicz, W. Kubiak, J. Szwarcfiter, Scheduling independent fixed-type tasks, in: R. Słowiński, J. Węglarz (eds.), *Advances in Project Scheduling*, Elsevier Science Publ., Amsterdam, 1989, 225-236.

Bla78   J. Błażewicz, Complexity of computer scheduling algorithms under resource constraints, *Proc. I Meeting AFCET - SMF on Applied Mathematics*, Palaiseau, 1978, 169-178.

BLRK83   J. Błażewicz, J. K. Lenstra, A. H. G. Rinnooy Kan, Scheduling subject to resource constraints: classification and complexity, *Discrete Appl. Math.* 5, 1983, 11-24.

CD73   E. G. Coffman Jr., P. J.Denning, *Operating Systems Theory*, Prentice-Hall, Englewood Cliffs, N.J., 1973.

CGJ84   E. G. Coffman Jr., M. R.Garey, D. S.Johnson, Approximation algorithms for bin-packing - an updated survey, in: G.Ausiello, M.Lucertini, P.Serafini (eds.), *Algorithms Design for Computer System Design*, Springer Verlag, Wien, 1984, 49-106.

CGJP83   E. G. Coffman Jr., M. R. Garey, D. S. Johnson, A. S. La Paugh, Scheduling file transfers in a distributed network, *Proc. 2nd ACM SIGACT-SIGOPS Symp. on Principles of Distributed Computing*, Montreal, 1983.

GG75   M. R. Garey, R. L.Graham, Bounds for multiprocessor scheduling with resource constraints, *SIAM J.Comput.* 4, 1975, 187-200.

GJ75   M. R. Garey, D. S.Johnson, Complexity results for multiprocessor scheduling under resource constraints, *SIAM J.Comput.* 4, 1975, 397-411.

Jan86   A. Janiak, Flow-shop scheduling with controllable operation processing times, in: H. P. Geering, M. Mansour (eds.), *Large Scale Systems: Theory and Applications*, Pergamon Press, 1986, 602-605.

Jan88a   A. Janiak, Single machine sequencing with linear models of jobs subject to precedence constraints, *Archiwum Aut. i Telem.* 33, 1988, 203-210.

Jan88b   A. Janiak, Permutacyjny problem przepływowy z liniowymi modelami operacji, Zeszyty Naukowe Politechniki. *Śląskiej. ser. Automatyka* 94, 1988, 125-138.

Jan88c   A. Janiak, Minimization of the total resource consumption in permutation flow-shop sequencing subject to a given makespan, *J. Modelling, Simulation and Control (AMSE Press)* 13, 1988, 1-11.

Jan88d   A. Janiak, General flow-shop scheduling with resource constraints, *Internat. J. Production Res.* 26, 1988, 1089-1103.

Jan89a   A. Janiak, Minimization of resource consumption under a given deadline in two-processor flow-shop scheduling problem, *Inform. Process. Lett.* 32, 1989, 101-112.

Jan89b   A. Janiak, Minimization of the blooming mill standstills - mathematical model. Suboptimal algorithms, *Zesz. Nauk. AGH s. Mechanika* 8, 1989, 37-49.

Jan91a   A. Janiak, Dokladne i przyblizone algorytmy szeregowania zadan i rozdzialu zasobow w dyskretnych procesach przemyslowych, Prace Naukowe Instytutu Cybernetyki Technicznej Politechniki Wroclawskiej 87, Monografie 20, Wroclaw, 1991.

Jan91b   A. Janiak, Single machine scheduling problem with a common deadline and resource dependent release dates, *European J. Oper. Res.* 53, 1991, 317-325.

JG87   J. Grabowski, A. Janiak, Job-shop scheduling with resource-time models of operations, *European J. Oper. Res.* 28, 1987, 58-73.

Kar84   N. Karmarkar, A new polynomial-time algorithm for linear programming, *Combinatorica* 4, 1984, 373-395.

KE75   O. Kariv, S. Even, An $O(n^2)$ algorithm for maximum matching in general graphs, *16th Annual Symp. on Foundations of Computer Science*, IEEE, 1975, 100-112.

KSS75   K. L. Krause, V. Y. Shen, H. D. Schwetman, Analysis of several task-scheduling algorithms for a model of multiprogramming computer systems, *J. Assoc. Comput. Mach.* 22, 1975, 522-550. Erratum: *J. Assoc. Comput. Mach.* 24, 1977, 527.

Law76   E. L. Lawler, *Combinatorial Optimization: Networks and Matroids*, Holt, Rinehant and Winston, New York 1976.

Len83   H. W. Lenstra, Jr., Integer programming with a fixed number of variables, *Math. Oper. Res.* 8, 1983, 538-548.

McN59   R. McNaughton, Scheduling with deadlines and loss functions, *Management Sci.* 12, 1959, 1-12.

NZ81   E. Nowicki, S. Zdrzalka, Optimal control of a complex of independent operations, *Internat. J. Systems Sci.* 12, 1981, 77-93.

NZ84a   E. Nowicki, S. Zdrzalka, Optimal control policies for resource allocation in an activity network, *European J. Oper. Res.* 16, 1984, 198-214.

NZ84b   E. Nowicki, S. Zdrzalka, Scheduling jobs with controllable processing times as an optimal control problem, *Internat. J. Control* 39, 1984, 839-848.

SW89   R. Słowiński, J. Węglarz (eds.), *Advances in Project Scheduling*, Elsevier, Amsterdam, 1989.

WBCS77   J. Węglarz, J. Błażewicz, W. Cellary, and R. Słowiński, An automatic revised simplex method for constrained resource network scheduling, *ACM Trans. Math. Software* 3, 295-300, 1977.

Weg80   J. Węglarz, Multiprocessor scheduling with memory allocation - a deterministic approach, *IEEE Trans. Comput.* C-29, 1980, 703-709.

Weg81   J. Węglarz, Project scheduling with continuously-divisible, doubly constrained resources, *Management Sci.* 27, 1981, 1040-1052.

Weg82   J. Węglarz, Modelling and control of dynamic resource allocation project scheduling systems, in: S. G. Tzafestas (ed.), *Optimization and Control of Dynamic Operational Research Models*, North-Holland, Amsterdam, 1982.

Weg89   J. Węglarz, Project scheduling under continuous processing speed vs. resource amount functions, 1989. Chapter II.5 in [SW 89].

Weg91   J. Węglarz, Synthesis problems in allocating continuous, doubly constrained resources, in: H. E. Bradley (ed.), *Operational Research'90 - Selected Papers from the 12th IFORS International Conference*, Pergamon Press, Oxford, 1991, 715-725.

8 Scheduling in Flexible Manufacturing Systems

8.1 Introductory Remarks

A new application area for machine scheduling theory comes from Flexible Manufacturing Systems (*FMSs*). This relatively new technology was introduced to improve the efficiency of a job shop while retaining its flexibility. An FMS can be defined as an integrated manufacturing system consisting of flexible machines equipped with tool magazines and linked by a material handling system, where all system components are under computer control [BY86a]. Existing FMSs mainly differ by the installed hardware concerning machine types, tool changing devices and material handling systems. Instances of machine types are dedicated machines or parallel multi-purpose ones. Tool changing devices can be designed to render automatic online tool transportation and assignment to the machines' magazines while the system is running. In other cases tool changes are only possible if the operations of the system are stopped. Most of the existing FMSs have automatic part transportation capabilities.

Different problems have to be solved in such an enviroment which comprise design, planning and scheduling. The vital factors influencing the solutions for the latter two are the FMS-hardware and especially the existing machine types and tool changing devices. In earlier (but still existing) FMSs NC-machines are used with limited versatility; several different machines are needed to process a part. Moreover the machines are not very reliable. For such systems shop scheduling models are applicable; in classical, static formulations they have been considered in Chapter 6. Recent developments in FMS-technology show that the machines become more versatile and reliable. Some FMSs already are implemented using mainly only one machine type. These general purpose machine tools make it possible to process a part from the beginning to the end using only one machine [Jai86]. A prerequisite to achieve this advantage without or with negligible setup times is a *tool changing system* that can transfer tools between the machines' tool magazines and the central tool storage area while all machines of the system are in operation. Some FMSs already fulfill this assumption and thus incorporate a high degree of flexibility. Results from queueing theory using closed queueing networks show that the expected production rate is maximized under a configuration which incorporates only general purpose machines [BY86b, SS85, SM85].

With the notation of machine scheduling theory this kind of FMS design can be represented by parallel machine models, and thus they were treated relatively broadly in Chapter 5. The most appropriate type of these models depends on the particular scheduling situation. All the machines might be identical or they have to be regarded as uniform or unrelated. Parts (i.e. jobs) might have due dates or deadlines, release times, or weights indicating their relative importance. The possibilities of part processing might be restricted by certain precedence constraints, or each operation (i.e. task) can be carried out independently of the others which are necessary for part completion.

Objectives might consist of minimizing schedule length, mean flow time or due date involving criteria. All these problem characteristics are well known from traditional machine scheduling theory, and had been discussed earlier.

Most of the FMS-scheduling problems have to take into account these problem formulations in a quite general framework and hence are *NP*-hard. Thus, with the view from today, they are computationally intractable for greater problem instances.

The difficulties in solving these problem types are sometimes overcome by considering the possibility of preempting part processing. As shown in former chapters, quite a lot of intractable problems are solvable in their preemptive versions in polynomial time. In the context of FMSs one has to differ between two kinds of preemptions. One occurs if the operation of a part is preempted and later resumed on the same machine (part-preemption). The other one appears if the operation of a part is preempted and then resumed at the same point of time or at a later time on another machine (part-machine-preemption). The consequences of these two kinds of preemption are different. Part-preemption can be carried out without inducing a change of machines and thus it does not need the use of the FMS material handling system. Part-machine-preemption requires its usage for part transportation from one machine to another. A second consequence comes from the buffer requirements. In either case of preemption storage capacity is needed for preempted and not yet finished parts. If it is possible to restrict the number and kind of preemptions to a desirable level, this approach is appealing. Some computationally intractable problem types are now efficiently solvable and for most measures of performance the quality of an optimal preemptive schedule is never worse than nonpreemptive one. To consider certain inspection, repair or maintenance requirements of the machine tools, processing availability restrictions have to be taken into account. The algorithmic background of these formulations can be found in [Sch84, Sch88] and were already discussed in Chapter 5. Some nondeterministic aspects of these issues will be studied in Chapter 9.

In the context of FMSs another model of scheduling problems is also of considerable importance. In many cases tools are a very expensive equipment and under such an assumption it is unlikely that each tool type is available in an unrestricted amount. If the supply of tools of some type is restricted, this situation leads to parallel machine models with resource constraints. In an FMS-environment the number of resource types will correspond to the number of tool types, the resource limits correspond to the number of available tools of each type and the resource requirements correspond to the number of tools of each type which are necessary to perform the operation under consideration. Models of this kind are extensively treated in [BCSW86], and some recent results had been given in Section 7.1.

There is another aspect which has to be considered in such an environment. In many cases of FMS production scheduling it is desired to minimize part movements inside the system to avoid congestion and unnecessary repositioning of parts which would occur if a part is processed by more than one machine or if it is preempted on the same machine. FMSs which consist mainly of general purpose machine tools have the prerequisite to achieve good results according to the above objectives. In the best case repositioning and machine changeovers can be avoided by assigning each part to only one machine where it is processed from the beginning to the end without preemption. A modeling approach to represent this requirement would result in a formulation where all operations which have to be performed at one part would be summed up resulting in one super-operation having different resource requirements at discrete points of time. From this treatment models for project scheduling would gain some importance [SW89]. A relaxed version of this approach to avoid unnecessary part transportation and repositioning has to consider the minimization of the number of preemptions in a given schedule.

Let us also mention that any FMS scheduling problem can be decomposed into single machine problems, as it was suggested in [RRT89]. Then the ideas and algorithms presented in Chapter 4 can be utilized.

From the above issues, we can conclude that traditional machine and project scheduling theory has a great impact on advanced FMS-environments. Besides this, different problems are raised by the new technology which require different or modified models and corresponding solution approaches. There are already many results from machine and project scheduling theory available which can also be used to support the scheduling of operations of an FMS efficiently, while some others still have to be developed (see [RS89] as a survey). Various modeling approaches are investigated in [Sch89], some more recent, selected models are investigated in the following three sections. We stress the scheduling point of view in making this selection, due to the character of this book, and, on the other hand, the prospectivity of the subject. Each of the three models selected opens some new directions for further investigations. The first one concerns flexible flow shops, where the flexibility means that there is more than one (parallel) machine at at least one machine center constituting a machining system. The second deals with dynamic job shops (i.e. such in which some events, particularly job arrivals, occur at unknown times) and with the approach solving a static scheduling problem at each time of the occurrence of such an event, and then implementing the solution on a rolling horizon basis. The third considers simultaneous task scheduling and vehicle routing in a class of FMS.

8.2 Scheduling Flexible Flow Shops

8.2.1 Problem Formulation

We consider the problem of scheduling n parts or jobs J_j, $j = 1, 2, \cdots, n$, through a manufacturing system that will be called a *flexible flow shop* (*FFS*), to minimize the schedule length. An FFS consists of $m \geq 2$ machine stages or centers with stage i having $k_i \geq 1$ identical parallel machines $P_{i1}, P_{i2}, \cdots, P_{ik_i}$ (see Figure 8.2.1). For job J_j vector $[p_{1j}, p_{2j}, \cdots, p_{mj}]^T$ of processing times is known, where $p_{ij} \geq 0$ for all i, j. Task T_{ij} of job J_j may be processed on any of the k_i machines. This is the generalization of the standard flow shop scheduling problem, whereas all the remaining assumptions remain unchanged (see Section 6.1). In particular, machines may remain idle and in-process inventory is allowed. This is important, since a restricted version of the problem was studied already by Salvador [Sal73] who presented a branch and bound algorithm for FFS with no-wait schedules and $p_{ij} > 0$ for all i, j. He identified the problem in the polymerization process where there are several effectively identical and thus interchangeable plants each of which can be considered as a flow shop. Of course, all situations where a parallel machine(s) is (are) added at at least one stage of a flow shop to solve a bottleneck problem or to increase the production capacity lead to the FFS scheduling. Another interesting application of the problem was described by Brah and Hunsucker [BH91] and concerns the running of a program on a computer where the three steps of compiling, linking and running are performed in a fixed sequence and we have several processors (softwares) at each step. Other real life examples exist in the electronics manufacturing.

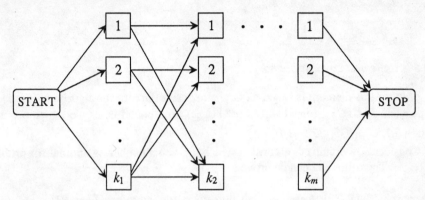

Figure 8.2.1 *Schematic representation of a flexible flow shop*

Heuristics for the general FFS scheduling problem (in the sense stated above) were developed by Wittrock [Wit85, Wit88], and by Kochbar and Morris [KM87]. The first paper deals with a periodic algorithm where a small set of jobs is scheduled and the schedule is repeated many times, whereas the second one presents a nonperiodic algorithm. The basic approach in both cases is to decompose the problem into three subproblems: machine allocation, sequencing and timing. The first subproblem is to determine which jobs will visit which machine at each stage. The second subproblem sequences jobs on each machine, and the third one consists of finding the times at which the jobs should enter the system. The heuristic algorithm developed by Kochbar and Morris considers setup times, finite buffers, blocking and starvation, machine down time, and current and subsequent state of the system. The heuristics tend to minimize the effect of setup times and blocking.

In the following sections we will present some heuristics for simple subproblems of our problem for which the worst and average case performance is known, and then a recently published branch and bound algorithm for the general problem.

8.2.2 Heuristics and their Performance

The results presented in this section were obtained by Sriskandarajah and Sethi [SS89]. In the sequel the FFS scheduling problem with m machine stages and k_i machines at stage i will be denoted by $Fm \mid k_1, k_2, \cdots, k_m \mid C_{\max}$.

Let us start with the problem $F2 \mid k_1 = 1, k_2 = k \geq 2 \mid C_{\max}$, and let us assume that the buffer between the machine stages has unlimited capacity. Firstly, consider the list scheduling algorithm in which a list of the job indices $1, 2, \cdots, n$ is given. Jobs enter the first machine stage (i.e. machine P_1) in the order defined by the list, form the queue between the stages and are processed in center 2, whenever a machine at this stage becomes available. C_{max} denotes the schedule length of the set of jobs when the list scheduling algorithm is applied, and C^*_{max} is the minimum possible schedule length of this set of jobs. Then the following theorem holds.

Theorem 8.2.1 [SS89] *For the list scheduling algorithm applied to the problem $Fm \mid k_{m-1} = 1, k_m = k \geq 2 \mid C_{max}$ we have*

$$C_{max}/C^*_{max} \leq m + 1 - \frac{1}{k},$$

and this is the best possible bound. □

The proof of this theorem is based on Grahams result [Gra66] for algorithms applied to the problem $Pm \mid \mid C_{max}$ (or $F1 \mid k_1 = k \geq 2 \mid C_{max}$). The bound is, as we remember from Section 5.1, $C_{max}/C^*_{max} \leq 2 - 1/k$.

Consider now Johnson's algorithm which, as we remember, is optimal for problem $F2 \mid \mid C_{max}$. The following can be proved.

Theorem 8.2.2 [SS89] *For Johnson's algorithm applied to problems $F2 \mid k_1 = 1, k_2 = k = 2 \mid C_{max}$ and $F2 \mid k_1 = 1, k_2 = k \geq 3 \mid C_{max}$ with $C_{max} \leq \sum_{j=1}^{n} p_{1j} + \max_{j}\{p_{2j}\}$ the following holds:*

$$C_{max}/C^*_{max} \leq 2$$

and this is the best possible bound. □

Theorem 8.2.3 [SS89] *For Johnson's algorithm applied to the problem $F2 \mid k_1 = 1, k_2 = k \geq 3 \mid C_{max}$ with $C_{max} > \sum_{j=1}^{n} p_{1j} + \max_{j}\{p_{2j}\}$ we have*

$$C_{max}/C^*_{max} \leq 1 + (2 - \frac{1}{k})(1 - \frac{1}{k}). \quad \square$$

Notice that the bounds obtained in Theorems 8.2.2 and 8.2.3 are better than those of Theorem 8.2.1.

Let us now pass to the problem $F2 \mid k_1 = k_2 = k \geq 2 \mid C_{max}$. The basic algorithm is the following.

Algorithm 8.2.4 *Heuristic H_a for $F2 \mid k_1 = k_2 = k \geq 2 \mid C_{max}$* [SS89].
begin
Partition the set of machines into k pairs $\{P_{11}, P_{21}\}, \{P_{12}, P_{22}\}, \cdots, \{P_{1k}, P_{2k}\}$, treating
　　each pair as an artificial machine P'_i, $i = 1, 2, \cdots, k$, respectively;
for each job $J_j \in \mathcal{J}$ **do** $p'_j := p_{1j} + p_{2j}$;
call Algorithm 5.1.2;
　　-- This problem is equivalent to the NP-hard problem $Pk \mid \mid C_{max}$ (see Section 5.1),
　　-- where a set of jobs with processing times p'_j is scheduled nonpreemptively
　　-- on a set of k artificial machines; list scheduling algorithms such as Algorithm 5.1.2

-- solve this problem heuristically.

for $i = 1$ **to** k **do call** Algorithm 6.1.1;

    -- This loop solves optimally each of the k flow shop problems with unlimited buffers,

    -- i.e. for each artificial machine P_i' the processing times p_i'

    -- assigned to it are distributed among the two respective machines P_{1i} and P_{2i}

end;

Let us note, that in the last **for** loop one could also use the Gilmore-Gomory algorithm (see Section 6.1), thus solving the k flow shop problems with the no-wait condition. The results obtained from hereon hold also for the FFS with no-wait restriction, i.e. for the case of no buffer between the machine stages. On the basis of the Graham's reasoning, in [SS89] the same bound as in Theorem 8.2.1 has been proved for H_a, and this bound remains unchanged even if a heuristic list scheduling algorithm is used in the last **for** loop. Since Algorithm 5.1.2 has the major influence on the worst case behavior of Algorithm H_a, in [SS89] another Algorithm, H_b, was proposed in which Algorithm 5.1.2 is replaced by the *LPT* algorithm. We know from Section 5.1 that in the worst case *LPT* is better than an arbitrary list scheduling algorithm for $Pm||C_{max}$. Thus, one can expect that for H_b a better bound exists than for H_a.

The exact bound R_{H_b} for H_b is not yet known, but Srishkandarajah and Sethi proved the following inequality for *it*,

$$\frac{7}{3} - \frac{2}{3k} \leq R_{H_b} \leq 3 - \frac{1}{k}.$$

The same authors proved that if *LPT* in H_b is replaced a better heuristic or even by an exact algorithm, the bound would still be $R_{H_b} \geq 2$. The bound 2 has also been obtained in [Lan87] for a heuristic which schedules jobs in nonincreasing order of p_{2j} in FFS with $m = 2$ and an unlimited buffer between the stages.

Computational experiments performed in [SS89] show that the average performance of the algorithms presented above is much better than their worst case behavior. However, further efforts are needed to construct heuristics with better bounds (i.e. less than 2).

8.2.3 Branch and Bound Algorithm

Below we present the branch and bound algorithm developed by Brah and Hunsucker in [BH91]. We start with the description of the bounding procedure. In addition to the notation already introduced we will use denotion $\mathcal{A}$ for a subset of jobs, i.e. $\mathcal{A} \subseteq \mathcal{J}$, and $\mathcal{A}'$ for $\mathcal{A} + \{J_q\}$, where $J_q \notin \mathcal{A}$. Three types of lower bounds have been proposed by the above authors: machine based bounds, job based bounds, and composite bounds. Before presenting these bounds let us desribe some basic concepts. As it is known, to find a lower bound on each branching node, two contiguous partial schedules must be considered. Let the first of these schedules involve all jobs on all machines through machine stage $i - 1$, along with the sequence of job set $\mathcal{A}$ at stage i. Denote this schedule by $S_i(\mathcal{A})$, and let $S_i(\mathcal{A}')$ be the schedule obtained from $S_i(\mathcal{A})$ by adding an unscheduled job J_q at stage i. The second partial schedule, $S_i'(\mathcal{J} - \mathcal{A}')$, consists of all the remaining jobs not contained in the schedule $S_i(\mathcal{A}')$ at stage i, and all jobs beyond stage i in an arbitrary order. A complete schedule of jobs at stage i and all the subsequent stages will be denoted by $S_i(\mathcal{A}')S_i'(\mathcal{J} - \mathcal{A}')$. For a given partial schedule $S_i(\mathcal{A})$ let $C[S_i(\mathcal{A}), l_i]$ denote the completion time of this schedule on machine P_{il_i}. Completion times of the partial schedule $S_i(\mathcal{A}')$ on machine P_{il_i}, $i = 1, 2, \cdots, m$, $l_i = 1, 2, \cdots, k_i$, can be calculated recursively by

$$
C[S_i(\mathcal{A}'), l] = \begin{cases} \max\{C[S_i(\mathcal{A}), l_i], C[S_{i-1}(\mathcal{A}'), l_{i-1}]\} + p_{iq} \\ \qquad \text{if } J_q \text{ is processed on } P_{il_i}, \\ C[S_i(\mathcal{A}), l_i] \qquad \text{otherwise}, \end{cases}
$$

where $C[S_0(\mathcal{A}), 0] = C[S_i(\varnothing), l_i] = 0$ for all i and $\mathcal{A}$, $C[S_0(\mathcal{A}), 0]$ being the start of processing time, and $C[S_i(\varnothing), l_i]$ being the completion time of the empty set at stage i. Thus, the schedule performance measure $C_{\max}$ is given by

$$
C_{\max} = \max_{l_m}\{C[S_m(\mathcal{J}), l_m]\}
$$

where $S_m(\mathcal{J})$ is the entire schedule of all jobs at the last stage m.

Let us consider now the *machine based bounds*, starting from the average completion time and processing requirement for stage i

$$
ACT[S_i(\mathcal{A}')] := \frac{1}{k_i}\sum_{l_i=1}^{k_i} C[S_i(\mathcal{A}'), l_i] + \frac{1}{k_i}\sum_{J_j \in \mathcal{J} - \mathcal{A}'} p_{ij}
$$

where the first term on the right hand side is the average interval over which the machines are already committed after scheduling job J_q at stage i, whereas the second term is the remaining average workload for the unprocessed jobs required on machines at stage i.

It is easy to verify that $ACT[S_i(\mathcal{A}')]$ is a lower bound on the completion time of all the jobs through stage i if i were the last stage of processing. Indeed, by definition

$$
ACT[S_i(\mathcal{A}')] \leq \max_{l_i}\{C_i(\mathcal{J}), l_i]\}
$$

and, since each job in $\mathcal{J} - \mathcal{A}'$ must be assigned to some machine at stage i,

$$
ACT[S_i(\mathcal{J})] = \frac{1}{k_i}\sum_{l_i=1}^{k_i} C[S_i(\mathcal{J}), l_i].
$$

Since the average is less than the maximum, we obtain the desired property.

Now let us notice that the maximum completion time of a scheduled workload,

$$
MCT[S_i(\mathcal{A}')] := \max_{l_i}\{C[S_i(\mathcal{A}'), l_i]\}
$$

is also a lower bound on the maximum completion time if i were the last stage. It is obvious that if it were possible to determine which job finished last at stage i, then adding the workload of that job to the remaining machines will give a lower bound on the schedule length. However, it is only possible to determine the set from which the last job comes. Namely, if $ACT[S_i(\mathcal{A}')] \geq MCT[S_i(\mathcal{A}')]$, then one of the remaining unscheduled jobs will be the last job finished at stage i, i.e. the job comes from the set $\mathcal{J} -$

$\mathcal{A}'$. Otherwise the last job may come from either the set $\mathcal{A}'$ or $\mathcal{J} - \mathcal{A}'$. This leads to the following machine based bound for the branching node at stage i

$$LBM[S_i(\mathcal{A}')] := \begin{cases} ACT[S_i(\mathcal{A}')] + \min\limits_{J_j \in \mathcal{J} - \mathcal{A}'} \sum\limits_{i'=i+1}^{m} p_{i'j} \\ \quad \text{if } ACT[S_i(\mathcal{A}')] \geq MCT[S_i(\mathcal{A}')], \\ MCT[S_i(\mathcal{A}')] + \min\limits_{J_j \in \mathcal{A}'} \sum\limits_{i'=i+1}^{m} p_{i'j} \\ \quad \text{otherwise.} \end{cases}$$

If the number of jobs is close to the number of machines at each stage, it can be advantageous to use the *job based bounds*. The calculation of these bounds are based on the remaining processing required of each unscheduled job at stage i, $i = 1, 2, \cdots, m$. However, the lower bound for the standard flow shop problem given by Gupta [Gup70] and Baker [Bak75] must be modified, since in FFS we have alternate routes for the jobs to process. A modification was constructed by considering the unscheduled jobs in the set $\mathcal{J} - \mathcal{A}'$ at stage i, which have to be completed at stage i and at the rest of the stages. Thus, if we add the maximum of times in this set to the smallest completion time of $S_i(\mathcal{A}')$, we obtain the lower bound for our problem

$$LBJ[S_i(\mathcal{A}')] := \min_{l_i}\{C[S_i(\mathcal{A}'), l_i]\} + \max_{J_j \in \mathcal{J} - \mathcal{A}'} \sum_{i=i}^{m} p_{ij}.$$

Baker [Bak75] suggests that job based bounds should be used in combination with machine based bounds, as it was proposed in [MB67] for a standard flow shop. Implementation of this suggestion in FFS leads to the following composite lower bound

$$LBC[C_i(\mathcal{A}')] := \max\{LBM[S_i(\mathcal{A}')], LBJ[S_i(\mathcal{A}')]\}.$$

Let us now pass to the description of the branching procedure for the scheduling problem. This procedure is a modification of the method developed by Bratley et al. [BFR75] for scheduling on parallel machines. At each stage i two decisions must be made: the assignment of the jobs to a machine P_{il}, and the scheduling of jobs on every machine at stage i. The enumeration is accomplished by generating a tree with two types of nodes: node (j) denotes that job J_j is scheduled on the current machine, whereas node $\boxed{j}$ denotes that J_j is scheduled on a new machine, which now becomes the current machine. The number of $\square$ nodes on each branch is equal to the number of parallel machines used by that branch, and thus must be less than or equal to k_i at stage i. The number of possible branches at each stage i was established by Brah in [Bra88] as

$$N(n, k_i) = \binom{n-1}{k_i-1} \frac{n!}{k_i!}.$$

Consequently, the total number of possible end nodes is equal to

$$S(n, m, \{k_i\}_{i=1}^{m}) = \prod_{i=1}^{m} \binom{n-1}{k_i-1} \frac{n!}{k_i!}.$$

For the construction of a tree for the problem, some definitions and rules at each stage i are useful. Let the level 0_i represent the root node at stage i, and $1_i, 2_i, \cdots, z_i$ represent different levels of the stage, with z_i being the terminal level of this stage. Of course, the total number of levels is nm. The necessary rules for the procedure generating the branching tree are the following.

Rule 1 Level 0_i contains only the dummy root node of stage i, $i = 1, 2, \cdots, m$ (each i is starting of a new stage).

Rule 2 Level 1_i contains the nodes $\boxed{1}, \boxed{2}, \cdots, \boxed{x}$, where $x = n - k_i + 1$ (any number larger than x would violate Rules 5 and 7).

Rule 3 A path from level 0_i to level j_i, $i = 1, 2, \cdots, m$, $j = 1, 2, \cdots, n$, may be extended to the level $(j+1)_i$ by any of the nodes $\boxed{1}, \boxed{2}, \cdots, \boxed{n}, ①, ②, \cdots, ⓝ$ provided the rules 4 to 7 are observed (all unscheduled jobs at stage i are candidates for $\square$ and $\bigcirc$ nodes as long as they do not violate Rules 4 to 7).

Rule 4 If $\boxed{l}$ or $ⓛ$ has previously appeared as a node at level j_i, then l may not be used to extend the path at that level (this assures that no job is scheduled twice at one stage).

Rule 5 $\boxed{l}$ may not be used to extend a path at level j_i, which already contains some node $\boxed{r}$ with $r > l$ (this is to avoid duplicate generation of sequences in the tree).

Rule 6 No path may be extended in such a way that it contains more than k_i $\square$ nodes at each stage i (this guarantees that no more than k_i machines are used at stage i).

Rule 7 No path may terminate in such a way that it contains less than k_i $\square$ nodes at each stage i unless the number of jobs is less than k_i (there is no advantage in keeping a machine idle if the processing cost is the same for all of the machines).

A sample tree representation of a problem with 4 jobs and 2 parallel machines is given in Figure 8.2.2. All of the end nodes can serve as a starting point for the next stage 0_{i+1} ($i < m$). All of the nodes at a subsequent stage may not be candidates due to their higher value of lower bounds, and thus not all of the nodes need to be explored. It may also be observed that all of the jobs at stage i will not be readily available at the next stage, and thus inserted idle time will increase their lower bounds and possibly remove them from further considerations. This will help to reduce the span of the tree. The number of search nodes could be further reduced, if the interest is in the subclass of active schedules called nondelay schedules. These are schedules in which no machine is kept idle when it could start processing some task.

The use of these schedules does not necessarily provide an optimal schedule, but the decrease in the number of the nodes searched gives a strong empirical motivation to do that, especially for large problems [Fre82].

Finally we describe the idea of the branch and bound algorithm for the problem. It uses a variation of the depth-first least lower bound search strategy, and is as follows.

LEVEL

0_i

1_i

2_i

3_i

4_i

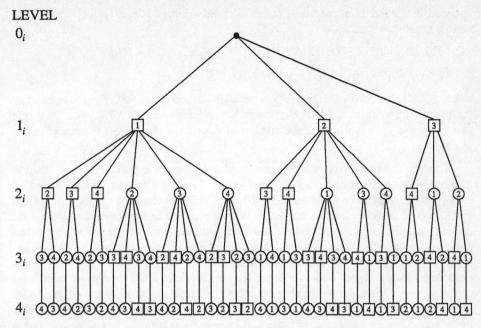

Figure 8.2.2 *Tree representation of four jobs on two parallel machines*

Step 1 Generate $n - k_1 + 1$ ☐ nodes at stage 1 and compute their lower bounds. Encode the information about the nodes and add them to the list of unprocessed nodes. Initialize counters (number of iterations, time) definining end of computation.

Step 2 Remove a node from the list of unprocessed nodes with the priority given to the deepest node in the tree with the least lower bound. Break ties arbitrarily.

Step 3 Procure all information about the retrieved node. If this is one of the end nodes of the tree go to Step 5, while if this is the last node in the list of unprocessed nodes then go to Step 6.

Step 4 Generate branches from the retrieved node and compute their lower bounds. Discard the nodes with lower bounds larger than the current upper bound. Add the remaining nodes to the list of unprocessed nodes and go to Step 2.

Step 5 Save the current complete schedule, as the best solution. If this is the last branch of the tree, or if the limit on the number of iterations or computation time has reached, then pass to the next step, otherwise go to Step 2.

Step 6 Print the results and stop.

As we see, the algorithm consists of three major parts: the branching tree generation, the lower bound computing, and the list processing part. The first two parts are based on the concepts described earlier with some modifications utilizing specific features of the problem. For the list processing part, the information is first coded for each branching node. If the lower bound is better than the best available C_{max} value of a complete solution (i.e. the current upper bound), provided it is available at the moment, the node is stored in the list of unprocessed nodes. The information stored for each branching node is the following:

$$KODE = NPR \times 1\,000\,000 + NPS \times 10\,000 + LSN \times 100 + JOB$$

$$LBND = NS \times 10\,000\,000 + NSCH \times 100\,000 + LB$$

where *JOB* is the index of the job, *NS* is the index of the stage, *NSCH* is the number in the processing sequence, *LB* is the lower bound of the node, *NPR* is the machine number in use, *NPS* is the sequence number of this machine, and *LSN* is number of the last □ nodes.

The stage and the level numbers are coded in the opposite manner to their position in the tree (the deepest node has the least value). Thus, the deepest node is stored on top of the list and can be retrieved first. If two or more nodes are at the same stage and level, the one with the least lower bound is retrieved first and processed. Once a node is retrieved, the corresponding information is decoded and compared with the last processed node data. If the node has gone down a step in the tree, the necessary information, like sequence position and completion time of the job on the retrieved node, is established and recorded. However, if the retrieved node is at a higher or the same level as the previous node, the working sequence and completion time matrix of the nodes lower than the present level and up to the level of the last node are re-initialized. The lower bound is then compared with the best known one, assuming it is available, and is either eliminated or branched on except when this is the last node in the tree. The qualifying nodes are stored in the list of unprocessed nodes according to the priority rule described in Step 2 of the algorithm. However, in case this is the last node in the tree, and it satisfies the lower bound comparison test, the working sequence position and job completion time matrix along with the completion time of the schedule is saved as the best known solution.

Of course, the algorithm described above is only a basic framework for further improvements and generalizations. For example, in order to improve the computation speed for large problems some elimination criteria, like the ones developed in [Bra88] can be used together with the lower bounds. The algorithm could also be applied for schedule performance measures other than the schedule length, if corresponding lower bounds would be elaborated. Moreover, the idea of the algorithm can be used in a heuristic way, e.g. by setting up a counter of the number of nodes to be fully explored or by defining a percentage improvement index on each new feasible solution.

8.3 Scheduling Dynamic Job Shops

8.3.1 Introductory Remarks

In this section we consider *dynamic job shops*, i.e. such in which job arrival times are unknown in advance, and we allow for the occurrence of other nondeterministic events such as machine breakdowns. The scheduling objective will be mean job tardiness which is important in many manufacturing systems, especially those that produce to specific customer orders. In low to medium volume of discrete manufacturing, typified by traditional job shops and more recently by flexible manufacturing systems, this objective was usually operationalized through the use of priority rules. A number of such rules were proposed in the literature, and a number of investigations were performed dealing with the relative effectiveness of various rules, e.g. in [Con65, BB82, KH82, BK83, VM87]. Some deeper tactical aspects of the interaction between priority rules and the methods of assigning due-dates were studied in [Bak84].

Below we will present a different approach to the problem, proposed recently by Raman, Talbot and Rachamadugu [RTR89a], and Raman and Talbot [RT92]. This approach decomposes the dynamic problem into a series of static problems. A static problem is generated at each occurrence of a nondeterministic event in the system, then solved entirely, and the solution is implemented on a rolling horizon basis. In this procedure the entire system is considered at each instance of the static problem, in contrast to priority rules which consider only one machine at a time. Of course, when compared with priority rules, this approach requires greater computational effort, but also leads to significantly better system performance. Taking into account the computing power available today, this cost seems to be worth to pay. Moreover, the idea of the approach is pretty general and can be implemented for other dynamic scheduling problems. Let us remind that the approach was originally used by Raman, Rachamadugu and Talbot [RRT89] for a single machine.

The static problem mentioned above can be solved in an exact or a heuristic way. An example of an exact method is a modification of the depth-first search branch and bound algorithm developed by Talbot [Tal82] for minimizing schedule length in a *project scheduling* problem. We will not describe this modification which is presented in [RT92] and used for benchmarking a heuristic method proposed in the same paper. This heuristic is especially interesting for practical applications, and thus will be described in more detail. It is based on decomposing the multiple machine problem, and constructing the schedule for the entire system around the bottleneck machine. For this purpose relative job priorities are established using task due dates (TDDs). However, in comparison with the traditional usage of task milestones, in this approach TDDs are derived by taking into account other jobs in the system, and TDDs assignment is combined with task scheduling. In the next two sections the heuristic algorithm will be described and results of computational experiments will be presented.

8.3.2 Heuristic Algorithm for the Static Problem

In papers dealing with priority rules applied to our scheduling problem it has been shown the superiority of decomposing job due dates into task due dates, and using TDDs for setting priorities. In particular, Baker [Bak84] found that the *Modified Task Due Date (MTD) rule* performs well across a range of due date tightness. It selects the task with the minimum MTD, where the MTD of task T_{ij} is calculated as

$$MTD_{ij} = \max (\tau + p_{ij}, d_{ij}), \tag{8.3.1}$$

and where τ is the time when the scheduling decision needs to be made and d_{ij} is the TDD of T_{ij}. Raman, Talbot and Rachamadugu [RTR89b] proved that for a given set of TDDs the total tardiness incurred by two adjacent tasks in a nondelay schedule on any given machine does not increase if they are resequenced according to the *MTD* rule. It means that if TDDs are set optimally, the *MTD* rule guarantees local optimality between adjacent tasks at any machine for a nondelay schedule. Most existing implementations of the *MTD* rule set TDDs by decomposing the total flow $d_j - p_j$ of job J_j where $p_j = \sum_{i=1}^{n_j} p_{ij}$, into individual task flows in a heuristic way. Vepsalainen and Morton [VM87] proposed to estimate each TDD by netting the lead time for the remaining tasks from the job due date. In this way the interactions of all jobs in the system are taken into account. The heuristic by Raman and Talbot also takes explicitly into account this interactions, and, moreover, considers TDD assignment and task scheduling simultaneously. Of course, the best set of TDDs is one which yields the best set of priorities, and thus the goodness of a given set of TDDs can be determined only when the system is scheduled simultaneously. In consequence, the heuristic is not a single pass method, but it considers global impact of each TDD assignment within a schedule improvement procedure. The initial solution is generated by the *MTD* rule with TDDs at the maximum values that they can assume without delaying the corresponding jobs. Machines are then considered one by one and an attempt is made to revise the schedule of tasks on a particular machine by modifying their TDDs. Jobs processed on all machines are ranked in the nonincreasing order of their tardiness. For any task in a given job with positive tardiness, first the interval for searching for the TDD is determined and for each possible value in this interval the entire system is rescheduled. The value which yields the minimum total tardiness is taken as the TDD for that task. This step is repeated for all other tasks of that job processed on the machine under consideration, for all other tardy jobs on that machine following their rank order, and for all machines in the system. The relative workload of a given machine is used to determine its criticality; the algorithm ranks all the machines from the most heavily loaded (number 1) and considers them in this order. Since the relative ranking of machines does not change, in the sequel they are numbered according to their rank.

In order to present the algorithm we need two additional denotations. The ordered sequence of jobs processed on P_k, $k = 1, 2, \cdots, m$ will be denoted by $\mathcal{J}_k$, the set of tasks of $J_j \in \mathcal{J}_k$ on P_k by $\mathcal{T}_{kj}$, and the number of tasks in $\mathcal{T}_{kj}$ by n_{kj}.

Algorithm 8.3.1 *Heuristic for the static job shop to minimize mean tardiness* [RT92].
begin   -- initialization
for each task T_{ij} **do** $d_{ij} := d_j - t_{ij} + p_{ij}$;
        -- a set of new task due dates has been assigned, taking into account the cumulative
        -- processing time t_{ij} of J_j up to and including task T_{ij}
call *MTD rule;*
        -- the initial sequence has been constructed
Order and number all the machines in nonincreasing order of their total workloads
        $\sum_{J_j \in \mathcal{J}_k} \sum_{T_{ij} \in \mathcal{T}_{kj}} p_{ij}$;
$r := 1$; $z(0) := \infty$; $z(1) := \sum_{j=1}^{n} D_j$;
        -- initial values of counters are set up
while $z(r) < z(r-1)$ **do**
        begin
        $\mathcal{P}_1 := \mathcal{P}$;
                -- the set of unscanned machines $\mathcal{P}_1$ is initially equal to the set of all machines $\mathcal{P}$

```
while  𝒫₁ ≠ ∅ do
    begin
    Find k* := min{k | Pₖ ∈ 𝒫₁};    -- machine Pₖ* is selected (scanned)
    while  𝒥ₖ* ≠ ∅ do
        begin
        Select Jⱼ* as the job with the largest tardiness among jobs belonging to
            𝒥ₖ*;
        for  l = 1 to nₖ*ⱼ* do
            begin    -- schedule revision
            Determine interval [aₗ,bₗ] of possible values for the TDD value dₗⱼ* of
                task Tₗⱼ*;
                -- this will be described separately
            for  x = aₗ to bₗ do
                begin
                Generate the due dates of other tasks of Jⱼ*;
                    -- this will be described separately
                call  MTD rule;
                    -- all machines are rescheduled
                Record total tardiness D(x) = Σⱼ Dⱼ;
                end;
            Find x such that D(x) = min;
            dₗⱼ* := x;
            Reassign due dates of other tasks of Jⱼ* accordingly;
                -- Task due dates are chosen so that the value of the total tardiness is
                -- minimized. This will be described separately
            end;
        for  j = 1 to n do
        Calculate Dⱼ;    -- New tardiness values are calculated
        𝒥ₖ* := 𝒥ₖ* − {Jⱼ*};
            -- The list of unscanned jobs on Pₖ* is updated
        end;
    𝒫₁ = 𝒫₁ − {Pₖ*};    -- The list of unscanned machines is updated
    end;
r := r + 1;
z(r):= Σⱼ₌₁ⁿ Dⱼ;
end;
end;
```

We now discuss in more details the schedule revision loop, the major part of the algorithm, which is illustrated in Figure 8.3.1. As we see, the solution tree is similar to a branch and bound search tree with the difference that each node represents a complete solution.

Given the initial solution, we start with machine P_1 (which has the maximum workload), and job J_j (say) with the maximum tardiness among all jobs in $\mathcal{J}_1$. Consider task $T_{1_1 j}$ whose initial TDD is $d_{1_1 j}$. The algorithm changes now this TDD to integer values in the interval $[L_1, U_1]$, where $L_1 = \sum_{l=1}^{1_1} p_{lj}$, $U_1 = d_j$. It follows from (8.3.1) that for any $d_{1j} < L_1$, the relative priority of $T_{1_1 j}$ remains unchanged, since L_1 is the earliest time by which $T_{1_1 j}$ can be completed.

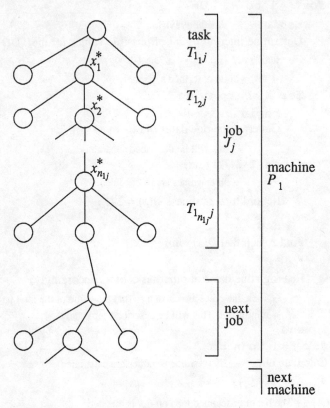

Figure 8.3.1 *Solution tree for the scheduling algorithm.*

Now, a descendant node is generated for each integer x in this interval. For a given x, the TDDs of other tasks of J_j are generated as follows

$$d_{ij} = d_{i-1\,j} + (x - p_{1_1 j}) p_{ij} / t_{1_1 - 1\,j}, \; i = 1, 2, \cdots, 1_1 - 1$$

and

$$d_{ij} = d_{i-1\,j} + (d_j - x) p_{ij} / (p_j - t_{1_1 j}), \; i = 1_1 + 1, 1_1 + 2, \cdots, n_j,$$

where $t_{ij} = \sum_{l=1}^{i} p_{lj}$. Thus, we split J_j into three "sub-jobs" $J_{j_1}, J_{j_2}, J_{j_3}$, where J_{j_1} consists of all tasks prior to $T_{1_1 j}$, J_{j_2} contains only $T_{1_1 j}$, and J_{j_3} comprises all tasks following $T_{1_1 j}$.

Due dates of all tasks within a sub-job are set independently of other sub-jobs. They are derived from the due date of the corresponding sub-job by assigning them flows proportional to their processing times, due dates of J_{j_1}, J_{j_2} and J_{j_3} being $x - p_{1_1 j}$, x, and d_j, respectively. TDDs of tasks of other jobs remain unchanched. The solution value for the descendant is determined by rescheduling all jobs at all machines for the revised set of TDDs using the *MTD* rule. The branch corresponding to the node with the minimum total tardiness is selected, and the TDD of $T_{1_1 j}$ is fixed at the corresponding value of x, say x_1^*. TDDs of all tasks of J_j preceding $T_{1_1 j}$ are updated as follows

$$d_{ij} = d_{i-1 j} + (x_1^* - p_{1_1 j}) t_{ij} / t_{1_1 - 1 j}, \ i = 1, 2, \cdots, 1_1 - 1 .$$

Next, the due date of task T_{1_2} is assigned. The interval scanned for $d_{1_2 j}$ is $[L_2, U_2]$ where $L_2 = \sum_{i = 1_1 + 1}^{1_2} t_{ij} + x_1^*$, $U_2 = d_j$. In the algorithm it is assumed $a_l = \lceil L_2 \rceil$ and $b_l = \lfloor U_2 \rfloor$. For a given value of x for the TDD of $T_{1_2 j}$, the due dates of tasks of J_{j_1}, excluding $T_{1_1 j}$, $T_{1_2 j}$ and those which precede $T_{1_1 j}$, are generated as follows

$$d_{ij} = d_{i-1 j} + (x - x_1^* - p_{1_2 j}) p_{ij} / (t_{1_2 - 1 j} - t_{1_1 j}), \ i = 1_1 + 1, \ 1_1 + 2, \cdots, 1_2 - 1$$

and

$$d_{ij} = d_{i-1 j} + (d_j - x) p_{ij} / (p_j - t_{1_2 j}), \ i = 1_2 + 1, \ 1_2 + 2, \cdots, n_j .$$

TDDs of tasks preceding and including $T_{1_1 j}$ remain unchanged.

In the general step, assume we are considering TDD reassignment of task T_{ij} at P_k (we omit index k for simplicity). Assume further that after investigating P_1 through P_{k-1}, and all tasks of J_j prior to T_{ij} on P_k, we have fixed the due dates of tasks $T_{\tilde{1}j}$, $T_{\tilde{2}j}, \cdots, T_{\tilde{z}j}$, Let T_{ij} be processed between $T_{\tilde{l}j}$ and $T_{\widetilde{l+1}j}$ with fixed due dates of x_l^* and x_{l+1}^*, respectively, i.e. the ordered sequence of tasks of J_j is $(T_{1j}, T_{2j}, \cdots, T_{\tilde{1}j}, \cdots, T_{\tilde{2}j}, \cdots, T_{\tilde{l}j}, \cdots, T_{ij}, \cdots, T_{\widetilde{l+1}j}, \cdots, T_{\tilde{z}j}, \cdots, T_{nj})$. Then, for assigning the TDD of T_{ij}, we need to consider only the interval $[\sum_{r=l+1}^{i} p_{rj} + x_l^*, x_{l+1}^* - p_{\widetilde{l+1}j}]$. Moreover, while reassigning the TDD of T_{ij}, TDDs need to be generated for only those tasks which are processed between $T_{\tilde{l}j}$ and $T_{\widetilde{l+1}j}$.

Of course, as the algorithm runs, the search interval becomes smaller. However, near the top of the tree, it can be quite wide. Thus, Raman and Talbot propose the following improvement of the search procedure. In general, while searching for the value x for a given task at any machine, we need theoretically consider the appropriate interval $[L, U]$ in unit steps. However, a task can only occupy a given number of positions α in any sequence. For a permutation schedule on a single machine we have $\alpha = n$, whereas in a job shop $\alpha > n$ because of the forced idle times on different machines. Nonetheless, it is usually much smaller than the number of different values of x. In consequence, TDDs, and thus total tardiness remains unchanged for many subintervals within $[L, U]$.

The procedure is a modification of the binary search method. Assume that we search in the interval $[L_0, U_0]$ (see Figure 8.3.2). First, we compute total tardiness $D(L_0)$ and $D(U_0)$ of all jobs for $x = L_0$ and x $= U_0$, respectively. Next, we divide the interval into two equal parts, compute the total tardiness in the midpoint of each half-interval, and so on. Within any generated interval, scanning for the next half-interval is initially done to the left, i.e. $U_i = \dfrac{L_0 + U_{i-1}}{2}$, $i = 1, 2, 3$, and terminates when a half-interval is fathomed, i.e. when the total tardiness at end-points and the midpoint of this interval are the same (e.g. $[L_0, U_3]$ in Figure 8.3.2).

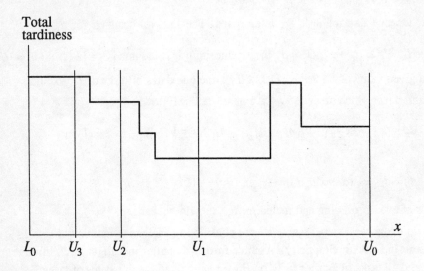

Figure 8.3.2 *A modification binary search procedure.*

Notice that this search procedure may not always find the best value of x. This is because it ignores (rather unlikely in real problems) changes in total tardiness within an interval, if the same tardiness is realized at both its end points and its midpoint.

After finishing of left-scanning, the procedure evaluates the most recently generated and unfathomed interval to its right. If the total tardiness at both end-points and the midpoint of that interval are not the same, another half-interval is generated and left scanning is resumed. The procedure stops when all half-intervals are fathomed.

Note that it is desirable to increase the upper limit of the search interval for the initial tasks of $\mathcal{J}_j$ from d_j to some arbitrarily large value (for example, the length of the initial solution). This follows from the fact that it can happen that the position of any task of a given job which corresponds to the minimum total tardiness results in that job itself being late. The presented search procedure reduces the computational complexity of each iteration from $O(m^2 N^3 \sum_{j=1}^{A} p_j)$ to $O(m^2 N^4)$, where $N = \sum_{j=1}^{A} n_j$.

8.3.3 Computational Experiments

Raman and Talbot [RT92] conducted extensive computational experiments to evaluate their algorithm (denoted *GSP - Global Scheduling Procedure*) for both static and dynamic problems.

For the static problem two sets of experiments were performed. The first compared *GSP* with the following priority rules known from literature: *SPT* (Shortest Processing Time), *EDD* (Earliest Due Date), *CRIT* (Critical Ratio), *MDD* (Modified Job Due Date), *MTD*, and *HYB* (Hybrid - see [RTR89a], uses *MTD* for scheduling jobs on nonbottleneck machines, and *MDD* on bottleneck machines), and with the exact algorithm running with a time trap of 15 sec. *GSP* provided the best results yielding an average improvement of 12.7% over the next best rule.

In the second set of experiments 100 problems (in four scenarios of 25 problems) were solved optimally as well as by the *GSP* algorithm. In majority of cases in each scenario *GSP* found the optimal solution. The performance of *GSP* relative to the optimum depends upon parameter ρ which determines the range of job due dates. *GSP* solutions are quite close to the optimum for large ρ, and the difference increases for smaller ρ.

Experiments for the dynamic problem were performed to study the effectiveness of implementing *GSP* solutions of the static problem on a rolling horizon basis. As we mentioned, in a dynamic environment a static problem is generated at each occurence of a nondeterministic event in the system, such as an arrival of a new job. At such point in time a tree shown in Figure 8.3.1 is generated taking into account the tasks already in process. Of course, at that time some machines can be busy - they are blocked out for the period of commitment since we deal with the nonpreemptive scheduling. The solution found by *GSP* is implemented until the next event occurs, as in the so-called reactive scheduling which will be discussed in more details in Chapter 9.

Flow	Balanced workloads			Unbalanced workloads		
	MTD	*GSP*	α	*MTD*	*GSP*	α
2	268	252	0.15	396	357	0.01
3	151	139	0.04	252	231	0.07
4	84	68	0.09	154	143	0.06
5	39	28	0.11	111	81	0.09

Table 8.3.1 *Experimental results for the dynamic problem.*

In the experiment job arrivals followed a Poisson process. Each job has assigned a due date that provided it a flow proportional to its processing time. Each job had a random routing through the system of 5 machines. Task processing times on each machine were sampled from a uniform distribution which varied to obtain two levels of relative machine workloads. The obtained machine utilizations ranged from 78% to 82% for the case of balanced workloads, and from 66% to 93% for unbalanced workloads. In both cases, the average shop utilization was about 80%. *GSP* was implemented with a time trap of 1.0 sec. per static problem, and compared with the same priority rules as in the case of the static problem experiment. The computational results are shown in

Table 8.3.1. Since among the priority rules *MTD* performed the best for all scenarios, it has been used as a banchmark. Also given in the table is the corresponding level of significance α for one-tailed tests concerning paired differences between *MTD* and *GSP*. As we see, *GSP* retains its effectiveness for all flows, and for both levels of workload balance, and this holds for $\alpha = 0.15$ or less.

8.4 Simultaneous Scheduling and Routing in some FMS

8.4.1 Problem Formulation

In FMS scheduling literature majority of papers deal with either part and machine scheduling or with Automated Guided Vehicle (AGV) routing separately. In this section both issues are considered together, and the objective is to construct a schedule of minimum length [BEFLW91].

The FMS under consideration has been implemented by one of the manufacturers producing parts for helicopters. A schematic view of the system is presented in Figure 8.4.1 and its description is as follows.

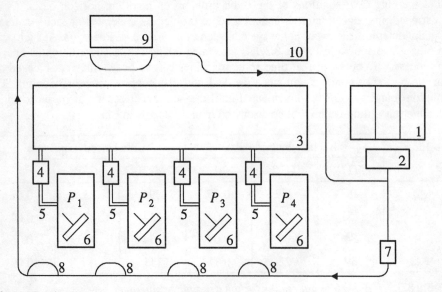

Figure 8.4.1 *An example FMS.*

Pieces of raw material from which the parts are machined are stored in the automated storage area AS (1). Whenever necessary, an appropriate piece of material is taken from the storage and loaded onto the pallet and vehicle at the stand (2). This task is performed automatically by computer controlled robots. Then, the piece is transported by an AGV (7) to the desired machine (6) where it is automatically unloaded at (8). Every machine in the system is capable of processing any machining task. This versatility is achieved by a large number of tools and fixtures that may be used by the machines. The tool magazines (4) of every machine have a capacity of up to 130 tools which are used for the various machining operations. The tools of the magazines are arranged in two layers so that the longer tools can occupy two vertical positions. The tools are changed automatically. Fixtures are changed manually. It should be noted that a large variety of almost 100 quite different parts can be produced by each of these machines in this particular FMS. Simpler part types require about 30 operations (and tools) and the most complicated parts need about 80 operations. Therefore, the tool magazines have sufficient capacity to stock the tools for one to several consecutive parts in a production schedule. In addition, the tools are loaded from a large automated central tool storage area (3) which is located closely to the machines. No tool competition is observed, since the storage area contains more than 2000 tools (including many multiple tools) and there are 4 NC-machines. The delivered raw material is mounted onto the appropriate fixture and processed by the tools which are changed according to a desired plan. The tool technology of this particular system allows the changing of the tools during execution of the jobs. This is used to eliminate the setup times of the tools required for the next job and occasionally a transfer of a tool to another machine (to validate completely the no-resource competition). The only (negligible) transition time in the FMS that could be observed was in fact the adjustment in size of the spindle that holds the tool whenever the next tool is exchanged with the previous one. After the completion the finished part exchanges its position with the raw material of the next job that is waiting for its processing. It is then automatically transported by an AGV to the inspection section (9). Parts which passed the inspection are transported and unloaded at the storage area (10).

We see that the above system is very versatile and this feature is gained by the usage of many tools and large tool magazines. As it was pointed out in Section 8.1, it is a common tendency of modern flexible manufacturing systems to become so versatile that most of the processes on a part can be accomplished by just one or at most two machine types. As a result many systems consist of identical parallel machines. On the other hand, the existence of a large number of tools in the system allows one not to consider resource (tool) competition. Hence, our problem here reduces in fact to that of simultaneous scheduling and routing of parts among parallel machines. The inspection stage can be postponed in that analysis, since it is performed separately on the first-come-first-served basis.

Following the above observations, we can model the considered FMS using elements described below. Given a set of n independent single-task jobs (parts) J_1, $J_2, \cdots, J_n$ with processing times p_j, $j = 1, 2, \cdots, n$, that are to be processed without preemptions on a set of m parallel identical machines $P_1, P_2, \cdots, P_n$, m not being a very large number. Here parallelism means that every machine is capable of processing any task. Setup times connected with changing tools are assumed to be zero since the latter can be changed on-line during the execution of tasks. Setup times resulting from changing part fixtures are included in the processing times.

As mentioned above, machines are identical except for their locations and thus they require different *delivery times*. Hence, we may assume that k $(k < m)$ AGVs V_1, $V_2, \cdots, V_k$, are to deliver pieces of raw material from the storage area to specified machines and the time associated with the delivery is equal to τ_i, $i = 1, 2, \cdots, m$. The delivery time includes loading time at the storage area and unloading time at the required machine, both times being equal to a. During each trip exactly one piece of raw material is delivered; this is due to the dimension of parts to be machined. After delivery of a piece of raw material the vehicle takes a pallet with a processed part (maybe from another machine), delivers it to the inspection stage and returns to the storage area (1). The round trip takes A units of time, including two loading and two unloading times. It is apparent that the most efficient usage of vehicles in the sense of a through-put rate for piece delivered is achieved when the vehicles are operating at a cyclic mode with cycle time equal to A. In order to avoid traffic congestion we assume that starting moments of consecutive vehicles at the storage area are delayed by a time units.

The problem is now to construct a schedule for machines and vehicles such that the whole job set is processed in a minimum time.

It is obvious that the general problem stated above is NP-hard, as it is already NP-hard for the nonpreemptive scheduling of two machines (see Section 5.1). In the following we will consider two variants of the problem. In the first, the *production schedule* (i.e. the assignment of jobs to machines) is assumed to be known, and the objective is to find a feasible schedule for vehicles. This problem can be solved in polynomial time. The second consists of finding a composite schedule, i.e. one taking into account simultaneous assignment of vehicles and machines to jobs.

8.4.2 Vehicle Scheduling for a Fixed Production Schedule

In this section we consider the problem of vehicle scheduling given a production schedule. Suppose an (optimal) nonpreemptive assignment of jobs to machines is given (cf. Figure 8.4.2). This assignment imposes certain deadlines d_j^i on delivery of pieces of raw material to particular machines, where d_j^i denotes the latest moment by which raw material for part J_j should be delivered to machine P_i. The lateness in delivery could result in exceeding the planned schedule length C. Below we describe an approach that allows us to check whether it is possible to deliver all the required pieces of raw material to their destinations (given some production schedule), and if so, a vehicle schedule will be constructed. Without loss of generality we may assume that at time 0 at every machine there is already a piece of material to produce the first part; otherwise one should appropriately delay starting times on consecutive machines (cf. Figure 8.4.3).

Our vehicle scheduling problem may now be formulated as follows. Given a set of deadlines $d_j^i, j = 1, 2, \cdots, n$, and delivery times from the storage area to particular machines $\tau_i, i = 1, 2, \cdots, m$, is that possible to deliver all the required pieces of raw material on time, i.e. before the respective deadlines. If the answer is positive, a feasible vehicle schedule should be constructed. In general, this is equivalent to determining a feasible solution to a *Vehicle Routing with Time Windows* (see e.g., [DLSS88]). Let J_0 and J_{n+1} be two dummy jobs representing the first departure and the last arrival of every vehicle, respectively. Also define two dummy machines P_0 and P_{m+1} on which J_0 and J_{n+1} are executed, respectively, and let $\tau_0 = 0$, $\tau_{m+1} = M$ where M is an arbitrary large number. Denote by $i(j)$ the index of the machine on which J_j is executed. For any two jobs $J_j, J_{j'}$, let $c_{jj'}$ be the travel time taken by a vehicle to make its delivery for job $J_{j'}$ immediately after its delivery for J_j

$$c_{jj'} = \begin{cases} \tau_{i(j')} - \tau_{i(j)} & \text{if } \tau_{i(j')} \geq \tau_{i(j)} \\ A - \tau_{i(j')} - \tau_{i(j)} & \text{if } \tau_{i(j')} < \tau_{i(j)} \\ & j, j' = 0, \cdots, n+1, j \neq j'. \end{cases}$$

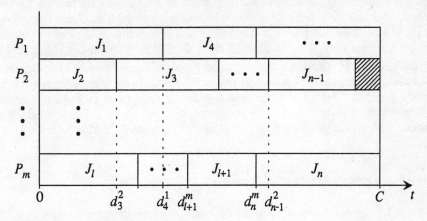

Figure 8.4.2 *An example production schedule.*

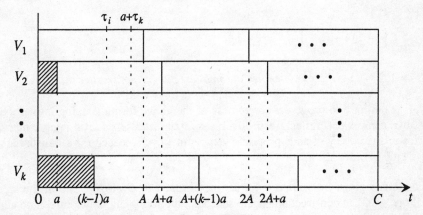

Figure 8.4.3 *An example vehicle schedule.*

If $\tau_j + c_{jj'} \leq \tau_{j'}$, define a binary variable $x_{jj'}$ equal to 1 if and only if a vehicle makes its delivery for $J_{j'}$ immediately after its delivery for J_j. Also, let u_j be a nonnegative variable denoting the latest possible delivery time of raw material for job J_j, $j = 1, \cdots, n$. The problem then consists of determining whether there exist values of the variables satisfying

$$\sum_{j=1}^{n} x_{0j} = \sum_{j=1}^{n} x_{j\,n+1} = k, \tag{8.4.1}$$

$$\sum_{j=0, j \neq l}^{n+1} x_{jl} = \sum_{j'=0, j' \neq l}^{n+1} x_{lj'} = 1, \qquad l = 1, \cdots, n, \tag{8.4.2}$$

$$u_j - u_{j'} + Mx_{jj'} \le M - c_{jj'}, \qquad\qquad j, j' = 1, \cdots, n, j \ne j', \qquad\qquad (8.4.3)$$

$$0 \le u_j \le d_j^i. \qquad\qquad\qquad\qquad\qquad\qquad\qquad\qquad\qquad (8.4.4)$$

In this formulation, constraint (8.4.1) specifies that k vehicles are used, while constraints (8.4.2) associate every operation with exactly one vehicle. Constraints (8.4.3) and (8.4.4) guarantee that the vehicle schedule will satisfy time feasibility constraints. They are imposed only if $x_{jj'}$ is defined. This feasibility problem is in general *NP*-complete [Sav85]. However, for our particular problem, it can be solved in polynomial time because we can use the cyclic property of the schedule for relatively easily checking of the feasibility condition of the vehicle schedule for a given production schedule. The first schedule does not need to be constructed. When checking this feasibility condition one uses the job latest transportation starting times defined as follows

$$s_j = d_j^i - \tau_i, \ j = 1, 2, \cdots, n.$$

The feasibility checking is given in Lemma 8.4.1.

Lemma 8.4.1 *For a given ordered set of latest transportation starting times* s_j, $s_j \le s_{j+1}, j = 1, 2, \cdots, n$, *one can construct a feasible transportation schedule for* k *vehicles if and only if*

$$s_j \ge (\lceil \frac{j}{k} \rceil - 1)A + [j - (\lceil \frac{j}{k} \rceil - 1)k - 1]a$$

for all $j = 1, 2, \cdots, n$, *where* $\lceil \frac{j}{k} \rceil$ *denotes the smallest integer not smaller than* j/k.

Proof. It is not hard to prove the correctness of the above formula taking into account that its two components reflect, respectively, the time necessary for an integer number of cycles and the delay of an appropriate vehicle in a cycle needed for a transportation of the jth job in order. $\square$

The conditions given in Lemma 8.4.1 can be checked in $O(n\log n)$ time in the worst case. If one wants to construct a feasible schedule, the following polynomial time algorithm will find it, whenever one exists. The basic idea behind the algorithm is to choose for transportation a job whose deadline, less corresponding delivery time, is minimum - i.e., the most urgent delivery at this moment. This approach is summarized by the following algorithm.

Algorithm 8.4.2 *for finding a feasible vehicle schedule given a production schedule* [BEFLW91].
begin
$t := 0; \ l := 0;$
for $j = 1$ **to** n **do**
Calculate job's J_j latest transportation starting time;   -- Initial values are set up
Sort all the jobs in nondecreasing values of their latest transportation starting times and
       renumber them in this order;
for $j = 1$ **to** n **do**

```
begin
   Calculate slack time of the remaining jobs; slⱼ := sⱼ−t;
   If any slack time is negative then stop;      -- No feasible vehicle schedule exists
   Load job Jⱼ onto an available vehicle;
   l := l+1;
   if l ≤ k−1 then t := t+a
   else
      begin
      t := t − (k−1)a + A;
      l := 0;
      end;
   end;      -- All jobs are loaded onto the vehicles
end;
```

A basic property of Algorithm 8.4.2 is proved in the following theorem.

Theorem 8.4.3 *Algorithm 8.4.2 finds a feasible transportation schedule whenever one exists.*

Proof. Suppose that Algorithm 8.4.2 fails to find a feasible transportation schedule while such a schedule S exists. In this case there must exist in S two jobs J_i and J_j such that $sl_i < sl_j$ and J_j has been transported first. It is not hard to see that exchanging these two jobs, i.e., J_i being transported first, we do not cause the infeasibility of the schedule. Now we can repeat the above pattern as long as such a pair of jobs violating the earliest slack time rule exists. After a finite number of such changes one gets a feasible schedule constructed according to the algorithm, which is a contradiction. □

Let us now calculate the complexity of Algorithm 8.4.2 considering the off-line performance of the algorithm. Then its most complex function is the ordering of jobs in nondecreasing order of their slack times. Thus, the overall complexity would be $O(n\log n)$. However, if one performs the algorithm in the on-line mode, then the selection of a job to be transported next requires only linear time, provided that an unordered sequence is used. In both cases a low order polynomial time algorithm is obtained. We see that the easiness of the problem depends mainly on its regular structure following the cyclic property of the vehicle schedule.

Example 8.4.4 To illustrate the use of the algorithm, consider the following example. Let m the number of machines, n the number of jobs, and k the number of vehicles be equal to 3, 9 and 2, respectively. Transportation times for respective machines are $\tau_1 = 1$, $\tau_1 = 1.5$, $\tau_1 = 2$, and cycle and loading and unloading times are $A = 3$, $a = 0.5$, respectively. A production schedule is given in Figure 8.4.4(a). Thus the deadlines are $d_5^1 = 3$, $d_7^1 = 7$, $d_6^2 = 6$, $d_8^2 = 7$, $d_4^3 = 2$, $d_9^3 = 8$. They result in the latest transportation starting times $s_4 = 0$, $s_5 = 2$, $s_6 = 4.5$, $s_7 = 6$, $s_8 = 5.5$, $s_9 = 6$. The corresponding vehicle schedule generated by Algorithm 8.4.2 is shown in Figure 8.4.4(b). Job J_9 is delivered too late and no feasible transportation schedule for the given production plan can be constructed. □

(a)

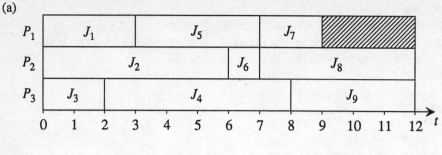

(b)

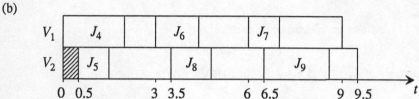

Figure 8.4.4 *Production and nonfeasible vehicle schedules*
(a) production schedule,
(b) vehicle schedule: J_9 is delivered too late.

The obvious question is now what to do if there is no feasible transportation schedule. The first approach consists of finding jobs in the transportation schedule that can be delayed without lengthening the schedule. If such an operation is found, other jobs that cannot be delayed are transported first. In our example (Figure 8.4.4(a)) job J_7 can be started later and instead J_9 can be assigned first to vehicle V_1. Such an exchange will not lengthen the schedule. However, it may also be the case that the production schedule reflects deadlines which cannot be exceeded, and therefore the jobs cannot be shifted. In such a situation, one may use an alternative production schedule, if one exists. As pointed out in [Sch89], it is often the case at the FMS planning stage that several such plans may be constructed, and the operator chooses one of them. If none can be realized because of a nonfeasible transportation schedule, the operator may decide to construct optimal production and vehicle schedules at the same time. One such approach based on dynamic programming is described in the next section.

8.4.3 Simultaneous Job and Vehicle Scheduling

In this section, the problem of simultaneous construction of production and vehicle schedules is discussed. As mentioned above, this problem is *NP*-hard, although not strongly *NP*-hard. Thus, a pseudopolynomial time algorithm based on dynamic programming can be constructed for its solution.

Assume that jobs are ordered in nonincreasing order of their processing times, i.e. $p_1 \geq p_1 \geq \cdots \geq p_{n-1} \geq p_n$. Such an ordering implies that longer jobs will be processed first and processing can take place on machines further from the storage area, which is a convenient fact from the viewpoint of vehicle scheduling.

Now let us formulate a dynamic programming algorithm using the ideas presented in [GLLRK79]. Define

$$
x_j(t_1, t_2, \cdots, t_m) = \begin{cases} \textbf{true} & \text{if jobs } J_1, J_2, \cdots, J_j \text{ can be scheduled on machines} \\ & P_1, P_2, \cdots, P_m \text{ in such a way that } P_i \text{ is busy in} \\ & \text{time interval } [0,\ t_i],\ i = 1, 2, \cdots, m \text{ (excluding} \\ & \text{possible } idle\ time \text{ following from vehicle} \\ & \text{scheduling), and the vehicle schedule is feasible} \\ \textbf{false} & \text{otherwise} \end{cases}
$$

where

$$
x_0(t_1, t_2, \cdots, t_m) = \begin{cases} \textbf{true} & \text{if } t_i = 0,\ i = 1, 2, \cdots, m \\ \textbf{false} & \text{otherwise.} \end{cases}
$$

Using these variables, the recursive equation can be written in the following form

$$
x_j(t_1, t_2, \cdots, t_m) =
$$

$$
\bigvee_{i=1}^{m} [x_{j-1}(t_1, t_2, \cdots, t_{i-1}, t_i - p_j, t_{i+1}, \cdots, t_m) \wedge Z_{ij}(t_1, t_2, \cdots, t_{i-1}, t_i, t_{i+1}, \cdots, t_m)]
$$

where

$$
Z_{ij}(t_1, t_2, \cdots, t_{i-1}, t_i, t_{i+1}, \cdots, t_m) = \begin{cases} \textbf{true} & \text{if } t_i - p_j - \tau_j \geq \\ & (\lceil \tfrac{j}{k} \rceil - 1)A + [j - (\lceil \tfrac{j}{k} \rceil - 1)k - 1]a \\ & \text{or } j \leq m \\ \textbf{false} & \text{otherwise} \end{cases}
$$

is the condition of vehicle schedule feasibility, given in Lemma 8.4.1.

Values of $x_j(\cdot)$ are computed for $t_i = 0, 1, \cdots, C$, $i = 1, 2, \cdots, m$, where C is an upper bound on the minimum schedule length C^*_{max}. Finally, C^*_{max} is determined as

$$
C^*_{max} = \min\{\max\{t_1, t_2, \cdots, t_m\} \mid x_n(t_1, t_2, \cdots, t_m) = \textbf{true}\}.
$$

The above algorithm solves our problem in $O(nC^m)$ time. Thus, for fixed m, it is a pseudopolynomial time algorithm, and can be used in practice, taking into account that m is rather small. To complete our discussion, let us consider once more the example from Section 8.4.2. The above dynamic programming approach yields schedules presented in Figure 8.4.5. We see that it is possible to complete all the jobs in 11 units and deliver them to machines in 8 units.

To end this section let us notice that various extensions of the model are possible and worth considering. Among them are those including different routes for particular vehicles, an inspection phase as the second stage machine, resource competition, and different criteria (e.g., maximum lateness). These issues are currently under investigation.

(a)

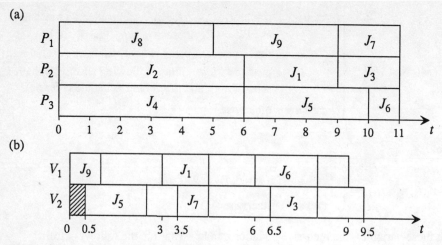

(b)

Figure 8.4.5   *Optimal production and vehicle schedule*
            (a) *production schedule,*
            (b) *vehicle schedule.*

References

Bak75   K. R. Baker, A comparative study of flow shop algorithms, *Oper. Res.* 23, 1975, 62-73.

Bak84   K. R. Baker, Sequencing rules and due date assignments in a job shop, *Management Sci.* 30, 1984, 1093-1104.

BB82   K. R. Baker, J. M. W. Bertrand, A dynamic priority rule for sequencing against due dates, *J. Oper. Management* 3, 1982, 37-42.

BCSW86   J. Błażewicz, W. Cellary, R. Słowiński, J. Węglarz, *Scheduling Under Resource Constraints - Deterministic Models*, J. C. Baltzer, Basel, 1986.

BEFLW91   J. Błażewicz, H. Eiselt, G. Finke, G. Laporte, J. Węglarz, Scheduling tasks and vehicles in a flexible manufacturing system, *Internat. J. FMS* 4, 1991, 5-16.

BFR75   P. Bratley, M. Florian, P. Robillard, Scheduling with earliest start and due date constraints on multiple machines, *Naval Res. Logist. Quart.* 22, 1975, 165-173.

BH91   S. A. Brah, J. L. Hunsucker, Branch and bound algorithm for the flow shop with multiple processors, *European J. Oper. Res.* 51, 1991, 88-99.

BK83   K. R. Baker, J. J. Kanet, Job shop scheduling with modified due dates, *J. Oper. Management* 4, 1983, 11-22.

Bra88   S. A. Brah, Scheduling in a flow shop with multiple processors, Unpublished Ph.D. Dissertation, University of Huston, Huston, TX, 1988, 30-33.

BY86a   J. A. Buzacott, D. D. Yao, Flexible manufacturing systems: a review of analytical models, *Management Sci.* 32, 1986, 890-905.

BY86b   J. A. Buzacott, D. D. Yao, On queueing network models for flexible manufacturing systems, *Queueing Systems* 1, 1986, 5-27.

Con65   R. W. Conway, Priority dispatching and job lateness in a job shop, *J. Industrial Engineering* 16, 1965, 123-130.

DLSS89   M. Desrochers, J. K. Lenstra, M. W. P. Savelsbergh, F. Soumis, Vehicle routing with time windows, in: B. L. Golden, A. A. Assad (eds.), *Vehicle Routing: Methods and Studies*, North-Holland, Amsterdam, 1988, 65-84.

Fre82   S. French, Sequencing and Scheduling: *An Introduction to the Mathematics of Job-Shop*, Wiley, J. New York, 1982.

GLLRK79   R. L. Graham, E. L. Lawler, J. K. Lenstra, and A.H.G. Rinnooy Kan, Optimization and approximation in deterministic sequencing and scheduling theory: A survey, *Ann. Discrete Math.* 5, 1979, 287-326.

Gra66   R. L. Graham, Bounds for certain multiprocessing anomalies, *Bell System Technical J.* 54, 1966, 1563-1581.

Gup70   J. N. D. Gupta, M-stage flowshop scheduling by branch and bound, *Opsearch* 7, 1970, 37-43.

Jai86   R. Jaikumar, Postindustrial manufacturing, *Harvard Buss. Rev.* Nov./Dec., 1986, 69-76.

KH82   J. J. Kanet, J. C. Hayya, Priority dispatching with operation due dates in a job shop, *J. Oper. Management* 2, 1982, 155-163.

KM87   S. Kochbar, R. J. T. Morris, Heuristic methods for flexible flow line scheduling, *J. Manuf. Systems* 6, 1987, 299-314.

Lan87   M. A. Langston, Improved LPT scheduling identical processor systems, *RAIRO Technique et Sci. Inform.* 1, 1982, 69-75.

MB67   G. B. McMahon, P. G. Burton, Flow shop scheduling with the branch and bound method, *Oper. Res.* 15, 1967, 473-481.

RRT89   N. Raman, R. V. Rachamadugu, F.B. Talbot, Real time scheduling of an automated manufacturing center, *European J. Oper. Res.* 40, 1989, 222-242.

RS89   R. Rachamadugu, K. Stecke, Classification and review of FMS scheduling procedures, Working Paper No 481C, The University of Michigan, School of Business Administration, Ann Arbor MI, 1989.

RT92   N. Raman, F. B. Talbot, The job shop tardiness problem: a decomposition approach, *European J. Oper. Res.*, 1992, to appear.

RTR89a   N. Raman, F. B. Talbot, R. V. Rachamadugu, Due date based scheduling in a general flexible manufacturing system, *J. Oper. Management* 8, 1989, 115-132.

RTR89b   N. Raman, F. B. Talbot, R. V. Rachamadugu, Scheduling a general flexible manufacturing system to minimize tardiness related costs, Working Paper # 89-1548, Bureau of Economic and Business Research, University of Illinois at Urbana - Champaign, Champaign, IL, 1989.

Sal73   M. S. Salvador, A solution of a special class of flowshop scheduling problems, *Proceedings of the Symposium on the theory of Scheduling and its Applications*, Springer-Verlag, Berlin, 1975, 83-91.

Sav85   M. W. P. Savelsbergh, Local search for routing problems with time windows, *Annals of Oper. Res.* 4, 1985, 285-305.

Sch84   G. Schmidt, Scheduling on semi-identical processors, *Z. Oper. Res. Theory* 28, 1984, 153-162.

Sch88   G. Schmidt, Scheduling independent tasks on semiidentical processors with deadlines, *J. Opl. Res. Soc.* 39, 1988, 271-277.

Sch89   G. Schmidt, *CAM: Algorithmen und Decision Support für die Fertigungssteuerung*, Springer Verlag, Berlin, 1989.

SM85   K. E. Stecke, T. L. Morin, The optimality of balancing workloads in certain types of flexible manufacturing systems, *European J. Oper. Res.* 20, 1985, 68-82.

SS85   K. E. Stecke, J. J. Solberg, The optimality of unbalancing both workloads and machine group sizes in closed queueing networks for multiserver queues, *Oper. Res.* 33, 1985, 882-910.

SS89   C. Sriskandarajah, S. P. Sethi, Scheduling algorithms for flexible flowshops: worst and average case performance, *European J. Oper. Res.* 43, 1989, 143-160.

SW89   R. Słowiński, J. Węglarz (eds.), *Advances in Project Scheduling*, Elsevier, Amsterdam, 1989.

Tal82   F. B. Talbot, Resource constrained project scheduling with time resource tradeoffs: the nonpreemptive case, *Management Sci.* 28, 1982, 1197-1210.

VM87   A. P. J. Vepsalainen, T. E. Morton, Priority rules for job shops with weighted tardiness costs, *Management Sci.* 33, 1987, 1035-1047.

Wit85   R. J. Wittrock, Scheduling algorithms for flexible flow lines, *IBM J. Res. Develop.* 29, 1985, 401-412.

Wit88   R. J. Wittrock, An adaptable scheduling algorithms for flexible flow lines, *Oper. Res.* 33, 1988, 445-453.

9 Knowledge-Based Scheduling

Within all activities of production management, *production scheduling* is a major part of production planning and control. By production management we mean all activities which are necessary to carry out production. The two main activities in this field are *production planning* and *production control*. Production scheduling is a common activity of these two areas because scheduling is needed not only on the planning level - as mainly treated in the preceding chapters - but also on the control level. From the different aspects of production scheduling problems we can further distinguish *predictive production scheduling* or *offline-planning* (*OFP*) and *reactive production scheduling* or *online-control* (*ONC*). Predictive production scheduling serves to provide guidance in achieving global coherence in the process of local decision making. Reactive production scheduling is concerned with revising predictive schedules when unexpected events force changes. OFP generates the requirements for ONC and ONC creates feedback to OFP. The relationship between these functions are shown in Figure 9.0.1.

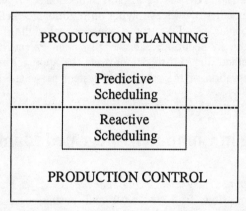

Figure 9.0.1 *Functions of production management.*

Problems of production scheduling can be modelled on the basis of distributed planning and control loops, where data from the actual manufacturing process are used. A further analysis of the problem shows that job release to and job traversing inside the manufacturing system are the main issues, not only for production control but also for short term production planning.

In practice, scheduling problems arising in manufacturing systems are of discrete, distributed, dynamic and stochastic nature and turn out to be very complex. So, for the majority of practical scheduling purposes simple algorithms are not available, and the manufacturing staff has to play the role of the main problem solver. On the other hand, some kind of Decision Support Systems (*DSS*) has been developed recently to solve these scheduling problems. There are different expressions for such support systems among which "Graphical Gantt Chart System" and the German expression "Leitstand" are most popular. Such a DSS is considered to be a shop floor scheduling system which can be regarded as a control post mainly designed for short term production scheduling. Many support systems of this type are available today.

Most of the existing shop floor production scheduling systems, however, have two major drawbacks. First, they do not effectively apply intelligence to the solution process, and second, they are not very efficient in solving scheduling problems in a distributed environment, i.e. when the production of different workshops has to be coordinated. In the following, we concentrate on designing a system that avoids the first drawback, i.e. we will introduce intelligence to the modeling and to the solution process of practical scheduling problems quite generally.

Later in this chapter we will suggest a special DSS designed for *short term production scheduling* that works on the planning and control level. It makes appropriate use of scheduling theory, knowledge-based and simulation techniques. The DSS introduced will also be called "*Intelligent Production Scheduling System*" or IPS in the following.

This chapter is organized as follows. First we give a short idea about the environment of production scheduling from the perspective of integrated problem solving in manufacturing (Section 9.1). Then, we review quite generally existing modeling and solution approaches for scheduling problems that are developed in the area of Artificial Intelligence (Section 9.2). We will be mainly concerned with constraint based scheduling either following an open interactive (Section 9.2.1) or a closed loop solution approach (Section 9.2.2). Based on this we suggest in Section 9.3 a system that integrates knowledge-based approaches and ideas relying on traditional scheduling theory. Considering the requirements of a DSS for production scheduling we design an IPS (Section 9.3.1). Finally, in Section 9.3.2 we present an extended example problem using a flexible manufacturing cell to demonstrate the approach, and establish some proposals for the integration of the scheduling system presented in the environment discussed in 9.1.

9.1 Scheduling in Computer Integrated Manufacturing

The concept of *Computer Integrated Manufacturing* (*CIM*) is based on the idea of combining information flow from technical and business areas of a production company [Har73]. All steps of activities, ranging from customer orders to product design, master production planning, detailed capacity planning, predictive and reactive scheduling, manufacturing and, finally, delivery contribute to the overall information flow. Hence a sophisticated common database support is essential for the effectiveness of the CIM system. Usually, the database will be distributed among the components of CIM To integrate all functions and data a powerful communication network is required. Examples of network architectures are hierarchical and loosely connected computer systems. Concepts of CIM are discussed in detail by e.g. Ranky [Ran86] and Scheer [Sch91].

To describe shortly the main structure of CIM systems, the more technically oriented components are *Computer Aided Design* (*CAD*) and *Computer Aided Process Planning* (*CAP*), often comprised as *Computer Aided Engineering* (*CAE*), *Computer Aided Manufacturing* (*CAM*), and *Computer Aided Quality Control* (*CAQ*). The concept of CIM is depicted in Figure 9.1.1 where edges represent data flows in either directions. In CAD, development and design of products is supported. This includes

technical or physical calculations and drafting. CAP supports the preparation for manufacturing through process planning and the generation of programs for numeric controlled machines. Manufacturing and assembly of products are supported by CAM
which is responsible for material and part transport, control of machines and transport
systems, and for supervising the manufacturing process. Requirements for product
quality and generation of quality review plans are delivered by CAQ. The objective of
the *Production Planning System* (*PPS*) is to take over all planning steps for customer
orders in the sense of material requirements and resource planning. Within CIM, the
IPS organizes the execution of all job- or task-oriented activities derived from customer orders.

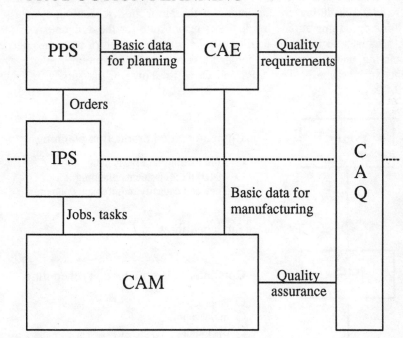

PRODUCTION PLANNING

PRODUCTION CONTROL

Figure 9.1.1 *The concept of CIM.*

Problems in production planning and control could theoretically be represented in a
single model. But even if all input data would be available and reliable this approach
would not be applicable in general because of prohibitive computing times to find a
solution. Therefore a practical approach is to solve the problems of production planning and control sequentially using a hierarchical scheme. The closer the investigated
problems are to the bottom of the hierarchy the shorter will be the time scale under
consideration and the more detailed the needed information. Problems on the top of the
hierarchy incorporate more aggregated data in connection with longer time scales. Decisions on higher levels serve as constraints on lower levels. Solutions for problems on
lower levels give feedback to problem solutions on higher levels. The relationship bet-

ween PPS, IPS and CAM can serve as an example for a hierarchy which incorporates three levels of problem solving. It is quite obvious that a hierarchical solution approach cannot guarantee optimality. The number of levels to be introduced in the hierarchy depends on the problem under consideration, but for the type of applications discussed here a model with separated tactical (PPS) and operational levels (IPS and CAM) seems appropriate. A computer system covering the different hierarchical levels is shown later in Figure 9.1.4.

In production planning the material and resource requirements of the customer orders are analyzed, and production data such as ready times, due dates or deadlines, and resource assignments are determined. In this way, a midterm or tactical production plan based on a list of customer orders to be released for the next manufacturing period is generated. This list also shows the actual production requirements. The production plan for short term scheduling are the inputs of the production scheduling system - here called IPS - on an operational level. IPS is responsible for the assignment of jobs or tasks to machines, to transport facilities, and for the provision of resources needed in manufacturing, and thus organizes job and task release for execution. In that way, IPS represents an interface between PPS and CAM as shown in the survey presented in Figure 9.1.2.

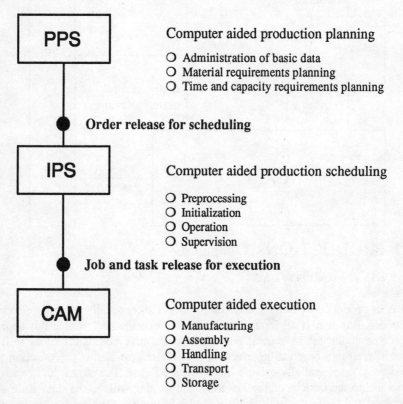

Figure 9.1.2 *Production planning, scheduling and execution.*

In detail, there are four major areas the IPS is responsible for [Sch89a].

(1) Preprocessing

Examination of production prerequisites: the customer orders will only be released for manufacturing if all needed resources such as materials, tools, machines, pallets, and NC-programs are available.

(2) System Initialization

The manufacturing system or parts thereof have to be set up such that processing of released orders can be started. Depending on the type of job, NC-programs have to be loaded, tools have to be mounted, and materials and equipment have to be made available at specified locations.

(3) System Operation

The main function of short term production scheduling is to decide about releasing jobs for entering the manufacturing system and how to traverse jobs inside the system in accordance with business objectives and production requirements.

(4) System Supervision and Monitoring

The current process data allow to check the progress of work continuously. The actual state of the system should always be observed, in order to be able to react quickly if deviations from a planned state are diagnosed.

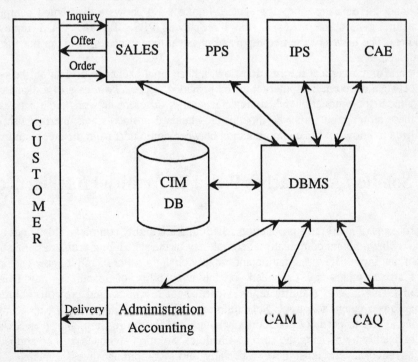

Figure 9.1.3 *CIM and the database.*

Offline planning (OFP) is concerned with preprocessing, system initialization and production scheduling on a *predictive level*, while online control (ONC) is focused mainly on production scheduling on a *reactive level* and on the level of system supervision and monitoring. Despite the fact that all these steps have to be performed by the IPS, following the purpose of this chapter we mainly concentrate on short term production scheduling on the predictive and the reactive level.

One of the most important necessities of CIM is an integrated database system. Although data are distributed among the various components of a CIM system, they should be logically centralized so that the whole system is virtually based on one database. The advantage of such an architectue would be redundancy avoidance which allows for easier maintenance of data and hence provides ways to assure consistency of data. This is a major activity of the *database management system* (*DBMS*). The idea of an integrated data management within CIM is shown in Figure 9.1.3.

The *computer architecture* for CIM follows the hierarchical approach of problem solving which has already been discussed earlier in this section. The hierarchy and can be represented as a tree structure that covers the following decision oriented levels of an enterprise: strategic planning, tactical planning, operational scheduling and manufacturing. At each level a host computer is coordinating one or more computers on the next lower level; actions at each level are carried out independently, as long as the requirements coming from the supervising level are not violated. The output of each subordinated level meets the requirements for correspondingly higher levels and provides feedback to the host. The deeper the level of the tree is, the more detailed are the processed data and the shorter has to be the computing time; in higher levels, on the other hand, the data are more aggregated. Figure 9.1.4 shows a distributed computer architecture, where the boxes of the three levels PPS, IPS and CAM represent computers. The leaves of the tree represent physical manufacturing and are not further investigated.

Apart from a vertical information flow, a horizontal exchange of data on the same level between different computers must be provided, especially in case of a distributed environment for production scheduling. Generally, different network architectures to meet these requirements may be thought of. Standard protocols and interfaces should be utilized to allow for the communication between computers from different vendors.

9.2 Solution Approaches Based on Artificial Intelligence

The problems of short term production scheduling are highly complex. This is not only caused by the inherent combinatorial complexity of the scheduling problem but also by the fact that input data are dynamic and rapidly changing. For example, new customer orders arrive, others are cancelled, or the availability of resources may change suddenly. This lack of stability requires permanent revisions, and previous solutions are due to permanent adaptions. Scheduling models for manufacturing processes must have the ability to partially predict the behaviour of the entire shop, and, if necessary, to react quickly by revising the current schedules. Solution approaches to be applied in such an environment must have especially short computing times, i.e. time- and resource-consuming models and methods are not appropriate on an operational level of production scheduling.

All models and methods for these purposes so far developed and partially reviewed in the preceding chapters are either of descriptive or of constructive nature. Descriptive models give an answer to the question "what happens if ⋯ ?", whereas constructive models try to answer the question "what has to happen so that ⋯ ?". Constructive models are used to find best possible or at least feasible solutions; descriptive models are used to evaluate decision alternatives or solution proposals, and thus help to get a deeper insight into the problem characteristics. Examples of descriptive models for production scheduling are queueing networks on an analytical and discrete simulation on an empirical basis; constructive models might use combinatorial optimization techniques or knowledge of human scheduling experts.

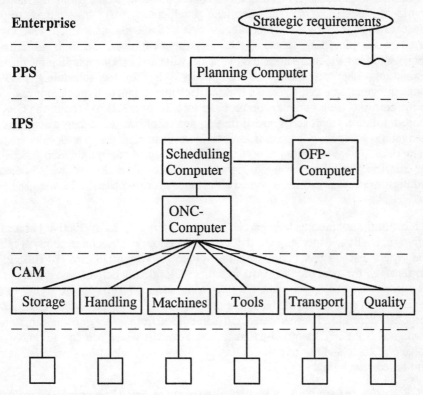

Figure 9.1.4 *Computer system in manufacturing.*

For production scheduling problems one advantage of descriptive models is the possibility to understand more about the dynamics of the system, whereas constructive models can be used to find solutions directly. Coupling both model types the advantages of each would be combined. The quality of a solution generated by constructive models could then be evaluated by descriptive ones. Using the results, the constructive models could be revised until an acceptable schedule is found. In many cases there is not enough knowledge available about the manufacturing system to build a constructive model from the scratch. In such situations descriptive models can be used to get the right understanding of the relevant problem parameters.

From another perspective there also exist approaches trying to change the system in order to fit into the scheduling model, others simplify the model in order to permit the use of a particular solution method. In the meantime more model realism is postulated. Information technology should be used to model the problem without distortion and destruction. In particular it can be assumed that in practical settings there exists not only one scheduling problem all the time and there is not only one solution approach to each problem, but there are different problems at different points in time which have to be treated in different ways. To build and solve these models both expert knowledge and "deep" methods coming from combinatorial optimization and scheduling theory should be applied for problem formulation, analysis and solution.

Solution approaches for scheduling problems mainly come from the fields of Operations Research (*OR*) and Artificial Intelligence (*AI*). In contrast to OR-approaches to scheduling, which are focused on *optimization* and which were mainly covered in the preceding chapters, AI relies on *satisfaction*, i.e. it is sufficient to generate solutions which are accepted by the decision maker. Disregarding the different paradigm of either disciplines the complexity status of the scheduling problems remains the same, as it can be shown that the decision variant of a problem is not easier than the corresponding optimization problem (see Section 2.2). Although the OR- and AI-based solution approaches are different, many efforts of either disciplines for investigating scheduling problems are similar; examples are the development of priority rules, the investigation of bottleneck resources and constraint based scheduling. With priority scheduling as a job- or task-oriented approach, and with bottleneck scheduling as a resource-oriented one, two extremes for rule-based schedule generation exist.

Most of the solution techniques can be applied not only for predictive but also for reactive scheduling. Especially for the latter case priotity rules concerning job release to the system and job traversing inside the system are very often used [BPH82, PI77]. Unfortunately, for most problem instances these rules do not deliver best possible solutions because they belong to the wide field of *heuristics*. Heuristics are trying to take advantage from special knowledge about the characteristics of the domain environment or problem description respectively and sometimes from analyzing the structure of known good solutions. Many AI-based approaches exist which use domain knowledge to solve predictive and reactive scheduling problems, especially when modelled as constraint-based scheduling.

OR approaches are built on numerical constraints, the AI approach is considering also non-numerical constraints distinguishing between *soft* and *hard constraints*. In this sense scheduling problems also can be considered as *constraint satisfaction problems* with respect to hard and soft constraints. Speaking of hard constraints we mean constraints which represent necessary conditions that must be obeyed. Among hard constraints are given precedence relations, routing conditions, resource availability, ready times, and setup times. In contrast to these, soft constraints such as desirable precedence constraints, due dates, work-in-process inventory, resource utilization, and a number of tool changes, represent rather *preferences* the decision maker wants to be considered. From an OR point of view they represent the aspect of optimization with respect to an objective function. Formulating these preferences as constraints too, will convert the optimization problem under consideration into a feasibility or a decision problem. In practical cases it turns out very often that it is less time consuming to decide on the feasibility of a solution than to give an answer to an optimization problem.

The *constraint satisfaction problem* (*CSP*) deals with the question of finding values for the variables of a set $X = \{x_1, \cdots, x_n\}$ such that a given collection C of constraints $c_1, \cdots, c_m$ is satisfied. Each variable x_i is assigned a domain z_i which defines the set of values x_i may assume. Each constraint is a subset of the Cartesian product $z_1 \times z_2 \times \cdots \times z_n$ that specifies conditions on the values of the variables $x_1, \cdots, x_n$. A subset $\mathcal{Y} \subseteq z_1 \times z_2 \times \cdots \times z_n$ is called a *feasible solution* of the constraint satisfaction problem if $\mathcal{Y}$ meets all constraints of C, i.e. if $\mathcal{Y} \subseteq \bigcap_{j=1}^{n} c_j$.

The analysis of a constraint satisfaction problem either leads to feasible solutions or to the result that for a given constraint set no such solution exists. In the latter case *conflict resolution* techniques have to be applied. The question induced by a constraint satisfaction problem is an *NP*-complete problem [GJ79] and one of the traditional approaches to solve it is backtracking. In order to detect *infeasibility* it is sometimes possible to avoid this computationally expensive approach by carrying out some preprocessing steps where conflicts between constraints are detected in advance.

For illustration purposes consider the following example problem with $X = \{x_1, x_2, x_3\}$, $z_1 = z_2 = z_3 = \{0, 1\}$, and $C = \{c_1, c_2, c_3\}$ representing the constraints

$$x_1 + x_2 = 1 \tag{9.2.1}$$

$$x_2 + x_3 = 1 \tag{9.2.2}$$

$$x_1 + x_3 = y \text{ for } y \in \{0, 2\}. \tag{9.2.3}$$

Feasible solutions for this example constraint satisfaction problem are given by $\mathcal{Y}_1 = \{(0, 1, 0)\}$ and $\mathcal{Y}_2 = \{(1, 0, 1)\}$. If a fourth constraint represented by

$$x_2 + x_3 = 0 \tag{9.2.4}$$

is added to C, conflicts arise between (9.2.2) and (9.2.4) and between (9.2.1), (9.2.3), and (9.2.4). From these we see that no feasible solution exists. Notice that no backtracking approach was needed to arrive at this result.

To solve constraint satisfaction problems most AI scheduling systems construct a search tree and apply some search technique to find a feasible solution. A common technique to find feasible solutions quickly is constraint directed search. The fundamental philosophy uses a priori *consistency checking techniques* [DP88, Fre78, Mac77, Mon74]. The basic concept is to prune the search space before unfeasible combinations of variable values are generated. This technique is also known as *constraint propagation*.

Apart from the discussed focus on constraints, AI emphasizes the role of domain specific knowledge in decomposing the initial problem according to several perspectives like bottleneck resources, hierarchies of constraints, conflicting subsets of constraints, while ignoring less important details. Existing AI-based scheduling systems differentiate between *knowledge representation* (models) and *scheduling methodology* (algorithms). They focus rather on a particular application than on general problems. The scheduling knowledge refers to the manufacturing system itself, to constraints and to objectives or preferences. Possible representation techniques are semantic networks (declarative knowledge), predicate logic (especially for constraints), production rules (procedural knowledge) and frames (all of it). Scheduling methodology used in AI is mainly based on production rules (operators), heuristic search (guides the application of operators), opportunistic reasoning (different views of problem solving, e.g. resource-based or job-based), hierarchical decomposition (subproblem solution, abstraction and distributed problem solving), pattern matching (e.g. using the status of the manufacturing system and given objectives for the application of priority rules), constraint propagation, reinforcement or relaxation techniques.

In the next two sections we describe two approaches which use AI-based solution techniques to give answers to production scheduling problems. In Section 9.2.1 we demonstrate interactive scheduling and in Section 9.2.2 we discuss some approaches using expert knowledge in the solution process of scheduling problems.

9.2.1 Interactive Scheduling

We now want to describe how an AI-based approach can be incorporated to solve predictive scheduling problems interactively. Following Schmidt [Sch89b], decomposable problems can be solved via a heuristic solution procedure based on a hierarchical "relax and enrich" strategy (*REST*) with lookahead capabilities. Using REST we start with a solution of some relaxed feasibility problem considering hard constraints only. Then we enrich the problem formulation stepwise by introducing preferences for the decision maker that can be regarded as soft constraints. Generally, we cannot expect that all of these preferences are met simultaneously. Some of them may cause conflicts. In this case we have to analyze all the preferences by some *conflict detection* procedure. Having discovered conflicting preferences we must decide which of them should be omitted in order to *resolve contradictions*. This way a feasible and acceptable solution can be generated.

REST seems to be appealing in a production scheduling environment for several reasons. The separation of hard constraints from preferences increases scheduling flexibility. Especially, preferences very often change over time so that plan revisions are necessary. If *relaxation* and *enrichment* techniques are applied, only some preferences have to be altered locally while very often major parts of the present schedule satisfying hard constraints can be kept unchanged. A similar argument applies for acceptable partial schedules which may be conserved and the solution procedure can concentrate on the unsatisfactory parts of the schedule only.

This problem treatment can be incorporated into the earlier mentioned DSS framework for production scheduling which then includes an *algorithmic* module to solve the problem under the set of hard constraints, and a *knowledge-based* module to take over the part of conflict detection and implementation of consistent preferences. Without loss of generality and for demonstration purposes only we want to assume in the following that the acceptability of a solution is the greater the more preferences are incorporated into the final schedule. Using this performance measure it is assumed that all preferences are of equal importance.

In this section we describe the basic ideas of REST quite generally and demonstrate its application using an example from precedence constrained scheduling. We start with a short discussion of the types of constraints we want to consider. Then we give an overview on how to detect conflicts between constraints and how to resolve them. Guided by a simple example we present the working features of a scheduling system which are based on REST.

Analyzing Conflicts

Conflicts occur among contradicory constraints. We assume that the given hard constraints are not contradictory among themselves and thus a feasible schedule exists which meets them. We further assume that conflicts can only be induced by the set of preferences. Then, there are two kinds of contradictions which have to be taken into account. On the one hand there are conflicts between the preferences and the hard constraints, and on the other hand there may be conflicts among preferences themselves. These conflicting interactions are mainly caused by time restrictions and limited resource availabilities. Following the strategy of REST we do not want to detect all of these conflicts in advance. Starting with a first feasible schedule wehave the possibility to analyze the relationship in greater detail.

According to the various kinds of possible contradictions we differentiate between unary, binary and k-ary conflicts. An *unary conflict* occurs if a single preference leads to an inconsistency with some hard constraints. A *binary conflict* occurs if two preferences are contradictory. An *k-ary conflict* occurs if a number k of preferences is inconsistent, i.e if for each preference PR of these k preferences there exists another preference being in conflict with PR. Moreover, we distinguish between the set LC of *logically conflicting* preferences, the set TC of *time conflicting* preferences, and the set RC of *resource conflicting* preferences. Logical conflicts between preferences occur if a set of desired task orderings is incompatible from a logical point of view. The analysis of logical conflicts can be carried out by representing the set of preferences by a directed graph $G = (T, LC)$ where T is the set of tasks and $LC \subseteq T \times T$ represents the preferred processing orders among them. Binary conflicts can be detected by pairwise comparisons of tasks. In order to discover k-ary conflicts, the relational product LC^k has to be considered.

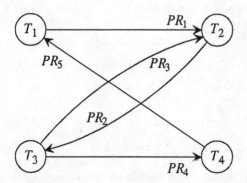

Figure 9.2.1 *$G = (T, LC)$ representing logical conflicts in Example 9.2.1.*

Example 9.2.1 To illustrate the analysis of conflicts we base the discussion in this section on an example problem where a set T of four tasks has to be scheduled. We start to concentrate on conflicts between preferences only. Let PR be a set of five preferences which suggest certain orderings between pairs of tasks. Let $\mathcal{T} = \{T_1, T_2, T_3, T_4\}$, $\mathcal{PR} = \{PR_1, PR_2, PR_3, PR_4, PR_5\}$ with $PR_1 = (T_1, T_2)$, $PR_2 = (T_2, T_3)$, $PR_3 = (T_3, T_2)$, $PR_4 = (T_3, T_4)$, and $PR_5 = (T_4, T_1)$. Logical conflicts in $G = (\mathcal{T}, \mathcal{LC})$ can be detected by finding all cycles of G (compare Figure 9.2.1). From this we will get the two logically conflicting sets $\mathcal{LC}_1 = \{PR_2, PR_3\}$ representing a binary conflict and $\mathcal{LC}_2 = \{PR_1, PR_2, PR_4, PR_5\}$ representing a 4-ary conflict. □

Time conflicts occur if a set of preferences is not consistent with time restrictions following from the initial solution obtained on the basis of the set of hard constraints. To detect time conflicts we must explicitly check all time conditions between the tasks. Hard constraints implying earliest beginning times EB_j, latest beginning times LB_j and processing times p_j restrict the preferences that can be realized. For each preference of type (T_u, T_v), we must assure that

$$EB_u + p_u \leq LB_v.\tag{9.2.5}$$

Otherwise, at least one of the time restrictions will be violated, and the corresponding preference causes a unary conflict. More generally, if a task sequence $(T_u, \cdots, T_v, T_w)$ is time compatible, then necessarily we have

$$Z_v + p_v \leq LB_w\tag{9.2.6}$$

where

$$Z_v = \max \left\{ EB_v, \max_{k=u}^{v-1} \left\{ EB_k + \sum_{j=k}^{v-1} p_j \right\} \right\}.$$

If (9.2.6) does not hold the time constraint coming from the last task of the chain will be violated.

Example 9.2.2 To clarify this let us again consider Example 9.2.1. Assume that each task T_j has a given earliest beginning time EB_j and a latest beginning time LB_j as specified together with processing times p_j in the following Table 9.2.1.

T_j	EB_j	LB_j	p_j
T_1	7	7	5
T_2	3	12	4
T_3	13	15	2
T_4	12	15	0

Table 9.2.1 *Time parameters for Example 9.2.1.*

The first consistency investigation refers to an unary check of feasibility of the single preferences PR_1, PR_2, PR_3, PR_4, and PR_5. We see that for preferences PR_3 and PR_5 the time constraints of (9.2.5) cannot be met and they thus lead to unary time conflicts. To check n-ary time conflicts for $n \geq 2$, we have to investigate time compatibility of the remaining preferences, PR_1, PR_2, and PR_4. These would suggest execution of the tasks in order (T_1, T_2, T_3, T_4). To verify feasibility of this sequence we have to check all its subsequences subject to (9.2.6). The subsequences of length 2 are time compatible as the only time conflicting sequences of length 2 are (T_3, T_2) and (T_4, T_1). Applying (9.2.6) to the whole sequence (T_1, T_2, T_3, T_4), we get $Z_3 = \max \{EB_3, EB_1 + p_1 + p_2, EB_2 + p_2\} = 16$ and $Z_3 + p_3 > LB_4$; thus preferences PR_1, PR_2 and PR_3 are creating a 3-ary time conflict. In the same way, the two subsequences of length 3 can be tested, and we get the result that (T_1, T_2, T_3) realizing preferences PR_1 and PR_2 are in time conflict, whereas (T_2, T_3, T_4) are not. So we end up with four time conflicting sets of preferences, the unary conflicts $\mathcal{TC}_1 = \{PR_3\}$ and $\mathcal{TC}_2 = \{PR_5\}$, the binary conflicts $\mathcal{TC}_3 = \{PR_1, PR_2\}$, and the 3-ary conflict $\mathcal{TC}_4 = \{PR_1, PR_2, PR_4\}$. $\square$

If the implementation of some preference causes a resource demand at some time t such that it exceeds resource limits at this time, i.e.

$$\Sigma_{T_t} R_k(T_j) > m_k, k = 1, \cdots, s, \tag{9.2.7}$$

then a resource conflict occurs. Here T_t denotes the set of tasks in process at time t, $R_k(T_j)$ the requirement of resource of type R_k of task T_j, and m_k the corresponding resource supply. Assume in Example 9.2.1 that $s = 1$, $m_1 = 1$, and $R_1(T_j) = 1$ for all $j = 1, \cdots, 4$. Taking the given time constraints of Example 9.2.2 into account, then from (9.2.7) we detect a unary conflict for PR_1 since T_2 cannot be processed in parallel with tasks T_3 and T_4. Thus an additional conflicting set $\mathcal{RC}_1 = \{PR_1\}$ is introduced.

Coping with Conflicts

Having detected the unary, binary and n-ary conflicting sets concerning logical, time and resource conflicts we have to find out if there is a solution schedule that meets all the restrictions coming from these conflicting sets. In general we have to find a subset $\mathcal{PR}'$ of the set $\mathcal{PR}$ of preferences of maximal cardinality such that none of the conflicting sets $\mathcal{LC}_i$, $\mathcal{TC}_j$, or $\mathcal{RC}_k$ of preferences is a subset of $\mathcal{PR}'$.

We want to represent preferences and conflicts between them by an undirected *conflict graph* $G = (\mathcal{PR}, \mathcal{E})$. The set $\mathcal{PR}$ of nodes represents all the given preferences and the set $\mathcal{E}$ of edges shows the conflicts between them.

To understand what we mean by such a representation let us investigate how to cope with the different classes of conflicts. For each single preference PR_i which is unary conflicting we introduce an edge $\{PR_i, PR_i\}$. For a binary conflicting pair PR_i and PR_j of preferences, we introduce an edge $\{PR_i, PR_j\}$. For each n-ary conflicting preference $\mathcal{PR} = \{PR_1, \cdots, PR_n\}$ ($n > 2$), introduce an edge-circuit $\{PR_n, PR_1\}$, $\{PR_i, PR_{i+1}\}$, $i = 1, \cdots, n-1$. In order to represent all classes of conflicts investigated so far we decompose $\mathcal{E}$ into the three sets of edges $\mathcal{E}_1$, $\mathcal{E}_2$ and $\mathcal{E}_3$, where $\mathcal{E}_1$ corresponds to the set of unary, $\mathcal{E}_2$ to the set of binary, and $\mathcal{E}_3$ to the set of n-ary conflicts, and $\mathcal{E}_1 \cup \mathcal{E}_2 \cup \mathcal{E}_3 = \mathcal{E}$. Set $\mathcal{E}_1$ includes all loops $\{PR_i, PR_i\}$, $\mathcal{E}_2$ includes all edges representing pairwise conflicts $\{PR_i, PR_j\}$, and $\mathcal{E}_3$ includes all edge cycles $\{PR_1, PR_2\}, \cdots, \{PR_{n-1}, PR_n\}$, $\{PR_n, PR_1\}$.

For Examples 9.2.1 and 9.2.2 we get the conflict graph representation with

$$\mathcal{E}_1 = \{\{PR_1, PR_1\}, \{PR_3, PR_3\}, \{PR_5, PR_5\}\},$$

$$\mathcal{E}_2 = \{\{PR_1, PR_2\}, \{PR_2, PR_3\}\},$$

$$\mathcal{E}_3 = \{\{PR_1, PR_2\}, \{PR_2, PR_4\}, \{PR_4, PR_5\}, \{PR_4, PR_1\}, \{PR_5, PR_1\}\},$$

as shown in Figure 9.2.2 where the dashed lines refer to binary conflicts.

According to our *measure of acceptability* we are interested in the maximum number of preferences that can be fulfilled without loosing feasibility. This is justified if all preferences are of equal importance. If the preferences have different weights we might be interested in finding all these preferences which do not cause a conflict and have maximum total weight. All these practical questions are *NP*-hard problems if we have to consider quite general instances of $\mathcal{E}_2$ and $\mathcal{E}_3$ [GJ79].

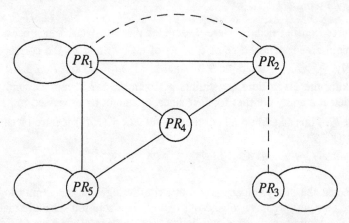

Figure 9.2.2 $G = (\mathcal{PR}, \mathcal{E})$ *representing conflicts for Example 9.2.1.*

In order to find $\mathcal{PR}'$ we have to choose a subset of $\mathcal{PR}$ such that for all nodes PR_u, $PR_v, \cdots, PR_w$ of $\mathcal{PR}'$, $\{PR_u, PR_u\}$ is not in $\mathcal{E}_1$, $\{PR_u, PR_v\}$ not in $\mathcal{E}_2$, and $\{PR_u, PR_v\}, \cdots, \{PR_w, PR_u\}$ are not in $\mathcal{E}_3$. Note that for any solution of the problem we can eliminate in advance all vertices $PR_x \in \mathcal{PR}$ with $\{PR_x, PR_x\} \in \mathcal{E}$ and all edges from $\mathcal{E}$ which are incident with some vertex PR_x such that $\{PR_x, PR_x\} \in \mathcal{E}$. These preferences PR_x can never be included into a feasible solution.

Working Features of an Interactive Scheduling System

The above described approach of REST with conflict detection mechanisms can be integrated into a DSS. Its general outline is shown in Figure 9.2.3.

The DSS consists of four major modules: problem analysis, schedule generation, conflict detection and evaluation. Their working features can be organized by incorporating four phases. The first phase starts with some problem analysis investigating the set of hard constraints which we have to take into account for any problem solution. Then, in the second phase a first feasible solution (basic schedule) is generated by ap-

plying some scheduling algorithm. The third phase takes over the part of a
set of preferences of task constraints and their interaction with the result
schedule via the conflict detection module. In the last phase a compatible sub...
constraints according to the objectives of the decision maker is determined, from w...
a provisional final schedule is generated and then evaluated. If the evaluation is
satisfactory a solution for the predictive scheduling problem is found; if not, the schedule has to be revised by considering new constraints from the decision maker. The loop
stops as soon as a satisfactory solution has been found.

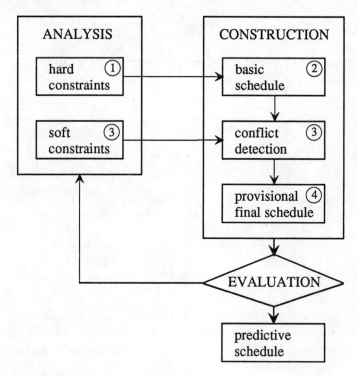

Figure 9.2.3 *A DSS for the REST-approach.*

The DSS can be extended to handle a dynamic environment. Whenever hard constraints have to be revised or the set of preferences is changing we can apply this approach on a rolling basis.

Example 9.2.3 To demonstrate the working feature of the scheduling system consider
a set of tasks $\mathcal{T} - \{T_1, T_2, T_3, T_4, T_5, T_6, T_7, T_8\}$. Hard constraints are shown in Figure
9.2.4(a) where processing times, earliest beginning times, and latest beginning times
are given as triples $(p_j; EB_j, LB_j)$ next to the task nodes, and precedence constraints are
specified. In addition, concurrent task execution is restricted by three types of resources
and resource requirements of the tasks are given by $R(T_1) = [0, 0, 0]$, $R(T_2) = [1, 1, 1]$,
$R(T_3) = [2, 4, 1]$, $R(T_4) = [0, 1, 1]$, $R(T_5) = [4, 2, 2]$, $R(T_6) = [2, 0, 2]$, $R(T_7) = [3, 5, 3]$,
$R(T_8) = [0, 0, 0]$, and total resource supply is $m = [5, 5, 5]$.

Having analyzed the hard constraints we generate a feasible basic schedule by applying some scheduling algorithm. The result is also shown in Figure 9.2.4(b). Feasibility of the schedule is gained by assigning a starting time s_j to each task such that $EB_j \leq s_j \leq LB_j$ and under the condition that the resource constraints are met.

(a)

(b)

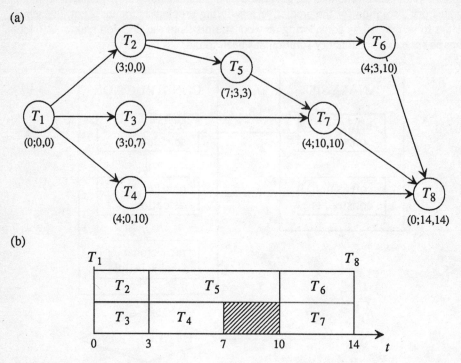

Figure 9.2.4 *Illustration of Example 9.2.2*
(a) *Tasks with precedence constraints and triples $(p_j; EB_j, EB_j)$ specifying processing times and earliest and latest beginning times,*
(b) *a basic schedule.*

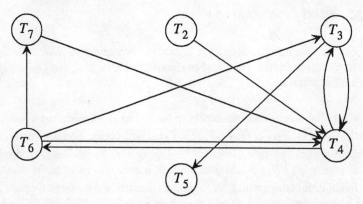

Figure 9.2.5 *$G = (T, \mathcal{LC})$ representing logical conflicts in Example 9.2.3.*

The problem can now be described using the terminology of the constraint satisfaction problem; the variables refer to the starting times of the tasks, their domains to the intervals of corresponding earliest and latest beginning times and the constraints to the set of preferences. Let the set of preferences be given by $\mathcal{PR} = \{PR_1, \cdots, PR_9\}$ with $PR_1 = (T_2, T_4)$, $PR_2 = (T_3, T_4)$, $PR_3 = (T_3, T_5)$, $PR_4 = (T_4, T_6)$, $PR_5 = (T_4, T_3)$, $PR_6 = (T_6, T_4)$, $PR_7 = (T_6, T_7)$, $PR_8 = (T_6, T_3)$, and $PR_9 = (T_7, T_4)$.

We start with the detection of logical conflicts. From the cycles of the graph in Figure 9.2.5 we get the logically conflicting sets $LC_1 = \{PR_2, PR_5\}$, $LC_2 = \{PR_4, PR_6\}$, $LC_3 = \{PR_2, PR_4, PR_8\}$, and $LC_4 = \{PR_4, PR_7, PR_9\}$.

An analysis of time constraints shows that there is only one unary conflict, $TC_1 = \{PR_9\}$. Next, task sequences of length greater than 2 have to be checked. Note that we only have to consider those task sequences which do not include any conflicting preferences already detected. From this we get the following sequences of tasks together with corresponding preferences,

(T_2, T_4, T_6): $\{PR_1, PR_4\}$, (T_2, T_4, T_6, T_7): $\{PR_1, PR_4, PR_7\}$,

(T_2, T_4, T_6, T_3): $\{PR_1, PR_4, PR_8\}$, $(T_2, T_4, T_6, T_3, T_5)$: $\{PR_1, PR_4, PR_8, PR_3\}$,

(T_2, T_4, T_3): $\{PR_1, PR_5\}$, (T_2, T_4, T_3, T_5): $\{PR_1, PR_5, PR_3\}$,

(T_3, T_4, T_6): $\{PR_2, PR_4\}$, (T_3, T_4, T_6, T_7): $\{PR_2, PR_4, PR_7\}$,

(T_4, T_6, T_7): $\{PR_4, PR_7\}$, (T_4, T_6, T_3): $\{PR_4, PR_8\}$,

(T_4, T_6, T_3, T_5): $\{PR_4, PR_8, PR_3\}$, (T_4, T_3, T_5): $\{PR_5, PR_3\}$,

(T_6, T_4, T_3): $\{PR_6, PR_5\}$, (T_6, T_4, T_3, T_5): $\{PR_6, PR_5, PR_3\}$,

(T_6, T_3, T_4): $\{PR_8, PR_2\}$, (T_6, T_3, T_5): $\{PR_8, PR_3\}$.

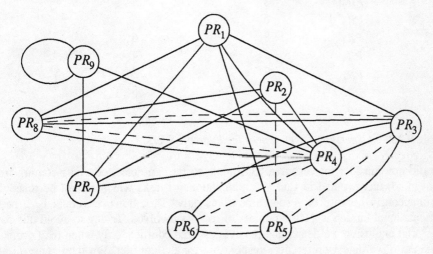

Figure 9.2.6 $G_c = (\mathcal{PR}, \mathcal{E})$ representing all conflicts for Example 9.2.2.

According to (9.2.6) we find the time conflicting sets $\mathcal{TC}_2 = \{PR_1, PR_4, PR_7\}$, $\mathcal{TC}_3 = \{PR_1, PR_4, PR_8\}$, $\mathcal{TC}_4 = \{PR_1, PR_4, PR_8, PR_3\}$, $\mathcal{TC}_5 = \{PR_1, PR_5, PR_3\}$, $\mathcal{TC}_6 = \{PR_2, PR_4, PR_7\}$, $\mathcal{TC}_7 = \{PR_4, PR_8\}$, $\mathcal{TC}_8 = \{PR_4, PR_8, PR_3\}$, $\mathcal{TC}_9 = \{PR_5, PR_3\}$, $\mathcal{TC}_{10} = \{PR_6, PR_5\}$, $\mathcal{TC}_{11} = \{PR_6, PR_5, PR_3\}$, and $\mathcal{TC}_{12} = \{PR_8, PR_3\}$. These conflicts are shown in the conflict graph $G_c = (\mathcal{PR}, \mathcal{E})$ of Figure 9.2.6 where again the dashed lines represent binary conflicts.

As already mentioned, for simplicity reasons we assume that all preferences are of equal importance. First we omit PR_9 in G_c because $\mathcal{TC}_1 = \{PR_9\}$ is a unary conflict. To solve the remaining problem we use a least commitment strategy in the following way. Let $(PR_{\alpha_1}, \cdots, PR_{\alpha_n})$ be a sequence ordered according to nondecreasing number of conflicts they create. In case of ties order nondecreasingly according to the number of conflicting preferences which are involved in these conflicts. If there are still ties order nondecreasingly according to index number of preferences. Now select a nonconflicting subset of preferences in the following way. Take the first preferences, $PR_{\alpha_1}, \cdots,$ PR_{α_i}, to the selected set as long as there are no conflicts introduced. When the next preference, $PR_{\alpha_{i+1}}$, is to be chosen check its compatibility to the already selected preferences $PR_{\alpha_1}, \cdots, PR_{\alpha_i}$. If $PR_{\alpha_{i+1}}$ is in conflict to one of them, then skip it and continue with $PR_{\alpha_{i+2}}$; otherwise add $PR_{\alpha_{i+1}}$ to the selected set and continue with $PR_{\alpha_{i+2}}$.

For the preferences of Example 9.2.3, Table 9.2.2 gives the number of conflicts and number of conflicting preferences. Thus, following the obove strategy, we would select the preferences PR_1, PR_2, PR_6, PR_7, and PR_8. The Gantt chart in Figure 9.2.7 shows the resulting schedule where the triples next to the tasks denote their resource requirements.

Preference	# Conflicts	# Conflicting Preferences
PR_1	4	5
PR_2	3	4
PR_3	6	5
PR_4	8	6
PR_5	5	4
PR_6	3	3
PR_7	2	3
PR_8	6	4

Table 9.2.2   *Ordering of preferences for Example 9.2.3.*

We did not consider the resource constraints so far. To detect conflicts coming from them in advance we had to find all combinations of tasks which cannot be scheduled simultaneously because of resource conflicts only. This, however, could be a heavy computational burden if a large number of tasks is involved. Trying to avoid this combinatorial explosion we detect and resolve resource conflicts only when they occur. In these cases we detect preferences responsible for the conflict. We then generate new conflicting sets of preferences and solve the resource conflict under consideration by applying the least commitment strategy described before. In this manner we proceed until a feasible solution is found.

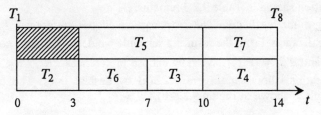

Figure 9.2.7 *Schedule for Example 9.2.3 without considering resource conflicts.*

(a)

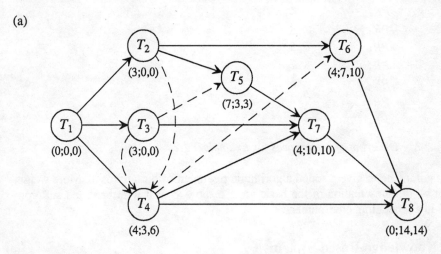

(b)

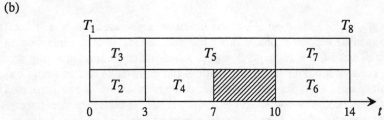

Figure 9.2.8 *Final schedule for Example 9.2.3*

    (a) *precedence graph of Figure 9.2.4(a) with additional hard constraints* (T_4, T_7),

    (b) *corresponding schedule.*

The schedule of Figure 9.2.7 shows among others a resource conflict for tasks T_4 and T_7. In order to prevent simultaneous execution of T_4 and T_7 we might introduce preference (T_4, T_7) or (T_7, T_4). Taking the time constraints into account we choose (T_4, T_7), and from now on we regard this preference as an additional hard constraint. Considering all resource conflicts of the schedule in Figure 9.2.7 in that way we will end up with a new precedence graph (see Figure 9.2.8(a)). The new precedences cause new sets of time conflicts to be added to the conflict sets determined earlier, $TC_{13} = \{PR_6\}$, $TC_{14} = \{PR_6, PR_5\}$ and $TC_{15} = \{PR_6, PR_5, PR_3\}$. Since preference PR_6 can be eliminated the situation shown in Table 9.2.3 remains.

According to the *least commitment* strategy we choose preferences PR_1, PR_5, PR_7 and PR_8 for realization. From the resulting schedule we detect resource conflicting sets $RC_1 = \{PR_5\}$ and $RC_2 = \{PR_7\}$. We now choose preferences PR_1, PR_2, PR_3 and PR_4 for implementation, shown in Figure 9.2.8(a) by dashed lines. The corresponding feasible schedule is shown in Figure 9.2.8(b).

Preference	# Conflicts	# Conflicting Preferences
PR_1	4	5
PR_2	3	4
PR_3	5	4
PR_4	7	5
PR_5	3	3
PR_7	2	3
PR_8	6	4

Table 9.2.3   *Ordering of preferences for Example* 9.2.2.

We did not intend to give a sound algorithmic treatment of our approach. More weight was put on the presentation of the basic ideas of how to deal with hard and soft constraints in a scheduling environment.

9.2.2 Knowledge-Based Systems

Expert Systems are special kinds of AI-based or knowledge-based systems. Expert systems are designed to support problem modeling and solving with the intention to simulate the capabilities of domain experts, e.g. problem understanding, problem solving, explaining the solution, knowledge acquisition, and knowledge restructuring. Expert systems mainly use two types of knowledge: *descriptive knowledge* or *facts*, and *procedural knowledge* or knowledge about the semantics behind facts. The *architecture* of expert systems consists of the four components storing knowledge, knowledge acquisition, explanation of results, and problem solution. In the following we will concentrate on problem solution.

There is an important difference between expert systems and conventional problem solving systems. In most expert systems the model of the problem description and basic elements of problem solving are stored in a knowledge base. The complete solution process is carried out by some inference modul interacting with the knowledge base. Conventional systems do not have this kind of seperated structure; they are rather a mixture of both parts in one program.

In order to implement an expert system one needs three types of *models*: a model of the domain, a model of the elementary steps to be taken, and a model of inference that defines the sequence of elementary steps in the process of problem solution. The domain is represented using descriptive knowledge about objects, their attributes and the relations between objects. In scheduling for example, objects are machines, jobs, tasks or tools, attributes are machine states, job and task characteristics or tool setup times, and relations could be precedence constraints or the subsumption of machines to machine types. The model of elementary steps uses production rules or other representations of procedural knowledge. For if-then rules there exists a unique input-output description. The model of inference uses combinations or sets of elementary steps to represent the solution process where a given start state is transformed to a desired goal state. This latter type of knowledge can be either knowledge of domain experts or domain independent knowledge.

The objective of the expert system approach is mainly to improve the modeling part of the solution process to get closer to reality. To give a better understanding of this view we refer to an example given by Kanet and Adelsberger [KA87]: "··· consider a simple scheduling situation in which there is a single machine to process jobs that arrive at different points in time within the planning period. The objective might be to find a schedule which minimizes mean tardiness. An algorithmic approach might entertain simplifying the formulation by first assuming all jobs to be immediately available for processing. This simplified problem would then be solved and perhaps some heuristic used to alter the solution so that the original assumption of dynamic arrivals is back in tack. The approach looks at reformulation as a means to 'divide et impera'. On the other hand a reformulative approach may ··· seek to find a 'richer' problem formulation. For example the question might be asked 'is working overtime a viable alternative?', or 'does there exist another machine that can accomplish this task?', or 'is there a subset of orders that are less critical than others?', and so on."

Systems for production scheduling should not only replicate the expert's schedule but extend the capabilities by doing more problem solving. In order to achieve this AI systems separate the scheduling model from the *solution procedure*. In [Fox90] the shop floor scheduling model described uses terms from AI. It is considered to be time based planning where tasks or jobs must be selected, sequenced, and assigned to resources and time intervals for execution. Another view is that of a *multi agent planning* problem, where each task or job represents a seperate agent for which a schedule is to be created; the agents are uncooperative, i.e. each is attempting to maximize its own goals. It is also claimed that expert systems appear inappropriate for the purpose of problem solution especially for two reasons: (1) problems like production scheduling tend to be so complex that they are beyond the cognitive capabilities of the human scheduler, and (2) even if the problem is relatively easy, factory environments change often enough so that any expertise built up over time becomes obsolete very quickly.

We believe that it is nevertheless possible to apply an expert system approach for the solution of production scheduling problems but with a different perspective on problem solving. Though, as already stated, expert systems are not appropriate for solving combinatorial search problems, they are quite reasonable for the *analysis* of models and their solutions. In this way expert systems can be used for building or selecting models for scheduling problems. An appropriate solution procedure can be selected for the model, and then the expert system can again support the evaluation of the solution.

The scheduling systems reviewed next are not expert systems in their purest sense and thus we will use the more general term *knowledge-based system*. *ISIS* [SFO86, Fox87, FS84], *OPIS* [SPPMM90] and *CORTES* [FS90] are a family of systems with the goal of modeling knowledge of the manufacturing environment using mainly constraints to support *constraint guided search*; knowledge about constraints is used in the attempt to decrease the underlying search space. The systems are designed for both, predictive and reactive scheduling. ISIS-1 uses pure constraint guided search, but was not very successful in solving practical scheduling problems. ISIS-2 uses a more sophisticated search technique. Search is divided into the four phases job selection, time analysis, resource analysis, and resource assignment. Each phase consists in turn of the three subphases pre-search analysis (model construction), search (construction of the solution), and post-search analysis (evaluation of the solution). In the job selection phase a priority rule is applied to select the next job from the given set of available jobs. This job is passed to the second phase. Here earliest start and latest finish times for each task of the job are calculated without taking the resource requirements into account. In phases three and four the assignment of resources and the calculation of the final start and finish times of all tasks of the job under consideration is carried out. The search is organized by some *beam search* method. Each solution is evaluated within a rule-based post-search analysis. ISIS-3 tries to schedule each job using more information from the shop floor, especially about bottleneck-resources. With this information the job-centered scheduling approach as it is realized in ISIS-2 was complemented by a resource-centered scheduler.

As the architecture of ISIS is inflexible as far as modifications of given schedules are concerned, a new scheduling system called OPIS-1 was developed. It uses a *blackboard approach* for the communication of the two knowledge sources analysis and decision. These use the blackboard as shared memory to post messages, partial results and any further information needed for the problem solution. The blackboard is the exclusive medium of communication. Within OPIS-1 the "analyzer" constructs a rough schedule using some *balancing heuristic* and then determines the bottlenecks. Decision is then taken by the resource and the job scheduler already implemented in ISIS-3. Search is centrally controlled. OPIS-1 is also capable to deal with reactive scheduling problems, because all events can be communicated through the blackboard. In OPIS-2 this event management is supported by two additional knowledge sources which are a "right shifter" and a "demand swapper". The first one is responsible for pushing jobs forward in the schedule, and the second for exchanging jobs. Within the OPIS systems it seems that the most difficult operation is to decide which knowledge source has to be activated.

The third system of the family we want to introduce briefly is CORTES. Whereas the ISIS systems are primarily job-based and OPIS switches between job-based and resource-based considerations, CORTES takes a task-oriented point of view, which provides morre flexibility at the cost of greater search effort. Within a five step heuristic procedure a task is assigned to some resource over some time interval.

Knowledge-based systems using an expert system approach should concentrate on finding good models for the problem domain and the description of elementary steps to be taken during the solution process. The solution process itself may be implemented by a different approach. One example for model development considering knowledge about the domain and elementary steps to be taken can be found in [SS90]. Here a reactive scheduling problem is solved along the same line as OPIS works using the following problem categorization: (1) machine breakdown, (2) rush jobs, (3) new batch of jobs, (4) material shortage, (5) labour absenteeism, (6) job completion at a machine, and (7) change in shift. Knowledge is modularized into independent knowledge sources, each of them designed to solve a specific problem. If a new event occurs it is passed to some meta-analyzer and then to the appropriate knowledge source to give a solution to the analyzed scheduling problem. For instance, the shortage of some specific raw material may result in the requirement of rearranging the jobs assigned to a particular machine. This could be achieved by using the human scheduler's heuristic or by an appropriate algorithm to determine some action to be taken.

As a representative for many other knowledge-based scheduling systems - see [Ata91] for a survey - we want to describe *SONIA* which integrates both predictive and reactive scheduling on the basis of hard and soft constraints [CPP88]. The scheduling system is designed to detect and react to inconsistencies (conflicts) between a predictive schedule and the actual events on the shop floor. SONIA consists of two analyzing components, a capacity analyzer and an analyzer of conflicts, and further more a predictive and a reactive component, each containing a set of heuristics, and a component for managing schedule descriptions.

For representing a schedule in SONIA the resources needed for processing jobs are described at various levels of detail. Individual resources like machines are elements of resource groups called work areas. Resource reservation constraints are associated with resources. To give an example for such a constraint, (*res*; t_1, t_2; *n*; *list-of-motives*) means that *n* resources from resource group *res* are not available during the time interval (t_1, t_2) for the reasons given in the *list-of-motives*.

Each job is characterized by a ready time, a due date, precedence constraints, and by a set of tasks, each having resource requirements. To describe the progress of work the notions of an actual status and a schedule status are introduced. The *actual status* is of either kind "completed", "in-process", "not started", and the *schedule status* can be "scheduled", "selected" or (deliberately) "ignored". There may also be temporal constraints for tasks. For example, such a constraint can be described by the expression (*time* $\leq t_1 t_2$; *k*) where t_1 and t_2 are points in time which respectively correspond to the start and the finish time of processing a task, and *k* represents the number of time units; if there have to be at least *t* time units between processing of tasks T_j and T_{j+1}, the corresponding expression would be (*time* $\leq$ (*end* T_j)(*start* T_{j+1}); *t*). To represent actual time values, the origin of time and the current time have to be known.

SONIA uses constraint propagation which enables the detection of inconsistencies or conflicts between predictive decisions and events happening on the shop floor. Let us assume that as a result of the predictive schedule it is known that task T_j could precede task T_{j+1} while the actual situation in the workshop is such that T_j is in schedule status "ignored" and T_{j+1} is in actual status "in process". From this we get an inconsistency between these temporal constraints describing the predictive schedule and the ones which come from the actual situation. The detection of conflicts through constraint propagation is carried out using propagation axioms which indicate how constraints and logic expressions can be combined and new constraints or conflicts can be derived. The axioms are utilized by an interpreter.

SONIA distinguishes between the three major kinds of conflicts delays, capacity conflicts and breakdowns. The class of delays contains all conflicts which result from unexpected delays. There are four subclasses to be considered, "Task Delay" if the expected finish time of a task cannot be respected, "Due-Date Delay" if the due date of a manufacturing job cannot be met, "Interruption Delay" if some task cannot be performed in a work shift determined by the predictive schedule, and "Global Tardiness Conflict" if it is not possible to process all of the selected tasks by the end of the current shift. The class of capacity conflicts refers to all conflicts that come from reservation constraints. There are three subclasses to be considered. If reservations for tasks have to be canceled because of breakdowns we speak of "Breakdown Capacity Conflicts". In case a resource is assigned to a task during a work shift where this resource is not available, an "Out-Of-Shift Conflict" occurs. A capacity conflict is an "Overload" if the number of tasks assigned to a resource during a given interval of time is greater than the available capacity. The third class consists of breakdowns which contains all subclasses from delays and capacity conflicts caused only by machine breakdowns. In the following we give a short overwiew of the main *components* of the SONIA system and its *control architecture*.

(i) *Predictive Components*

The predictive components are responsible for generating an off-line schedule and consist of a selection and an ordering component. First a set of tasks is selected and resources are assigned to them. The selection depends on other already selected tasks, shop status, open work shifts and jobs to be completed. Whenever a task is selected its schedule status is "selected" and the resulting constraints are created by the schedule management system. The ordering component then uses an iterative constraint satisfaction process utilizing heuristic rules. If conflicts arise during schedule generation, backtracking is carried out, i.e. actions coming from certain rules are withdrawn. If no feasible schedule can be found for all the selected tasks a choice is made for the tasks that have to be rejected. Their schedule status is set to "ignored" and the corresponding constraints are deleted.

(ii) *Reactive Components*

For reactive scheduling three approaches to resolve conflicts between the predictive schedule and the current situation on the shop floor are possible: Predictive components can generate a complete new schedule, the current schedule is modified globally forward from the current date, or local changes are made. The first approach is the case of predictive scheduling which already been described above. The easiest reaction to modify the current schedule is to reject tasks, setting their scheduling status to "ignored" and deleting all related constraints. Of course, the rejected task should be that one causing the conflicts. If several rejections are possible the problem gets far more difficult and applicable strategies have still to be developed. Re-scheduling forward from the current date is the third possibility of reaction considered here. In this case very often due dates or ends of work shifts have to be modified. An easy reaction would simply by a right shift of all tasks without modifying their ordering and the resource assignments. In a more sophisticated approach some heuristics are applied to change the order of tasks.

(iii) *Analysis Components*

The purpose of the analyzers is to determine which of the available predictive and reactive components should be applied for schedule generation and how they should be used. Currently, there are two analysis components implemented, a capacity analyzer and a conflict analyzer. The capacity analyzer has to detect bottleneck and underloaded resources. These detections lead to the application of scheduling heuristics, e.g. of the kind that the most critical resources have to be scheduled first; in the same sense, under-loaded resourses lead to the selection of additional tasks which can exploit the resources. The conflict analyzer chooses those available reactive components which are most efficient in terms of conflict resolution.

(iv) *Control Architecture*

Problem solving and evaluating knowledge have to be integrated and adjusted to the problem solving context. A blackboard architecture is used for these purposes. Each component can be considered as an independent knowledge source which offers its services as soon as predetermined conditions are satisfied. The blackboard architecture makes it possible to have a flexible system when new strategies and new components have to be added and integrated. The domain blackboard contains capacity of the resources determined by the capacity analyzer, conflicts which are updated by the schedule management, and results given by predictive and reactive components. The control blackboard contains the scheduling problem, the sub-problems to be solved, strategies like heuristic rules or meta-rules, an agenda where all the pending actions are listed, policies to choose the next pending action and a survey of actions which are currently processed.

SONIA is a knowledge-based scheduling system which relies on constraint satisfaction where the constraints come from the problem description and are then further propagated. It has a very flexible architecture, generates predictive and reactive schedules and integrates both solution approaches. A deficiency is that nothing can be said from an ex-ante point of view about the quality of the solutions generated by the conflict resolution techniques. Unfortunately also a judgement from an ex-post point of view is not possible because there is no empirical data available up to now which gives reference to some quality measure of the schedule. Also nothing is known about computing times. As far as we know, this lack of evaluation holds for many knowledge-based scheduling systems developed until today.

9.3 Integration of Knowledge and Algorithms

Short term production scheduling with its planning and control parts is done on the shop floor level supported by the shop floor scheduling system. Using data from an aggregated production plan a detailed decision is made in which sequence the jobs are released to the manufacturing system and how they traverse inside the system. The level of shop floor scheduling is the last step in which action can be taken on business needs for manufacturing.

One main difference between the predictive and the reactive scheduling level is the liability of the input data. For predictive scheduling input data are mainly based on expectations and assumptions. Unforeseen circumstances like rush orders, machine breakdowns, or illness of personal staff can only be considered statistically, if at all. The situation is completely different in reactive scheduling where actual data are available. If they are not in coincidence with the estimated data, situation-based revisions of previous decisions have to be made. Predictive scheduling alone without a reactive scheduling system is indeed of no great use. Offline schedules will mostly fail on the shop floor because of the inherent unpredictable and dynamic nature of a manufacturing environment.

Shop floor scheduling systems available commercially today are predominately data administration systems. Moreover, they register data and make data available from machines and the shop floor. Equipment and storage data are monitored and any interruptions in the manufacturing system are noted and partially diagnosed. Mainly routine operations are carried out by the shop floor scheduling system. Most of these systems support the production manager by offering him the preliminary tools necessary for the development of a paperless planning and control process. Additionally, some systems support him by offering various scheduling strategies. The current shop floor scheduling systems are good at data administration, but for the intelligent processing they are of not great help.

An intuitive job processing schedule, based solely upon the experience of skilled managers, does not take advantage of the potential strengths of an integrated IPS. Thus, the development of an intelligent system which integrates planning and control within scheduling for the entire operation and supports effectively the shop floor management, becomes necessary. Such a system could perform all of the functions of the current shop floor scheduling systems and would also be able to automatically produce good proposals for job processing schedules, which take deviations from the normal routine into consideration. It is also important in the development of alternative job processing schedules, that all effects on the overall production schedule are considered. With the help of such concepts the problems involved in initializing and operating a manufacturing system should be resolved. Because the solution to such problems generally presents a difficult problem by itself, even without considering the stochastic and dynamic aspects, it is not always possible to base an IPS only on the experience of manufacturing staff.

9.3.1 Intelligent Production Scheduling

Practical approaches to production scheduling on the planning and control level must take into account the dynamic and unpredictable environment of the shop floor. Due to business and technical considerations, most decisions must be made before all the necessary information has been gathered. Production scheduling must be organized in advance. The predictive schedule is the basis for production control; from this a reactive schedulein has to be able to handle unexpected events. In such a situation, one attempt is to adapt to future developments using a *chronological* and *functional hierarchy* within the decision making steps of production scheduling. This helps to create a presentation of the problem that considers all available information [Sch89a].

The chronological hierarchy leads to the separation of *offline planning* (*OFP*) and *online control* (*ONC*). Problems involved in production scheduling are further separated on a conceptual and a specific level in order to produce a functional hierarchy, too. The purpose of the chronological approach to prioritization is to be able to come to a decision through aggregated and detailed modelling, even if future information is inspecific or unavailable. Aside from fulfilling the functional needs of the organization, the basic concept behind the functional hierarchy is to get a better handle on the combinatorial difficulties that emerge from the attempt of simultaneously solving all problems arising in a manufacturing environment. The IPS should follow hierarchical concepts in both, the chronological and the functional respect. The advantage of such a procedure consists not only in getting a problem-specific approach for investigation of the actual decision problem, but also in the representation of the decision making process within the manufacturing organization.

Models and methods for the hierarchically structured scheduling of production with its planning and control parts have been developed over the years and are highly advanced; see e.g. [KSW86, Ku86, Ste85, LGW86]. However, they lack integration in the sense of providing a concept, which encompasses the entire planning and control process of scheduling. With our proposal for an IPS we try to bring these methods and models one step closer to practical application. The rudimentary techniques of solving predictive scheduling problems presented here work on a closed *Analysis-Construction-Evaluation loop* (*ACE loop*). This loop has a feedback mechanism creating an IPS on the levels of OFP and ONC. An overview over the system is shown in Figure 9.3.1.

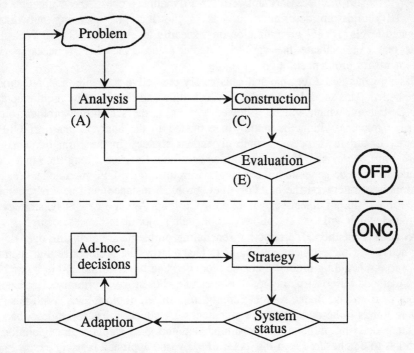

Figure 9.3.1 *Intelligent problem solving in manufacturing.*

The OFP module consists of an *analysis*, a *construction* and an *evaluation* component. First, the problem instance is analyzed (A) in terms of objectives, constraints and further characteristics. In order to do this the first step for (A) is to describe the manufacturing environment with the scheduling situation as detailed as possible. In a second step from this description a specific model has to be chosen from a set of scheduling models in the library of the system. The analysis component (A) is based upon knowledge-based approaches, such as those used for problems like classification within the realm of AI.

The problem analysis defines the parameters for the construction (C) phase. From the basic model obtained in (A), a solution for the scheduling problem is generated by (C) using some generic algorithms. The result is a complete schedule that has then to be evaluated by (E). Here the question has to be answered if the solution is implementable in the sense that manufacturing according to the proposed solution meets business objectives and fulfils all constraints coming from the application. If the evaluation is satisfactory to the user, the proposed solution will be implemented. If not, the process will repeat itself until the proposed solution delivers a desirable outcome or no more improvements appear to be possible in reasonable time. Note that the approach described in Section 9.2.1 where scheduling problems were solved interactively, is the special case of the ACE loop.

The construction component (C) of the ACE loop generates solutions for OFP. It bases its solution upon exact and heuristic problem solving methods. Unfortunately, with this approach we only can solve static representations of quite general problems. The dynamics of the production process can at best be only approximately represented. In order to obtain the necessary answers for a dynamic process, the evaluation component (E) builds up descriptive models in the form of queueing networks at aggregated levels [BY86] or simulation on a specific level [Bul82, Ca86]. With these models one can evaluate the various outcomes and from this if necessary new requirements for problem solution are set up.

Having generated a feasible and satisfactory predictive schedule the ONC module will be called. This module takes the OFP schedule and translates its requirements to an ONC strategy, which will be followed as long as the scheduling problem on the shop floor remains within the setting investigated in the analysis phase of OFP. If temporary disturbances occur, a time dependent strategy in the form of an ad-hoc decision must be devised. If the interruption continues for such a long time that a new schedule needs to be generated, the system will return to the OFP module and seek for an alternative strategy on the basis of a new problem instance with new requirements and possibly different objectives within the ACE loop. Again a new ONC strategy has to be found which will then be followed until again major disturbances occur.

As already mentioned, production scheduling problems are changing over time; a major activity of the problem analysis is to characterize the problem setting such that one or more scheduling problems can be modelled and the right method or a combination of methods for constructing a solution can be chosen from a library of scheduling methods or from knowledge sources coming from different disciplines. With this there are three things to be done; first the manufacturing situation has to be described, second the underlying problem has to be modelled and third an appropriate solution approach has to be chosen. From this point of view one approach is using expert knowledge to formulate and model the problem and then using "deep"-knowledge from the library to solve it.

The function of OFP is providing flexibility in the development and implementation of desirable production schedules. OFP applies algorithms which can either be selected from the library or may also be developed interactively on the basis of simulation runs using all components of the ACE loop. The main activity of the interaction of the three components is the resolution of conflicts which was already described in Section 9.2. Whenever the evaluation of some schedule generated by (C) is not satisfactory then there exists at least some conflict between the requirements or business objectives of a problem solution and the schedule generated so far.

The search for a suitable strategy within ONC should not be limited to routine situations, rather it should also consider e.g. breakdowns and their predictable consequences. ONC takes into consideration the scheduling requirements coming from OFP and the current state of the manufacturing system. To that end, it makes the short term adjustments, which are necessary to handle failures in elements of the system, the introduction of new requirements for manufacturing like rush jobs or the cancellation of jobs. An algorithmic reaction on this level of problem solving based on sophisticated combinatorial considerations is generally not possible because of prohibitive computing times of such an approach. Therefore, the competence of human problem solvers in reaching quality, realtime decisions is extremely important. An example for tackling this kind of problems by simple considerations within a rule-based system is presented in Table 9.3.1. First, concerning reactive scheduling, quite general questions with their answers are listed. For the answer to the third question the corresponding set of rule is given. We will discuss this example in greater detail in the next section.

OFP and ONC require suitable diagnostic experience for high quality decision making. Schedules generated in the past should be recorded and evaluated, for the purpose of using this experience to find solutions for actual problems to be solved. Knowledge-based systems, which could be able to achieve the quality of "self-learning", can make a significant contribution along these lines.

9.3.2 Integrated Problem Solving

In this section we first want to give an example to demonstrate the approach of integration algorithms and knowledge. For clarity purposes, the example is very simple. Let us assume, we have to operate a *flexible manufacturing cell* that consists of identically tooled machines. These kinds of cells are also called pools of machines. From the production planning system we know the set of jobs that have to be processed during the next period of time e.g. in the next shift. As we have identical machines we will now speak of tasks instead of jobs which have to be processed. The business need is that all tasks have to be finished at the end of the next eight hour shift. With this the problem is roughly stated.

Using further expert knowledge from scheduling theory for the analysis of the problem we get the following insights (see Chapter 5 for details).

(A1) The schedule length is influenced mainly by the sequence the tasks enter the system, by the decision to which machine an entering task is assigned next for manufacturing and by the position an assigned task is then given in the corresponding machine queue.

(A2) As all machines are identically tooled each task can be processed by all machines and with this also preemption of tasks between machines is allowed.

(A3) The business need of processing all tasks within the next eight hour shift can be translated in some scheduling objective which says that we want to minimize schedule length or makespan.

(A4) It is well known that for identical machines, independent tasks and the objective of minimizing makespan, schedules with preemptions of tasks exist which are never worse than schedules where task preemption is not allowed.

From knowledge sources (A1)-(A4) we conclude within the problem analysis to choose *McNaughton's rule* [McN59] (see Chapter 5) to construct a first possible schedule. From an evaluation of the generated schedule it turns out that all tasks could be

processed within the next shift. Another observation is that there is still enough spare
time to process additional tasks in the same shift.

Questions and answers for reactive scheduling

(1)   In which sequence should the jobs be
      introduced into the system?

   *Introduce jobs according to predetermined
   list of priorities!*

(2)   Which machines should process the jobs?

   *Always choose the machine which is
   presently processing the least work!*

(3)   How should the waiting line of jobs
      in front of a machine be processed?

   *Process tasks according to the current
   status of the machine, the queues and the system!*

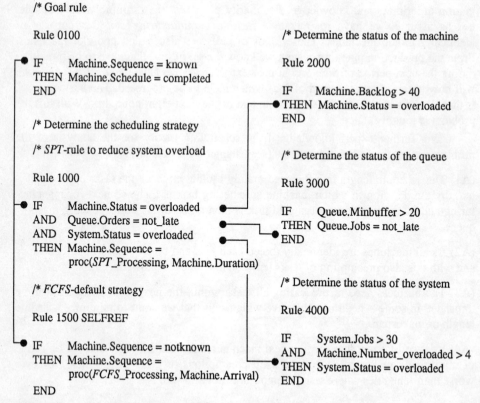

/* Goal rule

Rule 0100

IF   Machine.Sequence = known
THEN Machine.Schedule = completed
END

/* Determine the scheduling strategy

/* *SPT*-rule to reduce system overload

Rule 1000

IF   Machine.Status = overloaded
AND   Queue.Orders = not_late
AND   System.Status = overloaded
THEN Machine.Sequence =
         proc(*SPT*_Processing, Machine.Duration)

/* *FCFS*-default strategy

Rule 1500 SELFREF

IF   Machine.Sequence = notknown
THEN Machine.Sequence =
         proc(*FCFS*_Processing, Machine.Arrival)
END

/* Determine the status of the machine

Rule 2000

IF   Machine.Backlog > 40
THEN Machine.Status = overloaded
END

/* Determine the status of the queue

Rule 3000

IF   Queue.Minbuffer > 20
THEN Queue.Jobs = not_late
END

/* Determine the status of the system

Rule 4000

IF   System.Jobs > 30
AND   Machine.Number_overloaded > 4
THEN System.Status = overloaded
END

Table 9.3.1   *Example problem for reactive scheduling.*

To evaluate the dynamics of the above observations we simulate the schedule taking also transportation times of the preempted tasks to the different machines into account. From the results of simulation runs we now get a better understanding of the problem. It turns out that the schedule constructed by McNaughton's rule is not feasible, i.e. in conflict according to the restriction to finish all tasks within the coming shift. The transport times which were neglected during static schedule generation have a major impact on the problem solution.

From this we must analyze the problem again and with the results from the evaluation process we derive the fact that the implemented schedule should not have machine change-overs of any task, to avoid transport times between machines.

Based on this new constraint and further knowledge from scheduling theory we decide now to use the *longest processing time* (*LPT*) heuristic to schedule all tasks. It is shown in Section 5.1.1 that LPT gives good performance guarantees concerning schedule length and problem settings with identical machines. Transport times between machines do not have to be considered any more as each task is only assigned to one machine. Let us assume the evaluation of the LPT-schedule is satisfactory. Now, we use earliest start times and latest finish times for each task as constraints for ONC. These time intervals can be determined using the generated OFP-schedule. Moreover we translate the LPT rule into a more operational scheduling rule which says: release all the tasks in a nonincreasing order of processing times to the flexible manufacturing cell and always assign a task to the queue of a machine which has least total work to process. The machine itself selects tasks from its own queue according to a *first-come-first-served* (*FCFS*) strategy.

As long as the flexible manufacturing cell has no disturbances ONC can stick to the given LPT-strategy. Now, assume a machine breaks down and the tasks waiting in its queue have to be assigned to queues of the remaining machines. Let us further assume that under the new constraints not all the tasks can be finished in the current shift. From this a new objective occurs which says that as many tasks as possible should be finished. Now, FCFS would not be the appropriate scheduling strategy any longer; a suitable ad-hoc decision for local repair of the schedule has to be made. Finding this decision on the ONC-level means again to apply some problem analysis also in the sense of diagnosis and therapy, i.e. also ad-hoc decisions follow some analysis-construction sequence. If there is enough time available also some evaluation runs could be applied, but in general this is not the case. To demonstrate a possibility how the problem can be resolved similar rules as these from Table 9.3.1 could be used. For the changed situation, *shortest processing time* (*SPT*) rule would now be applied. The *SPT* rule is proposed due to the expectation that this rule helps to finish as many tasks as possible within the current shift. In case of further disturbances that cause major deviations from the current system status, OFP has to be reactivated for a global repair of the schedule.

At the end of this section we want to discuss shortly the relationship of our approach to solve production scheduling problems and the requirements of integrated problem solving. The IPS has to be connected to existing information systems of an enterprise. It has interfaces to the production planning systems on a tactical level of decision making and the real-time oriented CAM-systems. It takes and represents this part of the whole production scheduling system which carries out the feedback loop between planning and execution. The vertical decision flow is supplemented by a horizontal decision flow from CAE and CAQ. The position of the IPS within CIM is shown in Figure 9.3.2.

We gave a short introduction to an IPS which uses a closed loop solution approach; in the same framework an open loop combined with interactive scheduling is possible. In this case analysis is carried out mainly by the user, construction and evaluation are supported by the system. To that end a number of models and methods for analysis and construction have been devised, from which an appropriate selection should be possible. The modular and open architecture of the system offers the possibility of a step by step implementation which can be continuously adapted to changing requirements.

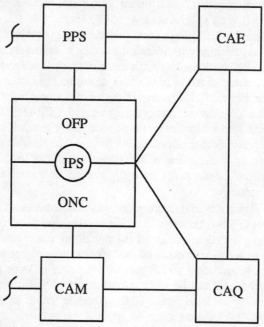

Figure 9.3.2 *IPS within CIM.*

A further application of the system lies in a distributed production scheduling environment. The considered manufacturing system has to be modeled and appropriately decomposed into subsystems. For the manufacturing system and each of its subsystems corresponding IPS apply, which are implemented on different computers connected by an appropriate communication network. The IPS on the top level of the manufacturing system serves as a ccordiantor of the subsystem IPS. Each IPS on the subsystem level works independently fulfilling the requirements from the master level and communicating also with the other IPS on this level. Only if major decisions have to be taken the master IPS is also involved.

References

Ata91   H. Atabakhsh, A survey for constraint based scheduling systems using an artificial intelligence approach, *Artif. Intell. Eng.* 6, 1991, 58-73.

BPH82   J. H. Blackstone, D. T. Phillips, G. L. Hogg, A state-of-the-art survey of dispatching rules for manufacturing job shop operations, *Int. J. Prod. Res.* 20, 1982, 27-45.

Bul82   W. Bulgren, *Discrete System Simulation*, Prentice-Hall, 1982.

BY86   J. A. Buzacott, D. D. Yao, FMS: a reveiw of analytical models, *Management Sci.* 32, 1986, 890-905.

Ca86   A. S. Carrie, The role of simulation in FMS, in: A. Kusiak (ed.), *Flexible Manufacturing Systems: Methods and Studies*, Elsevier, 1986, 191-208.

CPP88   A. Collinot, C. Le Pape, G. Pinoteau, SONIA: a knowledge-based scheduling system, *Artif. Intell. in Eng.* 3, 1988, 86-94.

DP88   R. Dechter, J. Pearl, Network-based heuristics for constraint-satisfaction problems, *Artificial Intelligence* 34, 1988, 1-38.

Fox87   M. S. Fox, *Constraint Directed Search: A Case Study of Job-Shop Scheduling*, Morgan Kaufmann, Los Altos 1987.

Fox90   M. S. Fox, Constraint-guided scheduling - a short history of research at CMU, *Computers in Industry* 14, 1990, 79-88

Fre78   E. C. Freuder, Synthesizing constraint expressions, *Comm. ACM* 11, 1978, 958-966.

FS84   M. S. Fox, S. F. Smith, ISIS - a knowledge-based system for factory scheduling, *Expert Systems* 1, 1984, 25-49.

FS90   M. S. Fox, K. Sycara, Overview of CORTES: a constraint based approach to production planning, scheduling and control, *Proc. 4th Int. Conf. Expert systems in Production and Operations Management*, 1990, 1-15

GJ79   M. R. Garey, D. S. Johnson, *Computers and Intractability: A Guide to the Theory of NP-Completeness*. W. H. Freeman, San Francisco, 1979.

Har73   J. Harrington, *Computer Integrated Manufacturing*, Industrial Press, New York, 1973.

KA87   J. J. Kanet, H. H. Adelsberger, Expert systems in production scheduling, *European J. Oper. Res.* 29, 1987, 51-59.

Kus86   A. Kusiak, Application of operational research models and techniques in flexible manufacturing systems, *European J. Oper. Res.* 24, 1986, 336-345.

KSW86   M. V. Kalkunte, S. C. Sarin, W. E. Wilhelm, Flexible Manufacturing Systems: A review of modelling approaches for design, justification and operation, in: A. Kusiak (ed.), *Flexible Manufacturing Systems: Methods and Studies*, Elsevier, 1986, 3-28.

LGW86   A. J. Van Looveren, L. F. Gelders, N. L. Van Wassenhove, A review of FMS planning models, in: A. Kusiak (ed.), *Modelling and Design of Flexible Manufacturing Systems*, Elsevier, 1986, 3-32.

Mac77   A. K. Mackworth, Consistency in networks of relations, *Artificial Intelligence* 8, 1977, 99-118.

McN59   R. McNaughton, Scheduling with deadlines and loss functions, *Management Sci.* 12, 1959, 1-12.

Mon74   U. Montanari, Networks of constraints: Fundamental properties and applications to picture processing, *Inform. Sci.* 7, 1974, 95-132.

PI77   S. S. Panwalkar, W. Iskander, A survey of scheduling rules, *Oper. Res.* 25, 1977, 45-61.

Ran86   P. G. Ranky, *Computer Integrated Manufacturing*, Prentice Hall, New York, 1986.

Sch89a   G. Schmidt, *CAM: Algorithmen und Decision Support für die Fertigungssteuerung*, Springer-Verlag, 1989.

Sch89b   G. Schmidt, Constraint satisfaction problems in project scheduling, in: R. Słowiński, J. Węglarz (eds.), *Advances in Project Scheduling*, Elsevier, 1989, 135-150.

Sch91   A.-W. Scheer, *CIM - Towards the Factory of the Future*, Springer-Verlag, 1991.

SFO86   S. F. Smith, M. S. Fox, P. S: Ow, Constructing and maintaining detailed production plans: investigations into the development of knowledge-based factory scheduling systems, *AI Magazine* 7, 1986, 45-61.

SPPMM90   S. F. Smith, S. O. Peng, J.-Y. Potvin, N. Muscettola, D. C. Matthys, An integrated framework for generating and revising factory schedules, *J. Opl. Res. Soc.* 41, 1990, 539-552

SS90   S. C. Sarin, R. R. Salgame, Development of a knowledge-based system for dynamic scheduling, *Int. J. Prod. Res.* 28, 1990, 1499-1512.

Ste85   K. E. Stecke, Design, planning, scheduling and control problems of flexible manufacturing systems, *Ann. Oper. Res.* 3, 1985, 3-121.

Index

Printing: Druckhaus Beltz, Hemsbach
Binding: Buchbinderei Kränkl, Heppenheim